DANCING IN CHAINS

The American Social Experience Series
GENERAL EDITOR: JAMES KIRBY MARTIN
EDITORS: PAULA S. FASS, STEVEN H. MINTZ,
CARL PRINCE, JAMES W. REED & PETER N. STEARNS

DANCING IN CHAINS

The Youth of William Dean Howells

RODNEY D. OLSEN

NEW YORK UNIVERSITY PRESS
NEW YORK AND LONDON
1991

boo 35669 11

Library of Congress Cataloging-in-Publication Data
Olsen, Rodney D.
Dancing in chains : the youth of William Dean Howells / Rodney D.
Olsen.
p. cm. — (The American social experience series ; 20)
Includes bibliographical references and index.
ISBN 0-8147-6172-0
1. Howells, William Dean, 1837–1920—Biography—Youth.
2. Novelists, American—19th century—Biography—Youth. 3. United
States—Social life and customs—1783–1865. 4. Critics—United
States—Biography. 5. Ohio—Social life and customs. I. Title.
II. Series.
PS2033.047 1990
818'.409—dc20
[B]   90-37916
CIP

New York University Press books are printed on acid-free paper,
and their binding materials are chosen for strength and durability.

For my father and mother,
W. Donald Olsen and Glenda Aamodt Olsen

If He could doubt on His triumphant cross,
  How much more I, in the defeat and loss
  Of seeing all my selfish dreams fulfilled,
  Of having lived the very life I willed,
Of being all that I desired to be?
My God, my God! Why hast thou forsaken me?

WILLIAM DEAN HOWELLS, 1894

Contents

Illustrations

Preface

William Dean Howells was the premier novelist of the nineteenth-century American middle class. He was a "domestic" novelist, master of the urban parlor scene, the setting reserved for tasteful display of affluence and elegant presentation of self. To outward appearances, Howells enjoyed a life of success and prosperity. Yet many of his novelistic characters lack the sense of security his middle-class readers associated with their parlors. Often Howells's characters do not feel "at home."

Although literary historians have significantly revised Howells's reputation as comforter of the middle class, the persistence of this image has prevented the fullest biographical and historical inquiry into the meaning of his life and career.[1] As a cultural historian informed by psychological perspectives and findings of the new social history, I am interested in Howells not only for what his life tells us about the making of William Dean Howells but also for what it reveals about the making of middle-class culture in the nineteenth century. In this study, I portray Howells's emotional, intellectual, and moral development. I discuss the psychological, social, and cultural influences that were the formative forces in his life. More ambitiously, I have tried to bring the coherence of lived experience to cultural analysis, demonstrating in Howells's life the interrelation of child-rearing practice, strategies of family survival, vocational aspirations, gender ideals, ideological experimentation, political commitment, moral belief, and spiritual doubt.

As a successful novelist and prominent social critic, Howells was not a typical nineteenth-century American in any simple sense, but he shared in experiences common to many families. In the years before the Civil War, middle-class Americans sanctified domestic scenes in an outpouring of lithographic prints and popular songs. Howells's uneasy characters express an emotion that had become prevalent by mid-century. An intense longing for a stable connection to home arose during the economic and social transformation that created the nineteenth-century middle class. With increasing momentum after the War of 1812, the formation of an integrated national market brought dramatic changes in traditional patterns of communal life, particularly in the North. As communal life began to erode, home acquired its deep, resonant appeal.

In the years before the Civil War, becoming middle class rather than being middle class was the experience of most Americans. Along with many other families, the Howells family struggled to accommodate the new with the old. While revering traditional values, they assimilated the emergent middle-class ethos of "civilized morality" with its ideals of self-control and individual success. Howells's early writings—his diaries, poetry, fiction, newspaper columns, and family letters—present a detailed self-portrait of childhood and youth, stages of life that were newly realized and rationalized to accord with the transformation of everyday life. The tensions of Howells's life and work, like those of many of his contemporaries, were rooted in this transitional period.

While I elaborate the personal meanings of Howells's words and actions, I pay particular attention to the public dimensions of his development. My primary psychological premises are drawn from Erik Erikson's conception of the identity crisis of youth with its precursors in childhood. An individual's identity, in Erikson's view, is formed from a complex interplay of personal, social, and cultural forces.[2] From the experiences of his early childhood, for instance, Howells developed a demanding conscience that was strongly rein-

forced by the affectionate child-rearing methods and the Swedenborgian religious beliefs of his family. At the same time, he was
influenced by conflicting sets of family values that responded to
the transformation of everyday life; one set emphasized mutual
aid, the other individual desire. As he later struggled to realize his
family's expectations in a literary career, he confronted competing
conceptions of the public good as well as competing literary ideologies.[3]

For Howells and for countless antebellum youth, home leaving
was a momentous time of life. Aspiring middle-class Americans
could no longer view the family as a "little commonwealth," a
relatively self-sufficient entity that prescribed the limits of individual desire and expectation. To accommodate the emergent order,
they made the family a place for strenuous beginnings, where
children absorbed the values and developed the talents that prepared them for accomplishments in the "outer world." For middle-
class Americans, home leaving became a necessary tribulation, a
hazardous rite of passage. They expected youth to face fearful tests
and temptations. They warned of fateful decisions. Howells's home-
leaving difficulties were compounded by his struggle for a literary
vocation and complicated by a powerful family claim. Unless he
believed the literary vocation offered the greatest possible usefulness to others, he could not escape terrible feelings of selfishness.
Howells's distress over his "selfish aim" to "succeed in literature"
was severe and enervating. But it represented an extreme instance
of vocational anxieties that affected many nineteenth-century
Americans who were troubled by "ambition."[4]

Howells's village of Jefferson, Ohio, was one of several localities
that channeled and challenged his literary aspirations. Solidly aligned
against slavery—eventually forming a phalanx of radical Republicans—Jeffersonians upheld a moral conception of politics that
seemed to diminish the authority of literature. Hesitation over his
political commitments contributed to Howells's bouts of hypochondria and vertigo. When he moved to Columbus, Ohio, taking
a position as a radical Republican journalist, he entered a literary

scene more sophisticated and enticing than he had known in his village. Although he tried to be both poet and agitator, he was more committed to literature. Howells's attraction to the new mass audience for literature, as an expansive realm of usefulness, added to his dilemmas. This largely female audience seemed to demand "sentimental" forms of literature that compromised his sense of manliness and moral action. Eventually Howells was drawn into the orbit of Boston, but acceptance by his Brahmin sponsors only suspended his struggles.

The pain of Howells's home leaving separated him irrevocably from the moral certainties he had been taught as a child. Contrary to his father, who believed in a moral universe where everyone had charge of his fate, Howells feared that individuals were prey to unknown malevolent forces. He often saw life itself as "desultory," ruled by caprice and chance rather than by discernible moral or spiritual laws. He suspected that seeking the good of others—the dominant imperative of his childhood and youth—might be futile and quixotic. Concerned primarily with the impact of Darwinian science, historians have not fully appreciated this kind of disillusionment and doubt. It derived as much from traumas of personal experience, from the "drift" caused by the disruption of traditional life, as from scientific dismemberment of religious belief.[5]

But the meaning of Howells's life is diminished if viewed simply in terms of his despair. Erikson suggests that the struggles of youth may set "commitments 'for life,' " commitments that are renewed and reassimilated, especially during times of crisis.[6] The climactic crisis of Howells's life should be understood in these terms—as a homecoming. During the late 1880s and early 1890s, Howells was plagued by the return of his youthful feeling that he was a "slave of selfishness." He resisted this feeling, not in the self-referential escapes popular with many of his contemporaries, but in concerted action that revitalized the communal ideals of his youth. In his writing, he drew attention to the ills of industrial capitalism, especially to the plight of the hungry and homeless. Dismayed by the estrangement of middle-class Americans from the democratic ethos of equality and fraternity, Howells urged his readers to realize their ties of mutual responsibility. He urged all who were prospering to recognize that they were eternally bound to all who were suffering.[7]

Acknowledgments

I am pleased to acknowledge a Lewis E. Atherton Research Grant from the history department of the University of Missouri at Columbia. The grant bears the name of my mentor—a masterful teacher, dedicated historian, and wise man. The history department at Missouri also aided my work with two Frank F. and Louise I. Stephens fellowships. Stan Johannesen started me on this project when he innocently said I might be interested in a book called *Identity: Youth and Crisis.* John and Martha Rainbolt encouraged my interest in psychological issues in our discussions and in the course I taught with John, who told me long before I realized it myself that I was writing this book. My advisor, Ed Purcell, kept me at my work with the right mixture of criticism and encouragement. Richard Hocks shared his meditations on American literature and confirmed my efforts beyond all my expectations. Rich Bopp, Susan Armeny, and Paul Langley were helpful critics and friends.

Jackson Lears has had a special influence on this study. While Jackson was completing *No Place of Grace,* he was reading my early drafts. Perhaps because of our similar interest in the emotional and intellectual odysseys of nineteenth-century Americans, Jackson maintained a light touch, urging me to give my insights greater emphasis. I thank Jackson for helping me to find my voice. And I thank Karen Lears for timely encouragement.

William White Howells expressed interest in my work on his grandfather from its beginnings, when he met me in his office at Harvard with the kind of welcome for which his grandfather was famous. Dave Nordloh, general editor of the Howells Edition at Indiana University, was a chance acquaintance during my first research trip to Cambridge. At Indiana, he placed a vast amount of Howells's writing and correspondence at my fingertips. I thank him for the many ways he facilitated my work during and after my visits to Bloomington and especially for his welcome of a historian's perspective on Howells. Many of the superbly edited Howells Edition texts became available while I was pursuing my work. The librarians at the Houghton Library at Harvard University, the Herrick Memorial Library at Alfred University, the Ohio Historical Society, the Massachusetts Historical Society, and the Rutherford B. Hayes Presidential Center were informative and helpful. In particular, I thank Norma Higgins of Alfred University for her extra efforts and for the friendly interest she took in my work.

This study was supported by an Andrew Mellon Postdoctoral Fellowship in the Humanities at Rice University, where I participated in a two-year seminar on the "Culture of Capitalism." While I was at Rice, Tom Haskell read my original manuscript and urged me toward greater precision. Bob Patton, Susan Gilman, Elizabeth Long, George Lipsitz, George Frederickson, and Mark Warren offered criticisms and encouragement. In the greater Houston community of scholars, I was lucky to find Steve Mintz and Tom Cole, with whom I shared interests in the history of the family and the life cycle. During the past year, being a colleague of Tom's at the Institute for the Medical Humanities has helped me put the finishing touches on my study. Recent readers in whole or part have helped me to improve my final thinking and writing. I thank Tom Bender, Ellen Moore, Bill Winslade, Jim Jones, and Bob Abzug. Colin Jones, director of New York University Press, has expertly guided me and the manuscript through the publication process.

My deepest thanks go to my parents, W. Donald Olsen and Glenda Aamodt Olsen, who have been wondrously constant in their support. My dedication of this book to them is a small return for all they have done for me. My sister, Sandra Olsen Looney, has been a model teacher and keeper of light. She has taught me how to write, and by her generous life, she has taught me what to write. My wife Florence's parents, John Crighton and Rebecca Wright Crighton, have always been encouraging. John's own devotion to the historian's craft has been an inspiration. Florence herself is a beautiful person and a tenacious copy editor. The best parts of this book are the places where I have satisfied her exquisite sense of fluency and subtlety.

—GALVESTON, TEXAS / ARLINGTON, VIRGINIA, JUNE 1989

PART I

Childhood

CHAPTER I

A Selfish Ideal of Glory

We who are nothing but self, and have no manner of being
Save in the sense of self, still have no other delight
Like the relief that comes with the blessed oblivion freeing
Self from self in the deep sleep of some dreamless night.
HOWELLS, 1894

In his autobiography *Years of My Youth* (1916), William Dean Howells recounted that his childhood village of Hamilton, Ohio, was a place of "almost unrivaled fitness" to be the home of boys who were swimmers, skaters, foragers, and enthusiasts of outdoor life. Two branches of the Great Miami River flowed through the village; at the heart of the village was the inviting basin of the Miami Canal. Close by were fields and woods. Public holidays seemed to come in rapid succession, while "Saturdays spread over half the week." After recording these lyrical memories, Howells* tried to recall how fear first came into his life. He noted that once a man in his village had died from hydrophobia. He tied this dire event to his father's jest that the victim wisely made his peace with God, before he called in the doctors. As Howells described his father, William Cooper Howells always seemed to see the best in everything, often to the consternation of his wife. His father viewed

---

* "Howells" always refers to William Dean Howells.

3

hellfire revivals with "kindly amusement." His Swedenborgian beliefs suggested that those who had chosen hell were happy with their choice. While he disliked religious controversy, he was stirred by the annexation of Texas and the Mexican War, events that posed the question whether the American nation would become entirely free or slave.[1]

Having sketched the joys of village life, a traumatic death, and his father's easy demeanor toward aspects of life that troubled others, especially his mother, Howells recorded his earliest memory of fear. He focused on a "tragical effect" he had once suffered from the "playfulness" of his father.

> My mother and he were walking together in the twilight, with me, a very small boy, following, and my father held out to me behind his back a rose which I understood I was to throw at my mother and startle her.
>
> My aim was unfortunately for me all too sure; the rose struck her head, and when she looked round and saw me offering to run away, she whirled on me and made me suffer for her fright in thinking my flower was a bat, while my father gravely entreated, "Mary, Mary!" She could not forgive me at once, and my heart remained sore, for my love of her was as passionate as the temper I had from her, but while it continued aching after I went to bed, she stole up-stairs to me and consoled me and told me how scared she had been, and hardly knew what she was doing; and all was well again between us.[2]

Howells had thrown a rose, a symbol of love, at the object of his deepest childish affection, his mother. His trust in his father's playful invitation had been met with summary punishment from his mother. Treating the same episode in a children's story he had published earlier, Howells described the punishment as a boxing of ears, a startling violation of the affectionate treatment that his father always favored over any harsh form of discipline.[3]

The most prominent themes in Howells's memory of the rose-throwing episode are associated with developmental difficulties that emerge in early childhood, about the time when "a very small boy" is old enough to tag after his parents. At this age, children have just acquired a proud sense of themselves as actors and initiators. They enjoy curious exploring and excited running about.

They feel self-sufficient and want to try things out. They are eager to follow their parents' enticements. A small boy imagines he can do everything his father can do. But very soon the child's exuberant sense of initiative is complicated by fears of punishment stemming partly from related sexual impulses. "The child indulges in fantasies of being a giant and a tiger, but in his dreams he runs in terror for dear life." At the time of the rose-throwing episode, Howells's imagination of grand designs, especially his desire to act like father toward mother, was becoming burdened with guilt. While he was ready to follow his father's playful invitation, he was vulnerable to his mother's angry reaction.[4]

How a child resolves the developmental difficulties of this phase of life has significant meaning for his anticipation of adult roles, whether he trusts himself and others, whether he feels sufficient to pursue and accomplish tasks. Another problem is accepting an emotional separation from his mother that is more decisive than his earlier separations. And most significantly for Howells, how a child deals with these difficulties establishes the lineaments of conscience. The child's primitive conscience can be unyielding and cruel, for it partly reflects a turning in of his aggressive impulses. Whether a child will be harshly punishing or fairly reasonable in his self-judgments depends upon his predispositions, family circumstances, and alleviations provided by parents and other ideal adults.[5]

The interrelated meanings of Howells's rose-throwing episode —especially its reference to the development of his conscience— become clearer in light of his earlier treatment of the episode in *The Flight of Pony Baker* (1902), a book-length story for children.[6] Stung by the boxing of ears he receives from his mother, Howells's stand-in, Pony Baker, decides to retaliate by running away with the circus. Pony imagines that one day he will return to his village as a famous circus performer, amazing everyone with his ability to ride three horses bareback. He will be, this sexually charged image suggests, powerfully self-sufficient. Pony imagines that his moment of triumph will be his retaliation, for, among his many admirers, he will choose to shun his mother.

As he elaborated his own childhood trauma, Howells portrayed how Pony Baker's impulsive self-confidence is replaced by disillusionment and terror. As his first step to stardom, Pony plans to join a circus that has arrived in his village. But as his departure nears, Pony begins to doubt his imagined prowess; he begins to feel he is as diminished as his name suggests. One night, his fears come alive in a dream. As he falls asleep, he seems to see the circus procession approaching his house. He runs outside to meet the wagons and feels himself floating above the ground. Then the magician suddenly appears. Pony has been told the magician aids runaway boys like himself, but Pony is frightened by his strange appearance: He wore "a tall, peaked hat, like a witch. He took up the whole street, he was so wide in the black glazed gown that hung from his arms when he stretched them out, for he seemed to be groping along that way, with his wand in one hand, like a blind man." Pony is even more alarmed by the magician's gruff and ominous words: "He kept saying in a kind of deep, shaking voice: 'It's all glory; it's all glory,' and the sound of those words froze Pony's blood." With these words, Howells invoked the specific kind of guilt encouraged in his childhood home. In Swedenborgian belief, seeking "glory" was the most abhorrent selfishness; it destroyed a person's usefulness and brought eternal damnation.[7]

Frightened by the magician's looming appearance and damning words, Pony tries to escape by shrinking up "so little" he will not be seen. When regression fails, he searches frantically for the knob of his front door but finds only a smooth wall. This hint of castration anxiety is elaborated through an abrupt transition in Pony's dream. Just when he is about to envelop Pony, the magician is transformed into Pony's father, who is standing beside Pony's bed consulting a doctor about Pony's sleepwalking. His father and the doctor have decided that Pony must be bled—a fearful remedy Howells had endured as a child in Hamilton.[8] As the doctor begins to prepare his lancet, Pony's mother suddenly calls and rouses him from his dream. With Pony awake and reconciled to his mother, Howells completed this remarkable re-creation of his own childhood trauma. Writing without knowledge of Freud's interpretation of fantasy and dreams, Howells had tapped a stream of symbolism, forcefully posing a retributive conscience and the threat of disfigurement against a small child's grand designs.

Parallel themes appear in Howells's discussion of the abusive corporal punishment he witnessed while attending common schools. He stated that such treatment always "outrages the young life confided to the love of the race."[9] Recollection of his outrage at these abuses called forth another painful memory:

> From the stress put upon behaving rather than believing in that home of mine we were made to feel that wicked words were of the quality of wicked deeds, and that when they came out of our mouths they depraved us, unless we took them back. I have not forgotten, with any detail of the time and place, a transgression of this sort which I was made to feel in its full significance. My mother had got supper, and my father was, as he often was, late for it, and while we waited impatiently for him, I came out with the shocking wish that he was dead. My mother instantly called me to account for it, and when my father came she felt bound to tell him what I had said. He could then have done no more than gravely give me the just measure of my offense; and his explanation and forgiveness were the sole event.[10]

The child's wish to become the sole object of his mother's attentions is reflected in Howells's innocent remark. His father had treated the offense with the affectionate regard he advocated for child rearing, a tactic that made Howells appreciate its "full significance." His mother's less tolerant reaction, like her reaction in the rose-throwing episode, complicated his feelings. While he wrote that he was not left with "an exaggerated sense of [his] sin," Howells nevertheless retained this painful memory, with all details of time and place, into the very last years of his life.[11]

William Cooper Howells emphasized reason in the raising of children. He had faith that understanding petulant actions in their "full significance" and in their "just measure" would disarm unreasonable anxieties. But the remedy of reason did not always suffice. Throughout his childhood, Howells repeatedly suffered from irrational fears and self-accusations. He experienced terrible nightmares that continued in his thoughts and tortured his waking hours. Fearful and hesitant, he "cowered along in the shadow of unreal dangers," everywhere imagining "shapes of doom and horror." Because he often "dwelt in a world of terrors," he was susceptible to the tricks and tauntings of his playmates, who took advantage of his fears. Furthermore, he suffered from his "abject terror of dying." When he began to write poems and stories, he sometimes would imagine a character dying. Then he would think that "he was that character, and [he] was going to die." His most agonizing fear, recurring during his adolescence, was of dying from hydrophobia like the man in his village. But he also suffered from his "fantastic scruples." Once when a schoolmate accused him of taking her pencil, he became "frantic with the mere dread of guilt." Despite his innocence, he could neither eat nor sleep until the issue was resolved. To ease his sufferings, his father reminded him of the need for reason, but Howells continued to magnify minor and imagined offenses.[12]

Howells's persistent fears and exacting scruples suggest that he struggled in childhood with a severe conscience. Other memories reveal associated childhood inhibitions. When he was nine or ten, Howells traveled with his father on the *New England No. 2*, the Ohio River steamboat piloted by one of his Dean uncles. Throughout their journey, Howells was troubled by his father's penchant to go ashore, stroll along the wharf, and distract himself by "sampling a book-peddler's wares, or [by] talking with this bystander or that." Howells refused to accompany his father on these forays. He clung to the steamboat rail, fearing that the boat might leave before his father returned.[13]

Each stop renewed Howells's anguish, as his father's "insatiable interest in every aspect of nature and human nature urged him ashore and kept him there till the last moment before the gangplank was drawn in." At last, Howells's misery "mounted to frenzy":

I was left mostly to myself, and I spent my time dreamily watching the ever-changing shore, so lost in its wild loveliness that once when I woke from my reverie the boat seemed to have changed her course, and to be going downstream instead of up. It was in this crisis that I saw my father descending the gang-plank, and while I was urging his return in mute agony, a boat came up outside of us to wait for her chance of landing. I looked and read on her wheel-house the name *New England,* and then I abandoned hope. By what fell necromancy I had been spirited from my uncle's boat to another I could not guess, but I had no doubt that the thing had happened, and I was flying down from the hurricane roof to leap aboard that boat from the lowermost deck when I met my uncle coming as quietly up the gangway as if nothing had happened. He asked what was the matter, and I gasped out the fact; he did not laugh; he had pity on me and gravely explained, "That boat is the *New England:* this is the *New England No. 2,*" and at these words I escaped with what was left of my reason.[14]

Though calmed by his uncle's words and his father's promise to account more exactly for his movements, Howells continued to resist his father's visits ashore to gather intelligence or to inspect glass foundries and rolling mills. He resisted as well when his father asked him for his impressions of the river landscape. "My lips were sealed," Howells explained, "for the generations cannot utter themselves to each other till the strongest need of utterance is past."[15]

The excursion on the Ohio River was Howells's most extended venture beyond the bounds of his home village and his first prolonged experience of the bustling, urban world. He vividly recalled the frightening clamor and confusion of steamboat enterprise he saw in Pittsburgh:

The wide slope of the landing was heaped with the merchandise putting off or taking on the boats, amidst the wild and whirling curses of the mates and the insensate rushes of the deck-hands staggering to and fro under their burdens. The swarming drays came and went with freight, and there were huckster carts of every sort; peddlers, especially of oranges, escaped with their lives among the hoofs and wheels, and through the din and turmoil passengers hurried aboard the boats.[16]

Scenes of dazzle and danger may have sparked Howells's fear of separation and encouraged him to cling to his father. His imagined separation from his father, moreover, can be understood in terms of his conflicted impulses, both as his wish to eliminate his father and as his urge to self-punishment. His inhibition in action and speech suggests the self-distrust born from such conflicts. Like many of his childhood memories, the steamboat incident indicates that Howells was susceptible to harsh demands of conscience. His self-accusations could be assuaged but not entirely eased by forces he identified as the protectors of his childhood—"a father's reason" and "a mother's love."[17]

Howells's evocative childhood memories do not stand alone. Their meaning is amplified by understanding other important influences on his early development. The family players in his individual drama were major characters. Their personalities and inclinations entered into his associations—his temperamentally optimistic father, his sometimes more fearful mother. Their religious and other beliefs also mattered—the Swedenborgian perspectives that warranted William Cooper Howells's comfort with the things his wife found troubling, the politics that he elevated to the forefront of his concern. The texture of village life mattered as well, portrayed by Howells as pristine but with a suggestion of its tenuousness. In its broader dimensions, Howells's story involves his family's reaction to the dominant forces of social and cultural change in the early nineteenth century.

An understanding of these broader dimensions of Howells's story can be approached in terms of generations, beginning with the hopes and dreams of his paternal grandfather. Joseph Howells had learned to build and operate woolen mills in Wales, yet in America he lost opportunities to parlay his skills into entrepreneurial success. As he became more and more dependent on others for his living, he yearned for a new start as a farmer. He had no experience in farming, but the seeming abundance of land fed his hunger for independence. His first venture set a discouraging pattern. Following the panic of 1819, he assumed land forfeited by a debtor. He bought forty acres of creek land near Steubenville, Ohio, for six hundred dollars on credit, using all of his cash for the initial payment. While the land offered mature orchards, fifteen acres was rocky hillside. The rest, his son William Cooper recalled, was "worn out and hopelessly poor." Rude improvements of a log barn and two log cabins had stripped the land of usable timber.[18]

Oblivious to flaws in his aspirations, Joseph Howells burdened his family with hopeless toil. He worked through the week at a Steubenville mill while his son William Cooper, a boy of twelve, managed the entire farm. Because his father could not afford draft horses, William Cooper tried to work the fields with ponies. Many tasks of planting, cultivation, and harvest required hired help, reducing family returns to "a mere trifle over expenses." To retrieve his losses, Joseph Howells bought ewes, hoping they would bear lambs. But the ewes proved infertile, and their wool brought less than the cost of their feed. The accumulation of his disappointments finally forced Joseph Howells to forfeit his land. In the following years, however, he tried farming four more times with similar results. "Had a farm [been] given to him, ready stocked," William Cooper ruefully concluded, "he would scarcely have been able to live on it." [19]

Although William Cooper Howells resented his father's failures in farming, he shared his father's penchant for illusory hopes. Starting late in the printing trade, he was anxious for immediate success. In 1828, when he turned twenty-one, he gave up fitful work as a journeyman printer and began his own publication, a political and literary miscellany called the *Gleaner*. He found few subscribers, even after renaming his newspaper the *Eclectic Observer and Workingman's Advocate* and enhancing its contentious Owenite flavor. Quitting his newspaper, he gathered his remaining resources for the publication of a massive book, *The Rise, Progress and Downfall of Aristocracy*, by a utopian reformer named William Matthers. [20]

Anticipating fabulous financial success, William Cooper Howells married Mary Dean in July 1831. He was soon forced to acknowledge, however, that the book was an utter failure and that Matthers would never pay pittance for expenses. "I found," he recalled, "that, compared with [Matthers] in his hopefulness, I had the coldest of common sense." Nevertheless, in succeeding years, William Cooper Howells continued to be enticed by his "constant tempter, Hope." As he pursued a living, first as a journeyman printer and then as a newspaper editor, he now and then tried to realize his dream of grander success. And like his father before him, he brought suffering to his family.[21] To endure his difficulties and sustain his hopes, William Cooper Howells developed a "buoyant expectation of the best in everything." "He believed," wrote his son William Dean, "that you could do what you wished to do if you wished it potently enough."[22]

An exaggerated ideal of individual will was not an eccentricity of the Howells family. Undeterred faith in the autonomous individual had gained widespread acceptance among antebellum Americans through changes in the structure of economic opportunity. Gaining momentum after the War of 1812 and accelerating during the 1830s, converging developments provided the basis for an integrated national market stretching from the eastern seaboard to the Mississippi River. Augmented by increased immigration, population began to concentrate in commercial cities, creating an urban demand for extensive cash-crop agriculture and expanded services. A series of military campaigns defeated Indian resistance east of the Mississippi River and opened the way for a swelling tide of western migration. Travel and the exchange of goods were facilitated by vast improvements in transportation as local and regional markets were joined by a chain of canals, roads, and railroad tracks. Steamboats sped regular traffic along the Ohio and Mississippi rivers from Pittsburgh to New Orleans. The construction of telegraph lines permitted rapid communications. Bankers, brokers, and other middlemen formed intricate networks of finance, credit, and distribution. The incipient development of manufacturing began to supply a larger variety of wants, from brooms to books. All this activity was fueled by a huge international demand for cotton textiles, which provided the final impetus for creating an integrated national market. By the 1850s this national market was in place, with ties to the South but developed most extensively in the North.[23]

The Howells family's ventures in farming and publishing were part of the "go-ahead" excitement stimulated by creation of the national market. Their enthusiasm was shared by politicians and publicists who sang ardent hymns to the new opportunities. Andrew Jackson—representing for many Americans a charismatic figure of unflinching will, the very embodiment of autonomous individualism—declared that Americans were now "unconstrained" to develop the "power and faculties of man in their highest perfection." Echoed by many others, this expansive faith fed democratic impulses and inspired communal ventures like the Owenite experiments William Cooper Howells defended in his *Eclectic Observer*. But antebellum Americans, including William Cooper Howells, also understood unconstrained pursuit of perfection to mean the individual quest for acquisitive success.[24] Fabled examples of wealthy entrepreneurs—diverse individuals such as John Jacob Astor who was celebrated by Washington Irving, or P. T. Barnum who celebrated himself—seemed to prove that anyone could achieve a grand success simply through the exercise of will.[25]

Yet, as Joseph and William Cooper Howells discovered, everyday realities often denied the belief that force of will was all-sufficient. Merchant capitalists, substantial farmers, and land speculators garnered the greatest returns from the new economic environment. Wealth increasingly lodged in the hands of those who possessed considerable financial means. Arduous labor, hazardous risks, and small economic gains were the common experiences of many antebellum Americans. Their visions of fabulous economic success grew dim. Even modest aspirations, like those of Joseph and William Cooper Howells, were prey to defeat. Americans, observed Alexis de Tocqueville, pursued success with "secret disquietude." A good part of their anxiety came from "vague dread" that somehow they had missed the main chance, that in a "go-ahead" society they had been left behind.[26]

Although disparities between grandly imagined success and disappointing everyday realities accentuated the anxieties of antebellum Americans like Joseph and William Cooper Howells, their ambivalence had a more profound basis. The emergence of more extensive forms of economic activity challenged traditional values of communal life. Before the early nineteenth century, most families engaged in limited market exchange while sustaining household production. People lived around small towns and villages; they were bound in networks of family, friends, and associates; their face-to-face involvements covered the full range of life, from work to worship. A patriarchal order augmented by strong religious sanctions reinforced mutual obligations throughout the life cycle, from rearing the young to caring for the aged. This corporate, communal world was never absolutely realized. It contained increasingly diverse and contending groups, and as it eroded it acquired a nostalgic glow that denied its repressive features. But before the early nineteenth century, the corporate community provided the basis of life for most Americans and claimed their allegiance.[27]

As the corporate community lost ground, antebellum Americans were caught between the world of their immediate experience—the world of "home"—and the "greater world" of the emerging national market.[28] Well-to-do families might traverse these two worlds without too much difficulty, but families of the "middling sort" like the Howells family—small farmers, shopkeepers, and artisans—felt especially vulnerable in the shifting economic circumstances. Troubled by the feeling of living in two different worlds with incommensurate demands, they began to devote more attention to the survival and safety of their children. Tensions were played out in many cultural, social, and political realms, but the province of family life was perhaps the most critical.[29] Earlier parents had raised children to follow in their own footsteps, to preserve values of kin, craft, church, and community. Children might leave home, but they were not apt to go beyond the reach of parental guidance. Often they stayed within a day's ride. With the changing opportunities, children might settle at greater distances and show less concern about family values. Joseph Howells wanted his son to stay in the family, contribute to the family's welfare, and worship in the family's way. But William Cooper left home at his earliest chance for his own purposes—to gain his economic and spiritual independence.

The phantom shape of the world beyond home intensified parental worries. Personal fate appeared subject to the decisions of "strangers." Fear of being controlled by these unknown others focused on the "confidence man" whose guises proliferated in popular stories. Although the rhetoric of the self-made man offered some reassurance of individual autonomy, unease concerning personal freedom deeply affected antebellum Americans. Periodic panics and depressions beginning in 1819, 1837, and 1857 brought home the message that individuals were dependent on distant, impersonal forces. Ultimately this message eroded trust in a secure moral order where individuals were accountable for their actions.[30]

Parents had once prepared children for a well-known world confirmed and sustained by strong spiritual convictions; now they were forced to account for an unfamiliar world that threatened their most sacred beliefs. Control over children became freighted with critical meaning. Because schooling and professional training were still in the making, not becoming common until the 1850s, these institutions seemed inadequate safeguards. Even after formal education became available, antebellum parents relied on traditional means of control, particularly intense forms of child-rearing practice and religious instruction. To harness the wayward inclinations of his son, Joseph Howells augmented his moral instruction with coercive Methodist camp meetings. He told William Cooper that he expected him "to become religious," a fervent Methodist, if he wished to stay in the family. But William Cooper wished to break away.[31]

The questioning of patriarchal authority during the American Revolution had stimulated debate over the rearing of children. Acceleration of economic development during the early nineteenth century spread this debate to a broad population. The overtly coercive measures favored by Joseph Howells lost favor as they failed to bind children to parental decrees. Middling parents began to shift their child-rearing preferences to affectionate persuasion and loving explanation. Complicating the emotional relations between parents and children, these subtle methods fostered children's self-control as a substitute for immediate family and communal controls. The fabled self-made man emerged as the new variety of family-made man, not the family heir who had received the estate, but the family hope who had deeply internalized the ethos of self-control.[32]

The child-rearing literature of the 1830s—the decade of Howells's birth—emphasized affectionate persuasion and loving example as the means of self-control. A "system of early and practical self-control" was essential, Theodore Dwight observed in *The Father's Book*, because the child would be "his own disciplinarian through life." The poetess and moralist Lydia H. Sigourney was among the many writers who seconded this emphasis. In *Letters to Mothers*, she contended that the "science of self-government" was "the great end of education."[33] The reiterated ideal of self-control formed the cornerstone of the emergent middle-class value system of "civilized morality." For the aspiring middle class, self-control became the summa of all advice, the antidote for all ills.[34]

The ideal of self-control could serve different, and sometimes divergent purposes. For antebellum Americans seeking new opportunities, it could help rationalize autonomous individualism and further the quest for acquisitive success. But within many families, parents also taught children the ideal of self-control to strengthen resistance to the erosion of traditional communal values.[35] Stirred by a vision of new opportunities, William Cooper Howells reared his son William Dean to achieve a grand success in the world beyond home. While encouraging his son's ambitions, however, he taught him that success was nothing in itself. Unless pursued primarily for the benefit of others, the ideal of success was a damning "ideal of glory."

The word *glory* emerged in Howells's later self-accusations, appearing with full force when he imagined the looming magician who threatened Pony Baker. Howells used this word without acknowledging or apparently recognizing that it expressed the core of his father's religious convictions. By 1837, when his second son, William Dean, was born in the "coal-smoky town" of Martinsville, Ohio, William Cooper Howells had thrown off evangelical Methodism. Believing Methodism had distracted his father from the "business of life," William Cooper Howells had found a more congenial faith in Swedenborgianism. The writings of the philoso-pher-mystic Emanuel Swedenborg suited William Cooper How-ells's optimistic temperament. Swedenborg described an absolute "moral universe" that ensured the ultimate triumph of good over evil while allowing each individual control over his fate. In the Swedenborgian scheme, salvation was entirely voluntary. As the "sovereign chooser" of his own destiny, an individual might fur-ther the good of all and initiate a heavenly serenity within himself. For William Cooper Howells, Swedenborgianism "served to an-swer every question and satisfy every need of his spirit."[36]

For those who lacked William Cooper Howells's tranquil assur-ance of salvation, however, Swedenborgianism intensified fears of damnation. Swedenborgian belief encouraged painful soul-search-ing, the constant questioning of desires and intentions for hints of self-love. "If a man directs his love wholly to himself," William Cooper Howells explained in the *Retina*, the Swedenborgian news-paper he edited when his son William Dean was ages six and seven, "he immediately demands the love and submission of others to him; and seeks to render them subservient to his wishes and grati-fications. To this desire we know there [are] no bounds, and from it must grow contentions, oppositions, wars and fightings of every kind; in short, from this root of self-love springs all moral evil."[37]

Although emphasis on the "voluntary principle of man" tied William Cooper Howells's Swedenborgian faith to autonomous individualism, Swedenborgians understood that exercise of the will was "perilous." In William Cooper Howells's vivid metaphor, in-dividual freedom "poised man upon the most delicately-balanced verge, where the power to turn either way was so easily exerted as to require unceasing vigilance to exercise it for good, and where equilibrium when lost was extremely hard to recover." Any "un-due action" of self, he pointed out, destroyed all potential for good: "The least turning in upon himself of the power to love would turn the balance against man; and then his selfhood, in the delight of his freedom, would be tempted into excesses, and evil would spring from such excess in its rankest growth. To love oneself for the sake of self is to hate all others who do not minister to that love

—not only by *loving* us, but by *serving* us. Man thus sets himself up as a god; and demanding others to serve and worship him, defies God Himself—as his enemy."[38]

Swedenborg emphasized that even those who sought the light of heaven could surround themselves with darkness: "For he that loves divine truths for the sake of his own glory regards himself and not the Lord." An ideal of "usefulness" was the only way to resist the perils of self-love. "It seems to have been the first order of Providence respecting us," wrote William Cooper Howells, with no sense of violating the idea of voluntarism, "that we should be so bound to each other that no man can be independent. Our inevitable duties in some way relate to others; and even what we do for ourselves, if rightly done[,] is done for others." This Swedenborgian concept of self-control assimilated traditional communal notions of mutual responsibility.[39]

Lessons in Swedenborgian self-control began early in the Howells family. William Cooper Howells believed children received truth with greater delight than adults; heaven seemed "nearer" to children. But hell was in equal proximity. Howells once heard his father explain Swedenborg's frightening conception of hell to a neighbor. William Cooper Howells pointed out that each person cast himself into hell "if he loved the evil rather than the good, and that no mercy could [save him] without destroying him, for a man's love was his very self." According to Swedenborg's notion of "ruling love," salvation or damnation was fated in every choice. To avoid damnation and self-destruction, Howells resolved that "he would do his poor best to love the good."[40]

William Cooper Howells taught that redeeming usefulness could be accomplished in the family and the world at large. He put his children to work in the family's printing office for their "souls' sake," enacting his belief that "every one should fulfil a use." When Howells tired at his compositor's tasks, his father reminded him that "the angels in the highest heaven delighted in uses."[41] Throughout Howells's childhood, William Cooper Howells demonstrated the communal dimension of Swedenborgian usefulness in his antislavery activities. Shifting from Conscience Whig to Free

Soiler to radical Republican, he set an example of usefulness that extended to the whole nation.

With its antisacramental and ethical emphasis, Swedenborgianism mirrored the secular tendency to substitute self-control for religious authority and to understand moral purpose as social utility. The central Swedenborgian term, *usefulness*, increasingly replaced *righteousness* in the vocabulary of the aspiring middle class. Henry Ward Beecher used the term to encourage "industry" and discourage "idleness": "All efforts without the design of usefulness," he warned in *Lectures to Young Men*, "are of the nature of Idleness."[42] But Swedenborgian demands went far beyond conventional cautions. Mere social utility could not ensure salvation, usefulness was damning if performed from a love of self, and rankest evil resulted from the "least turning in" of love.

The same intensity entered into the ideal of "moral nurture" that William Cooper Howells shared with advice writers. Earlier Calvinists had enjoined a strict breaking of the child's will to subdue expressions of original sin, but nineteenth-century moralists encouraged a gentle bending of the child's will to cultivate correct choices. Although the voluntarism encouraged by moral nurture supported autonomous individualism, affectionate means could significantly restrict a child's freedom. The advice writer Heman Humphrey grasped the power of affectionate means when he intoned, "there is no constraint like that of love."[43]

Many stories and articles that William Cooper Howells selected for his Swedenborgian newspaper emphasized affectionate means of child rearing and religious instruction. "Let a mother approve of a child's conduct whenever she can," one article suggested. "Let her show that his good behavior makes her sincerely happy. Let her reward him for his effort to please by smiles and affection. In this way she will nourish in her child's heart some of the noblest and most desirable feelings of our nature."[44] Later in life, when his daughter Annie lost patience with his granddaughter Vevie and asked for his counsel, William Cooper Howells summarized his attitude toward child rearing. His advice touched all the themes of moral nurture—the need to use gentle persuasion, the need to bend rather than break the will, the need to encourage correct choices, and the need to establish loving constraints. Annie had resorted to a "whipping" when the little girl refused to dress:

It is a good plan to let the anger of a child cool down, [William Cooper Howells suggested,] so that they may get out of the fighting state, and listen to what you propose. The "obstinacy" of children is "force of character" when they grow up. It is a bad plan to break it up and yet you must control and direct. It might have been a good plan to have told her that she had to submit to your direction, in that you would not dress her; but rather than whip her, which was painful to you as well as to her, you would leave her undressed till the girl did it. She would have got tired and hungry at last, and then come to your terms. The point is to let her know that you want her to submit willingly; but that *you* were to have *your* way in the event. But dear Annie, I do not know what to tell you, better than to use all the reasoning, and all the force of affection you can.[45]

"Force of affection" precisely conveys the mingling of love and constraint emphasized by advocates for civilized morality. William Cooper Howells was particularly sensitive to the force of affection because his child-rearing principles were set against his father's more overtly coercive practices. Shifting from quiet Quaker worship to "shouting" Methodism, his father had thrust him into long camp meetings designed to force conversion. William Cooper Howells had silently submitted to conversion in the mourner's circle at age fourteen, an early age reflecting evangelicals' nervousness over children about to leave home. But he never experienced genuine "enjoyment," the renewal of conversion feeling that proved inward conviction. He became a secret Owenite atheist, breaking with Methodism when he finally left home. During his "wander years" as a journeyman printer, he was attracted to Swedenborgianism, a faith that shared the Quaker emphasis on gradual means of spiritual instruction. He decided that his children would never suffer the kind of coercion he had experienced as a child. He would guide rather than compel them to choose salvation; he would store their memories with "truths that will direct their affections to proper objects."[46]

William Cooper Howells's rebellious trust in affectionate measures is revealed by an incident Howells recalled in his autobiography. His grandfather had discovered the Howells boys breaking the Sabbath, loitering beside the river and throwing stones at the body of a dead dog lodged in driftwood. Expecting a sharp reprimand or at least a good talking-to, the grandfather marched them home and reported the affront to Howells's father. But after a brief reproof, William Cooper Howells gently concluded, "Boys, consider yourselves soundly thrashed." His ironic words rebuked his own father's coercive practices and endorsed the affectionate measures he had put in their place.[47]

Another incident from Howells's autobiography demonstrates the effectiveness of his father's gentle approach. At age four or five, Howells traced an engraving of a bull on greased paper and proclaimed that he had drawn the picture himself. When his brother called him a liar, their quarrel came to their father's attention. William Cooper Howells ended the dispute by accepting his son's fib as the truth. Howells stated that his father always believed "people are more apt to be true if you trust them than if you doubt them." Encouraging free choice within the constraints of love, his father gave Howells "a far worse conscience than if [he] had whipped him." Howells recalled that for a long time afterward he was "very miserable about that bull."[48] As a "forgiving parent" who despised the "rod of correction," William Cooper Howells fostered the substitute authority of conscience. Agreeing with middle-class moralists, he trusted that conscience would guide his children into the outer world and preserve their chances for both success and salvation.[49] Conscience would make them miserable for their least assertions of selfishness, just as it had made Howells miserable for his fib about the bull.

Swedenborgian teachings and affectionate child rearing channeled Howells's self-accusations into an abhorrence of self-love. But additional family circumstances apparently made him particularly susceptible to severe demands of conscience. In Howells's story of Pony Baker, the father tells Pony that his mother should not be blamed for her actions. He explains that lately she has been "ner-

vous."[50] Howells chose the word "nervous" carefully, for it recalled his own sufferings in adolescence and, more grievously, the
decline and death from "nervous prostration" of his gifted daughter
Winifred.[51] Mary Howells's nervousness seems to have peaked just
when her son was most vulnerable to self-accusations. Threatening
changes in Mary Howells's life—particularly separation from her
kin—may have caused her to act abruptly and without reflection,
as she did in the rose-throwing incident.

William Cooper Howells's idealized notion of family life was to
make a "heaven on earth in his beloved and loving home," but his
adherence to Swedenborgianism encouraged a more restricted and
lonely family style than Mary Howells desired. Before her marriage, she had been converted to evangelical Methodism, honored
as "the first one of [her] large family to profess faith in Jesus." The
communal worship of her earlier years was an extension of the
peace and security she felt in her family as the eldest daughter
among nine children. With considerable difficulty, Mary Howells
had to adjust to the more solitary life thrust upon her by her
marriage. Like other antebellum Americans, William Cooper
Howells was excited by the idea that new economic opportunities
were opening around him. Mary Howells discovered that pursuit
of these opportunities set families in motions that revolved more
around spouses than around kin.[52]

During the early years of her marriage, Mary Howells endured
separation from her Dean kin while her husband wandered from
town to town looking for permanent work as a printer. When
William Cooper Howells's efforts reached an impasse in 1836, his
father-in-law, John Dean, proposed that William, Mary, and their
small son, Joseph, settle on an adjacent lot in the eastern Ohio
village of Martinsville. Agreeing with John Dean that it was "A
Very hard thing to labor for Naught," William Cooper Howells
accepted his invitation. Although her father sickened and died a
short time later, Mary Howells felt relieved to be at home and free
of the loneliness she always suffered when apart from her kin. In
1837 her second son, William Dean, was born within the supportive circle of her mother and sisters. In later life, Mary Howells

recalled the pleasure she took in her second child, whose "little body was so be[a]utifully moulded[,] so perfectly sym[m]etrical," whose "hands were exquisit[ely] rounded on their backs like little pin cushions."[53]

By 1839, however, Mary Howells's peace and security were at risk as her husband became more and more restless. In the aftermath of the financial panic, William Cooper Howells began looking for new opportunities to replace the flagging house-painting business he had begun in Martinsville. He found a far better chance than he had expected, as editor of the *Intelligencer*, a Whig newspaper in Hamilton, a village on the far western side of Ohio, near Cincinnati. The offer renewed his optimistic assessment of economic opportunities. But Mary Howells wished to stay with her kin, and she resisted the move. She refused her permission to sell the house they had built in Martinsville, a decision her husband always resented because he believed it hindered their chances for financial success in Hamilton. Though she did not change her decision on the house, Mary Howells finally followed her husband to Hamilton. They brought three small children to the village, for a daughter, Victoria, had been born two years before. At this time, their son William Dean was nearly three years old.[54]

By the time Howells reached age six in 1843, his mother had borne two more children—Samuel and Aurelia—and soon she was pregnant with her sixth child. Managing her growing household apart from the traditional aid and encouragement of her kin was undoubtedly a strain. But her distress and loneliness were accentuated by pressure to relinquish her communal Methodist worship for unceremonious Swedenborgian readings in her home. The presence in Hamilton of William Cooper Howells's Methodist father offered no support because father and son were fervently divided on religious questions. Every Sunday afternoon they would "have it out," distressing Mary Howells with the heat of their arguments. The grandfather grieved for the eternal fate of grandchildren he feared damned without a Methodist conversion. He communicated his fears to his grandchildren, caressing them and lamenting out of his pity, "Poor thing, poor thing!" Despite pres-

sures from his father, however, William Cooper Howells adamantly set the "New Church" of Swedenborg against the "Old
Church" of Methodism. He scorned Methodism as a faith that led
not to salvation but to "spiritual barrenness." As long as Mary
Howells continued a Methodist, she silently sided against her
husband in a distressing quarrel.[55]

Mary Howells's sense of estrangement and loneliness in Hamilton was reinforced by her husband's opposition to slavery. Antislavery was an eccentric and dangerous stand in Hamilton, a part
of southern Ohio regarded as the "South Carolina of the North."
Just to the south in Cincinnati, antiabolitionist mobs rioted in
1836, 1841, and 1843, directing their animus against newspaper
editors they considered "white traitors" and "amalgamationists."
Contrary to abolitionists, William Cooper Howells believed moral
suasion would fail to end slavery unless allied with political means.
Nonetheless, his sentiment against slavery and his kin associations
identified him with the abolitionist cause. His father was a well-
known abolitionist whose opinions had hurried him from the
Wheeling, Virginia, area. In 1836, William Cooper Howells's cousin
Edward had been working for James Birney on the *Philanthropist* in
Cincinnati when an antiabolitionist mob destroyed the newspaper's
press. In 1841, when William Cooper Howells condemned a Dayton mob that had killed a man at an abolitionist rally, his newspaper rivals seized the chance to accuse him of secret abolitionism.
He denied the charge but failed to quiet his opponents. In this
atmosphere of heightened rhetoric and threatened violence, Mary
Howells's anxieties intensified. She began to long inconsolably for
her Martinsville kin.[56]

Howells recalled that sometimes his mother's apprehensions
provoked "an insupportable crisis," followed by her departure on
one of her "homesick visits Up-the-River." Whenever she fled to
Martinsville, she left her children in the charge of a girl who
became "lastingly abhorrent" to her son. The girl made an "insipid
milk-gravy" that ruined the beefsteak, and she had recurrent nightmares punctuated with "a sort of wild involuntary yodeling."
Howells remembered that when his mother returned and released

him from this strange tormentor, she "always came back more contented with the home which she herself was for us." But as a child he resented her absences. His "perversely eclectic memory" registered his mother's explanation for becoming more contented —she said, "one could burn wood in Hamilton, but had to burn coal [in Martinsville], where everything was smutched by it."[57] Howells undoubtedly felt better reasons required his mother's presence in Hamilton: He was in Hamilton, and he needed protection from her threatening replacement.

A dreamlike, punitive mother figure who spoiled food and disrupted sleep, the yodeling girl represents the kind of magical self-reproach exacted by the conscience of a young child. She denied Howells fundamental expressions of mother's love—pleasing food and soothing sleep. The girl may have taken on frightening features because Howells feared that his mother's absence was really abandonment, a punishment he deserved for his passionate impulses. His mother's absence raised tormenting feelings, while her presence temporarily dispelled his fears. Howells recalled a supportive mother figure in his memory of the celebration that occurred when his mother returned from another visit to Martinsville, a visit that had included him. She threw herself onto the lush grass and "tossed and frolicked with her little ones like a girl." This image endured through the years, Howells wrote in his autobiography, "while all the phantasmagory of spectres has long vanished away."[58]

Like many nineteenth-century Americans, Howells regarded his mother not only as "the centre of home" but also as "home itself."[59] But mother and home provided Howells with an imperfect sense of security. During crucial times in Howells's early childhood, Mary Howells felt estranged from home and failed to ease her son's natural tensions. Growing up under the influence of Swedenborgianism and affectionate child rearing, he developed a conscience that constantly tested his individual desires for hints of self-love. These childhood experiences set him against mainstream middle-class beliefs. In the rhetoric of autonomous individualism, self-control produced a disciplined, energetic individual, able to take hold of market opportunities and work for the general welfare while pursuing his own self-interest. But Howells found atonement possible only through *selfless* devotion to the good of all. Only this commitment could still the voice that told him he was "nothing but self"—isolated, unpitied, and without salvation.[60]

CHAPTER 2

A Kind of Double Life

Every boy is two or three boys, or twenty or thirty different kinds
of boys in one; he is all the time living many lives and forming
many characters; but it is a good thing if he can keep one life and
one character when he gets to be a man. He may turn out to be like
an onion when he is grown up, and be nothing but hulls, that you
keep peeling off, one after another, till you think you have got down
to the heart, at last, and then you have got down to nothing.

HOWELLS, 1890

When he faltered in his later efforts to realize his father's ideal of
usefulness, Howells often expressed his despair in Swedenborgian
imagery. Remembering his earliest literary experiments in his autobiography *A Boy's Town* (1890), he contrasted his elder brother
Joseph's "ideal of usefulness" with his own "ideal of glory." Refer-
ring to himself as "my boy," Howells asserted that "his brother
was a calm light of common-sense, of justice, of truth, while [my
boy] was a fantastic flicker of gaudy purposes which he wished to
make shine before men in their fulfilment. His brother was always
doing for him and for the younger children; while my boy only
did for himself." [1] The experiences of Howells's later childhood
encouraged this deep ambivalence toward his literary aspirations.
As his family struggled to secure and maintain middle-class status,

Howells had frequent occasion to feel that his literary desires were "selfish," that they failed to serve his family's best interests.

Historians of antebellum America have detected an emergent family style that focused on vocational choice as the means of ascent to the middle class. As land acquisition became more and more difficult, parents typically directed sons toward the expanding clerical and professional occupations. Parents of narrower means sometimes found it necessary to concentrate resources on a single son, reviving the traditional practice of maintaining the patrimony intact. Parents expected their other children—and almost always their daughters—to accept this preferment. The single son selected for advancement became the family hope, the embodiment in material and symbolic terms of his family's desire for a prosperous and secure future.[2]

This middling style of developing the family hope contrasted with another adaptation of traditional family life. In earlier times, parents had typically subordinated the desires of individual children to the immediate material needs of the family. Everyday working responsibilities that supported the whole family overrode individual expectations of independent futures, which were entirely the prerogative of parents. Children's moral duties were tied to the ethic of mutual aid rather than to self-development.[3]

Families without resources to cultivate even a single child as the family hope continued to rely on mutual aid as a necessary means of survival. But families aspiring to the secure middle class began to associate mutual aid with diminished, working-class status. Many working-class families followed the traditional practice of stretching household boundaries to include boarders and lodgers—apprentices and others who contributed labor or "ready money" for the family's immediate support. Middle-class families, on the other hand, began to exclude boarders and lodgers from their households to provide the privacy and concentrated attention that promoted the vocational strivings of their individual children.[4]

The child's choice of vocation took on great consequence for antebellum families, becoming a sign of class status for children and parents alike. Few parents left vocational choice entirely to their child's "self-cultivated" discretion, as some advice writers such as Horace Greeley suggested. Most parents were less sanguine than Greeley concerning their child's capacity to choose correctly. They made vocational choice a matter of intense emotional negotiation, especially with the child selected as the family hope.[5]

In the Howells family, middle-class hopes concentrated on the inclinations of William Dean, whose love of literature offered a vision of ascent beyond clerical and professional occupations to headier realms of usefulness. Although Howells worked in his father's shop as soon as he was able, William Cooper Howells encouraged his son to imagine a grand future as a literary artist. But economic circumstances frequently forced William Cooper Howells to rely heavily on children's labor. Because his family lapsed from strategies that preferred him as the family hope, Howells sometimes found his expectations sharply contradicted. These dismaying moments accentuated his feeling that he was leading a "kind of double life," that one part of him supported the mutual needs of his family while another part of him sought to fulfill a selfish ambition in literature.[6]

"I should be interested to know now," Howells wrote in one of his autobiographies, "how the notion of authorship first crept into my mind, but I do not in the least know."[7] As a small child, however, he first imagined creating literature when he began to imitate the "loveliness" of the poetry his father frequently read aloud to the family. William Cooper Howells often selected passages from Swedenborg, but he routinely ended a day's labor with verses from secular poets such as James Thomson, Thomas Moore, Robert Burns, and Walter Scott. Howells's earliest memory of these occasions appears in A Boy's Town: "The first book my boy remembered to have heard him read was Moore's 'Lalla Rookh,' of which he formed but a vague notion, though while he struggled after its meaning he took all its music in, and began at once to make rhymes of his own. He had no conception of literature except the pleasure there was in making it; and he had no outlook into the world of it, which must have been pretty open to his father."[8]

Reading aloud to his family, William Cooper Howells followed a traditional style of devotional practice that reinforced the notion that the husband and father was God's representative in the home and responsible for his family's salvation. By the early nineteenth century, literature had become a means to this end. William Cooper Howells believed literature and especially poetry were suffused with spiritual meaning. Poetry, he wrote later in life, looks "inward to the soul. . . . Its range is universal. Whatever we think, or love, whatever we imagine or know; whether of Earth or Heaven, our highest conceptions of it are told in poetry." Like many antebellum Americans, William Cooper Howells granted literature a spiritual authority once exclusively reserved for sacred scripture and devotional texts.[9] Following Swedenborg's suggestion that everything earthly had spiritual "use," he included secular poems and stories in the *Retina* for the religious instruction of young children. He brought this combination of the religious and secular lessons home in his daily readings to his family, tying "Memorable Relations" from Swedenborg to spiritual expressions in poetry.[10]

This association of literature and religion was reinforced when the Howells family entertained itinerant Swedenborgian ministers. Howells recalled an awe-inspiring occasion when he declaimed Fitz-Greene Halleck's "Marco Bozzaris" before one of these "personally sacred" beings, whose influence seemed to free him "from the fear in which his days seem mostly to have been passed."[11] Understood as a spiritual offering, literature provided similar consolation. It helped to heal the emotional wounds of Howells's earlier childhood, strengthening him against his torturing nightmares and self-accusations. Literature, Howells began to sense, might offer personal atonement.

Yet Howells did not find total self-affirmation in his earliest attempts to create literature. While describing the harsh punishments meted out by schoolmasters in *A Boy's Town*, he shifted to an occasion when he had joined his fascination for literature to the

1. In 1917, Clifton Johnson photographed scenes to illustrate Howells's autobiography *Years of My Youth*. Little remained of the past in Hamilton, Ohio, but remnants of the Miami Canal. "In the warm summer nights of that southerly latitude," Howells fondly recalled, "the water swarmed with laughing, shouting, screaming boys, who plunged from the banks and rioted in the delicious water, diving and ducking, flying and following. . . . They turned somersaults from the decks of the canal-boats; some of the boys could turn double somersaults."

Swedenborgian conception of evil.[12] One day, to ease his boredom in the common school, he flipped to the back of his grammar and discovered the rules of prosody. He felt immediately as if "heaven had opened to him." He now possessed the means that allowed him to enter his father's sacred world. "The music which he had followed through those poems his father read was no longer a mystery," Howells wrote; "he had its key, its secret; he might hope to wield its charm, to lay its spell upon others." He mastered the rules at first reading and immediately composed a poem describing heaven. After school, he hurried home to present his poem as an offering to his father.

Although he was impressed by his son's precocious effort, William Cooper Howells raised a fine point about Swedenborgian belief. Drawing from his current controversies with Universalists, he remarked that the poem represented heaven in the sky, and he wished his son "to realize that heaven was a *state* and not a *place*, and that we could have it in this world as well as the next." Swedenborgians believed in continuity between earthly and heavenly states; spiritual perfection commenced when one renounced the love of self for the love of others. Heaven like hell was an immediate reality, here and now, fated in every choice. Howells promised always to remember the true nature of heaven, but he knew that many of the poets his father read put heaven in the sky, and he thought he could do likewise, "no matter what Swedenborg said." His father's didactic response left Howells feeling resentful. "[My Boy] revered Swedenborg," Howells recalled; "he had a religious awe of the seer's lithograph portrait in full-bottom wig which hung in the front-room, but he did not see how even Swedenborg could have helped calling heaven a place if he had been making poetry." [13]

William Cooper Howells's sectarian precision concerning heaven overrode his usual sensitivity. He confused his son's understanding that poetry naturally expressed spiritual truth. To reaffirm pride in his accomplishment, Howells rebelliously questioned Swedenborg's supreme authority — symbolized judicially in the seer's full-bottom-wig portrait. But pride was a dangerous emotion in a Swedenborgian universe. The prosody incident undoubtedly provoked Howells's self-accusations and reinforced his tendency to associate all self-assertion, even devotional literary expression, with malignant self-love.

While distrust of his literary desires remained a disturbing undercurrent, other experiences tended to diminish this feeling and support Howells's notion that creating literature was a redemptive act. In the family printing office where he had been put to use for the sake of his soul, Howells discovered that certain kinds of literary eloquence were much admired. Listening to his father's fervent talk around the editorial desk, Howells was drawn into a vibrant arena of public debate where language was a powerful instrument of moral action. His father's opposition to the Mexican War sealed this association. "In a community hot with wild Democratic zeal for the invasion, and often flown with whiskey against the enemies of the war," Howells recalled, "he fought it steadily . . . and spared neither men no[r] measures in his denunciations." On one occasion, William Cooper Howells read aloud from James Russell Lowell's *Biglow Papers*, enjoying the poet's satiric condemnations of the war's absurdities. He celebrated Thomas Corwin's diatribe against the war with even more enthusiasm. Howells helped to set the speech in type, memorizing Corwin's fearful prophecy that a vengeful God would punish all the American warriors who ventured onto Mexican soil. Howells's daily work in the printing office—where he quickly became the "most proficient" helper among the children—encouraged him to feel that he was worthy because his work was devoted to the production of righteous words.[14]

As Howells began to imagine literature as a sanctified vocation, his father made the choice of a literary career nearly inevitable by investing his son with hopes he had once cherished for himself. The time soon passed when William Cooper Howells considered his son's literary productions primarily as opportunities for religious instruction. When Howells demonstrated a true love of poetry, his father became his enthusiastic literary guide, encouraging him to read the poets and writers he most adored himself. William Cooper Howells believed his own literary talents had been wasted by the "slavish" labor of his youth. He had composed a few poems and written a melodrama on the War of 1812 that had failed after a single performance. In the *Gleaner*, he had tried his hand at literary publishing. Discouraged with the "political yoke" he had assumed as a Whig editor, he longed for a position more commensurate with the boundless opportunities he sensed around him. In 1844 he broke his association with the *Intelligencer* and began more fulfilling work as editor of the *Retina*. But after a few months his religious forum failed, and he made an embarrassing return to his political newspaper. In the wake of this disappointment, he renewed his optimism by eagerly promoting his son's literary interests.[15]

Howells recalled that in himself, more than in the other children, his father "divined and encouraged the love of poetry." Through subtle attentions, William Cooper Howells selected his son Will to achieve the grand success he himself had found elusive. "The time came early in our companionship," Howells observed, "when he thought fit to tell me that he regarded me as different from other boys my age; and I had a very great and sweet happiness without alloy of vanity, from his serious and considered words. He did not say that he expected great things of me; though I had to check his fondness in offering my poor endeavors for the recognition of print." William Cooper Howells's enthusiastic actions for his "teachable and gentle" son undoubtedly overrode his occasional words of caution. While circumstances had prevented his own accomplishment of "great things," it would not be the same for his son.[16]

Still, William Cooper Howells's avid promotion of his son's literary interests expressed a degree of latent jealousy. "He was always prouder than I of what I did unaided," Howells wrote of his father; "he believed I could do everything without help."[17] With his father's encouragement to proceed on his own, Howells struggled to learn subjects he could have mastered easily with slight instruction. Insisting on the sufficiency of self-help, William Cooper Howells never taught his son the rudiments of grammar, even though he had once written a primer for schoolchildren. Howells wondered if his father had expected him to learn grammar by the "principle of heredity."[18] A force as powerful as heredity was involved—the communication of unfulfilled desire from one generation to the next. "Having had so little help in my studies," Howells explained, "I had a stupid pride in refusing all, even such as I might have availed myself of, without shame, in books."[19] Only the most exaggerated ideal of self-sufficiency ruled out all help from books, but the faith Howells accepted from his father had this effect.

As he molded himself in his father's image, Howells began a struggle for autonomous achievement that was intensified by his father's sense of unbounded opportunities and complicated by his father's aggressive belief in the sufficiency of individual effort. At the same time, Howells's Swedenborgian conscience compelled him to test every self-assertion for hints of damning self-love. The expectation that he accomplish all by himself, without selfish regard for himself, while subordinating himself to the good of others, helps to explain Howells's desperate confusion during his youthful pursuit of a literary vocation. In the midst of his youthful struggles, his father, then confined to his newspaper tasks, wrote proudly to a friend, "Will is so much a continuation and development of my own aspirations and efforts that he seems almost myself."[20]

Selected by his father to fulfill his dream of success, Howells often received the emotional and material preferment granted the family hope. But in the Howells family, strategies of individual development were tenuously maintained against the strategies of mutual aid needed for day-to-day survival. In the country towns and small cities where William Cooper Howells sought a livelihood, printing had a deserved "repute for insolvency." Howells remembered journeymen printers who arrived out of nowhere at his father's office; if no work were available for a dollar a day, a hat was passed around the office, and the journeyman vanished with his meager take. Because newspaper subscriptions and advertising rarely paid expenses, printer-editors like William Cooper Howells fared little better. Their fate depended on the slim margin that came from political patronage. Twice during Howells's childhood, his father's advocacy of antislavery—minority opinion in the Whig party—scuttled his newspaper and set the family on the road.[21]

William Cooper Howells minimized the desperate realities of his trade and secured his "happy doubt of disaster" through traditional strategies of family survival.[22] The risks of the trade made printing in small towns and cities a household industry. Although Howells was allowed to choose between the common school and the printing office when he became old enough to work at age six or seven, his "choice" was fated by family necessity. Children were valued laborers. They saved the board of apprentices and the wages of journeymen. William and Mary Howells felt no urge to follow the middle-class strategy of family limitation; they added a new child

to their household every two years between 1837 and 1846. Howells was the second eldest child of a family that eventually numbered five brothers and three sisters, a work force appropriate for
the printing trade.[23]

Since only Howells and his brother Joseph were old enough to
work the print shop in Hamilton, his father followed the custom-
ary practice of enlarging his household with journeymen and apprentice "printer-boys." Howells recalled several printer boys who
lived in their Hamilton home. These printer boys became like
brothers and shared equally in daily tasks. When the cow was
abroad, everyone gave chase. Printer boys submitted to the same
paternal authority as the Howells children and received the same
instruction in Swedenborgian self-control: "I am very grateful to
you," one former printer boy wrote to William Cooper Howells,
"& shall try never to do an act that you would be ashamed of your
own boys for doing."[24] Household production and the boarding of
journeymen and printer boys was a way of life set apart from the
practices of the aspiring middle class. The middle-class ideal was a
family geared to the development of individual children, a family
enclosed in privacy, without boarders or other "strangers."[25]

William Cooper and Mary Howells expected their children to
be "duteous," to devote their labor to the welfare of the whole
family. They gave their children useful tasks to perform and taught
them to share. The children were "denied oftener than they were
indulged." Scarce family resources required that they make the
most of rare treats. Once their father brought three glorious oranges home from Cincinnati, and the children had to split the
oranges into five shares. William Cooper Howells preached frugal-
ity and sometimes abstinence. During hard times, his children did
without undershirts and made do with ragged clothes. Yet he was
always eager to indulge the literary appetites of his son Will. He
also granted him precious time. To pursue his literary studies,
Howells left the printing office early in the day and sealed himself
in a small study set aside for his exclusive use. Later William
Cooper Howells encouraged his son's writing by printing poems in

his own newspaper and pressing poems upon his journalistic friends.[26]

Cultivation of Howells's literary ambitions required sacrifices from other family members. The chief burden for picking up the slack in the printing office fell to Joseph, who clearly resented the favor shown his younger brother. Once Joseph commandeered Will's literary diary and wrote in the margin beside a poem, "Thus you see the Poetry bust rite out of the young poet, like a biled tater does out of the skin."[27] Joseph's teasing was often good-natured fun, but his earthy deflation of poetic pretension reveals Joseph's sense of the different futures assigned himself and his brother Will. Joseph was to take his father's place as a practical printer, working for the mutual survival of the family, if necessary through the sacrifice of his individual desires. His brother Will was to pursue his individual inclinations because he was destined for usefulness in larger spheres. Joseph was to be the family stalwart who would satisfy laboring necessities; Will was to be the family hope who would fulfill middle-class aspirations.

The message designating Howells the family hope was communicated with imperfect clarity. Encouraged to be an individual of special accomplishment who would be served by family support and sacrifice, Howells was also expected to respond to his family's immediate needs. He was aware of living a "kind of double life," of having an "inward being that was not the least like [his] outward being, but that somehow seemed to be [his] real self, whether it truly was so or not." His inward being resided in "a world of dreams, of hopes, of purposes" that came from his reading and writing, but his outward being was attached to everyday tasks that contributed to family survival.[28] During most of his childhood in Hamilton, Howells controlled his double-lived feelings. Then, as he recalled, the "skies changed."[29]

In 1848, William Cooper Howells refused to endorse Zachary Taylor, the Whig nominee for president, because Taylor was a slave-holding Southerner and a hero of the Mexican War. His decision to vote Free Soil rather than support "slave propagandism" cost him his standing in the Whig party and his editorship of the newspaper that provided the livelihood for a family that now numbered seven children with the addition of a daughter, Anne, and a son, John. His father's decision, Howells related, was an example of his "unconscious courage," a phrase that suggests Howells's feeling that his father had been foolish as well as brave.[30]

After he relinquished the *Intelligencer*, William Cooper Howells "amused his hopeful ingenuity" for several months, imagining entrepreneurial possibilities. He toyed with various money-making schemes, including the dream of turning milkweed into paper, while Joseph and Will kept the family solvent working as newspaper compositors. Deciding finally in the spring of 1849 that his only chance was another newspaper, William Cooper Howells returned as a renegade to his party. He put his note on the Dayton *Transcript*, a newspaper he immediately turned to antislavery Whiggery in competition with the mainstream Whig newspaper, the Dayton *Journal*.[31]

Without hope of party patronage, William Cooper Howells attempted to overcome his indebtedness by force of hard family labor. To broaden the newspaper's appeal, he added daily and weekly editions to the triweekly paper. Much of the task of printing the new editions fell to Joseph and Will. In Hamilton printing-office chores had been Howells's "delight"—the activity that truly revealed his "ruling love." In Dayton, however, printing-office chores became Howells's "oppression." At age twelve he worked six days a week from five in the morning until eleven at night, delivering papers, setting type, and collecting telegraph dispatches. "When Sunday came, and I could sleep as late as I liked," Howells recalled, "it was bliss such as I cannot tell to lie and rest, and rest, and rest!"[32]

Howells described the eighteen months his family spent in Dayton as "heavy years," "toil-years," "Boeotian years." His exaggeration of the actual time and its stupefying effect reflects his suffering. Being useful without relief left him little time to satisfy the longings of his inward self. He attended a few plays during the first days in Dayton, but throughout the whole period he read only a single significant book, Charlotte Brontë's *Jane Eyre*. This intense, gothic romance merged in his mind with the current spiritualist hysteria set off by the Rochester "Knockings." As he read the novel, he tried to ignore his sensation that spirits were near at hand, jangling pictures on the wall of his room.[33]

Renewed fearfulness of a world alive with malignant forces was further stimulated by the cholera epidemic that swiftly killed two hundred people in Dayton during the summer of 1849. As Howells watched funeral after funeral pass his door, the "brooding horror of the pestilence sank deep into [his] morbid soul." President Taylor called for a day of fasting to cleanse the nation of its sins, for the moral theory of disease identified the scourge as a visitation upon the damned. Word of this interpretation probably added to Howells's alarm when he suffered a "slight" attack himself. His mother decided to prepare him for death. She told him heaven was a better place where he would be loved more fully than on earth. But Howells became so distraught that she had to reassure him that he was in no danger of dying.[34]

In the midst of a family crisis, suffering from insecurity and fearing the scourge of the cholera, Mary Howells dissented from her husband's Swedenborgian notion that heaven was a state to be enjoyed in the present and for all time. Her Methodism allowed that submission to an "all-wise and good Providence" provided the only comfort for the earthly travail of suffering and death.[35] Mary Howells had returned to her Methodist faith because the move to Dayton had been traumatic, eroding the communal ties and feeling of respectability she had finally established in Hamilton. Dayton was a rapidly growing commercial city with "less neighborhood" than Hamilton. An afternoon tea no longer seemed possible, let alone a more communal gathering like a quilting. Through the week, Mary Howells managed a large household that included two journeymen printers. Her sole outing came on Sunday evening when the family visited her husband's brother Israel, a prosperous druggist in Dayton. Howells remembered his uncle's home as a vision of "worldly splendor," a notion he probably absorbed from his mother's admiration of its middle-class adornments, especially the parlor with piano, lace curtains, and haircloth chairs.[36]

As Mary Howells began to long for these emblems of middle-class security, her husband grew estranged from the individualistic and entrepreneurial assumptions of the middle-class ethos. In the midst of his difficulties, William Cooper Howells turned assertively to communal values. Influenced by his Swedenborgian beliefs and working-class movements in the East, he developed a radical critique of the national market society. He proclaimed that "radicalism" was essential for the "redemption of mankind" and proposed redistribution of land and abolition of interest to annul the "tyranny of the land[ed] and monied capitalists."[37] He believed one reform—the exemption of family homesteads from collection for debt—was especially important, for it would check "the restless spirit of adventure which is now drying up almost every domestic sentiment":

[Protecting family homesteads] will give birth to an affection for home and its associations, and elicit a new and more intimate patriotic relation to the State. It will tend to localize our people and attach them to the soil; and direct the accumulation of wealth in small hands to the form of the greatest usefulness. . . . It will call forth more domestic taste, and increase the comforts [of] home; and thus be the most direct means of elevating the masses of the community. It will tend to build up neighborly attachments, and establish endearments in social life that will be worth more to any people than the mines of California.[38]

As envisioned by William Cooper Howells, domestic sentiment would help to check the acquisitive spirit and reconstitute the traditional ethos of mutual aid. He cared less than Mary Howells for the "cane-seat-chair things" that would make the home a private refuge in an alien world.[39]

In addition to his long hours in the printing office and the loss of his time for literature, Howells suffered from his parents' tensions. His mother's despair recalled difficult moments of his earlier childhood when she had left the family for the haven of Martinsville. Before long, his anxieties coalesced in an episode he described as incredible for the "hard-heartedness" it revealed in his boyish

2. Mary Dean Howells, ca. 1846, fashionably dressed during her later days in Hamilton. "In the hard life of her childhood in the backwoods," Howells stated, "she was sent to an academy in the nearest town, but in the instant anguish of homesickness she walked ten miles back to the log-cabin where at night, as she would tell us, you could hear the wolves howling."

self. His parents had befriended a seduced and abandoned seamstress. They provided her with meals and included her in family
pleasures. Everyone but Howells welcomed her into the family
circle: "I would not take a dish from her at table, or hand her one;
I would not speak to her, if I could help it, or look at her; I left the
room when she came into it; and I expressed by every cruelty short
of words my righteous condemnation." His persistent persecution
of the girl ended when she confessed her pain to his parents, who
put him to "bitter shame" for his behavior.[40]

Troubled by the reawakening of his own sexual impulses, Howells acted out a ritual of middle-class respectability that went far
beyond the teachings of his parents. His condemnation of the
seamstress mirrored the most severe strictures of middle-class moralists, who viewed all sexual liaisons outside of marriage as abhorrent violations of self-control and offered little quarter to injured
parties. Presenting himself as a middle-class moralist—one of
"adamantine conscience," as he later put it—Howells set himself
apart from the seamstress as someone who possessed perfect control over his sexual impulses.[41]

But Howells's persecution of the seamstress also dramatized his
resentment of his family's lapse from strategies that nurtured him
as the family hope. The girl's presence in the family signaled that
neither his desire for privacy nor his expectation of exclusive care
would be honored in the difficult economic circumstances of Dayton. Forced to practice strict self-control himself by working beyond his physical strength and by burying his literary longings,
Howells undoubtedly harbored bitter thoughts concerning his usefulness to the family. This silent dissent from the ethic of mutual
aid made him vulnerable to self-accusations of selfishness. The
seamstress's publicly shameful violation of self-control gave him
the opportunity to vent his guilty feelings. By questioning why
she should be living with them, "like one of ourselves," he declared
his absolute virtue in Swedenborgian as well as sexual terms.[42]

Although his experiences in Dayton reinforced and complicated
his double-lived feelings, Howells was released from his anxiety
and bitterness when the *Transcript* failed after eighteen months of

unprofitable labor. William Cooper Howells celebrated the "inevitable break" with a day of swimming with his sons, but he was left in a difficult position. Having to depend again on family labor, he found employment for his sons in a German printing office. At the same time, he grew increasingly estranged from his political party. After the passage of the Fugitive Slave Law in September 1850, he severed all connections with the Whigs and considered his alternatives. Freed from the "political yoke" that had long frustrated him, he was inspired to make the most of necessity. He decided to carry his Swedenborgian principles further by putting his radical communal beliefs into practice. He planned a communal association modeled on worker cooperatives that would form around the nucleus of his kin, bringing together the families of his father and three brothers.[43]

William Cooper Howells's communal utopia was to reunite a scattered kin network. The economic basis of the commune on the Little Miami River was to be a milling privilege purchased by Israel, the prosperous druggist. Before his father and brothers arrived, William Cooper Howells was to establish a going concern. In late fall, to the great relief of his sons, who renounced the printing business forever, he moved his family to Eureka Mills, a name he chose to contrast his venture with quests for California gold. At Eureka Mills, William Cooper Howells hoped to recover more precious riches—"neighborly attachments" and "endearments in social life"—to oppose the acquisitive spirit.[44]

The move to Eureka Mills turned his family further away from its middle-class aspirations, but Howells regained his role as the family hope in the midst of the communal enterprise. At Eureka Mills, he recalled, the "stress of toil, with the shadow of failure darkening all, fell from me like the horror of an evil dream." He brought up the "long arrears of play" and renewed his devotion to literature. He started his diary, studied Spanish, and searched the barrels of paperback books that his father had brought from Dayton. His family's primitive log cabin had a gable window in the loft, and there he privately read Shakespeare, Scott, and other exemplars of the literary life. He developed a special kinship with

the wandering adventures of Don Quixote and began to think of
Cervantes as his "confidential friend." Delivered from pressures of
work and given the time he needed to experiment with literature,
Howells no longer suffered extraordinary fears. For once, he fondly
remembered, the surrounding solitude "had no terrors for the
childish fancy." With growing confidence, he devoted himself more
and more exclusively to his literary "delights."[45]

While the Howells children responded to the primitive conditions of log-cabin living with fascination and joyous abandon, the
transition was difficult for their parents. William Cooper Howells
was pleased and gratified sharing work with neighbors, but his
need for ready money complicated preparation of the commune.
Mary Howells's tensions were more pronounced. She could not
reconcile herself to the family's further descent from middle-class
respectability. Struggling with arduous open-hearth cooking and
enduring the constant grunting of pigs that jostled outside for a
warm position near the cabin's chimney, she felt renewed impulses
to flee up the river to Martinsville. Her husband persuaded her to
stay and comforted her by promising a frame house with middle-
class features of a parlor, dining room, and library. Her brother
Alexander urged her to resist her discontent: "When you look
around you," he wrote, "you see a great many you would not
exchange situations with."[46]

The divergent desires of his mother and father eventually disrupted Howells's serenity. The added cost of preparing a frame
house with middle-class comforts evidently depleted resources and
led to the family decision to remove Howells temporarily from his
literary delights. In the language of the printing trade, he was a
"good compositor, swift and clean," and when the family learned
of opportunities for ready money in Xenia and later in Dayton, the
family council "justly" decided he must go. The family ethic of
mutual aid supported this kind of occasional home leaving. While
no one else in the family seriously questioned the move, Howells
silently resisted the idea. The mere prospect of leaving Eureka
Mills "pierced [his] heart."[47]

Even before he was placed in the first printing shop, Howells was engulfed by an "anguish of homesickness." All the way to Xenia, he concentrated on the home he was leaving: "I had every fact of the cabin life before me; what each of the children was doing, especially the younger ones, and what, above all, my mother was doing, and how she was looking; and I saw the wretched little phantasm of myself moving about among them." After a brief introduction to his work and lodgings, he adamantly refused to stay in Xenia and agreed only after his father arranged additional work for Joseph. Giving up hope for ready money, William Cooper Howells placed his sons together in a hotel. Howells's frenzied homesickness had aborted his usefulness to his family. But when the work was done and he returned to Eureka Mills, he was "welcomed as from a year's absence."[48]

The second opportunity in a Dayton print shop seemed less risky because Howells would be in a familiar city and could stay with his uncle Israel. Nevertheless, his anguish immediately resurfaced once he arrived in Dayton. He managed to subdue his tears only by gulping great quantities of water. Finally, his alarmed uncle sent him home, where he arrived feeling as if he had been "saved from death." Although he had lost a second opportunity for ready money, his family welcomed him once more as an "honored guest." All that day, he was treated as "company." His mother was most solicitous, responding with special tenderness to a malady she had suffered frequently herself. "Doubtless she knew that it would have been better for me to have conquered myself," Howells reflected, "but my defeat was dearer to her than my triumph could have been."[49]

By sending him to work in Xenia and Dayton, Howells's family had violated his belief that he was the family hope as well as his sense of readiness for the journey away from home. His powerful feelings of resentment provoked the resistance he expressed through his homesickness. But his rebellion from family duty was certainly accompanied by feelings of selfishness that provoked his sense of abandonment—the fantasized punishment he had suffered in his earlier years. His image of himself as a "little phantasm" moving among the younger children represented his yearning for return

3. The photographer Clifton Johnson found Eureka Mills deserted. Fire had razed the mills, the dam had crumbled, and the millrace had become a dry ditch. The name itself had been forgotten. The site nevertheless suggested the beauty that Howells as a boy had associated with an oceanic sense of wonder, the feeling, as he later described it, "that whatever perishes there is something in us that cannot die, that divinely regrets, divinely hopes."

and restoration. Had he been able to make this "little phantasm" real, Howells would have been once more a small child reunited with his mother's nurturing presence. At the same time, he would have been freed from his duties of work and returned to his literary delights.[50]

Howells's homesickness episodes actually mixed considerable triumph with defeat. His anguish gave him the appearance of an innocent sufferer rather than a selfish resister, but more significantly for his place in his family, his homesickness established a covert language of psychological fragility that communicated his aggressive demands. In the past, his parents had given him special treatment as the family hope—particularly freedom from work—to prepare for his future accomplishments. Finding himself without this support, Howells naturally felt abandoned and unconsciously imitated his mother's homesickness. Mary Howells had always offered the "rich compensation" of special favor when any child became ill; she could not help being even more responsive when her son showed signs of her own malady.[51] The sympathy and solicitude Howells received from his family sealed a silent pact: If they would respond to his needs, he would fulfill their dreams.

Scarcity of ready money scuttled William Cooper Howells's communal experiment at Eureka Mills in the fall of 1851. Israel's poor health and his failure to sell his Dayton drugstore meant the loss of the commune's chief financial supporter. Faced again with a struggle for survival, William Cooper Howells drew deeper from his fund of optimism and returned to the dominant social order. Since he could find work neither as an editor nor as a practical printer, he finally accepted a position on the *Ohio State Journal* in Columbus as a recorder of legislative debate. Will gained work in the same office as a compositor. Joseph, after several months on the river training to be a pilot with his Dean uncles, reluctantly resumed his role as family stalwart. Another in his "succession of sacrifices," Joseph's work in a grocery raised the family's income to seventeen dollars a week. On this sparse sum and with the initial aid of neighbors in Columbus, the family—enlarged by the birth of the eighth child, Henry—managed to survive.[52]

Although the move to Columbus ended the leisurely literary pleasures he had enjoyed at Eureka Mills, Howells yielded rather easily to his fate. Throughout his family's stay in Columbus, he displayed growing confidence. His diary—where he parodied his terror of dogs that made him "stir [his] stumps"—shows fears kept in abeyance. His work at a larger printing office provided him with congenial companions his own age, and the work itself was not as burdensome as in the past. He now possessed all the time he needed for his literary studies.[53] Howells was also supported by his family's clearer recognition—following the homesickness episodes—that he was the family hope. "A definite literary ambition grew up in me," he recalled, "and in the long reveries of the afternoon, when I was distributing my case, I fashioned a future of overpowering magnificence and undying celebrity. I should be ashamed to say what literary triumphs I achieved in those preposterous deliriums."[54]

At this time, William Cooper Howells reaffirmed his expectations for his son by smuggling one of Howells's poems, "Old Winter loose thy hold on us," into the *Ohio State Journal*. At first, Howells was embarrassed by this public exposure, but when the Cincinnati *Gazette* picked up his poem in the exchanges and reprinted it with a brief identifying comment, he confided to his diary, "Just think of that—called me a 'poet.' " Still, public recognition as a poet was difficult to bear because it opened him to ridicule from his fellow printers. In one instance, they patted him on the head while reciting lines from another poem he had written that depicted an emigrant's farewell to his "good old house dog." With the help of his father, Howells endured these gibes, and his humiliation was short-lived.[55]

Words from his grandfather struck deeper at Howells's sense of self. Even though Joseph Howells believed novels aroused fearful temptations, he thought poetry might serve spiritual purposes. He lavishly praised his grandson's poem "Old Winter" but added a troubling qualification. "We were much gratifyed to read the specimen of poetry by Dear Willie that you sent us," Joseph Howells asserted. "Oh that He may remember that it was from God that He [received] this tallent. May He use it to His Glory & praise, with all the endowments of his mind so that He may answer the [question] of his being. May the Lord save Him [from] Vanity & make Him a burning and shineing light." Throughout his life, Howells remembered the admonition of his Methodist grandfather as a damning Swedenborgian judgment. Glorifying God through his poetry, Howells recalled, was something "I had so little notion of doing in a selfish ideal of my own glory."[56]

Literature remained a realm of hazardous self-assertion, but Howells continued to identify literature with his atonement. He had met his "first real poet," an assistant editor at the *Ohio State Journal* named Florus B. Plimpton, whose poems occasionally appeared in the newspaper. But Howells did not consider Plimpton's verses very worthy. His impulse was to look beyond the models of his immediate society for the highest possible sanction. Howells chose Alexander Pope as his primary literary ideal, and "out-Poping Pope" became the single purpose of his study and writing. As a model, Pope had many advantages. He had risen to fame without formal schooling and had managed to live solely by literature. At age sixteen, Pope had launched his literary career with a series of pastoral poems supported by subscription. Two years ahead of Pope's schedule, Howells began a mock-heroic epic of his own, "with a whole apparatus of swains and shepherdesses, purling brooks, enamelled meads, rolling years." Adhering to Pope's insistence on strictly formal poetry, Howells developed a "fanaticism for methodical verse."[57]

Howells admired Pope's discipline in life as well as in poetry. "The poor man's life," he later noted, "was as weak and crooked as his frail, tormented body, but he had a dauntless spirit, and he fought his way against odds that might well have appalled a stronger nature."[58] Inspired by his identification with the dauntless Pope, Howells began to ease away from the double-lived feelings that had troubled him in Hamilton, Dayton, and Eureka Mills. A diary entry from these days in Columbus suggests his self-confidence. Howells had accompanied his father on a visit to the state asylum for the insane, where he noticed a physician, small in stature like himself, reading poetry to a group of inmates. Later he recorded the moment in his diary:

Here *was* a motley crowd, some of them lying at full length on the floor, others standing up and walking about, while crownless hats and dilapidated shirt-bosoms were the order of the day. In the midst of these terrible men, who [were] thoughtless as the brute, and ferocious as the tiger, stood a small man, (the assistant-physician) whom they could have torn limb from limb in a moment. Here was a beautiful instance of the power of mind over brute force. He was reading poetry to them, and these men totally bereft of reason, [were] listening like little children to the sweet cadence of verse.[59]

Recalling Howells's untroubled association with the wondrous verses his father had read to him as a child in Hamilton, this passage conveys the positive value Howells attached to the literary vocation while his family remained in Columbus. Literature, his partly chosen, partly ordained field of usefulness, might be surrounded by brutish forces—exaggerated fears, self-accusations, and double-lived feelings. Nevertheless, Howells sensed that through literature he might someday allay these difficulties and grandly demonstrate his worthiness.

PART II

Youth

CHAPTER 3

An Instance of Nervous Prostration

I should not mind being old, so much, if I always had the young, sure grip of myself. What I hate is this dreamy fumbling about my own identity, in which I detect myself at odd times. It seems sometimes as if it were somebody else, and I sometimes wish it were. But it will have to go on, and I must get what help I can out of the fact that it always *has* gone on. I think I could deal with the present, bad and bothering as it is, if it were not for visions of the past in which I appear to be mostly running about, full of sound and fury signifying nothing.

HOWELLS, 1902

In the spring of 1852, the skies changed again for the Howells family. Working as recorder of legislative debate, William Cooper Howells formed friendships with Free Soil politicians from the Western Reserve. Impressed by his antislavery battles in southern Ohio, Laban Sherman, a state senator from Ashtabula, suggested that he contact Henry Fassett, editor of the *Ashtabula Sentinel*. Because of his poor health, Fassett desired a partner. Anxious to resume editing and provide his family with a secure living, William Cooper Howells put his promise on a half share of the newspaper. He was now on solid antislavery ground. The *Sentinel* was the voice of the antislavery agitator Joshua Giddings, who had represented northeast Ohio in Congress for fourteen years. In addition, the paper reached a large constituency. While the average country newspaper claimed only four to five hundred subscribers, the *Sentinel* possessed nearly sixteen hundred.[1]

Giddings and other Ashtabula Free Soilers planned to extend the newspaper's influence. After six months in the lakeside village of Ashtabula, the Howells family moved to the county seat of Jefferson, supported by a group of Free Soil lawyers and farmers, who had bought out Fassett and modernized the enterprise by purchasing a steam press and new types. They intended to consolidate Free Soil gains from the 1852 elections and counter the influence of the Conneaut *Reporter*, the voice of United States Senator Benjamin Wade. Giddings and Wade were fellow citizens of Jefferson, where they had once shared a thriving law practice. Both abhorred slavery, but they had become bitter political rivals when Wade remained in the Whig party after the nomination of Taylor in 1848. Giddings believed Wade had sacrificed moral principle to party prestige and patronage, and he meant to confine Wade's voice to Conneaut by throwing the refurbished *Sentinel* "into every corner of the county."[2]

When the Howells family arrived in Jefferson, they found two brick buildings, unpainted houses, and boards laid down for sidewalks. This raw appearance did not discourage them, for it matched their sense of new beginnings. They soon began payments on a house, naming it "Saints' Rest" in honor of Mary Howells's desire for peace and security. The whole family turned to the task of making the newspaper pay. Joseph gave up his effort to avoid the printing business, and two years later he signed the note that made the *Sentinel* entirely a Howells enterprise. Although years passed before the newspaper and house were free and clear, Howells recalled these first days in Jefferson with nostalgia. The harsh winters made his compositing tasks arduous, since he had to thaw frozen types against the heated stove. But difficulties of work were alleviated by his feeling that his labor was not being wasted on a desperate cause.[3]

His family's renewed confidence helped to confirm Howells's status as the family hope. Once they settled into Jefferson, he initiated a strict routine and followed it faithfully. Each day he set several thousand ems of type, completing the task by early afternoon. The rest of the day and evening belonged to him. Cloistered at home in a small space beneath the staircase, he concentrated on literary study. He meant to master five languages—Greek, Latin, German, French, and Spanish—complete a biography of his beloved Cervantes, and surpass the literary accomplishments of Alexander Pope, especially in poetry. Since his father filled out the newspaper with *belles lettres*, the *Sentinel* became Howells's commonplace book where he offered selections from favorite writers. In the newspaper, he also tested his critical mettle and presented his own works in progress.[4]

Escape from privation and broadening literary ambitions made Howells's early adolescence a golden time. But this period also ushered in a difficult phase of dark episodes. Howells termed the most troubling of these episodes an instance of "nervous prostration." During the late spring of 1854 when he was seventeen, he overheard a doctor speak knowingly about hydrophobia. The doctor emphasized the silent course of the disease: " 'Works round in your system,' he said, 'for seven years or more, and then it breaks out and kills you.' " Although his father insisted he would never die from a dog bite he had suffered as a young child, Howells began to imagine climactic symptoms. "The splash of water anywhere was a sound I had to set my teeth against, lest the dreaded spasms should seize me," he recalled; "my fancy turned the scent of the forest fires burning round the village into the subjective odor of smoke which stifles the victim. I had no release from my obsession, except in the dreamless sleep which I fell into exhausted at night, or in that little instant of waking in the morning, when I had not yet had time to gather my terrors about me, or to begin the frenzied stress of my effort to experience the thing I dreaded."[5]

When Howells's anxieties persisted into the summer, his father released him from his compositing duties at the *Sentinel*. Howells

set off on long hikes and accompanied his father on business jour-
neys. His father explained that he was suffering from hypochondria, a delusion of disease he had experienced himself as a youth
without ill effects. But Howells was not persuaded, and soon his
fears provoked a crisis. Staying with his father at a country inn, he
awoke in a panic, splashed himself with water, and ran from the
room to await convulsions. He was relieved when these signs of
hydrophobia did not appear. As the summer heat receded, he
gradually overcame his anxieties. He knew his fears were illusory,
Howells recalled, but he was "helpless in the nervous prostration
which science, or our poor village medicine, was yet many years
from knowing or imagining."[6]

With the term *nervous prostration*, Howells tied his adolescent
breakdown to his contemporaries' understanding of nervous disorder. By the late nineteenth century, physicians such as James
Jackson Putnam, S. Weir Mitchell, and Mary Putnam Jacobi had
established a somatic theory to explain why "nervousness" was
afflicting many Americans. Giving self-control medical legitimacy,
they contended that every individual inherited a capacity for "nervous force" that required the most careful use. They warned that
excessive expenditures and abnormal imbalances of nervous force
could lead to fatigue, exhaustion, and death. The popularizer George
Beard emphasized that the competitive tenor of American life,
especially in occupations requiring "brain work," put people at
risk.[7] Howells considered nervous prostration a compelling explanation for his adolescent breakdown. His daughter Winifred had
been treated for nervous prostration by both Putnam and Mitchell.
The famous "rest cure" devised by Mitchell had failed to save her.
Howells believed Winifred had wasted away because of her cruel
inheritance of insufficient nervous force.[8]

While the theory of nervous prostration failed the scrutiny of
twentieth-century medicine, historians have learned to read nineteenth-century episodes of nervous prostration as signs of psychic
and cultural tensions. Nervous complaints expressed anxiety over
the loss of autonomous selfhood in modern urban-industrial society. The sense that modern life in some way *caused* nervous disor-

der led more and more people to question the middle-class ideal of self-control, the cornerstone of civilized morality. By the end of the nineteenth century, new therapeutic ideologies had begun to replace self-control with self-revitalization, an ideal more suited to the emerging consumer society.[9]

Many of the anxieties nineteenth-century Americans interpreted as "nervous prostration" were rooted in the shifting economic and social landscape of antebellum America. Close contemporaries of Howells, Jacobi and Beard had constructed their theories of nervousness from their own lives. Both had suffered vague nervous ailments in childhood and a succession of nervous crises in adolescence.[10] Many other individuals raised under the aegis of civilized morality could testify to similar experiences, especially to nervous episodes that had marked the onset of youth as they began to translate the moral lessons of childhood into virtuous adulthood.

The economic and social changes of the early nineteenth century made the period we now call adolescence a "nervous" time of life.[11] With the development of extensive market relations, parents began to prepare their children for a distant world away from home. Until age-graded schooling became more accepted in the 1850s, parents had little support in this effort. At the same time, emphasis on autonomous achievement undercut traditional deference to family authority. Subordination in spiritual matters weakened as well. Shifting responsibility for salvation from God to man, evangelical Protestants diminished God's sovereignty and undermined the spiritual guardianship of fathers.[12] Nevertheless, parental and spiritual authority was sustained by the strong emotional ties formed in childhood through moral nurture.

Anxious for the future and tied, sometimes guiltily, to the past, many antebellum youths suffered intense ambivalence. The ideal of self-control could accentuate their difficulties by adding a sense of failure to their confusion. Sometimes these feelings continued into adulthood. While nervous breakdowns beyond adolescence had complex immediate causes, they often involved renewed conflict over the divided commitments of youth. Joshua Giddings, the most prominent citizen in Jefferson, was a persistent nervous sufferer and seeker of cures. Plagued by "hypo" during his earlier career as a lawyer and land speculator, Giddings gained tenuous control over his malady when he shifted to antislavery politics. Becoming an antislavery agitator moderated Giddings's evangelical rebellion against his Calvinist upbringing and helped to keep his nervousness at bay.[13]

Howells's comparable "hypo" reveals the beginning of his struggle to accommodate the demands of childhood with the expanded possibilities he confronted as an adolescent. His breakdown was an extreme instance of an experience that was increasingly common among children of the middle class—a crisis marking the time when young people began to feel the need to resolve their past tensions and fortify their present commitments so that they could separate themselves from their families. Howells's struggle reflected the rigorous Swedenborgian version of self-control he had accepted during his childhood. Reconciling his individual desires with his conscience proved to be a hazardous undertaking.

A year before his traumatic breakdown, Howells had signaled the beginning of his adolescent distress. During his childhood, he had once awakened in the night with the pale light of the moon shining about him "in a very strange and phantasmal way." He thought immediately that he would die at age sixteen. His fear of this presentiment persisted. When he approached his sixteenth birthday, he began to anticipate his death. To await the fateful hour, he asked his mother the exact time of his birth. She said four o'clock in the morning. At the appointed time, Howells approached the family clock to witness the tolling of his death knell. But his father had taken the precaution to set the clock ahead, so he could tell his son that he had already lived beyond his sixteenth birthday. To calm him further, his father reasoned that since he was now in his seventeenth year, he could not possibly die at age sixteen. The family drama served its purpose. As he began to feel his adolescent anxieties, Howells reassured himself that he could depend on the solicitude of his parents, who responded with the same sympathy they had demonstrated during his homesickness episodes at Eureka Mills.[14]

At age sixteen, Howells could no longer consider himself a child. He had reached the time his parents anticipated when they began to nurture his capacity for civilized self-control, the time when he was to make the commitments that realized his role as the family hope.[15] Howells's fantasy of dying alerted his parents to his need for support, but the task of realizing his grand sense of literary vocation was a burden he was to carry alone, as an independent person destined to break free from home. By the time of his "nervous prostration" one year later, it was clear that he was failing in his effort to become an autonomous individual.

One source of Howells's troubles was his growing belief that he lacked proper means to accomplish the "greatest things" in literature. He had adhered to his father's insistence on self-help, but his unaided efforts seemed to have reached the "vanishing-point." While he proceeded "by accident or experiment," his efforts sometimes woefully misfired. His father had given him a thick manual on the romance languages, calling it a "sixteen-bladed grammar" for its advertised claims of ease and completeness. In fact, the book was poorly made. Howells discovered that it rendered all examples in the English word order, an "imposition" that confused his study and wasted his time.[16]

To make up his deficiencies, Howells compromised his father's ideal of self-help. He sought instruction from fellow villagers but found no true teacher. An elderly minister agreed to help with his Latin studies. But when Howells began his recitation, the minister nodded to sleep. "It still seems to me lamentable," Howells reflected, "that I should have had to grope my way and so imperfectly find it where a little light from another's lamp would have instantly shown it."[17]

Howells's longing for formal schooling provoked a family crisis when he asked his parents to send him to Grand River Institute, an academy in nearby Austinburg. The family concluded, mainly through the urging of Joseph, that they could afford neither the fees nor the loss of Will's labor from the printing office, which saved them the wages and board of a journeyman printer. His parents lamented this sacrifice of their son's ambition—and his status as the family hope—though his father was "easier consoled" because he believed his son could continue to rely on self-help.[18]

The family veto, Howells recalled, was not an "unjust hardship." He conveyed his disappointment so forcefully, however, that Joseph always regretted his responsibility for this "irreparable wrong." Past encouragement had fostered Howells's expectation of an academy education. As "colleges of the middling classes," academies kept costs within the range of their clientele. Scholarship students at Grand River Institute paid five to ten dollars for a thirteen-week term. By subordinating Howells's desire for schooling to the task of paying for the newspaper and house, his family inadvertently demoted him from his status as the family hope. Secretly disputing their decision, he felt more and more selfish.[19]

The decision made Howells doubly aware that his literary aspirations clashed with his family's primary goals. They endured considerable deprivation in Jefferson to pay off "debts which would not be denied" on the newspaper and the house. "What could poor father have been thinking of?" Howells asked Joseph in later life. "I never had an undershirt till after my terrible rheumatic fever." Besides stinting on clothes, the family relied on a steady diet of cheap salt pork, and improvised materials and means in the printing office. As before, they boarded journeymen and printer boys to preserve scarce cash.[20]

Nevertheless, Howells was allowed "a certain discretion" in purchasing books. He had free access to a few books and magazines, including the English reviews, through the *Sentinel*, and his father traded advertisements for used books from a Cleveland bookseller. But Howells's precious Spanish books required cash. They came directly from Roe Lockwood and Son of New York, a firm that supplied him with all his wishes. The firm even procured the official grammar of the Spanish Academy all the way from Madrid.[21]

4. Saints' Rest, the Howells family house in Jefferson. "Its possession," Howells wrote, "had been the poetry of my mother's hardworking, loving life, and no doubt she had watched with hope and fear the maturing of each of the notes for it, with the interest they bore, until the last was paid off. In my father's buoyant expectation of the best in everything, I do not think he had any misgiving of the event."

Because he indulged no other pleasure, Howells may not have felt that spending money on Spanish books was selfish. But his lighter burden of work at the printing office became a focus of family tension. "Hard words" were spoken by Will and his brother Joseph, who wanted Will to exact "the same devotion in our common work that [Joseph's] conscience exacted of himself." Unlike Will, who departed early in the afternoon for his literary study, Joseph worked "far into every night."[22]

In the months before his breakdown, Howells's study became secret and sequestered. Retaliating for his lost education, he "savagely absented [him]self" from his family and excluded them from his private literary domain. Determined to overcome all obstacles to his ambition by self-help alone, he jealously guarded his time. When friends came by his house serenading, he greeted them, dazed from his studies. But he refused to join their revelry. He stayed aloof from other village entertainments as well, breaking his resolve only for self-improvement. He joined older villagers in the Lyceum Legislature, where he was elected reporter of the mock proceedings. In his reports, he chided his absent peers, who seemed drawn to "oysters" and "hoe downs" more than things of the mind.[23]

Howells later regretted that he had not joined more fully in the life enjoyed by younger villagers. "My ambition was my barrier from the living world around me," he recalled; "I could not beat my way from it into that; it kept me absent and hampered me in the vain effort to be part of the reality I have always tried to portray." Yet Howells did not stay completely aloof. He felt a strong urge to reveal his private literary self to his fellow villagers. His effort proved disconcerting and distressing. While some people in his village "accepted [literature] as a real interest," few thought literature a worthwhile vocation.[24]

Outside the circle of his family, Howells consorted with a "group of middle-aged cronies," a triumvirate that formed his main literary companionship. Their chief was a disabled Englishman named William Goodrich, a Charles Dickens fanatic who was fond of the pathos that flavored his countryman's novels. Goodrich's demeanor was "misanthropical," but he managed to scrimp a living by building organs and working as a handyman. Another literary friend was a consumptive jack-of-all-trades named Wadsworth, an avid reader of the English essayists, from whom he acquired his "vividly profane and pyrotechnically witty" style of speech. The last member of Howells's coterie was a "pale" poet, also a consumptive, who managed the small book section of William Allen's drugstore. Although these sick and infirm literary friends admitted Howells to their drugstore bantering, loaned him books, and praised his writing when it appeared in the *Sentinel*, none represented mainstream village opinion. In fact, they prided themselves a militant minority. Goodrich won distinction by professing to despise democracy. He also claimed to vote with the proslavery Democrats, though he considered slavery "the scandal and reproach of the American name."[25]

In addition to the book section of Allen's drugstore, the *Sentinel* printing office provided a setting for literary talk. Yet only a single journeyman fully shared Howells's love of literature. Jim Williams was six years older than Howells and aspired beyond the printing office to a career as professor of languages in a Western college. He became Howells's "boon" companion and a peer group of one as they studied Cervantes, Shakespeare, and the several languages that would fit them for their literary vocations. To confound fellow villagers and assert their self-importance, they conversed conspicuously in Latin. During the time Jim Williams could free himself from the journeyman's trade, Howells felt less need of his drugstore triumvirate.[26]

Beyond Howells's circle of eccentric friends, little passion for literature existed in Jefferson. Howells protested that he was not thought "altogether queer" for his devotion to literature, but he once heard of an evening session at the dry-goods-and-grocery store where consensus opinion declared he "would be nowhere in a horse-trade." Besides horse traders and other practical-minded citizens, evangelical Protestants distrusted literature, sharing the suspicion of Howells's Methodist grandfather that novel readers trifled with the devil.[27]

Most readers in Jefferson did not, like Howells, cultivate literary tastes from the English reviews. The *Sentinel* published a stream of sentimental stories and poetry from female writers in the county, with a contribution from Celestia Colby appearing nearly every week. Howells expressed contempt for the "lachrymose" writing sent to the *Sentinel* by women, but he stayed equally aloof from the typical literary tastes of men. His brother Joseph enjoyed the sea stories of Frederick Marryat and the Indian narratives of Emerson Bennett. These adventure novels were "blood-puddings" for which

5. Howells, in 1856 at age eighteen, with his literary friend William
Goodrich on his right and a farmer named Miller on his left. The passion
that Goodrich displayed in his appreciation of Dickens he also brought to
his music. "It was fine," wrote Howells, "to see him as he sat before [an
organ he had built himself], with his long, tremulous hands outstretched
to the keys, his noble head thrown back and his sensitive face lifted in the
rapture of his music."

Howells "cared absolutely nothing." Joseph, for his part, associated his brother Will's mysterious illnesses with his strange reading
of "heavy, morbid books."[28]

Among the respectable middle class in Jefferson, those who
supported lyceums for themselves and academy training for their
children, literature was undoubtedly accepted as a means of personal cultivation or diversion. A small library open to the public
was kept in the office of a local lawyer. Benjamin Wade was
reputed to be a reader of the English reviews, even though he
retained an evangelical distrust of the theater and viewed Shake-

speare as "gross and barbarous." A few other villagers occasionally commended or encouraged Howells's literary aspirations. A woman who admired his "studious ways and gentle sedate manner" rewarded him appropriately with a set of Addison and Steele's *Spectator*.[29]

As a vocation that would command lifelong devotion, however, literature was deemed absolutely frivolous by the most forceful leaders of respectable opinion. When Joshua Giddings learned that his sons had begun to read novels, he fired off a letter filled with "pain & mortification and disappointed hope," despairing at their disregard of "proper" and "useful" studies. Though Howells intended to become a poet after the manner of Alexander Pope—to Howells the highest and worthiest of aspirations—all literary vocations were suspect in respectable village circles. Despite his intense ambition to become a scholar of languages, Jim Williams carried a "stigma of real laziness" in the village. Giddings warned his sons that dalliance with novels threatened similar disrepute. He feared novel reading would leave them "destitute of the proper knowledge to make yourself respected & beloved."[30]

In Jefferson and in Ashtabula County, the way to become respected and beloved was not to study literature but to join the bar and establish a reputation as a foe of slavery. Giddings exhorted his sons to give themselves wholly to the law: "Think of that & nothing else. Study that & nothing else. Read that & nothing else."[31] In contrast to Howells's vague sense of a literary career, formed from his reading and sustained by journals that arrived from a distance at Allen's drugstore, law offered a vision of useful endeavor embedded in the everyday life of the immediate community.

Law had a reputation in Jefferson that transcended the prejudices that prevailed elsewhere. Lawyers made up the Jefferson elite. They ranked among the wealthiest villagers and dominated positions of civic leadership. Giddings and Wade owned the two finest houses in the village. Giddings was the first person in Jefferson to purchase a piano. To Jeffersonians, these emblems of respectable middle-class status were fairly earned, for the most successful lawyers in the village had all begun poor. As a young man, Giddings had struggled on a hardscrabble farm, while Wade had started as a laborer on the Erie Canal. Giddings, Wade, and other members of the Jefferson bar had begun their rise by reading law in village offices. As they worked the rounds of county and district courts, they established regional contacts that extended their influence. Later they had gone into politics, winning county posts and prominent party positions. A fair number had gone further, successfully running for the state legislature. The pinnacle of ambition was election to the United States Congress, where Giddings, Wade, and Wade's brother Edward had gained renown for their agitation against slavery.[32]

If you wanted to be "somebody" in Jefferson, Howells admitted, the thing to do was "to read law and crowd forward in political life." Part of the affinity that drew Howells to Jim Williams was their mutual disdain for this "common ideal" of their village.[33] It was natural that they should react defensively to careers that were highly regarded and fully integrated into the everyday life of Jefferson. Because law and politics represented the most forceful vocational and ideological options available to young men, these careers offered strong, implicit criticism of the vaguer, literary strivings of Howells and his friend.

Law and politics were all the more forceful because they were associated with antislavery. Jefferson was a focal point of the Western Reserve, one of the few antislavery enclaves in Northern society. The principal discourse of the village adapted traditional republican themes of vigilance to purposes of antislavery agitation, elaborating a conspiratorial threat to "life, liberty, and the pursuit of happiness" from the Southern "slave power." "Slavery's gullet is large, and its roaring vociferous," warned William Cooper Howells. "The gluttonous monster will never be satiated until it has devoured us, or we have thrust the knife deep into its horrid heart."[34]

In Jefferson and the Western Reserve, antislavery politics was also a "holy cause." Antislavery agitation subsumed religious worship among civic leaders like Giddings, who attacked religious sects for their "infidel" toleration of slavery and emphasized that "religion should be a daily and habitual virtue." Giddings's church was his "Republican Church." His vision closely approximated the Swedenborgian morality of William Cooper Howells. Both believed that faith in a moral universe must be expressed in action: "In our relations with our fellows," William Cooper Howells observed in support of Giddings's attack on "infidel" sects, "we are never free from the obligations of the higher law, which binds us to do to others as we would have them do to us."[35]

Antislavery agitation fulfilled William Cooper Howells's belief in Swedenborgian usefulness and expressed his feeling that he was "never free" from moral obligation. As he channeled his religious zeal into Free Soil and later into radical Republican politics, he added the force of family authority to the dominant ideological and vocational options in Jefferson. Combining individual assertion with the communal imperative to do good for others, antislavery agitation helped middle-class Northerners like William Cooper Howells rationalize their problematic sense of individual autonomy. We should be aroused to throw off the degradation of slavery, he told his fellow villagers, "by the clanking of our own fetters."[36]

Merged with antislavery agitation, law and politics opened a field of action that seemed free of ambivalence and devoted to high ideals. Howells needed to believe that literature was comparably worthy, but dramatic changes in the political climate had made his task difficult. While Howells was anxiously pursuing his literary study, the party system that had contained the onslaughts of antislavery agitation for more than a decade began to unravel. In January 1854, Stephen Douglas introduced his Nebraska bill, authorizing the organization of Kansas and Nebraska territories on the basis of "popular sovereignty," a scheme antislavery forces viewed as a culminating ploy of the "slave power" conspiracy. "Indignation Meetings" in Jefferson and other antislavery strongholds directed intense opposition. "A blow may now be struck for liberty," William Cooper Howells told those who assembled in Jefferson, "which if forborne will leave us hopelessly bound for all time."[37]

During the spring and summer of Howells's breakdown year, the "Nebraska fraud" dominated community concern. A rhetorical refrain emphasized action to resist the "encroachments of the Slave-holding Aristocracy." Douglas's plan of territorial organization by popular sovereignty forced Wade's break with the Whigs. He shifted his support to the movement initiated by Giddings and other antislavery politicians to form a party embracing all opposition to Douglas. William Cooper Howells hoped that this coalition of "Independent Democrats" would evolve into an antislavery party with a broad national base. "Energy, zeal, persevering action, is the watchword," he asserted. "With these we conquer. Without them we fail."[38]

In the months preceding Howells's breakdown, the public atmosphere in Jefferson was charged with talk of political commitment. The tendency of events did not support someone seeking public approval for the vocation of poet. The political crisis most certainly weakened Howells's ability to stave off the deepening sense of selfishness aroused by his family's decision to keep him in the printing office. His self-preoccupation seemed all the more selfish when his father and other political leaders were calling for immediate political action on the behalf of others, beginning with the slave and extending to the entire nation. William Cooper Howells declared that failure to act for the slave was unmistakable evidence of "selfishness."[39]

In the midst of the Nebraska crisis, Howells's work took on an all-or-nothing urgency. He would do all that he wished against all odds; he would succeed at once to cast away all doubts. Howells maintained his resolve to master five languages, though he went at them "blindly and blunderingly." He felt more anxiety, however, over his inability to meet the severe standard he had set for his writing, particularly for his poetry. "Far into the night," Howells related, "I clung to my labored failures in rhyme while I listened for the ticking of the death-watch in the walls of my little study; or

6. Joshua R. Giddings, ca. mid-1850s. William Cooper Howells described Giddings's moral example: "He was earnestly enlisted for the rights of man; and when he talked of freedom, he meant it; and carried that purpose into the acts of his public and private life, with a perseverance that *commanded* the respect of even those whose schemes were thwarted by it; and won the admiration of all who appreciate the value of *continual* well doing."

if I had imagined, in my imitations of others' fiction, some character that the poet devoted to an early death, I helplessly identified myself with that character, and expected his fate."[40]

While resisting these self-punishing thoughts, Howells imagined that at least he was suffering for literature. He was comforted to think that his death would summon mourners to lament the loss of his unrealized genius. "At the same time that I was so horribly afraid of dying," he recalled, "I could have composed an epitaph which would have moved others to tears for my untimely fate." By midsummer, his anticipation of dying romantically as an unrealized genius had lapsed into his "incessant, inexorable" fear of dying tortuously from hydrophobia.[41]

Death and rumors of death may have released the full force of Howells's fears. In early March his favorite uncle, Israel, weakened by a long bout with consumption, suffered a devastating stroke. Israel's death in mid-May unsettled all within the extended Howells family. Then in mid-July, a cholera scare spread throughout the West, reminding Howells of his sufferings in Dayton. William Cooper Howells alarmed his readers by reporting that cholera was "daily making its appearance in the villages." Another disturbing report of death, verified in several instances, described packs of marauding dogs that were killing sheep and other domestic animals in the countryside around Jefferson.[42]

The thought of vicious dogs lurking at the edges of his village evoked Howells's childhood terror of hydrophobia. He had first learned of the disease at age four in Hamilton when a drayman named David Bowers was bitten by a rabid dog. Bowers's excruciating death was reported in disturbing, melodramatic detail by his brother-in-law Isaac Saunders in four columns of the *Intelligencer*. The Bowers incident became part of Howells family lore. Howells's grandfather had helped Bowers settle accounts with God. Howells's father had seized the moment to propose a general slaughter of dogs to protect public health. William Cooper Howells had insisted that no good dog could ever "atone for the loss of a good citizen."[43]

Bowers's traumatic death had occurred just when Howells as a small child was becoming susceptible to fears of punishment, and undoubtedly hydrophobia seemed to him the most dire punishment. The symptoms that obsessed Howells during his adolescent breakdown—a subjective sense of stifling smoke and violent convulsions induced by splashes of water—were prominent elements in Bowers's story. The story also fully credited the popular belief Howells heard again in Jefferson, that hydrophobia could lie dormant many years before suddenly emerging and killing its victim.

Fear of hydrophobia naturally expressed Howells's psychic tensions. Since early childhood, Howells had sought atonement in his literary ambitions. Accomplishing great things in literature had become his way of resisting self-accusations. When he entered adolescence, he began to feel severe frustrations. From his perspective, his unaided study had reached the "vanishing-point," his literary ambitions opposed his family's immediate financial needs, and his desire for a literary vocation found little support in a community dedicated to antislavery agitation. Doubting whether he could ever secure his sense of literary vocation, Howells began to suffer intense feelings of selfishness. These persistent feelings finally recalled the self-annihilating impulses he had experienced as a small child, and he focused his anxieties on tortuous death from hydrophobia.

Howells's fear of hydrophobia was all the more devastating because he associated it with abandonment. During his childhood in Hamilton, his mother's homesick visits had accentuated his fear of abandonment. Abandonment had seemed the punishment he deserved for his imagined wrongs. Incidents in his later childhood had tied abandonment to his fear of hydrophobia. Once, after being nipped by a dog, Howells had run home to an empty house. His overpowering sense of abandonment had frightfully augmented his impulse to self-punishment. "I had heard of excising a snake-bite to keep the venom from spreading," Howells remembered, "and I would now have cut out the place with my knife, if I had known how."[44]

Withdrawn from his family and his village, dealing with his vocational anxieties as best he could by himself, Howells probably felt as abandoned as he had at the onset of his earlier episodes of terror. Although his fear of hydrophobia expressed his sense of abandonment, it was also a forceful plea for help. It elaborated the covert language of psychological fragility that had served him during his homesickness episodes at Eureka Mills. In the past, his father had responded sensitively to his anxieties and had reasoned him out of his fears. Howells probably gained some comfort by identifying himself with the story of Bowers's death, for the drayman's suffering had drawn the sympathetic attention of his father, his grandfather, and the entire village of Hamilton.

Most likely Howells's breakdown was not noticed by most of his fellow villagers, for his recovery was strictly a family affair. Released from the printing office, he no longer endured the daily judgmental scrutiny of Joseph, whose resentment of his literary afternoons and evenings had spilled out in angry words. Significantly, his departure from the printing office was a "forced respite," viewed by the entire family as a necessary break and not a selfish desertion. His father rehearsed, as often as Howells asked, his own youthful suffering from hypochondria, a fear of consumption that accompanied his effort to escape the printing trade by studying medicine. He later liked to say that he "studied Medicine until he knew so much about it that he did not believe anything in it." But actually he had left his studies because of persistent anxieties over illness. William Cooper Howells pointed out that these anxieties were like his son's—they were unfounded, and they soon disappeared.[45]

Howells's sister Aurelia, however, remembered that William Cooper Howells gave his story of conquering hypochondria a didactic turn. Father had settled in his mind that he would die, she recalled, "until he heard mother weeping to [grandfather Dean], when [grandfather] told her he 'did not think poor William could get well!' And father decided that he would!"[46] William Cooper Howells's sympathy contained a remnant of his ambivalence toward his son's literary aspirations. His account of his own youthful troubles implied that his son could resolve his crisis simply through self-help, through a more determined assertion of reason and will.

Howells accepted his father's challenge: "In self-defense I learnt to practice a psychological juggle," he recalled; "I came to deal with my own state of mind as another would deal with it, and to combat my fears as if they were alien."[47]

Another kind of self-healing aided Howells's recovery. His anticipations of involuntary rage and spasmodic convulsions were forceful symbolic representations of his loss of autonomy. Acting out these symptoms reversed his feeling of being in control of forces outside himself and beyond his command. He was able to "own" this threat to his identity through his private ritual of self-representation.[48] Psychological reversal by breaking down was a desperate grasping for autonomy or self-control, but nervous prostration was becoming a respectable option for increasing numbers of middle-class Americans, who sought relief from their tensions in water-cure establishments and health spas. A water curist had recently brought the fad to Jefferson, taking up ground near the Grand River in Austinburg. Howells's uncle Joseph, who operated a drugstore in Hamilton, urged him to apply the universal water-cure remedy—frequent baths and vigorous rubbings with a coarse wet towel.[49] Being a nervous invalid might be respectable—Giddings himself was publicly known as a sufferer from "hypo"—but it was nevertheless a dubious distinction in a community dedicated to energetic antislavery agitation.

Uncle Joseph also recommended the suspension of all study and writing, but Howells could not halt the routine that sustained his literary aspirations and his vision of moral usefulness. While he rested from his frustrating study of languages, he became even more omnivorous in his reading, devouring book after book to escape his malady. In this frenzied manner, he read through Dickens's novels for the first time, finding intentions that fortified his own sense of literature's moral importance. Dickens, he pointed out to *Sentinel* readers, has "never varnished vice or gilded meanness. He has struck terrible blows at established iniquity."[50]

Following his hypochondriacal breakdown, Howells defended literature against all criticism. When he noticed George W. Curtis's *Potiphar Papers* for the *Sentinel*, he observed that Curtis sought "to kindle in the hearts of his readers a generous love of virtue, and a generous hatred of vice; to unveil hypocrisy, and strip from pretense its guads and frippery; to present simplicity and truth to the mind in their most beautiful forms; to contrast with these the vileness of affectation and deceit; to attack the familiar abuses of every-day life in their strong[h]olds, and to uphold whatever is high and worthy, with equal firmness."[51] The merit of literature, by Howells's description, equaled if it did not surpass the merit of law and politics.

Howells dismissed pretenders to literary authority with equal assertiveness, reserving special scorn for sentimental poets whose work appeared in exchange newspapers and sometimes invaded the *Sentinel*. Most of these poetic offerings struck him as "harrowingly weak" and best consigned to the stove. He took pains to separate his own tastes from women writers whom he caricatured as "Sibi-lanta" and "Sombra." He warned readers, "Any writer of ordinary merit can write 'machine poetry,' but not one in a thousand can produce a real poem."[52]

Sometimes Howells revealed a more hesitant demeanor. In an experiment he dropped after a single trial, he adopted a cloying, apologetic manner for a column of literary gossip, "You and I." Inviting readers to join him in his "quiet corner of the newspaper" for "easy talks" removed from the "mingled sea of news and poli-tics [that] tumbles heavily outside," he cautioned that the tranquil-lity of his "little cove" might put them to sleep. Inspired by his current fascination with Ik Marvel's *Dream Life* and *Reveries of a Bachelor*, Howells posed as a retiring self-satirist who gossiped on the "less noisy themes" of the day. This appeal to mutual sympa-thy, removed from public engagement and devoid of moral crite-ria, had little potential to affirm the authority of the literary voca-tion. The Ik Marvel persona was another instance of psychological reversal—a defense against his feeling that his literary intentions would sweep him into an inconsequential, unread corner of the newspaper.[53]

The Ik Marvel persona contrasted with another confidential

mask Howells adopted later in the same column—the snob he had encountered in the novels of Thackeray. Although he had earlier described Thackeray as a writer who "loves whatever is beautiful and good, and hates whatever is base and mean," Howells made a mistaken appeal to fellow feeling when he adopted Thackeray's haughty manner. "By the way, do you not think we rather overdo the use of the word *lady?*" he inquired. "I am not the least bit aristocratic, and I think anyone who works for a living quite as worthy and respectable as those who do not. Yet I confess that I could not help laughing when I heard a laundress spoken of as the lady who did the washing!" Even Goodrich, the professed despiser of democracy, thought Howells's passion for Thackeray strange and almost "a moral defect." But Thackeray provided Howells with a self-affirmation he eagerly desired. Thackeray "seemed to promise me in his contempt of the world," he remembered, "a refuge from the shame I felt for my own want of figure in it."[54]

As Howells searched for a satisfying way to represent the moral importance of literature, the political tensions in Jefferson began to subside. The off-year elections in October demonstrated surprising success for antislavery forces. The fusion party some were now calling Republican had established a formidable resistance against Douglas's Nebraska Democrats. William Cooper Howells celebrated the victory with a call to vigilance that his son must have read with discomfort: "The battles of a party—and particularly a party in the right—are like the battles of an individual with himself," his father observed. "They are daily—hourly. Mischiefs, evils, wrongs of all kinds are coming up every day, and must be met and conquered. This success is but the beginning." William Cooper Howells's summer-long struggle with his son's irrational fear of death certainly informed this statement; it reasserted William Cooper Howells's faith in the sufficiency of individual will.[55]

With the moderation of political tensions and the passing of the dog-days summer heat—a condition believed to provoke rages of hydrophobia—Howells returned to a semblance of health. Describing the relieving change of seasons in a poem he entitled "Midnight Rain," he presented images of accomplished peace that contrasted with his father's allusions to perpetual combat. Just as a gentle rain soothes the parched earth, Howells wrote, the return of health relaxes "tensioned nerves," encourages "gentle sleep," and allows a "pleasing languor" to spread "throughout the soul."[56] Howells had survived his hypochondriacal breakdown. Although he later viewed this emotional trial as the most traumatic of his life, his breakdown had saved him from a fate he identified with death—the burying of his literary hopes. His breakdown had allowed him time to resurrect his failing initiative so that he could continue to pursue his literary ambitions.

Howells's Jefferson breakdown was the beginning of a prolonged identity crisis that extended into his later twenties. The tenuous, compromised close of his struggles at age twenty-eight foreshadowed his lifelong "dreamy fumbling" about his own identity and fated his return in the 1880s and 1890s to the unsettled problems of his youth. In retrospect, Howells was certain that his adolescent breakdown had altered his life: "I must always be a different man from that I could have been but for that dreadful year," he stated twelve years later. Throughout his life, he continued to regard his youthful instance of "nervous prostration" as a formative experience, having deep personal consequences for "both good and evil."[57]

Many thoughtful people of Howells's generation lost trust in themselves and trust in their faith through comparable tests of personal experience. As a consequence of his youthful ordeal, Howells began to see reality as anomalous or chancelike and began to contrast this perception with his father's belief in a moral universe. Guided by his Swedenborgianism, William Cooper Howells was sure that right and good would ultimately triumph, and wrong and evil would inevitably fail. He believed, furthermore, that every individual possessed perfect autonomy; every individual was "always master of the greatest happiness possible."[58]

But Howells began to distrust his father's vision. "I can see that doing all by myself[,] I was not truly a law to myself," he later reflected, "but only a sort of helpless force."[59] Howells began to consider that if individuals lacked perfect control, they lacked moral freedom and were not responsible for good or evil actions. If no final accounting were possible, the moral universe of his father was in desperate disarray. While plunging into Dickens's novels, Howells found the representation of his father's moral universe:

While I read [Dickens], I was in a world where the right came out best, as I believe it will yet do in this world, and where merit was crowned with the success which I believe will yet attend it in our daily life, untrammelled by social convention or economic circumstance. In that world of his, in the ideal world, to which the real world must finally conform itself, I dwelt among the shows of things, but under a Providence that governed all things to a good end, and where neither wealth nor birth could avail against virtue or right.[60]

The qualifying voice in this passage concluded with a blunt caveat: "Of course it was in a way all crude enough," Howells said of Dickens's moral universe, "and was already contradicted by experience in the small sphere of my own being."[61] Howells was a perceptive self-observer. His traumatic adolescent breakdown changed him forever by loosening his hold on moral surety and initiating his doubts.

CHAPTER 4

The Umbrella Man

We are just beginning to discern that certain conceptions of our relations to our fellow-men, once formulated in generalities which met with a dramatic acceptation from the world, and were then rejected by it as mere rhetoric, have really a vital truth in them, and that if they have ever seemed false it was because of the false conditions in which we still live. Equality and fraternity, these are the ideals which once moved the world, and then fell into despite and mockery, as unrealities; but now they assert themselves in our hearts once more.

HOWELLS, 1895

Many people in Jefferson accepted republican ideals of equality and fraternity as actual expressions of village life, however much a truly democratic ethos clashed with notions of middle-class respectability gaining popularity with the village elite. Joshua Giddings was among those Jeffersonians who idealized and spiritualized their community. During his business travels, Giddings longed for home, especially on Sundays when he retired to his hotel room and contemplated his disagreeable situation. He was disturbed that the din of bargaining continued on the Lord's Day, when everything should be at rest. He felt the contrast of Jefferson, recalling its "sweet[-]natured silence, that throws around the Sabbath a loveliness & sanctity so grateful to the Christian feelings." Giddings abided separation from his village with less anxiety and soul-searching once he channeled his religious impulses into antislavery agitation. For Giddings, resisting the "slave power" in Washington meant asserting village morality, a role that intensified his pride in the "humble unassuming neighbors" who had chosen him their representative.[1]

The mutual feeling that Jefferson constituted a distinct moral community was confirmed for Giddings and his neighbors in 1841. Censured for challenging the exclusion of antislavery petitions from Congress, he resigned his seat to run for reelection. Jeffersonians, along with other citizens of the Western Reserve, returned him to Washington with a resounding victory. The victory confirmed Giddings's sense that morality began in his home village: "I am bound to make myself useful to my family first[,] then to my friends, my neighbors, the public[,] and so far as God gives me talents and opportunity[,] I am bound to extend my usefullness to the nation and the world." By the time the Howells family arrived in Jefferson, "Old Gid" had become a living symbol of a communal village world that sustained this expansive ideal of moral commitment.[2]

Like the majority of antebellum Americans, Jeffersonians looked first to their village for guidance and direction, despite their increasing involvement in a national market and the controversies of national political parties. In fact, their faith in village morality was intensified as these national forces challenged their trust in local autonomy. Giddings and other antislavery agitators warned that the "slave power" conspiracy posed an immediate danger to "free labor" communities like Jefferson.[3] Another threat to communal life—from store-bought goods—was less well defined but just as keenly felt. William Cooper Howells was adept at fashioning wooden types and other devices for his newspaper, and he once made a reliable barometer that he highly prized. He linked handmade goods to moral meanings. "If you want boots or shoes," he cautioned his readers, "buy of your neighbor[s], who *make*, in preference to those who *sell* them." He believed that patronizing a local artisan would sustain "a thrifty neighbor, with well[-]educated children, himself intelligent and elevated in the social scale, and consequently an agreeable associate." The *Sentinel*'s advertisements for store-bought goods might be taken as the opposite advice, but William Cooper Howells sensed that neglecting local artisans might seriously undermine Jefferson's moral consensus.[4]

The perception of threats from the outside world, from the "slave power" or store-bought goods, sharpened the moral meaning of locality for antebellum Americans. This heightened consciousness had significant implications for Howells's literary aspirations. Although he had formed tastes and modes of judgment that reflected the cosmopolitan world of his reading—the universal Republic of Letters that included Cervantes's Spain and Thackeray's England—he could not easily ignore the cherished ideals of his village. Dual allegiance had troubled him before, especially during his family's migratory years when his literary desires seemed set against his family's economic needs. During his adolescence, however, his sense of living a double life took on new and perplexing dimensions. In the years immediately following his breakdown, Howells became acutely aware that the local world of Jefferson exerted formidable power over his desire for literary success in the greater world.

In November 1854, with the easing of his hypochondria, Howells launched an ambitious effort to reconcile his literary ambitions with the life of his village, offering Jefferson readers a precocious serial story in the *Sentinel* entitled, "The Independent Candidate." He announced his desire to make his serial a reflection of the life near at hand by adding the subtitle, "A Story of To Day."[5] The tale Howells began to weave, putting it directly into type at his compositor's case, involved political intrigue, youthful love, and hereditary insanity.

Following the examples of Dickens's *Bleak House* and Thackeray's *Pendennis*, Howells elaborated a cast of characters around a flexible plot drawn from local politics. George Berson, a strong force in the Whig party, has been outmaneuvered at the Elks County convention by the Errington clique, which has obtained the party legislative nomination for Berson's rival, Cuffins. Berson has bolted the party to run as an independent candidate and has enlisted his cousin Wat Larrie to stump for him in the hostile, old-line Whig village of Beauville. To aid Wat, Berson has gathered a motley group of supporters, including the tavern keeper Trooze and the lawyer Sliprie. Early in the serial, Howells forewarned readers that Berson's family suffers from hereditary insanity, a secret that the unscrupulous Cuffins intends to reveal during the campaign. The serial follows the intrigues of the candidates, with intermittent episodes of Wat's spooning and Berson's home life. Though much of the story is told by an author-narrator, Howells also described events through Wat, who frequently records his experiences in "voluminous epistles."

Howells started his serial confidently, but he was soon wondering how to sustain his cast of characters and his convoluted plots. He was more disturbed by the thought that readers were growing impatient with his serial. In the *Sentinel* office, he had heard an "old farmer" say he would be glad when "that there continued story was through."[6] While struggling with dialogue and action, Howells began to contend with his imagined reader. He opened the third installment of his serial with a section labeled "Rather Diadactical," where he personified his sense of village criticism in a character he called "Old Smith."

In the "Rather Diadactical" section, Howells's author-narrator explains his high-minded intentions. He wants his tale to be "the most beautiful, lovely, and discreet story that ever was penned." He promises he will never follow the melodramatic ploys of popular writers like George Lippard and Emerson Bennett, who regularly kill off troublesome characters with a mere stroke of the pen. At this point, Old Smith emerges and interrupts the narrator, telling him that if he wants to please his readers so much, why doesn't he just "invent a postmaster, and have him run over by a stage-coach. I would!" Shocked and perturbed by Old Smith's unseemly attack, the author-narrator responds with calm argument until his critic relents. Nevertheless, Old Smith gets the last word. When the author-narrator laments that every local politician will

think he is being described in the character Berson, Old Smith
offers a chilling rejoinder: "O! console yourself with the thought
that they probably don't read your story."[7]

Old Smith's choice of a postmaster to be sacrificed to a stage-
coach was not random or unmeaning. Postmasters were symbols
of oppression, appointees of Franklin Pierce and adherents of the
proslavery Democratic party. Howells's author-narrator had
countered by ignoring party loyalty and appealing to humane
feelings. Was not the local postmaster, he asked, "most amiable,
polite and courteous"? This tactic failed to settle the political currents raised by Howells's story. He had described George Berson
as an "independent candidate," a designation that suggested the
turmoil of the preceding year when Giddings and other "Independent Democrats" had formed a fusion party pledged to antislavery.[8] Howells had also invoked long-standing tensions of local
politics by setting his independent candidate against the Errington
clique that ruled old-line Whig territory in Elks County. The
Conneaut *Reporter*, part of Benjamin Wade's coterie, sustained an
old-line Whig demeanor under its editor, D. C. Allen, despite
Wade's advocacy of fusion.[9] Howells surmised that readers would
be puzzled by these unmistakable allusions to local politics.

Readers had reason for confusion. Cuffins, the old-line Whig
candidate, is ready to smear George Berson, the independent, with
his secret of hereditary insanity, but Berson is hardly admirable.
Though his independent candidacy identifies him with an actual
politics of moral integrity, Berson is thoroughly corrupt. He relies
chiefly on flattery and small bribes to gain self-interested and
conniving supporters. Even their compatriot Wat admits they are
"a sorry pack of Yahoos." Berson cynically rationalizes his corrup-
tion by asserting, "Candidates generally get the name of liars and
humbugs, anyhow—so they have to be liars and humbugs when it
pays." In contrast to the antislavery politics of Jefferson, Howells's
campaign lacks moral purpose. No politician in his story has the
intentions of Giddings or Wade. Berson and Cuffins simply seek
personal aggrandizement.

Howells indicted other characters drawn from the world of his village. He was especially acerbic with lawyers, portrayed in the character of Sliprie, a "scoundrel-thief." Wat warns that while Sliprie has a broad, rich laugh, "it is as treacherous as a pitfall covered with flowers." Wat himself bears watching. In the beginning of the story, he is likeable and well meaning, but he has recently passed the bar and started on the downward path. As a fledgling lawyer, he has acquired a fondness for "bullying and brow-beating" witnesses. The only sympathetic figure from Howells's local political world is the editor, Doan, modeled after his father, who refuses to smear Berson with the charge of insanity. But Howells added a caveat even with Doan, attributing his moral integrity to his financial security. "The *Messenger* is paid for," Doan asserts to his tempter Cuffins, "and it shall never be used as a means to blast any man's character while in my hands."

The seamy world of "The Independent Candidate" contrasts with the moral atmosphere of Jefferson, where politicians, lawyers, and editors backed a party to end slavery forever. Part of Howells's difficulties with his story derived from his arm's-length treatment of local political issues. Allowed the discretions of fiction, he fell back on a general indictment of political chicanery. This tactic furthered the vague and meandering tendency of his story. Without the moral issues that animated his village, "The Independent Candidate" became a blank tablet on which Howells wrote out his secret animus toward the dominance of politics over literature.

As he lost confidence in his story, Howells reverted to the clumsy devices he despised in melodramatic novels. George Berson wins the election but is speedily dispatched by hereditary insanity. Dismissed earlier for his moral corruptibility, Wat Larrie makes an awkward last appearance. His drunken intrusion into Berson's house provokes the outburst that confirms the candidate's demented condition.

"The Independent Candidate" ended in muddle and collapse, principally because Howells found no authoritative answer for Old Smith's nagging question about the political meaning of his story. But the debate with Old Smith raised another issue of moral commitment that Howells found perplexing. Old Smith is a device Howells borrowed from a style of vernacular humor rooted in oral tradition. Vernacular humorists confronted refined, gentlemanly characters, representing the respectable, middle-class ethos of self-control, with passionate, dialect-speaking characters, representing the waning communal world. The confrontation subjects the gentleman to the leveling wit of the vernacular character and asserts democratic feeling over genteel pretension.[10]

Sympathetic use of vernacular characters and language expressed Howells's regard for the communal habits and democratic ideals still dominant in Jefferson. Old Smith, Howells's version of a vernacular character, speaks dialect only slightly, but he bristles with an urge to profanity that the refined author-narrator takes pains to forestall. The author-narrator finally subdues his antagonist, but not before Old Smith has the last word—the assertion that no one may be reading the story. With this gesture, Howells admitted that the democratic authority of the vernacular had command over his writing.

Howells made this admission with much ambivalence. In his debates with his friend Goodrich, he had taken the side of Thackeray against Dickens, defending Thackeray's more refined diction. Thackeray appealed to Howells's aesthetic pride, his ability to distinguish himself from his fellow villagers by his reading tastes and his writing experiments. He admired Dickens as well, especially for his sympathetic portrayal of desperate, forgotten lives. "The dumb lips of hoveled and prisoned wretchedness," he had written, "have found an utterance through [Dickens]."[11] Drawing inspiration from both Thackeray and Dickens in writing "The Independent Candidate," Howells shaded his allegiance toward Thackeray, assuming the manner of a refined author-narrator and using Wat Larrie to satirize the common or vernacular speech of other characters.

Through much of his story, Howells chose refinement without hesitation. Wat stands amazed at the language of the Dickens-like tavern keeper John Trooze. Considering the "cussedness" of women, Trooze asserts, " 'I used to think sparkin' was a mighty fine thing, but blame me if the slangin' and bangin' and whangin' *sence*, ain[']t enough to make up for it.' " Howells created a small retinue of Dickens-like characters who fall under the censorious eye of either the author-narrator or Wat Larrie for their uncouth ways and barbarous words.

Yet Howells also presented common, colloquial language without explicit or implied ridicule. "Punch up the *Herald* man. He ought to come out savage," says Wat, suggesting that strong editorials are needed to help Berson's candidacy. Howells appreciated the colloquial language of the middle level, if not the tavern-keeper level, of village society. He was aware that the choice of words declared allegiance to a larger community, and he was hostile to verbal pretension and inauthentic usage. Commenting on the assertions of one villager, Howells's author-narrator notes, "His use of huge words, where homely mon[o]syllables would do quite as well, is enough to prove him a savant alone. The daw who rigged himself out with peacock's feathers, was a very silly bird, and the donkey who played lion was a great ass." Although this villager, Moro Gilky, is another Dickens parody, Howells struck closer to home in a scene where Wat Larrie confronts a vernacular character.

Howells's author-narrator often resorts to the style of sentimental magazine sketches meant for middle-class audiences. He is especially prone to the "melting mood" appropriate for elevated rhapsodies over landscape scenes.[12] And despite occasional lapses into colloquial speech, his protagonist Wat Larrie usually maintains a similar middle-class style of refined diction to distinguish himself from the Troozes of village society. In one signal instance, however, Howells turned the tables and imagined a ritual humiliation that stripped Wat Larrie of dignity. Wat relates in a letter that while stumping for Berson in the old-line Whig village of Beauville, he addressed a hostile crowd gathered at the schoolhouse. Carried away by his rhetorical flair, he boldly challenged an old-line Whig to step forward if such a being dared exist. He was surprised to discover one did—"A hulking, burly, beef-butchering varlet." To restrain the butcher, Wat resorted to the "bullying and brow-beating" he was learning as a lawyer:

I must have been half crazy, or I would have seen that I was on dangerous ground.—But while the butcher waxed redder and angrier, I only attacked him with renewed gust. At last he burst into tears, and dashed toward me. There was not a great deal of time to think, but I did a great deal of thinking, nevertheless. There was a pitcher of water on the desk before me, and I let the butcher have that at once. I also bestowed two candles and sticks upon him and the "Sacred Songster," which lay within reach. I was about to launch "Webster's Unabridged," when my antagonist closed upon me. Somebody got awfully thrashed. I could not tell who, exactly, but I do not think it was the butcher.

Meanwhile, the fellows near the door kept up a deafening yell, and discharged volleys of eggs at the speaker. I cried enough,—I state the fact without shame, for I might have said *plenty* with good reason—and the butcher allowed me to rise. I cast about me for my hat. I found it after a while, but it was so fearfully cocked that I could not wear it. Bareheaded and reeking, I made for an opening in that accursed room. But there was none to be found. Utterly bewildered, I ran hither and thither. At length I caught a glimmer of the night without, and dashed ahead in that direction. It was the door.—A great ruffian was stationed on the threshold after the manner of the Colossus of Rhodes. I ran between his legs, and upset the monster.

How cool the damp night breezes were!—I breathed them as eagerly as a thirsty man quaffs the thrilling waters of a desert spring. But I had no time to sentimentalize. I cut across lots, and was soon out of sight.

In this scene, Howells imaginatively employed the device of confrontation. His portrayal of Wat Larrie's humiliation has a sharp colloquial, if not completely vernacular, flavor. His depiction of middle-class refinement brought low is especially deft. The common triumphs over the refined through humorous reversals, beginning with the butcher bursting into tears, an act of "melting" sensitivity usually reserved for the cultivated middle class in its raptures over landscape scenes. In a pinch, Wat finds his high-toned oratory useless. Water pitcher, sacred songster, and Webster's unabridged, representing middle-class verities of lyceum, church, and schoolhouse, have lost all value except as missiles to beat back his opponent. With humiliation imminent, Wat tries to save face, posing a verbal distinction between *enough* and *plenty*. But the inarticulate butcher triumphs easily over the polished Wat. Howells's final touch is a clear qualification of the language of middle-class refinement. Pausing outside the schoolhouse, Wat has a momentary urge to rhapsodize the beautiful night scene in the conventional sentimental manner. But remembering his plight, he represses this urge and reverts to the colloquial: "I cut across lots, and was soon out of sight."

Had he written this passage with a deeper vernacular perspective, Howells would have been more interested in the butcher's point of view. If his allegiance to his village had risen above his allegiance to his reading, he might have allowed the butcher a distinctive vernacular voice. Despite his ambivalence, Howells demonstrated an inchoate form of the vernacular in his satirization of middle-class refinement and in his appreciation of colloquial language.[13] By the time he wrote this passage, however, his experiment with local and vernacular themes had become heavy on his hands. He had begun to share the feeling of public humiliation he depicted for Wat Larrie. Like Wat, he desired to cut across lots and get out of sight.

Considering his "strange disaster" with "The Independent Candidate," Howells felt his serial was neither "badly conceived" nor "attempted upon lines that were mistaken." But he never returned to his story, "so great was the shame and anguish." "It was," he declared, "like some dreadful dream one has of finding one's self in battle without the courage needed to carry one creditably through the action, or on the stage unprepared by study of the part which one is to appear in."[14] These images of shameful exposure suggest his perplexity concerning "that mythical creature, my reader." Recognition for the moral importance and communal value of the literary vocation seemed unavailable through a novel representing village life.

But Howells remained resolute. He had survived his terrible hypochondria of the previous summer; he meant to survive this calamity as well. His resilience is reflected in a tall tale he abruptly introduced into his serial one installment before his hasty retreat. Prompted by his description of Cuffins strolling with an umbrella, Howells began to satirize the middle-class respectability of quiet and meek men who never part with their umbrellas. Then, just as suddenly, he shifted to a lively account of Mr. Stub, the quintes-sential "Man-with-an-Umbrella man." Mr. Stub's umbrella is more than a symbol of careful, middle-class deportment. His umbrella frequently becomes an intrusive irritant to respectable villagers. It supports his chin when he glares down lecturers; it pokes members of the lecture audience in the ribs. On market days, his umbrella is a terrible menace, upsetting neatly arranged egg baskets and coffee stands. Mr. Stub, the umbrella man, perfectly expressed Howells's ambivalence toward the vernacular, for Mr. Stub com-bines the middle-class appearance of respectability with the ver-nacular style of leveling confrontation.

Appearances are deceiving in Howells's tall tale. Mr. Stub is not all that he seems at first glance, while his umbrella is extraordinary beyond anyone's imagining. The narrator describes the fantastic moment when it is revealed as a "Demon Umbrella":

Can I ever forget the moment when Mr Stub appeared on the roof of the burning house, with his Umbrella under his arm. The red flames leaped from the burning casements, as if to dash themselves upon the crowd, and roared and cracked with unearthly glee.—There seemed to be no escape; and a shudder ran through the mighty throng below, as Mr Stub stepped jauntily to the edge of the roof. He must needs fling himself down. Everybody thought so. What was their astonishment to see Mr Stub raise his Umbrella, and sheltering himself beneath it, jump from the eave into subtle air. He hovered over the house for a moment, and then drifting to the leeward, soared easily up toward the clouds. Every eye was strained to watch the flight of the devoted man. The Umbrella waxed smaller and smaller, and at last, with coat-tails flapping frantically, Mr Stub faded from sight.—He never came down; and perished, no doubt, a victim to his own Umbrella!—Every Man-with-an-Umbrella does not go up like a balloon. Yet there is a dreadful mystery hanging about such people, which may well excite in the boldest heart a willingness to give them the whole sidewalk.

The middle-class symbol of the umbrella becomes, in Howells's telling, a magician's wand making all things possible. Invested with demon potency, the umbrella is a close equivalent to a pen. In the course of his tale, Howells assumed the persona of Mr. Stub. He playfully mocked his own short stature in his hero's name while investing Mr. Stub with his own difficulties and desires. Like Mr. Stub, Howells had poked at his fellow villagers with his story, exposing their foibles and shortcomings with his satirical pen. He hoped that his story would elevate him to heights of praise and appreciation. But like Mr. Stub, he was left on a burning edifice— his story in disarray. Possibly he had felt the death wish represented by Mr. Stub's imminent destruction.

But Howells's umbrella man is a magician of transformation who can escape thoughts of death and resolve all double-lived feelings. On the one hand, he represents an insubstantial sense of identity, the kind of unease that resulted from Howells's failure to provoke a confirming response from his village. Mr. Stub's airy identity makes him vulnerable to the draft that carries him away. Yet Howells's umbrella man is able to affirm life on the brink of death. His step from the ledge astonishes the throng, and all eyes follow his miraculous escape, as he floats far beyond the confines of his village. Suffering public humiliation for his failed serial, Howells wished for a similar disappearance into "subtle air." Escape by means of his demon pen might leave the same aura of mysterious power. Should he reappear, still in the guise of a meek man, it would be wise for villagers to offer him "the whole sidewalk."

Howells's tall tale combined his impulse to escape with his determination to persist. Floating away from his troubles meant ignoring the promptings of his Swedenborgian conscience, which required a moral, communal context for the literary vocation. While the fate of "The Independent Candidate" seemed to diminish the possibility that Jeffersonians would sanction his desires, Howells allowed for total fulfillment. Like his umbrella man, he might return in triumph to his village. For the moment, however, retreat seemed best. After his failure in prose, Howells sought the sanctuary of poetry. Once he abandoned "The Independent Candidate," he immersed himself in James Russell Lowell's "Lectures on English Poetry." In January and February 1855, reports of the lectures appeared in the Boston *Advertiser*. By the time Howells had closed his story, the reports had begun to arrive in the news-paper exchanges.[15]

Lowell's lectures soothed Howells's wounded feelings. Al-though Lowell toppled Pope from Howells's highest esteem by describing him as the founder of the "artificial style" in poetry, the lectures sketched a grandiose alternative. According to Lowell, the true poet guarded the divine ideal that imbued all of life. From his eminent perspective, the poet could maintain a certain reserve; the poet could rebuke the bad and base indirectly by "making us feel what delight there is in the good and fair." While exalted above ordinary mortals in his contemplation of the ideal, Lowell's poet was enough engaged in the present to "h[o]ld up a mirror to contemporary life" and to draw inspiration from common speech —the talk of the street and the workshop.[16]

Despite Lowell's liking for common speech—such as the Yan-kee dialect that had inspired his creation of Hosea Biglow, the scourge of the Mexican War—Howells could read Lowell's lec-tures to justify a distanced relation to Jefferson villagers and talk. Withdrawal could be justified by the poet's sympathy with the "higher society" of universal being and his scholarly understanding of past ages.[17] This strategy reflected the compromises exemplary romantic poets had made with the industrializing market society. Inspired by the expanded influence possible with a multitude of readers, romantic poets were nonetheless disturbed by their depen-dence on commercial relations with a faceless audience. By retreat-ing to the realm of the ideal, they retained their assumption of priestly devotion to common life.[18]

The literary tastes Howells demonstrated in the succeeding months had no touch of local experience or language. He returned to his study, put Old Smith out-of-doors, and made his private domain a refuge for the poet and scholar. He wrote poems repre-senting the poet alone, communing with transcendent nature. In the *Sentinel*, he reprinted a passage from Lowell's lectures that asserted the "divine validity of number, proportion, and harmony," all apparent in a state of nature, chastened of social relations. He concentrated on the English reviews, emblems of scholarly refinement, to cultivate a "pure and sound literary taste." When a writer in *Blackwood's* attacked American language for its "uncouth phrases," Howells mounted a counteroffensive based on American refinement. He contended that English usage was actually more "barbarous" and cited the scholarly understanding of language possessed by America's principal writers—Irving, Prescott, Bryant, and Longfellow.[19]

Strident pride in the accomplishments of American scholar-poets was insufficient to sustain Howells for very long. He had hoped "The Independent Candidate" might provide a way to live by literature. He was well aware that Dickens earned an extravagant yearly income, reported at nearly one hundred thousand dollars, by writing serial novels.[20] "The Independent Candidate" had been a double failure. Neither moral confirmation nor a bare living was available from writing that found no readers. Howells had been warned that poetry could never earn his livelihood. On invitation from William Cooper Howells, the editor of the *Ohio Farmer* had inspected Howells's literary wares and accepted a poem for publication. When Howells confessed that he hoped the editor would employ him permanently to write poems and sketches, Joseph scoffed, "He would never pay you three dollars a week in the world for that."[21]

If he could not live *by* literature, Howells meant to live *for* literature. In May 1855, he grandly recorded in his diary that he was "quitting the printing-office, and entering upon the study of the law, as well as forming a kind of new epoch in my life."[22] Howells began reading law with Senator Benjamin Wade. But he had completed little more than a volume and a half of Blackstone's *Commentaries*, the work of a month, when the stress became too exhausting: "The strain was great enough when I had merely the work in the printing-office," Howells recalled; "but now I came home from my Blackstone mentally fagged, and I could not take up the authors whom at the bottom of my heart I loved so much better." He was distressed by the prospect of becoming a lawyer and nothing else. He had become disheartened after reading Blackstone's assertion that the law was a "jealous mistress" permitting no other affection. Without explaining to Senator Wade, Howells abandoned the law and returned to the printing office with a feeling of "ecstatic relief."[23]

No one, aside from his friend Goodrich, understood Howells's motives. After his humiliation with "The Independent Candidate," he had grown more reserved. He preferred disrepute to revelation of his "secret hope" of living for literature. He did not prefer it so much, however, that he could face Senator Wade, a man famous for his "fiery eyes" and "scowling mien." Wade was an acknowledged master of oratorical confrontation. Prepared for any clash with his Southern enemies, Wade practiced with a pistol in his front yard. Howells avoided encountering the senator in the streets. Then the "terrible moment" arrived when Wade picked up his newspaper in the *Sentinel* office. "[Senator Wade] looked me over in my general effect of base mechanical," Howells recalled, "and asked me if I had given up the law; I had only to answer him I had, and our conference ended."[24]

Howells's retreat from the law added to his feeling of public humiliation and confused his imagined literary prospects. While lawyers were highly respected in Jefferson and had prominent standing in social circles beyond the village, Howells understood that refined literary society would never respect a printer-poet.[25] His "base mechanical" trade diminished his status and forced him back upon his family, where no place existed for his future. Joseph was destined to become editor of the *Sentinel*; Will was expected to succeed elsewhere. If he stayed at home and worked at the *Sentinel*, Howells would always feel he had failed and would always be subordinate to Joseph, an unnerving prospect given their recent quarrels.

Trying to take pride in his mechanical trade, Howells commented in the *Sentinel* on the fine printing of the English reviews, judged by his eye as "a craftsman." He and Jim Williams had once talked of working a printing office in nearby Pennsylvania, but they could not muster "courage to offer even promises to pay for it." The journeyman printer's precarious life was even more alien to Howells's literary hopes. Recent expedients for survival adopted at the *Sentinel*—the steam press and cheaper labor of female compositors—typified changes that had made journeyman printing extremely hazardous.[26]

Estranged from his village and trapped in the printer's trade, Howells began to experience terrible headaches. To escape his tensions, he buried himself in an ambitious scholarly project—translation from the Spanish of the sixteenth-century picaresque tale *Lazarillo de Tormes*. This translation sustained his aspirations as a scholar-poet and gave him the company of the tale's hero, the crafty rogue servant Lazarillo, who is buffeted by tormenting masters. Lazarillo survives, returning deceit for deceit and blow for blow. Like Howells's umbrella man, Lazarillo is a master of transformation who turns disasters to his advantage.[27]

Publication of Lazarillo's adventures, Howells imagined, might be the means of his own transformation. J. P. Jewett and Company, the house that had produced Harriet Beecher Stowe's amazing best-seller, *Uncle Tom's Cabin*, operated a branch office in Cleveland. Howells accompanied his father to Cleveland with the intention of offering his manuscript, but he faltered at the company's doors. "I was half blind with one of the headaches that tormented me in those days," he recalled, "and I turned my sick eyes from the sign 'J. P. Jewett & Co., Publishers,' which held me fascinated, and went home without at least having my much-dreamed-of version of *Lazarillo* refused." Howells's headache saved him from what might have been another humiliating defeat. His translation of *Lazarillo* was the thread that held his hopes for a literary career; he could not chance having it cut away.[28]

While his trip to Cleveland had not accomplished all that he wished, Howells gained more than sufficient recompense when he found a copy of a book that was "moving polite youth in the East." Tennyson's *Maud* fulfilled its reputation as "passionate love poem, full of burning social protest and indignation." Howells was astonished to discover his own alienated feelings exemplified by the poem's world-weary protagonist. At the beginning of *Maud*, the youthful hero, "a poetic soul," is morbidly self-absorbed. He broods over his rural isolation and despises himself as "languid and base."

As his ranting drives him toward insanity and suicide, he is saved by his longings for the beautiful Maud, whom Tennyson offered as a restorative vision of perfect love.[29]

Reading *Maud* lifted Howells "above life." It seemed the "finest poem [he] had read." He imagined that no one but himself understood Tennyson's subtle meanings. To sustain this feeling of intimacy, he immediately sent off for an edition of Tennyson's complete poems. When it arrived, he read it "night and day, in-doors and out." At the same time, he gathered together everything personal he could learn about the poet. His fascination for Tennyson, Howells recalled, alleviated his "melancholy from ill-health" and his "anxiety for the future in which I must make my own place in the world." Tennyson's poetry transposed these worries into the "substance of literature," where they could be deflected, transformed, and allayed.[30]

Tennyson suggested a poetic strategy, furthermore, that was more earthbound than Lowell's. "He who translates the divine into the vulgar, the spiritual into the sensual," Lowell had contended, "is the reverse of a poet."[31] Because Tennyson portrayed the poet's morbidity as part of his spiritual aspiration, Howells had authoritative support for representing his personal turmoil in poetry. The balancing requirement was the longing for restoration and perfect love that characterized the hero of *Maud*. Howells was strengthened by Tennyson's descriptions of "divine despair."[32] How the poet was to perform service for others by looking intensely into himself was not clear, but for the moment Howells reveled in Tennyson's every word.

Wanting to share his enthusiasm for Tennyson, Howells found a listener close at hand. By this time, he had put away his "ungracious reserves" and admitted his sister Victoria into his literary domain. Victoria secretly nurtured her own literary aspirations, but she was eager to encourage her brother's literary dreams. The eldest of his sisters, Victoria was known in the family for her "unselfish devotion." Howells could imagine that she offered the perfect love Tennyson had described in *Maud*. Their mutual devotion helped to mitigate tensions Howells felt concerning family duty. His relationship with Victoria did not provoke the harsh self-judgments he felt with his brother Joseph.[33] At this time, Howells also gained a measure of toleration from Joseph, who acknowledged "by his few spare words" the beauty of lines Howells read from Tennyson's poem *The Princess*.[34] Joseph's forbearance did not approach perfect love, but it partially eased hostilities over family duties that persisted from their print-shop quarrels.

While Howells was finding solace in Tennyson and support from his family, his father began preparing him for a career in political journalism. The elections of the previous fall had narrowly established Republican control of the state government, with a Republican governor, Solomon P. Chase, and a majority in both branches of the state legislature. William Cooper Howells's support of the Republican ticket in Ashtabula County had been rewarded with a clerkship in the State House of Representatives. The position required a four-month absence in Columbus. When the legislative session began in January 1856, Joseph continued to supervise the printing of the *Sentinel*. Sole charge of the editorial side of the newspaper was given to Will. As temporary editor, Howells promptly expanded the newspaper's literary coverage. He also began a rapprochement with the moral ideals of Jefferson by lending his literary skills to antislavery agitation.[35]

Elevated from the compositor's table to the editorial desk, Howells became a vigorous voice for ascendant antislavery Republicanism. In his first editorial, he announced his allegiance to Chase: "Ohio, the first Democracy in the world, can at last point to an executive who is the expression, the faithful incarnation, of her own great soul." In his subsequent writing, Howells displayed his agitator's skills. He directed telling barbs at D. C. Allen, the diehard Whig editor of the Conneaut *Reporter*. He extolled the village hero, "Old Gid," describing him as a model of "sublimity and moral greatness."[36] In one signal instance, Howells blended literature with political journalism by developing an elaborate literary conceit to support the coming Republican convention in Pittsburgh:

Unfaltering and straight-forward *Action*, from the beginning to the middle, and from the middle to the end, is as much the life of the Republican movement, as it is of the complete and finished drama. There must be no episodes to mar the singleness of its grandeur, and distract the mind from the great denouement that it strives to bring about. Every one must play his part without regard to the "South Americans" in the pit, or the Union Savers in the boxes. The former are not to be tickled by covert allusions and *double-entendres*, nor the latter lulled by lugubrious and pseudo patriotic harangues. The denationalization of Slavery is the catastrophe of the drama in which we all bear parts, and each must press steadily on with this only aim in view.[37]

Concluding with the adjournment of the legislature in May, Howells's editorial role at the *Sentinel* gave him a sense of important standing in his village. Political journalism involved long hours and pressing deadlines, but it did not leave him exhausted as did the study of law. He was prepared to accept his father's scheme to open his way into the larger world. The next year when William Cooper Howells returned to his legislative post in Columbus, Will would travel with him. Victoria would come as well to provide homelike companionship. His father had arranged to write legislative reports for the Cincinnati *Gazette*, but he planned to substitute Will and reveal Will's identity once the reports gained favor. Anticipating the beginning of the legislative session, Howells relished the idea of acting the hero in a tale of concealed identity and dramatic revelation.[38]

With his immediate future set, Howells weathered a new crisis of political commitment. In late May 1856, Jeffersonians were aroused by accounts of the beating of the antislavery senator Charles Sumner by the Southerner Preston Brooks, paired with descriptions of the sacking of Lawrence, Kansas, by proslavery forces. Both events seemed thrusts of the "slave power" conspiracy, requiring resistance from "Sons of Revolutionary sires." "There never was a time like the present since the Revolution," William Cooper Howells told his fellow villagers. "A single move by the slavocracy in any densely settled part of the country would light the torch of civil war at once." Through the summer and fall, reports from "bleeding Kansas" described "butcheries" perpetuated by proslavery ruffians. Indignation meetings raised money to support "an armed emigration to Kansas" that would join free-state forces under James Lane. Harvey Greene, a former printer boy in the Howells family, wrote bristling letters from Kansas urging participation in the struggle. "You ought to be here," he advised the Howells brothers, "to realize a little of war life."[39]

The martial fervor was hard to resist, but talk of an armed expedition to Kansas faded as villagers concentrated on the campaign of the first Republican presidential nominee, John C. Fremont. Victory for the Democrat James Buchanan, William Cooper Howells emphasized, would solidify the "slavocracy," whose tyranny would penetrate even to Jefferson: "The postmaster who now insults us by words or signs, will be backed up with a power that will crush us into submission, or leave us to adopt the one alternative left to Revolutionists." The time for tolerance toward Democratic postmasters had passed. Howells added his voice to the election fervor. He composed a Republican campaign lyric, asserting that Fremont's victory would ensure that Kansas would be "Uncursed by the tread of the Slave!"[40]

Although Fremont fell short of the presidency, antislavery Republicans considered the election a "victorious defeat." The election demonstrated party solidarity throughout the North, prefiguring a national triumph in 1860. Fremont had swept Ohio on the strength of a huge Republican plurality in the Western Reserve. In Ashtabula County alone, Republicans polled 4,163 votes. William Cooper Howells proclaimed that the county was "polluted by the presence of but 975 traitors to liberty and 223 Judas Iscariots," voters who remained Democrats and Know-Nothings. "We stand," he observed to his fellow villagers, "in proud pre-eminence on this great question of Liberty."[41]

By the time of the Fremont campaign, Howells had accommodated himself to the expectations of his village. Antislavery Republicanism had provided a "Holy Cause" and a public role approved by his neighbors. During the Kansas turmoil, Howells had read George W. Curtis's lecture, "The Duty of the American Scholar to Politics and the Times." Curtis described bleeding Kansas as the scholar's Thermopylae. He challenged the scholar to speak out and dispel his reputation as a pale recluse and impractical dreamer. The domain of the scholar was not his study alone, Curtis suggested, for the scholar's words carried enormous consequence in the world at large. Clarion calls to action by mere politicians, Howells reflected, might not have touched him so deeply, but Curtis was the "citizen of a world far greater than theirs, a light of the universal republic of letters, who was willing and eager to stand or fall with the just cause, and that was all in all to me."[42]

Invigorated by Curtis's vision of scholarly agitation, Howells looked forward to the beginning of the state legislative session in January 1857. He imagined that, like his fabled umbrella man, he would rise above all the strange maladies and confusions he had suffered in Jefferson. A career in literature appeared congruent with village ideals of equality and fraternity. Howells was aware, however, that part of his being was at odds with the role of scholarly agitator. In the passionate and divinely despairing hero of Tennyson's *Maud*, he had found a self-portrait that was equally compelling.

CHAPTER 5

Striving away from Home

All who have lived with their eyes open have seen life itself as
desultory and capricious at the most momentous junctures.

HOWELLS, 1891

Although elated over his journalistic and literary prospects, Howells was anxious about leaving home. He recalled the pain he
suffered at Eureka Mills when he twice failed to endure separation
from his family. His anxieties were reinforced by family stories.
His grandfather and father recounted their fitful wanderings. His
mother related how her terrible homesickness made her schooling
impossible. His brother Joseph returned from his steamboating
venture telling of illness and frustration.[1]

Howells had written a success tale that countered family stories
of desperation and failure. In "A Tale of Love and Politics: Adventures of a Printer Boy" (1853), he imagined an alter ego named
George Wentworth who strives and succeeds, rising to fame and
fortune. An orphan unencumbered by inherited advantages, George
confidently sets forth into the world. Though courageous and
devoted to work, traits advice writers identified with success, George
needs chance or luck to accomplish his aims. He saves a rich man's
daughter from drowning and is rewarded with a substantial nest
egg; he writes anonymous editorials supporting the rich man for

political office and wins his benefactor's complete favor when his
authorship is accidentally revealed. His reward this time is marriage to the daughter. True to the typical success tale, Howells
emphasized benevolent chances. Those who proved worthy, his
success tale promised, would survive the hazards of leaving home.[2]

The hazards faced by home-leaving youth symbolized some of
the deepest anxieties of the antebellum middle class. Attempts to
govern youth or invest them with habits of self-control were partly
responses to adult fears that the outside world was hostile to
traditional moral values.[3] Advice writers typically described home
leaving as a voyage on a "stormy and dangerous ocean." This
"nautical metaphor" represented writers' own imagination of a
boundless world, where nothing would be prohibited and everything would be possible. Youth might succumb to "strangers,"
confidence men, or other purveyors of temptation and vice. "Early
departure from the homestead is a moral crisis that many of our
youth do not show themselves able to meet," one writer warned.
"It comes at a tender age, when judgment is weakest and passion
and impulse is strongest." Advice writers emphasized strenuous
self-control to avoid "juvenile depravity." "Reformation," one writer
insisted, "must come from *within*. . . . It must commence with the
soul."[4]

Advice writers' worries about home-leaving youth were reinforced by separation anxieties that appear to have been widespread
among antebellum Americans. Such anxieties encourage recourse
to early childhood fantasies—grandiosity and idealization—that
temporarily support a cohesive sense of self. Children, whose separation anxieties are most acute, first imagine they are grandiose—
supremely powerful and without need. When this fantasy inevitably fails, they begin to idealize another person, usually their mother,
and imagine they are merged with an all-powerful protector.[5] In
antebellum middle-class culture, the ideology of autonomous individualism projected a compelling fantasy of grandiosity, represented most vividly by the figure of the self-made man. The other
fantasy of idealization was represented in the sentimental portrayal
of home, concentrating on the image of the comforting, all-forgiv-

ing mother. Heightened separation anxieties are evident as well in funereal imagery representing death as the ultimate symbol of self-disintegration.[6]

Howells later declared that stoical acceptance of pain was the only way to endure the anxieties and traumas of home leaving. "The youth," he observed, "is always striving away from his home and the things of [home]. With whatever pain he suffers through the longing for them, he must deny them; he must cleave to the world and the things of [the world]; that is his fate, that is the condition of all achievement and advancement for him."[7] Unlike the experience of his hero George Wentworth, Howells's home leaving was a prolonged ordeal that released all the fears he had tried to suppress. Howells's separation from his family and his village seemed to unleash the malevolent power of chance, reinforcing his perception that he was living in a "desultory and capricious" world with no discernible moral order.

In a home-leaving story he wrote soon after his ordeal, Howells recanted the faith in benevolent chances that informed his depiction of George Wentworth's rise to success. In this tale, George Wentworth is replaced by another alter ego named Luke Beazley, who looks back rather than forward. At the moment of his home leaving, Luke Beazley realizes that his experience will be traumatic, for it requires the irreparable loss of an idealized protector. He knows his home leaving will separate him forever from his mother, in whose care "he had always found unfathomable love and pity and refuge."[8]

In early January 1857, the plan to secure Howells's place in political journalism took shape with the opening of the legislative session in Columbus. To impress the editors of the Cincinnati *Gazette*, William Cooper Howells gathered inside information for his son's reports. Mindful of a prejudice toward youth, he signed the initial reports with his own pseudonym, "Jeffersonian." But soon Howells's reporting found favor on its own merit, and he was launched auspiciously into political journalism.[9]

By living with his father and his sister Victoria in Columbus's

Goodale House, Howells had taken a significant portion of home with him on his journey into the world. Victoria encouraged literary projects he pursued with his earlier zest. In his ample leisure away from the legislative corridors, Howells made the State Library his "personal resort." Through the winter months, he and Victoria read many volumes of Zschokke's tales, finished Bulwer's novels, and started on De Quincey's essays. Jefferson had been a "prison," but Columbus seemed "a metropolis of the mind."[10]

Howells believed he was poised on the verge of a "great world of wealth, of fashion, of haughtily and dazzlingly, blindingly brilliant society." He and Victoria had envisioned literary society from sheet music illustrated with a company of "superbly comparisoned people." A fellow printer claimed experience in literary society and advised Howells to "face the proudest down and make audacity do the part of the courage [he] was lacking." Homey dances at Goodale House fell short of the expected grandeur, but Howells continued to associate his literary ambition with entrance into social circles more "polite" than those in Jefferson.[11]

Disappointment over the common level of his social experiences did not bother Howells for long. His nights were devoted to literary study, his days were filled with legislative debate. He had privileges that flattered him immensely—a desk on the Senate floor "as good as any Senator's" and entrée to any part of the beautiful State House. The "dignity" of his surroundings mirrored his grand sense of self-esteem: "I seemed to share personally in [the dignity] as I mounted the stately marble stairway from the noble rotunda or passed through the ample corridors from the Senate to the House when it needed not even a nod to the sergeant-at-arms to gain me access to the floor; a nonchalant glance was enough." In Jefferson, Howells believed he was stagnating in a dreary backwater, surrounded by people hostile to his literary intentions. In Columbus, he could be as literary as he wished. Moreover, he was finding that political journalism offered compatible duties that were "the most important in the world."[12]

Before his breakdown in Jefferson, Howells felt convicted of irredeemable selfishness. Now he was contributing ten dollars a week to pay off the family debt and was doing important service for others as a radical Republican agitator. His letters went south to Cincinnati and Hamilton County, the seat of Democratic conservatism and Ohio's proslavery stronghold. He might help to radicalize the Cincinnati *Gazette*, a newspaper ostensibly independent and usually hesitant regarding slavery. Prepared with the radical weapons of "cutting satire" and "indignant eloquence," Howells was alive to opportunities for agitation that appeared amid the plethora of legislative detail.[13]

Howells seized occasions to parry the main opposition "dodge," the Democratic effort to identify the Republican party with Garrisonian abolitionism and to label all resistance to slavery disunionist. When the Mississippi legislature asked the Ohio Senate to second a resolution blaming the Kansas troubles on the antislavery movement, Howells described the paper with utmost contempt. It contained, he asserted, "all the insufferable insolence of manner and epithet in regard to the agitation of slavery, which it is the peculiar gift of Southern fanaticism to assume." When Ohio Democrats decried Comeouter petitions that annually proposed disunion, hoping to link Comeouters to Republicans, Howells refused to take the bait. He pointed out that while Democrats spilled crocodile tears for the Union, Comeouters were sincere but "mistaken enthusiasts." Far less danger to the Union existed "in the mild madness of Garrisonian zealots, who neither fight nor vote," he concluded, "than in the violence, ruffianism, and avowed disunionism of the Democratic party at the South and the unrebuking silence of that organization at the North."[14]

The political atmosphere of Jefferson had thoroughly attuned Howells to radical measures and means. He supported Negro suffrage to cancel the "ludicrous distinction between black and white." He admonished Republicans to avoid temperance legislation that might undermine "the success of a party aiming at far mightier reforms."[15] His most promising opportunity for agitation developed early in the session. During House debate, John Slough, a conservative Democrat from Hamilton County, was rebuked by Darius Cadwell, a radical Republican from Jefferson. In response,

Slough struck Cadwell in the face. Known to be "rather quick," Cadwell "remained cool." He submitted the matter to the House. Republicans intended to expel Slough and replace him with a moderate not tied to the conservative "Miami Tribe" that ruled Democratic politics in Hamilton County.[16]

Through his day-by-day accounts of the expulsion effort, Howells assumed an important role in the radical Republican agitation. He drew the attention of Slough's constituency to the similarity between the Slough affair and the notorious beating of the radical Charles Sumner by the Southerner Preston Brooks, which had occurred on the floor of the United States Senate the previous spring. Admitting that the blow struck Cadwell was comparatively slight, Howells observed that it was "struck with the same lawless disregard of the sanctity of the place as animated Brooks, and a like contempt for his fellow-members which prevented any after apology." Slough's expulsion was fated by the Republican majority, but his defeat by an independent in the special election came as a surprise. Howells had reason for self-congratulation. His persistent reports of Slough's prevarications had pushed the Cincinnati *Gazette* to endorse the independent.[17]

Late in March, following the Slough affair, Howells received a visitor from Cincinnati. Edmund Babb, an editor at the *Gazette*, was a strange, energetic man, who spoke so indistinctly that Howells had trouble comprehending "the incredible thing he was proposing." Howells discovered that his father's "journalistic plan" had prospered to perfection. Babb offered a full-time position at twice the salary Howells was making in Columbus. Believing this "the greatest piece of good fortune," he hurried to Cincinnati, confident that this new opportunity promised the fulfillment of his hopes. "Already, I am grown fond of this big bustling city," he wrote his brother Joseph soon after his arrival. "The everlasting and furious rushing up and down, and to and fro, pleases me, and I like nothing better than to stroll about the streets alone; and stealthily contemplate the shop windows and orange stands, and speculate on the people I meet."[18]

Howells was not long in Cincinnati before his bravado began to fade. On 19 April he wrote his father that he "unfeignedly" desired to return home to Jefferson, and by early May he was there, disconsolate in his fallen estate.[19] He had remained in Cincinnati barely a month, but he had lost the self-confidence he had enjoyed throughout the previous winter. Returning to Jefferson reunited Howells with his earlier perplexities and self-accusations. Yet by abandoning his journalistic opportunity at the *Gazette*, Howells asserted his determination to become all that he desired to be, no matter the hazard, no matter the psychological cost.

Edmund Babb had proven a true friend, "untiringly kind and attentive." He had provided lodgings in his disheveled chamber above the newspaper office and had begun to teach Howells the journalistic ropes. Howells was to be the new "local," the reporter who covered the police courts and city government. This news was often sordid and violent: the local's column from 24 March to 1 April contained accounts of wife beatings, assaults, robberies, confidence schemes, the arrest of "Magdalens," an attempted suicide, a brawl on Canal Street, and the murder of "Chicken Mike," a local huckster. Howells made a single night's round of the police courts and witnessed for himself the "ravings of a drunken woman." He recalled that he was so "ignorant of life" that he believed that the unescorted shop clerks he saw in restaurants were probably prostitutes. Shaken by his experiences, Howells accepted the warnings of alarmist advice writers. But he did not have to imagine the horrors of city life; vice and viciousness daily appeared on police-court dockets.[20]

Howells later regretted that he had foregone this "university of the streets and police stations, with its faculty of patrolmen and ward politicians and saloon-keepers." But at the age of twenty, he felt the city's underside was destructive to his literary ideals. Vice and viciousness were the fare of sensational novelists like George Lippard, not the elevating, spiritual concerns of Tennyson. Some of the local's duties were less abhorrent than mundane. He reported the laying of sewage lines and the paving of roads. However useful, such reporting did not match the opportunities of the previous winter when Howells had engaged in serious antislavery agitation.[21]

In the midst of his disappointments, Howells began to feel his "old malady" of homesickness. Because Cincinnati was the heart of Democratic conservatism, he made no friends apart from Babb, and except for a few lectures he attended as relief from the dismaying street life, he missed the attractive cultural activities of the city. Babb was the final unsettling influence. He was the first of several journalists Howells met who were "abandoned" to their work. Howells finished his duties around midnight, but Babb returned to his chambers hours later when the newspaper went to press. Memories of his Dayton labors came flooding back, sealing Howells's determination to give up the "money chance" offered by the *Gazette*. It appeared to be no more than a money chance, allowing little opportunity to live for literature.[22]

Before leaving for Jefferson, Howells flirted with an offer from Thomas Brown, editor of the *Ohio Farmer* in Cleveland. Although this possibility seemed a "God-send" for a moment, he had no hope that overworking there, doing "so much for so little," would be any better than in Cincinnati. Yet returning to Jefferson was just as troubling. "I should like well enough to be at home," he wrote Victoria, "but I don[']t want to go back to live at Jefferson any more—which sentiment, were it known in that village, would ruin me." He knew that from the viewpoint of many Jeffersonians, he would have the appearance of a twice-failed son. He had been given opportunities to succeed in law and journalism, but by returning to his print-shop duties, he would be resuming boy's work at home.[23]

Understating his feelings, Howells later described his return to Jefferson as "not cheerful." Performing familiar tasks under dubious public notice was demeaning, but not as torturing as his feeling that he had failed his family. "I must not conceal," Howells recalled, "the disappointment which my father delicately concealed when I returned and took up my old work in the printing-office." His abortive home leaving had frustrated his father's elaborate "journalistic plan" and had eliminated a salary that eased the family debt. Although sympathetic to trials of homesickness, Howells's mother was similarly disappointed. She always encouraged her children to seize and "improve" opportunities for advancement beyond Jefferson.[24]

The literary efforts Howells now began did not reduce his guilt. "I sent off poems and they came back," he recalled; "I offered little translations from the Spanish that nobody wanted." He sought relief in his old lamentation. "As I pass up and down the streets of this not-to-be-sufficiently-detested village," he was soon saying, "and consider that there is not one in it (saving my own kin) for whom I care a hands turning, and that all in it are about that much interested in me, I feel a kind of selfish content that I would not exchange for the sensations of gratified vanity."[25]

The phrase "selfish content" belied Howells's satisfaction and expressed the core of his predicament. He needed to find contentment unalloyed by selfishness. To ready himself for the work he had abandoned in Cincinnati, he wrote a column for the *Sentinel* on "Local and Other Matters," where he reported unsavory news from surrounding country towns—a barn burning, an assault at a spiritualist meeting. But his initial verve as the *Sentinel*'s "local" soon disappeared, and he finally dropped his reporting altogether.[26] Howells's heart lay in his literary work. Despite the lack of response to his poems and translations, he plunged ahead, filling every hour outside his *Sentinel* duties with literature and more literature.

Putting aside his other projects, Howells concentrated on the German language. He piled up translations from German for the newspaper, but he kept at recitations from Ollendorf primarily to read Heinrich Heine, the German poet who had possessed his soul. He had found Heine enticing since reading George Eliot's assessment in the *Westminster Review* the year before. Since returning to Jefferson, however, he was "in a fever" to read Heine "with as little delay as possible." To his delight, he discovered someone in his village who could help. "He is a book binder," Howells proclaimed to his cousin Dune Dean, "and a learned and well[-] read man—thoroughly Teutonic, and an enthusiast about German literature." Otto Limbeck, his new literary friend, was a refugee of the 1848 revolutions. Although Limbeck understood very little English and Howells very little German, every evening they met in the *Sentinel* office to hammer out translations, word by word, until late at night when the bookbinder tired. Savoring Heine's fantastic mixture of prose and poetry, reality and dream, Howells ambled home, imagining that the darkened Jefferson street was out of Heine's wonderful *Reisebilder*. At home he persisted in his studies until becoming exhausted and drifting off to "slumbers which were often a mere phantasmagory" of Heine's imagery.[27]

Heine's influence, Howells later stated, "in its good time saved my life." Heine proved just that vital as the last and most formative literary ideal of Howells's youth. Howells was immediately entranced by the notion that Heine was a poet, even more beleaguered than Pope or Tennyson, who succeeded against desperate odds. Several years earlier, the *Sentinel* had reprinted a description of Heine's progressive paralysis: "It may be said," the writer concluded, "[Heine] lives only on the brain and tongue—the man is a mere corpse—the poet alone survives."[28]

Howells was exhilarated by Heine's suggestion that poetry transcended all the wretchedness of life. Writing his cousin shortly after beginning *Die Harzreise* in *Reisebilder I*, Howells exclaimed,

I have not read much—beyond this sublime sentiment, which Heine quotes from another German. Isn't it fine?—listen:
"Nothing is continual, but Change; nothing eternal but Death. Every beat of the heart gives us a wound, and Life were an endless bleeding, if it were not for Poetry. Poetry gives us what nature denies us: a golden time that rusts not; a spring that fades not; unclouded fortune and everlasting Youth."
Without knowing or thinking whether this would please you as much as it has pleased me, I have given you the benefit of the greatest thought that I have yet read outside our own language. The sweet German of it runs in my head all the while.[29]

Heine's motto from Ludwig Börne was an incantation against Howells's home-leaving difficulties. As he continued to read *Die Harzreise*, he must have found an amulet in every line. Heine's persona in this imaginary picaresque journey is a troubled poet closely drawn from his own life. Stagnating in the provincial city of Göttingen, where Heine felt cramped in the study of law, the poet-persona determines to leave. Encountering adventures in reality and dream, he resolves to overcome all enemies of the poetic imagination. Heine's diatribes against his law professors, who "philosophized away all the brightness of life," probably struck Howells as just, for he too had found the law hostile to his literary intentions. Heine was equally severe with the melancholy that immersed the poet-persona in despair. The struggles of *Die Harzreise* end with apotheosis, as the poet-persona, no longer able to "tell where irony ends and heaven begins," asserts freedom for the poetic imagination, an affirmation that Howells fervently desired for himself.[30]

Heine's assertion of poetic freedom at the end of *Die Harzreise* failed to dispel the gloom that preceded it. The final sense of the work is tenuous optimism. "To be free in everything, that was his ideal," Howells later wrote to Heine, "and [this ideal] was no doubt the effect of being too often free in nothing." The predominating tension of the *Reisebilder* is freedom threatened by confinement. *Die Harzreise*, in particular, universalized the all-or-nothing struggle for autonomy that sometimes emerges in youth. Heine seemed to be Howells's peer in sufferings endured by youthful poets. That these sufferings could occasion the supreme jesting in which Heine "unpacked all the insult of his soul" came to Howells as a cheering revelation.[31]

During the next few years, Howells thoroughly imbibed Heine's intoxicating prose and poetry, finding "a greater sympathy" in Heine than he had experienced with either Pope or Tennyson. "His potent spirit," Howells recalled, "became immediately so wholly my 'control,' as the mediums say, that my poems might as well have been communications from him so far as any authority of my own was concerned." But even though he considered Heine's influence decisive and profound, he had difficulty accounting for its precise significance. He once informed his readers that he had written an essay that perfectly captured Heine's essence, but this essay had strangely vanished.[32] While paying homage to Heine's elusiveness, Howells suggested that his youthful fascination with the poet, once so powerful and animating, was similarly difficult to pin down. Enough remained in memory, however, for Howells to intimate its nature. Against confinement that Howells described as "dancing in chains," Heine represented liberation.

"[Heine] undid my hands, which I had taken so much pains to tie behind my back," Howells explained, "and he forever persuaded me that though it may be ingenious and surprising to dance in chains, it is neither pretty nor useful." The chains he referred to here were the formal constraints of Augustan literary practice that he had learned from Pope. He had thought that "the expression of literature must be different from the expression of life; that it must be an attitude, a pose, with something of state or at least formality in it." Heine showed him to the contrary "that the life of literature was from the springs of the best common speech, and that the nearer it could be made to conform, in voice, look, and gait, to graceful, easy, picturesque and humorous or impassioned talk, the better it was." By the phrase "expression of life," Howells meant language itself, particularly the vernacular speech that represented the talk of common life.[33]

But Heine did not immediately free Howells to become a vernacular writer, for Howells retained painful memories of his humiliation with "The Independent Candidate." In another passage, Howells suggested a different kind of liberation and allowed broader meaning to the phrase "expression of life." Heine, he said, had fused the "gyves in which I was trying so hard to dance": "What I liked then was regularity, uniformity, exactness. I did not conceive of literature as the expression of life, and I could not imagine that it ought to be desultory, mutable, and unfixed, even if at the risk of some vagueness." This passage suggests that Heine's writings offered Howells a way to represent his own felt experience. Heine's "changeful, lawless, natural" style legitimized Howells's feeling that life itself was "desultory, mutable, and unfixed." Life, like talk, he asserted a short time later, was "perfectly desultory."[34]

Heine confirmed Howells's belief that the writer could learn "to run, to leap for joy, to dance," no matter the desultory and threatening nature of life itself. Dancing is notably present in Heine's writings, where it suggests liberation from all restraints. In *Florentinische Nächte*, a street dancer disregards the "affected unities and artificialities" of classical dance with its "danced alexandrines," a reference to Augustan style that Howells would have grasped immediately. Instead of relying on classical dance—"ideal realities and lies"—the street dancer trembles and gyrates in strange motions that seem "like words of a peculiar language that endeavored to communicate peculiar meanings." Several instances of "dancing in chains" also occur in Heine's writings. The most suggestive instance is the frenzied dancing of manacled slaves in his poem "Das Sklavenschiff." [35]

Howells's identification with Heine involved issues of autonomy like those evoked for antebellum Northerners by the image of the manacled slave. Howells's heaviest chain was his feeling that he was minutely responsible for his "evils." Within a Swedenborgian moral universe with its "ends, causes, and effects in an indissoluble connection," no action, thought, or feeling escaped final judgment. [36] If, on the other hand, the universe were not the divinely ordered realm that Swedenborg described, if it revealed only change, endless bleeding, and death, as the motto to *Die Harzreise* declared, then the individual's moral responsibility for his every thought and deed was an illusion or at least an unproven thesis. Nothing is more contrary to the moral universe of Swedenborg than the capricious universe represented by Heine. The *Reisebilder*, especially, portrays the tenuousness of all things, a point Heine made explicitly when he described the world as the dream of a "half-tipsy god." Momentarily when this god wakes, Heine declared, all the random appearances taken to be life will vanish into "nothingness." [37]

The appearance of a desultory world, posing the possibility of "nothingness," delivered Howells from damning self-judgment. The idea that no one is responsible within a desultory world eased the guilt Howells felt for the "selfish" thoughts and deeds that served his literary ambitions. "The final effect of all my lessons from [Heine]," Howells decided, "was to find myself, and to be for good or evil whatsoever I really was." But this self-affirmation was extremely fragile. Insofar as Heine sanctioned self-concern in ways that violated the claims of Howells's Swedenborgian conscience, his influence could never be entirely positive. For the moment, however, Heine suggested liberation: "If he chained me to himself," Howells wrote of Heine, "he freed me from all other bondage."[38]

Following his discovery of Heine, Howells was often depressed and sometimes desperate, but Heine's example, more forcefully than Tennyson's, expanded Howells's lonely condition to a realm of universal thought and feeling. Heine's assertion of self-sufficient freedom was exhilarating. Yet Heine's moments of bitterness and despair suggested that self-sufficient freedom could never be sustained. In Heine's writings, as in romantic writings generally, the grandiose sense of being omnipotent and without need oscillated with an urge to merge with an idealized whole, with transcendent nature or with the universal processes of history. Such idealized wholeness was as illusory as grandiose freedom, but the version represented in Heine enabled Howells to rationalize his sense of literary vocation without denying the claims of his Swedenborgian conscience.

For many young men of Howells's generation, Ralph Waldo Emerson was the premier exemplar of the literary life, offering a vision of the scholar as a solitary contemplative in union with transcendent nature. In his journal, Emerson identified the essence of his instruction: "In all my lectures, I have taught one doctrine, namely, the infinitude of the private man." Emerson argued for a radical form of "self-reliance," anchored in his belief that reflective inwardness provided access to the "currents of the Universal Being," where the solitary individual and especially the poet could joyfully contemplate flux and contradiction in anticipation of an all-embracing unity.[39] While others found Emerson's vision illuminating, Howells found it remote. He recalled that Emerson seemed "somehow, beyond and above my ken, a presence of force and beauty and wisdom." To some extent, Howells shared the notion popular outside of college circles—where Emerson gained his greatest acceptance with young men—that Emerson was "a hopeless mystic" who dwelt in the "ethereal heights."[40]

Heine's poet differed substantially from Emerson's and better represented Howells's own experience. Emerson described reflective inwardness as a condition of serenity and joy, but for Heine it was doleful, a sign of the poet's martyrdom. The passages Howells had chosen to reprint from George Eliot's article on Heine asserted the German's view that the world was a "great lazaretto" and the poet the principal sufferer. Similarly, for the Heinesque poet, the apparent flux of the universe portended division more than unity, a division that the poet experienced far more than ordinary individuals.[41]

Feelings of inner division were nonetheless the basis for the Heinesque poet's meaningful relation to a world outside himself, to society and universal history. With the Hegelian perspectives of his generation, Heine placed his poet within a scheme of progressive history. The poet's inner struggles reflected the core tensions of the age. His inner turmoil was the caldron of history where the process of synthesis occurred. His subjective brooding was "a consecrated means whereby to attain a heavenly end." Unlike Emerson, however, Heine had difficulty trusting that division would ever end. In Heine's writing there is "barely hope" for the achievement of a new, all-inclusive unity.[42]

Heine differed from Emerson in another important way for Howells. In his public writings, Emerson seemed to subordinate society to the divine meditations of the poet and even to eliminate society altogether as a subject of consideration. For Heine, on the other hand, society was always a force, the ground of the poet's beliefs and the source of his alienation. In the transitional age of the present, no poet could ignore the demands of society. Revolutionary strife involved the poet willy-nilly with his fellows. Furthermore, the poet had been brought to earth. Like the Greek gods whom Heine portrayed as exiled in the present, earning their keep in plebeian occupations, the poet had lost general assent to his divinity.[43]

As early as his initial reading of the *Reisebilder* in the summer of 1857, as he worked through the poet's writings word by word, Howells may have found Heine's effort to relate the poet to society and universal history congenial. In the hero of Tennyson's *Maud*, Howells had already met the poet as a self-involved sufferer, and he was prepared to understand the dimension of universal history from August Wilhelm Schlegel's *Lectures on Dramatic Art and Poetry*, a study he had read enthusiastically. In Schlegel's "luminous" discussion of the "glorious course" of romanticism from ancient times to the present, Howells discovered an account of Heine's poet. Schlegel, who had been Heine's teacher and an important influence in his youth, described the attitude of the modern, divided poet as sorrowful *Sehnsucht*, or longing, for "new and marvelous births."[44]

When Howells "pinned [his] faith" to Schlegel earlier in Jefferson, he had prepared himself for Heine. The present age, according to Heine, demanded a poetry expressing the "intensest self-consciousness" and the "feeling of personality," a poetry that was "subjective, lyrical, and reflective." Intense subjectivity offered the poet's only hope for a positive relation to society and the world at large. Later in his youth, Howells described the characteristic theme of this poetry as "the deep ineffable sadness of this age's subjective thought—the vain yearning, the sorrowful [S]ehnsucht, the under current of the life that bears upon its surface only the busy fleets of traffic."[45]

Despite the bitterness that punctuated Heine's poems, especially in their "devastating last lines," Heinesque *Sehnsucht* gave Howells a poetic strategy that suited his psychological needs.[46] Sorrowful longing combined romantic urges to grandiosity and idealization while acknowledging a sense of discontinuity that was missing from Emersonian inwardness. Sorrowful longing was also set against disreputable forms of romantic expression, such as Byronesque egoism. Longfellow argued that the cult of Byron had fostered "sullen misanthropy and irreligious gloom . . . until at length every city, town, and village had its little Byron, its self-tormenting scoffer at morality, its gloomy misanthropist in song."[47] More easily than Byronesque egoism, Heine's poetic strategy could be accommodated with Swedenborgian belief and morality. Heine asserted that concentration on self was not destructive; it was required for the poet's usefulness. Within the flux of universal history, the poet's concentration on self might someday work the greatest good. Comprehending tensions between Howells's experience and the moral imperatives of Swedenborgianism, Heine's poetic strategy provided Howells with a sustaining rationale for his sense of literary vocation.

Eventually Howells absorbed Heine's sense of the poet's positive relation to society and universal history, but Howells was initially drawn to Heine's suggestion that the poet could endure all vicissitudes. In his letter to his cousin Dune Dean, celebrating his discovery of Heine, Howells elaborated a theory of absolute self-sufficiency with Heinesque hauteur:

It is in oneself that one finds the true f[e]licity. If my tooth aches, my friend doesn't lessen my pain by groaning in company with me, let his exertions be never so disinterested and sincere. Neither shall I, by taking snuff, make him to sneeze. As it is with pain so it is with pleasure. No one surrounded by the perfectest happiness feels one happy sentiment unless something has occurred to him to put him in good humour. There are those who will tell you an atmosphere of any emotion, joy or grief, will fill you with sympathetic feelings. Gammon and stuff! A death causes (the thought is horrible, but true, as I know by observation) nothing but jesting and merriment outside of the circle whom it affects immediately; and there are some scenes of happiness that enrage and disgust the beholder. It is my belief that since there can be no effect without a cause, there cannot be a cause in one soul and an effect in another.[48]

Retaining cause and effect but obliterating Swedenborgian bonds of sympathy, Howells's theory was admittedly an attempt to console his "present loneliness." He set his letter aside, later adding a postscript terming his speculations "twaddle—which I am specially gifted to write." His previous remarks now seemed the product of a fitful mood because he had received word that his position as legislative correspondent for the Cincinnati *Gazette* had been renewed for the coming winter.[49]

Through the fall of 1857 as he waited for the legislative session to begin with the new year, Howells followed the protective routine he had begun in the summer, concentrating on his study of German and keeping primarily to himself. He filled the *Sentinel* with his German translations, including "Am fernen Horizonte" from Heine's *Die Heimkehr*, which he printed with the title "A Fragment." His title indicates that he had grasped Heine's notion that life consisted of broken strands that might someday form an entirety. In a poem he entitled "The Autumn-Land," he tested his own ability to express romantic *Sehnsucht*, posing emblems of the "brief November day"—"sorrowing birds," "songless birds," and "stricken elms"—against the yearnings of the "summer-mourning soul."[50]

Howells's growing understanding of the Heinesque poet did not stifle his apprehension that a second home leaving might prove as disastrous as his first. He had reached a dead end in Cincinnati and no longer saw journalism as his saving grace. Toward the end of October, he expressed his anxieties in a letter to Victoria, who was visiting in Pittsburgh. He admitted that his posture of "selfish content" was tenuously maintained against feelings of "sin and misery":

I'm in such a state of mind, not to say sin and misery, as hardly to be able to write. In the morning I get up in a stew, and boil and simmer all day, and go to bed sodden, and ferociously misanthropical. An hundred times a day, I give myself to the devil for having come back to Jefferson, when neither sickness nor starvation drove me; and as often I take myself to task for a discontented fool. For I know very well that had I remained in Cincinnati or Cleveland, I would have discovered as clearly as I have here, that I was in the worst possible situation, the most uncomfortable, the most unprofitable and unpromising. It's a taint of the blood. Here I am, *at home*,—to me the dearest of all places on earth—to begin with. I have books—the best friends. I have time—the most precious thing. No one molests me nor makes me afraid. I sit under my own vine and fig tree (figurative) and cock up my feet on my own secretary (reality). Yet I am not happy. I am not reasonable. They are fools or humbugs who say man *reasons*. Gammon! He wishes for, he grumbles at. The horse who shakes himself free of the wrinkles and recollections of his harness, and gratefully crops the grass, *reasons* more.

The present question with me, for instance, is, how am I to make a living? I bore myself continually about [it], conjuring up possible unpleasant predicaments, and give myself no rest. I am proud, vain, and poor. I want to make money, and be rich and grand. But I don't know that I shall live an hour—a minute! O it was the loftiest and holiest wisdom that bade us take no thought for the morrow and to consider the lilies of the field! If a man were to pray for the *summum bonum*, he would pray; Give me heart to enjoy this hour. Alas for me! Here I might be happy, yet here I am wretched. I want to be out in the world, though I know that I am not formed to battle with life. I want to succeed, yet I am of too indolent a nature to begin. — I want to be admired and looked up to, when I might be loved. — I know myself, and I speak by the card, when I pronounce myself *a mistake*.[51]

Though he relished his self-description, Howells concluded with heartfelt conviction. He pronounced himself "a mistake" because he was failing to sustain his sense of literary vocation under conditions of Heinesque self-sufficiency. His resolve, signified by his summer pseudonym, "Geoffrey Constant," had given way to the kind of self-recrimination that had foreshadowed his earlier breakdown. He was probably learning German and reading Heine with his earlier disregard of late-night hours, for by the middle of November he had succumbed to an illness he recalled as "my terrible rheumatic fever." Although his symptoms suggest he was painfully ill, within a week he was well enough to excuse his silence. "And now," he wrote friends, "do you expect an invalid— as I set up to be—to give you any village gossip?" If he had reverted to the defensive strategy of illness, his break had provided a needed psychic respite, readying him for his second encounter with the outside world. His uncle Samuel Dean's promise of a steamboat trip following the close of the legislative session also helped to restore him.[52]

Howells was fully prepared to succeed in his second home leaving. To strengthen his resolve, he chose an appropriate pseudonym from Longfellow's "Spanish Student," signing his political reports "Chispa," after the hero's rogue servant, a picaro like Lazarillo equal to any and all chances. But shortly after his return to Columbus, he encountered a strange and frustrating difficulty: "I woke to find the room going round me like a wheel. It was the beginning of a vertigo which lasted for six months." Although his vertigo was possibly an effect of his earlier illness, Howells felt it in an exaggerated way. All of his remedies were designed for a "nervous" ailment. Exercise in a gymnasium gave him temporary relief, but his vertigo recurred and finally forced him to suspend his legislative duties. For twenty days his father filled his post while Howells visited relatives in his childhood home of Hamilton. But there too the ground about him "waved and billowed."[53]

Resuming his Columbus duties, Howells attempted to succeed through sheer determination, the remedy usually proposed by his father. By the middle of March, however, before the end of the legislative session, he returned reluctantly to Jefferson.[54] He had fought against this result, for failure to succeed in his second home leaving was an extremely dismal prospect. Returning to Jefferson had become acceptable only because his circumstances in Columbus had posed an even greater threat.

Vertigo expressed Howells's dizzying sense of living in a desultory world and being commanded by powers outside himself. Associated with the earliest feelings of disequilibrium infants experience in their mothers' arms, vertigo also may have expressed the return of his separation anxieties.[55] A further meaning may have been suggested to Howells by an incident in Heine's *Die Harzreise*. The poet-persona is perched on a tall rock of granite, grandly surveying the countryside, when he loses his balance and barely avoids a dangerous fall by clutching to the iron cross that crowns the rock. The incident is an instance of Heine's bitter self-irony. Heine is a poet, supposedly a superior being. But he must earn his living as a lawyer, and becoming a lawyer requires that he renounce his Jewish heritage and convert to Christianity.[56] During his second home leaving, Howells recognized a similar disparity between his ideal aspirations and his actual circumstances.

When he first arrived in Columbus for his second stint as a

legislative correspondent, Howells had found much to please him. His ardor for Heine led him to Columbus's German community, where he formed friendships with several families, lunched at a beer saloon, took fencing lessons, and attended plays. He pushed his study as fiercely as before, expanding his appreciation to other German writers, including Goethe, Schiller, and Uhland. He read more of De Quincey, developing a "deep sympathy with certain morbid moods and experiences so like [his] own." He decided that De Quincey was peculiarly "allied to the German" in thought and feeling. The most auspicious moment in his Germanization came when he was introduced to a woman who had actually known Heine personally, but Howells suffered "indescribable disappointment" when she failed to radiate the ambience of Parisian literary society. Her talk of Heine did not correspond to the image of Heine that Howells held in his imagination.[57]

To concentrate on all things German, Howells pressed his legislative duties hard. Free time was precious, for his responsibilities had increased since the previous winter. He now sent reports to the *Sentinel* and the Cleveland *Herald* as well as to the Cincinnati *Gazette*. He labored to give each report its own particular slant.[58] He may have met these responsibilities easily the year before, but now he was no longer animated by unquestioning eagerness. Journalism no longer seemed his gateway to literature. His hesitations were all the more troubling because the political changes of the previous year had redoubled the need for radical vigilance. Republicans had suffered a series of setbacks beginning with the Dred Scott decision in March 1857. Most seriously, in the fall elections Republicans suffered more than Democrats from the economic slide that began with the Panic, losing decisively across the North. In Ohio, Chase narrowly won reelection, but Republicans lost both legislative houses. The Democratic majority was planning to repeal the antislavery measures passed the previous year, particularly the "Jail Bill" that radical Republicans designed to frustrate enforcement of the Fugitive Slave Law by prohibiting the incarceration of fugitive slaves in Ohio.[59]

As he began his reporting, Howells meant to defend the antislavery cause as vigorously as the best radical agitator. Going right to the attack, he treated the Democrats with a satiric flair enhanced by his immersion in Heine. He reported their rapaciousness for office, their oafish crudities and profanities, their discourteous attempts to squelch the Republican opposition. Only twenty days into the session, however, when the Republican effort to save the Jail Bill was just beginning, Howells withdrew. While his father assumed his duties, he sought relief from his vertigo. But he did not feel so impaired that he found it necessary to curb his literary studies.[60]

Howells probably returned to the legislature with revitalized hope that he could forge a unity between politics and literature. He lampooned Democrats even more unsparingly, but his attacks reveal a personal animus that may have been prompted by his increasing difficulties. His principal target was William H. Safford, the Democratic senator who led the assault on the Jail Bill. "He sits on the main aisle in the Chamber," Howells wrote with satiric contempt, "and he ran about in it like one distracted, thrashing the wind with arms 'of wild rejection' and swaying his body to and fro and lifting himself upon the toes of his boots, and stooping and surging up again, during the course of his speech, like an India rubber man with a severe attack of colic." At first Safford was not disposed to let this ridicule pass. Threatening Howells's expulsion, he demanded immediate "corrections." In mock-respectful replies, Howells compounded his offense, but Safford finally let the matter slide.[61]

Following his imbroglio with Safford, Howells directed a new thrust at Representative Hunter Brooke, a Hamilton County Democrat, reporting Brooke's remarks derisive of the Cincinnati press. "I expect," Howells declared, "that Mr. Brooke will rise to a question of privilege, tomorrow morning, and demand my expulsion for telling you the foregoing. I do it at my peril, for all reporters have had a fair warning not to put anything into their letters of a nature discreditable to this legislature." Although remonstrances from Brooke followed, they never led to Howells's expulsion.[62]

This result may well have disappointed Howells. His baiting of Safford and Brooke suggests that he was trying to exceed their toleration. The reporter for the Cincinnati *Commercial* had been barred from the House for similar insults.[63] By pushing his agitation to the extreme, Howells may have been seeking an honorable way out of his reporter's duties so that he could devote himself fully to literature. Had either Democrat called for his expulsion, he would have returned to Jefferson a martyr to the radical cause rather than a nervous sufferer from vertigo. As it was, he left for home in early March without a respectable excuse.

Reaching the manly age of twenty-one, Howells returned again to boyish tasks. He assumed at least the outward appearance of maturity by cultivating a moustache and imperial. He could not disguise his feelings from himself. Recognizing that his security at home represented his defeat in the greater world, he sought what little comfort remained in his old lamentation: "It is one of the best things to be at home," he wrote a friend; "but yet the little village is fearfully dull to me. Only the presence of Vic., and the frequent deploring of our hard lot . . . make it at all tolerable for me." Howells had less opportunity for his usual escape from his feelings because his father insisted that he curtail his late-night study for the sake of his health.[64]

Little in Howells's situation affirmed the self-sufficiency Heine imagined for poets. During his period of rest, he was excused from heavy compositing labors, but he continued clipping the English reviews for the *Sentinel*, including one passage that ironically represented his dilemma. The writer asserted that literary pursuits were "more independent of the will of others, more independent of the will of circumstances, than almost any other enjoyment." Howells fell back on advice-book admonitions to strive and succeed; he resolved to rise at once in the mornings and proceed immediately to his tasks. Soon he resumed his intense reading as well as his copious translations. He could follow his father's order to avoid study only by taking to the woods, where tramping "day after day," he tried to forget his vertigo and the perplexities of his home leaving. With the thawing snow, he anticipated the coming

of May when he was to be "respited" for a month on his uncle's
Ohio River steamboat.[65]

Despite the bitter experience of the preceding year—two inglo-
rious returns to Jefferson from abortive forays into the world—
Howells was no less tenacious in his determination to fulfill his
literary intentions. His river trip on his uncle's stern-wheeler, the
Cambridge, in the spring of 1858 became an important time of
restoration and rededication. Freed from immediate demands on
his usefulness, he could indulge his imagination as fully as he
wished and test whether Heine's guise of a traveler in the *Reisebilder*
was one he could assume for himself. In the letters Howells began
writing for the *Sentinel* describing his progress down "La Belle
Rivière," the most resounding note is his celebration of idleness.
Discovering to his delight that steamboat travel afforded the freedom he had craved in Columbus, he reported that "the cabin
passenger is a limited monarch, going where he pleases, and saying
and doing nearly the things he lists."[66]

Heine's *Reisebilder* sanctioned the widest range of imaginative
meandering. From Pittsburgh to St. Louis, Howells searched the
shoreline, alert to scenes that might generate various kinds of
literary response. Inevitably, as the *Cambridge* edged toward the
junction of rivers at Cairo, he saw evidence in the river towns that
fit his radical Republican notions of contrasting civilizations North
and South. The Northern side seemed a pastoral landscape, showing energy and enterprise, while the Southern side seemed "squalid"
and swarming with loafers. The Ohio itself, as it flowed south,
took on the enervation of a civilization founded on slavery. At its
confluence with the Mississippi at Cairo, it appeared "gross, swol-
len and bloated, like some vagabond profligate."[67]

Tiring of contrasts between North and South by the time the
Cambridge reached St. Louis, Howells was anxious to experiment
with other modes of writing. He released a pent-up desire to
rhapsodize the past when he found a sufficiently picturesque Spanish bell bearing the date A.D. 808. He indulged another inclination
by offering a description, from the safe distance of the *Cambridge*'s

guard rail, of the drinking dens, "loathsome pitfalls," that lined the
wharf. He observed the arrival of the "strange woman," whose
wiles and dangers were fabled in countless advice books. "She
drinks with [the revelers] again and again," Howells wrote. "She
dances before them, and they go mad with obscene glee. Shouts[,]
cries, oaths, and curses issue from the dens where they are crowded
together; and the uproar grows more furious, till all sounds are
blended in a frightful clamor. Now let the belated passer have a
care; for these men are ripe for robbery and murder; and there is
much chance that he will figure in the morning papers as one of
the parties in a case of 'Brutal Assassination.' " Howells had other
opportunities to indulge a sensational manner, but once was apparently enough. When the *Cambridge* left St. Louis for its return to
Pittsburgh, he was happy to escape "imprisonment" in the city
and turn his mind to loftier things.[68]

The river itself inspired Howells to emulate the kind of writing
that interested him most. Brooding over the changing and chance
appearances of the river landscape, he yearned to be pleased by the
"exquisite" emotion, described by Heine as almost painful, that
any fleeting form of "perfect beauty" could suggest. The river
moonrise offered one such form, inducing Heinesque reverie and
the emotion of vain longing: "It seemed as if one might, leaving
earth behind, walk on [the moon's reflection], in a rapturous dream,
out into the Morning Land, and forever forget the toils, cares, and
vexations of life in a sweet oblivion."[69] Howells cultivated a yearning for sweet, painful repose, the stance of the Heinesque poet in
his most affirmative mood:

Sweet are my last days' memories of the mighty river. For all along
our course the young water-willows, thickset among the cottonwood,
laded the charmed winds with delicate fragrance, and every little breeze
blew as if from paradise. —So it is, they say,—at this enchanted season
of the year—from the Egyptian metropolis [Cairo], to the mouth of the
Red River. The vast region through which the river sweeps away, is a
Lotus-Land of perfume, where the luxurious sense of the traveler is fed
upon odors sweeter than the breath of Hybla. Lapped in a dreamy
revery, I hung upon the guard and, "watching the tender curving lines of
creamy spray," almost thought to see "about the keel,"

"The mild-eyed, melancholy Lotus Eaters come."
bearing in their languid hands, branches
      —"of that enchanted stem
Laden with flowers and fruit."

But in reality there was little else to see than immense quantities of driftwood, with which the river was almost covered.[70]

Howells's interruption of his reverie suggests his protorealist urge to cut down extravagant emotions. But his slightly bitter undercutting primarily reflects a break—similar to Heine's "devastating last lines"—that expressed Howells's sense of a desultory world in which disruptive appearances could not be contained within any total, positive vision.

By the time the *Cambridge* was returning up the Ohio, Howells had successfully tested his ability to become a Heinesque traveler. He had also gained his respite. From St. Louis he had written his family of only one slight recurrence of his "old trouble of the head." He had grown more and more tired of repose. At a dreary river town, he had exchanged a glance of recognition with a group of loafers. The charm of the lazy river life was waning. Howells looked forward to reengaging the "toils, cares, and vexations of life" on different terrain.[71]

Becoming a legislative reporter was no longer an option. To prevent the recurrence of the difficulties that had called him away from his own duties, William Cooper Howells had suggested that the Cincinnati *Gazette* hire someone besides his son. Looking for alternatives, Howells sent off a flurry of inquiries. He proposed writing a column with the personally significant title of "Desultoria" for the radical Republican *National Era*, but the offer must have seemed too frivolous for a newspaper that was a principal organ of antislavery. When he seemed to have exhausted all possibilities, his father drew together duties dealing with subscription, advertising, and stationery, providing him with a face-saving position as the *Sentinel*'s business manager. Howells must have reflected bitterly how his situation fulfilled Heine's prediction that the poet, like the exiled Greek gods, could survive in the present only as a drudge in a humdrum job.[72]

His bookbinder friend, Otto Limbeck, rescued Howells from despair by loaning him a novel that helped to sustain him in his "prisoning environment." *Afraja*, by Theodore Mügge, described a young Dane who was seeking his fortune in the northern fisheries. "There was a supreme moment," Howells recalled, "when he was sailing through the fiords, and finding himself apparently locked in by their mountain walls without sign or hope of escape, but somehow always escaping by some unimagined channel, and keeping on. The lesson for him was one of trust and courage; and I, who seemed to be then shut in upon a mountain-walled fiord without inlet or outlet, took the lesson home and promised myself not to lose heart again." He did not have long to test his resolve, for "suddenly," as he remembered, "the whole world opened to me through what had seemed an impenetrable wall." In the middle of November, the newly reorganized *Ohio State Journal*, the voice of the state's radical Republicans, offered Howells a place as an assistant editor. He eagerly "forgot [his] ills" and accepted.[73]

From this seemingly chance event, Howells did not gain a sense of revitalized optimism comparable to his father's professed belief that everything worked for the best. The image of impenetrable walls in *Afraja* accorded more with the sense of life Howells derived from his home-leaving experience and his reading of Heine. During the fall, Howells had written a poem he entitled "The Mysteries." Rather than "trust and courage," the faith of his father, the poem expressed doubt and anxiety. The first mystery, learned in childhood but eased by mother's love, is "Death." The second mystery, learned by strife in the world, is "Life." The second mystery must be endured without consolation.[74]

8. William Cooper Howells, ca. 1856. After his father's death in 1894, Howells wrote, "[My father] brought to the study of persons and things his peculiarly genial intelligence. It was not merely that he saw them clearly, but that he saw them kindly. The unfriendly eye always loses what is best in a prospect, and his eye was never unfriendly."

9. Mary Dean Howells, ca. 1856. Though she missed her children terribly when they were away from home, Mary Howells told them to make their opportunities count. "It is you[r] duty to improve every advantage you have," she wrote Victoria, who was visiting in Pittsburgh. "I want you to see and hear every thing that will have tendency to elevate and improve your mind[.] [R]ead all the good and usefull books you can get. . . . [I]f your cousin Lizzie can help you any in your music I hope you will improve the chance for when you get home again the chances will be poor enough."

10. Joseph Alexander Howells, ca. 1856. Joseph was disappointed that he never fulfilled the "ambition of [his] life" to become a steamboat pilot. But helping the family, he said, "shut off all hope in that direction." His frustration may have influenced his decision to keep his brother Will in the print shop rather than send him to an academy when Howells was seventeen. Joseph felt guilty throughout his life for this "irreparable wrong." Howells forgave Joseph several times, even in a line he included in his brother's epitaph: "There needs no room for blame. Blame there was none."

11. Victoria Mellor Howells, ca. 1856. Likened by her family to the eldest daughter in John Greenleaf Whittier's *Snow-Bound*, who kept "with many light disguise / The secret of self-sacrifice," Victoria spent most of her life caring for her father and for her retarded brother, Henry. She was married briefly, but her husband left her. She nurtured literary ambitions like her brother Will, but she never found a producer for her play, "The Sheriff's Daughter."

12. Three of the younger Howells children, ca. 1846. From the left, the children are probably Victoria, Samuel, and Aurelia. Annie Howells, who was two years younger than Aurelia, recalled that her brother Will loved to entertain the children by impersonating figures from fiction. Their special favorite was the "Fat Boy" from Dickens: "With puffed out cheeks, he would stare at us with fixed eyes, and a gorged expression, to our wild delight."

13. Anne Thomas Howells, ca. 1863. During the years of the Civil War, Annie kept a journal, where she recorded her frustration at being distant from momentous events. "Northerners still languish in foul prisons, and fight beneath the burning southern sun," she wrote. "We in our quiet home feel none of war[']s desolation, not even a dear one is in danger, and at night we sleep as securely, and peacefully—lulled by the wind[']s soft lullaby—as if no such thing as Death walked over the land and marked his victims with rapid hand."

14. Henry Israel Howells, ca. 1856. The younger children were warned never to disturb their brother Will during his studies, but Howells made an exception with his retarded brother, Henry. Annie Howells believed that during these moments Henry gained "a soothing calm for his tortured nerves."

15. Howells with his brother John Butler Howells, ca. 1859–60. After his brother Johnny began attending Cleveland Institute in 1863, Howells offered advice: "Don't be taken with the shallow folly that anything which your conscience tells you is bad, can be brave or fine. You'll find a great many brilliant fellows in this world who are also vicious. You must not believe that it is their vice gives them brilliancy."

CHAPTER 6

———

Woman's Sphere

[Women of all ages] are the most devoted novel-readers, the most intelligent . . . and the most influential, by far. It is the man of feminine refinement and of feminine culture, with us so much greater than masculine culture, who loves fiction. . . . Business men, I fancy, seldom read novels at all; they read newspapers.

HOWELLS, 1899

Recalling her brother's home-leaving struggles, Howells's sister Aurelia wrote that "though a home boy, he was not cowardly, and at a suitable time of his life he went out and took his place in the world, and kept it." In November 1858, Howells made his decisive break from home when he assumed his position as assistant editor on the *Ohio State Journal* in Columbus. Friendly newspaper accounts described him as "studious and talented," someone who was a "Printing Office graduate, the best College from which to receive an editorial diploma." [1] Howells never returned home again under the humiliating conditions of the previous two years. Nevertheless, home remained a forceful reminder of family claims he could never forsake. Home was also associated with other claims on his sense of identity.

In the didactic writings and popular stories of civilized morality, home was depicted as "woman's sphere," the exclusive realm of

women, while the outer world was described as the exclusive realm
of men. This split reflected pressures exerted upon local community life by development of the national market. The concept of
"woman's sphere" helped to accommodate antebellum Americans
to the segmentation of home and work by reinforcing a rigid
differentiation of gender roles. Women took on daily chores of
child care and home maintenance as well as moral oversight; men
became "breadwinners" fated to struggle for autonomous success.
As self-sacrificing redeemers, women were to preserve the home as
a refuge, a haven of peace and love, set against the ruthless competition and spiritual waste associated with the outside world.[2]

This differentiation of gender roles was idealized by middle-
class writers. William Cooper Howells believed the idea of separate
spheres expressed natural equality: "The sexes are distinct and
their spheres of action and duties are distinct, and superiority over
the other, does not attach to either. In man's mind the understanding and judgment are most fully developed but in woman's mind
the affections and perceptive faculties are the strongest. . . . Who
shall say that judgment is a superior faculty to affection, or that
affection is above judgmen[t]?" But the new differentiation of gender roles was coercive for both men and women. The concept of
"woman's sphere" trivialized even as it idealized women's work,
sanctioning women's subordination within the altered economic
order. Men who failed to achieve the ideal of "manly" independence could be designated "cowards" or "home boys," the terms
that came easily to Aurelia Howells when she alluded to her
brother's home-leaving difficulties.[3]

In *A Boy's Town*, Howells portrayed his experience of initiation
ceremonies, tests of courage, and practices of conformity that prepared boys to become aggressive, self-assertive men. In one instance he was goaded by his fellows to run down and strike a timid
boy "in his imploring face" for some violation of the boyhood code.
He was overcome by shame for violating the values he had been
taught at home, but those who failed to live by the boyhood code
were called "girl-boys," a taunt Howells successfully avoided. Acceptance exacted costs. Besides guilt suffered for "brutal" actions,

welcome among his fellows required concealment of his literary desires. Howells painfully learned that they thought it "soft" or feminine to write poetry.[4]

The strictures of middle-class, civilized morality were partly meant to chasten the "savage" inclinations of the boyhood code, harnessing aggressive behavior for the practical affairs of men. But the dominant attitude toward poetry remained unchanged in the transition to manhood. In middle-class culture, all forms of imaginative literature were linked to "woman's sphere," considered too decorative or ethereal to have important consequences in the lives of "true men." Insofar as literature was associated with spiritual and ethical concerns, it was deemed appropriately consigned to women, who were increasingly considered the natural custodians of religion and morality.[5]

While in Jefferson, Howells had inveighed against the sentimental idiom favored by women who sent poems and stories to the *Sentinel;* he had asserted his equality with lawyers, politicians, and other so-called practical men. These skirmishes were preliminary to the more formative conflict that began in Columbus. Howells described his two-and-a-half years in the Ohio State capital as the "heyd[a]y of life" and the "blossom of [his] youth."[6] Although these years were exhilarating and expansive, they were also the time when he confronted the constricting gender ideals of his culture and tried to solve, once and for all, the problem of becoming both a literary and a "true" man.

At the *State Journal,* Howells was restored to the forefront of antislavery agitation. Republicans had triumphed in the 1858 state elections, and to herald the party's return to power, a new management had rescued the *State Journal* from faltering finances, spruced up its design, and dedicated it to "genuine Republicanism." Howells's employer, Henry D. Cooke, proved to be "the easiest of easy gentlemen," disposed to let his editorial staff of three run the newspaper while he lobbied in the legislative corridors. At first it appeared that Howells would have to perform the same duties that had distressed him in Cincinnati, but Cooke found a young man named Harris who doted on the local's "sundry ascents into various dingy Justice of Peaces' offices and hopeful visits to rowdy saloons." Howells's "senior," Samuel R. Reed, assumed the major responsibility for the newspaper's prodigious output of political commentary. As Reed's "lieutenant," Howells now and then contributed a "leader" to the political columns, but only on his own inclination and usually with a decided literary inspiration.[7]

For one resolved to be an "exclusively literary spirit," Howells found his situation at the *State Journal* surprisingly congenial. His primary duty was to skim the news from the tide of exchange newspapers and journals that deluged his desk every day and to arrange a column with his own comments under the title "News and Humors of the Mails." He recalled, not wholly in jest, that he accomplished this task with great flair, "wielding scissors of metropolitan brilliancy." He counted nothing alien within the great range of "politics, morals, literature or religion," an amplitude that allowed him to hone the "sharp tooth" of his radical Republicanism with a barb directed at "some frenzy of proslavery ethics" and, at the same time, to expound on the latest "gossip" of the literary scene. Eventually his items of literary gossip spilled into a column of their own. His journalistic duties provided the opportunity to balance the roles of scholar and agitator. It probably fortified Howells to learn that Heine had become a newspaper paragraphist to support his poetry. Further encouragement came from Reed, who tolerated his literary inspirations, allowing even his "self-betrayals"—his poems—to pass notice unscathed.[8]

Although he cared nothing for Howells's poetic "effusiveness," Reed admired Shakespeare, Dickens, and the Old Testament—the great resources for his agitator's language of satiric ridicule and righteous indignation. Howells found that Reed shared his taste for the theater and would accompany him to the makeshift enterprise on State Street, whose productions Reed enjoyed as much for their vulnerability to his "droll" commentary as for their realization of dramatic intention. For Reed, literature was not the sum of all that was precious in life, but a source of allusion that enhanced his aggressive, masculine deportment and a fund of material that offered occasion for his assertive mockery. No doubt the theater appealed to him in part because it lay outside the boundaries of respectable middle-class entertainments. In appearance, Reed violated the middle-class norm by dressing the dandy, and he was professedly a religious skeptic who conspicuously solemnized his philosophy in long Sunday walks.[9]

Reed's masculine style of opposition and irony appealed to Howells, but Howells could not assent to Reed's narrow appreciation of literature as simply a vehicle for sarcastic asides. Reed was too much Howells's senior in age and rank, however, to have force as a peer. His influence was not so great as other companions Howells found in Columbus who were part of the great influx of antebellum youth seeking urban employment as clerks and professionals, the kind of young men whose numbers and freedom from traditional restraints frightened the advice givers of civilized morality. Contrary to portraits in the advice books, the young men Howells knew best were a decorous and studious lot. They formed what he later called his "College" group, so named for their common residence in the Starling Medical College, a magnificent edifice of mixed Gothic and Tudor design that the panic of 1858 had partly transformed into a boardinghouse. One-third of Howells's weekly ten-dollar salary went to live at the College, but it provided him with a "charming state of animal comfort," augmented by pleasing male conviviality.[10]

Howells was amazed to find that his roommate, Artemus T. Fullerton, was also a poet. Although Fullerton was reading law, he had already published two poems in the *Atlantic Monthly*, for which he had been paid the grand sum of twenty-five dollars a page. Fullerton modeled his poetry on Browning's and needled Howells by claiming that Heine was a mere imitator of Sterne, making Howells an imitator of an imitator. Such remarks were part of the "richly personal" jesting that Howells fondly remembered as the norm of the College.[11]

Another law student, James M. Comly, possessed a "literary bent" similar to Fullerton's. Comly furnished his room with *Cornhill Magazine* and the London *Saturday Review* to follow the doings

of Thackeray, the literary rage of the moment. Soon after meeting
Comly, Howells told Victoria that Comly was his "present Jim
Williams," a boon companion with whom he could share his aspirations. Neither Fullerton nor Comly meant to sustain a literary
vocation, but they were ready for literary talk mixed with personal
reflection. They became Howells's companions in the ultimate of
social pleasures—evening calls where they met the young women
of Columbus society, women who in their dresses were like "silken
balloons walking." Following these calls, the young men usually
retired to Ambos's restaurant on High Street to recount their
experiences over a hearty oyster supper.[12]

Fullerton, Comly, and other young men Howells met at the
College represented a masculine style that allowed a place for
literature, but not exactly the place that Howells most cherished.
Although they shared Howells's literary interests more fully than
Reed, the Collegians imposed definite limits on their appreciation.
Comly did not assent to poetry, apparently believing the satiric
mode of Thackeray's novels more congruent with masculine demeanor. This tension between Howells and his friend surfaced
when Howells published a poem he called "The Poet's Friends,"
representing a bird sweetly singing to dull, uncomprehending cat-
tle. Howells unwittingly revealed that he had Comly in mind by
repeatedly insisting to him that the poem was "entirely dramatic,"
or imagined. Comly declined to feel insulted, but he never did take
Howells's poetry very seriously. Fullerton, despite being a published poet, also excluded poetry from the realm of manly affairs.
When he left Columbus for Peoria to begin his legal practice, he
made Howells promise that no mention of his Browningesque
poems would appear in the *State Journal*'s notice of his departure.
Fearing that he would be injured in his new career, Fullerton
capitulated to the prejudices of his culture: Poetry might be tolerated as a dalliance of youth, but it was best left behind when one
entered the realm of men.[13]

Howells had a single peer who shared his literary passions
without reserve. John J. Piatt had worked with Howells as a
compositor earlier in Columbus at the *State Journal*, where they

had once warred with wet sponges, an event Howells had celebrated in verse. On meeting again as young men, they were delighted to find that they both were aspiring poets nurturing their
ambitions while working on newspapers. They provided each other
with distant support, for Piatt had obtained the "literary and mis-
cellaneous" department on the Louisville *Journal*. But Piatt sometimes visited Howells in Columbus, and they communicated through
their columns, where they "puffed" each other's work and defended it against detractors. They both admired the "beautifully
sad" German poets headed by Heine and were reading intensely
along the same lines. Piatt was the one male confidant to whom
Howells could report the unabashed record of his poetic development, especially those "curious revelations of self" wherein he
most felt his growth. Piatt offered the further encouragement of
literary competition, for like Fullerton he had published a poem in
the *Atlantic Monthly*. Only "something worthy" of the *Atlantic*,
Howells decided, would establish his equality with his literary
friend.[14]

In contrast to Piatt, the young men of Howells's Columbus
social set mainly concerned themselves with literature to "please
the fair." Being well read in the literature of the day, especially the
latest serialized novels, was a necessary entrée and often a real
advantage in the evening soirees that moved from the parlor of one
young woman to that of another. For most young men, knowledge
of refined literature was a key that opened "woman's sphere."
Literature drew intense interest as a means of flirtation and courting. Armed with opinions concerning the current episodes of
Thackeray's serial novel *The Newcomes*, a young man was assured
that he would be able to do more than blankly stare at his beloved.
At the very least, literature provided a neutral ground of conversation between young men and women who had learned to regard
each other as polar opposites. Young men who demonstrated a
command of literary wit and analysis gained particular favor among
young women as well as among their older female chaperones.[15]

In this masculine competition, Howells excelled. A young woman
who met him at this time remembered, "His ready wit and bril-

liant conversational powers made him a welcome visitor everywhere. Stepping to a book-case, he was wont to take down a
volume of Thackeray or Dickens, and, hastily scanning its pages,
entertain a roomful with the drollery of his remarks." Nothing in
Howells's autobiographies called forth more evocative lyricism than
his memories of those occasions among the "gentle and cultivated"
women of Columbus society, who allowed him to do unreservedly
what he desired to do above all else, "always and evermore . . . to
think and dream and talk literature and literature only." [16]

Although he had not entered the "great world of wealth, of
fashion, of haughtily and dazzlingly, blindingly brilliant society"
that he once imagined surrounded literature, Howells had become
part of "good society" in Columbus, a social circle that set a
respectable middle-class tone. He owed his elevation in status to
his radical Republicanism, for the leaders of this social circle were
Governor Chase and his daughter Kate, who presided over the
social affairs of her widowed father. Governor Chase naturally
took a proprietary interest toward the editorial staff of the *State
Journal*. When he learned that Howells had not made a single New
Year's call, whereas Fullerton had made fifty-one, he conspired
with his daughter to bring Howells out at the next Chase recep-
tion. Thereafter Howells became a fixture in "good society"—
mostly Republican houses that to his immense delight turned out
to be also "literary houses." [17]

Howells enjoyed his new associates, especially the literary women
he met in Columbus parlors, settings reserved for displays of
middle-class respectability. To preserve domestic values from the
manipulation and misrepresentation associated with the outside
commercial world, advice writers urged cultivation of "sincere"
parlor manners and warned against charlatans who would disguise
their true intentions. The tension between the cult of sincerity and
fear of disguise was acted out in parlor games like charades, one of
the first tests Howells passed in Columbus society. Following a
dinner with Governor Chase, he was challenged to abandon all
pretense and show his true self when Kate Chase assigned him the
first dissyllable of "Canterbury Bell." No one who cantered for the

pleasure of others could cling to false pride. All of Howells's new associates appeared to be free of artifice. Everyone he met in parlor games, dances, and literary discussions, Howells told Victoria, seemed "single hearted and sincere—perhaps," he added, "because I am so myself, and I enjoy me in nearly all companies." [18]

The women Howells met in Columbus parlors immeasurably strengthened his resolve to be a poet. "I was taken at the best I meant as well as the best I was," he recalled, and the best he meant was to be the "author of things destined to eclipse all literature hitherto attempted." When he desired a purely literary occasion, he preferred the company of older women, who demonstrated a more sophisticated literary taste and were not apt to ask the favors sometimes requested by younger women, such as asking him to underline all the agreeable passages of *Adam Bede*. With older women, the conversation was likely to be "kind and earnest," rather than bantering and flirtatious. Older women were less competitive and more appreciative of his literary "feats." They considered literature a compelling interest in itself, not a means for finding a suitor. Whether from younger or older women, however, admiration of any sort was deeply gratifying to Howells. In Columbus society, he found a supportive feminine intimacy that previously consisted only of his sister Victoria. This intimacy always represented his ideal vision of the reading audience that was the principal arbiter of literary taste in nineteenth-century America. [19]

When he recalled his association with literary women in Columbus, however, Howells returned to his sense of being double lived. Outwardly he appeared to be a young journalist desiring to advance in his field; inwardly he was nothing other than a poet. Often the "face of the poet was saved by the audacity of the paragrapher." To "most men, men of affairs, men of the more serious callings," he was the writer of "sharp" social and political commentary rather than the writer of "soft" verses after the manner of Heinrich Heine. The subtle devaluation of the literary vocation that Howells felt in the hesitations and indifference of his friends Reed, Fullerton, and Comly was more explicitly expressed among men in Columbus who were the "hardest-headed." The affirmation Howells received from literary women reinforced his realization that literature was not considered useful by masculine standards. And judged by his Swedenborgian conscience, what was not useful was necessarily selfish.[20]

For the time being, Howells kept his ambivalence beneath the surface. In his letters to Victoria, his most intimate and accepting confidante, however, he made no pretense that he hoped for anything but literary success. His frequent reports to his sister, including a journal written solely for her eyes, voiced his heady aesthetic elation and recited his many "little triumphs." Some of his more literary contributions to the *State Journal*, notably "Bobby," a sketch of a misunderstood but intrepid adolescent boy, had won approval around Columbus. His sudden acclaim was "unspeakably sweet," Howells wrote Victoria. Moreover, he was finding other markets for his prose sketches. "I can sell, now," he told her confidently, "just as much as I will write."[21]

In the wake of his exultant optimism, Howells felt released from the stifling atmosphere he associated with his village. "O, how genially I come out in this ray of sunlight, after being frozen up so many years in Jefferson," he exclaimed to Victoria. "All my faculties expand, and the gloom leaves me, that haunted me forever." Still, the chancelike disappointments of his recent home leaving made him cautious. "All the time," he admitted, "I say to myself, you fool, don't let all this elate you. You have achieved your present little notoriety without desert, and you may suddenly lose it the same way."[22]

Howells confronted his anxieties in the poems he wrote during his "brief noonings" and late at night, as he worked out the meaning of his Heinesque persona.[23] But he pursued his writing with growing assurance that time was on his side and that an informed audience near at hand would appreciate his intentions. For the moment, he felt freed from the perplexities he had suffered in Jefferson. The umbrella man had floated into Columbus, and at least in certain quarters, he had been granted the whole sidewalk.

The new self-assurance Howells derived from his Columbus experiences is evident in his sketch "Bobby." Intractable and defiant of familial authority throughout his twelve years, Bobby has been pronounced a "worthless fellow" by his father, while his mother has sighed over him. But Bobby can endure all misgivings from his family, for he is determined and indomitable, a "cast-iron boy." Whatever he will be in the future, concluded Howells's narrator, "he will be with his whole heart, which is a great and good heart, as I say in defiance of his relatives."[24] Howells, in fact, needed the cast-iron resolve he attributed to Bobby to avoid censure of his good heart, for his vocational strivings were still framed within a Swedenborgian moral universe. The voice of his conscience was constantly joined by voices from home that reminded him of his obligations.

Although she had been his steadfast sympathizer ever since his Jefferson breakdown, Victoria found it difficult to accept merely a vicarious enjoyment of his new successes. Their mutual imagining of the future had included the glittering cosmopolitan life that her brother now seemed to be experiencing alone in Columbus. Victoria had hoped, when she had accompanied him to Columbus earlier, that she might find newspaper correspondence of her own to establish her independence as a writer. But William Cooper Howells had not sought opportunities for his daughter. Victoria was confined once more to a domestic sphere in Jefferson, a "destiny of dishes and cookies," as Howells described it during these years. He had assured her that he intended eventually to rescue his kindred from "bondage" in the Jefferson "Egypt."[25]

Victoria's dissatisfactions culminated in a lamenting letter, provoked by Howells's optimistic estimates of the income he could make selling sketches. He responded by asserting that the time for rescue was not yet at hand, for he could "barely manage to live" on his slender salary. To quiet her longings for society, he professed to find its charms waning and cited her advantages in Jefferson—books, music, and gardening, within the family circle. To forestall his feelings of selfishness, he pleaded limitations that one sex has in understanding the other and turned his guilt toward

Victoria by stating that her letter had intensified a depression he had been suffering all day.[26]

Howells's initial successes had released pent-up desires at home. He had promised that any money he made in the "outside way" of selling sketches would not be "used selfishly." The demands from home had come almost immediately. In addition to contributions toward the family debt, his mother wanted a carpet and other household items. Johnny desired a shotgun. Annie and Aurelia longed for at least a visit to the much-discussed metropolis. Sam assumed that his brother would support him in Columbus while he looked for employment.[27]

But Howells was not making the money he expected from sketches, and even his salary was beginning to be paid fitfully. His income had to support certain needs that sustained his literary aspirations. To appear correctly attired in Columbus society, for instance, required a dress coat, white gloves, and proper boots. When Joseph, the family's exemplar of unselfishness and self-sacrifice, visited Columbus, Howells continued his nightly rounds to literary soirees while his brother routinely retired to bed. Casting a barb at Joseph's grammar, Howells complained that Joseph seemed " 'kinder not to take no interest' " in his activities. "I felt so dissatisfied and disappointed when he went away," he confessed, "that if I had been a girl, I suppose I should have taken 'a good cry.' "[28]

Although he felt emasculated by Joseph's unwavering devotion to family purposes, Howells aggressively defended his literary aspirations. Hearing that Joseph was grumbling about his neglect of family duties, he sent thirty dollars home and promised to send more whenever asked. He listed his expenses, making sure to include those for books and for the clothes he wore making calls. "I can't go about the city streets looking as shabbily as Joe does at home," he retorted.[29] Without the shield of his journalism and the encouragement he received from the women of Columbus society, Howells could not have replied so forcefully to the implication that he was living a selfish life.

To think that he had violated family expectations made Howells uneasy. Besides feeling selfish, he sometimes realized that he had ignored the communal ideals cherished in his family and in his village. Because literature in Columbus was the concern of "good society," admittance to the parlors where it was discussed required a social status above the working class. Howells knew that if he were still a printer in his father's shop, no one in Columbus society would receive him.[30]

Howells's inattention to communal ideals was brought home by an accusation of "forgetting kindness." In 1850 when his family came to Columbus from Eureka Mills, they shared the house of another family. After returning to Columbus, Howells avoided this family, until his father arrived and proposed a visit. The mother of the family greeted Howells with "ironical surprise" and remarked that he had lost sight of humble friends since becoming a journalist. Later Howells tried to blame the woman for her sharp words, but his father would not allow him this escape.[31]

The social distinctions that separated Howells's old and new friends were clear. These distinctions were formalized in expectations of dress, parlor decorum, and customs like the exchange of visiting cards. Howells had been pleased to attend a party that was considered "extremely aristocratic." Only persons of the "first-chopest description" had been invited. One of the literary houses he frequented was furnished with servants in livery. When he and Reed entered the State Street theater, he knew they were stepping across a social boundary. Ethnic boundaries had become more apparent as well. Howells continued to see his old German acquaintances, but he did not meet them as frequently or freely as before. He learned that the German community in Columbus was held apart, except when it came to Republican politics.[32]

Tensions with his family and the democratic ethos of his village plagued Howells from time to time in Columbus, making it necessary for him to assume the demeanor of a "cast-iron" boy to preserve the sense of his "good heart." His political involvement was vulnerable to censure as well, so long as he considered it primarily a masculine mask that hid him from disrepute as a feminized lover of literature. But Howells was not content to accept his society's prejudices against literature. Literature was the realm of his redemption, his greatest use to others. He was determined to demonstrate that the literary vocation was an endeavor as manly as any other.

In his very first reference to the literary vocation in the *State Journal's* columns, Howells assumed the commanding air of his cast-iron-boy persona. A letter had arrived at his desk from "a young man of education and talent," asking for assistance in securing employment that was "literary and remunerative." Little more than a month had passed since Howells had ventured hopeful epistles of his own. Now he dismissed the expectations of another home-leaving youth with a flourish of condescension for his "inexperience of the ways of the world":

> There is no such employment for a young man—unless remunerative can be taken in "hope deferred which maketh the heart sick." Literary employment is rarely remunerative in the world's sense, even to men who are known widely. Works for newspapers or magazines [are] reasonably paid for, but those who are not regular editors must have other employment, or they will find a demand for cheap boarding houses and second-hand clothing stores very imperative. The literary men of America who are not pecuniarily independent of labor—are Editors, Professors, Preachers, Lawyers, Doctors, Teachers, Mechanics, Merchants, or Farmers.[33]

Howells was not disposed to indulge guileless fancies that mirrored the expectations of his immediate past. The purely literary man, he was now sure, was an anomaly in America. The true literary man was necessarily wedded to practical professions, even to the law. But Howells's assertions had excluded the most successful writers of the time. Many literary women had won a huge following that eagerly read their books. In the making of his literary identity, Howells could not ignore the success of "sentimental" women writers like Susan Warner, Maria Cummins, and "Fanny Fern."[34]

The 1850s marked a significant change in the status of writers.

"During this period," a historian of literary publishing has observed, "writing ceased to be a part-time avocation and became a profession capable of supporting authors in middle-class respectability." The spread of efficient railway transportation westward to the Mississippi River allowed for the consolidation of a Northern literary market geared to the tastes of Protestant women. Common schools and the lyceum circuit helped to expand this mass reading audience. Increased circulation of newspapers and magazines sustained the habit of reading and publicized authors and their books. Publishers, after a long period of economic chaos, established control over the manufacture, distribution, and promotion of literature in the Northern market. Their efforts were spurred by phenomenal "best sellers." New techniques of the book trade—including full-page advertisements, celebrity blurbs, and literary "gossip"—raised the standard to fifty thousand sales.[35]

The "sentimental" tastes of the new mass audience were complexly related to the developing national market, mixing resistance and accommodation to the emerging order. In its idealization of home and mother, the sentimental idiom sought to preserve a sense of affectionate bonds amid the erosion of local community life. In effect, the sentimental idiom projected idealized emotional feelings associated with family and community ties onto a public sphere that appeared vast, abstract, and threatening. While the sentimental idiom promised domestication of the public sphere, however, it helped to rationalize a narrow domestic role for women, posing moral "influence"—self-sacrifice and silent suffering—as their only means of expression and redress. Although some women used the ideology of domesticity—particularly its elevation of women's moral influence—to argue for extending their oversight beyond the home, sentimental writing also fostered an enervating, though glorified, passivity. Employing a language of familiarity to assuage the sense of living in an impersonal, alien world, the sentimental idiom could serve divergent ends.[36] But its potential for accommodation compromised its power of resistance. To a greater degree than other cultural expressions touched by immediate economic and social changes, the sentimental idiom evoked unappeasable longings for wholeness that could encourage a sense of helplessness and acquiescence.[37]

As he began to conceive of his audience in Columbus, Howells sensed the hazards of the sentimental idiom. Sentimental postures were the antithesis of the active, ethical engagement necessary for Swedenborgian usefulness, while the association of the sentimental idiom with popular women writers emphasized confinement to "woman's sphere." For literary men, choice of the sentimental idiom threatened a sure sense of gender identity. Many male commentators saw sentimentalism as a grotesque inversion of the demeanor expected of "true men."

Howells revealed little outward concern with female writers he identified as sentimental. Skimming sentimental domestic novels as the *State Journal*'s book reviewer, he was sometimes enticed by their "delightful liveliness and raciness of style and incident." Domestic novels were complex texts in which the sentimental impulse warred with a host of contrary and subversive impulses. Perhaps because he sensed more than he was willing to take on, Howells kept his distance. He maintained defensively that domestic novels showed "transcendent power in nothing."[38] For Howells, sentimental writing appeared more open to challenge in *New York Ledger*, a popular story weekly published by Robert Bonner. The *Ledger* had gained an extraordinary following. Between 1856 and 1860, its circulation climbed from eighty thousand to four hundred thousand, representing the largest readership of a single literary journal. Bonner followed a simple formula for success. He retained the best-known sentimentalists, including Lydia Sigourney and Fanny Fern, mixed their writing with stories of thrilling adventure by Sylvanus Cobb and Emerson Bennett, and publicized his product in noisy advertising campaigns.[39]

While Howells generally confined his comments on the *Ledger*'s female writers to patronizing asides, he was preoccupied with male writers who were their collaborators. Like the Northern men with Southern principles who drew his most unsparing scorn as a radical Republican, male sentimentalists were the enemies closest to home. Travestying Bonner's advertising style—"Edward Everett writes for it!"—Howells denounced the desertion of male writers to the *Ledger* ranks. He found it appropriate that Bonner peddled his writers like Dr. Roback's Scandinavian Remedies, for underneath the extravagant claims he discerned a patent-medicine literature, a cure-all for nothing.[40]

John Godfrey Saxe was Howells's whipping boy among *Ledger* contributors. One of the *Ledger*'s principal male poets, Saxe reportedly had gained readers of "more refined taste." While Howells professed indifference to uncultivated readers who habitually feasted on the *Ledger*'s "gross mud-honey," he found it lamentable that refined readers had shown interest in Saxe during his recent tour. In the grand style of P. T. Barnum, Saxe had promoted himself with a humbug review, describing his poem "Love" as an omnibus production that treated "love material, patriotic, philanthropic, sexual, and divine." But Howells found Saxe's sentiment unmoving and his poetry pure "bosh":

Whose brain was ever cleared by the sharp lightning of his *esprit?* Whose eyes were ever dazzled by the glitter of his satiric blade? He selects those whom people already despise for the display of his prowess, and fires volleys of purposeless puns at them. Long-haired reformers and silly, crack-brained women, are his game. He cannot grapple a great wrong and fight it.[41]

It is not surprising that Howells directed so much scorn at someone he depicted as utterly unimportant. His protest of Saxe's "shallow and spurious merit" acknowledged that the *Ledger* poet was no lightweight with the new mass audience.[42] Saxe highlighted a dilemma Howells began to feel in Columbus as his vision of usefulness expanded from pleasing a local readership to influencing the new mass audience: How was he to assume an active moral posture toward his society—to "grapple a great wrong and fight it" —when his words were addressed to a coterie of refined readers. Despite his dismissal of readers who feasted on "gross mud-honey," Howells was attracted to the new mass audience as a means for demonstrating that his desire to live for literature was not a selfish desire.

The vitriol Howells poured into his attack on Saxe was a measure of the claim exerted on him by the new mass audience. His first reaction was to deny this claim, to purge himself of all association by means of dismissive ridicule. He unleashed his full powers of derision when he turned to a figure more consequential than Saxe, a representative of the new mass audience itself, the male reader of the *Ledger*, whom he styled "Dick Dowdy." Though an inveterate backslapper, cigar smoker, and beer drinker, Dick Dowdy, as his name suggests, is a man who has assumed tastes understood as feminine. His brash manner fails to conceal that he is a "sentimental and tender[-]hearted fellow" addicted to elaborately colored, highly ornamental clothing. Dick Dowdy is a walking rainbow, sporting a farrago of ill-chosen fashions. He wears an "intensely vulgar calico shirt-bosom," a "sanguine collar," a "vest of lively colors," cashmere trousers, "extravagantly stubbed boots," a raglan coat, and saffron gloves. When he removes his gloves, he reveals that his fingers are adorned with rings.[43]

Dick Dowdy's loud attire violates all the rules of quiet, sincere dress Howells had mastered for his entrance into Columbus society. Compared with respectable middle-class attire, Dick Dowdy's clothes are bold-faced lies, as disreputable as his boast that the miniature in his ring is an image of his "woman," when it turns out to be a picture of his sister. But Dick Dowdy lacks the cunning to manipulate appearances for social advantage. He is not the hypocrite who would invade the parlor under false pretenses, the kind of insincere person condemned in books of advice and etiquette. Dick Dowdy is an inauthentic person of another kind. He has duped no one but himself. Howells presented his masquerade as a farce revealing that Dick Dowdy has uncritically absorbed all the false ideals of his culture.

The clownish clothes worn by Dick Dowdy are signs of his credulity. He is drawn as well to gaudy theatrical performances, such as the bombastic acting of Edwin Forrest and the tantalizing dancing of "little Zephyr Frisk." For Howells, however, Dick Dowdy's fondness for the *Ledger* school in literature proved that Dick was profoundly unable to distinguish between the beautiful and the tawdry. Although he privately admires Fanny Fern, Dick reserves public praise for John Godfrey Saxe. Because he believes Saxe is almost "the greatest writer that ever lived," he has accosted the *State Journal*'s literary editor for an "infernal mean" notice of Saxe. In defense, the editor buries himself in his exchanges until Dick Dowdy saunters off to the saloon.

Howells desired to wish his imagined *Ledger* reader entirely away, but Dick Dowdy had a nagging persistence. Abandoning all of his vernacular sympathies, Howells released the full measure of his derision: "Poor, coarse, cheap, shallow, shabby, aimless, foolish young fellow!" he exclaimed. He administered his *coup de grâce* by consigning Dick Dowdy to spiritual oblivion. "In the celestial wisdom of creation," he told his exemplary sentimental reader, "everything is said to have its use; but yours, we confess, we cannot divine." Dick Dowdy seemed to confound the moral order of a Swedenborgian universe, but the loss, Howells asserted, was entirely Dick Dowdy's:

Alas for you! whom nature has made so dull, that you even mistake your existence for a true living. To your soul, has never come any thought of the beautiful, the lofty, the good! You are hopelessly shut out from all gentle joys, all quiet sweetness drawn from books, all communication of God's beautiful creation, all the sun-crowned summits on which others stand, commanding wide prospects of pure and worthy happiness!

This rise to the sun-crowned summits, reflecting assertions sprinkled throughout Heine's *Reisebilder*, was essentially an expression of Howells's wavering security. His commanding air defined a lonely condition. If the Dick Dowdys of the new mass audience remained indifferent to him and enamored of poets like Saxe, he could never perform the greatest good for the greatest number.

When he returned to his essay ten years later, Howells was dismayed by its "innocent wickedness." He must have especially regretted his haughty closing line: "Ah! poor Dick Dowdy!" This patronizing assertion of his youth was the negative image of a statement that expressed his growing commitment to the lives of ordinary people as the source and inspiration of his writing: "Ah! poor Real Life, which I love."[44] Development of the new mass audience had complicated Howells's vocational aspirations. Its existence challenged writers to conceive of their vocation in broadened perspective, heightening their sense of moral potency. Under the dispensation of an expanding literary market, Howells and other writers could believe that their preoccupation with moral meanings might have implication for all of society, that their statements might contain not merely "individual and local" truths, but "general and operative" truths as well. Swelling readership encouraged writers to imagine, more expectantly than before, that they could become "guiding light[s] of the common life."[45]

The problem was Dick Dowdy. From reports of the acclaim enjoyed by writers like John Godfrey Saxe, Howells surmised that Dick Dowdy was a gaudy clown. But his imagined reader had another guise, half-consciously apprehended, that was far more threatening: As a representative of the mass reading audience, he seemed part of a faceless crowd. The relations between writers and readers in the new literary marketplace were distant and impersonal; these relations were mediated and obscured by publishers and distributors of books. The sense of rupture that plagued antebellum Americans in their general relations with the emerging national market was accentuated for writers who depended on the mass audience. Some writers chose to assert their self-sufficiency, positing a realm of absolute value—in the cosmos or in the soul— where self-affirmation did not depend on the sympathetic response of readers. Other writers chose the sentimental idiom as a means to bind writer and reader together in an idealized intimacy that staved off writers' feelings of alienation.

Howells's essay on Dick Dowdy disavowed the sentimental idiom. His Heinesque persona offered the temporary escape of disdainful negation, for in his assertive moods, Heine stated that the godlike poet did not have to truckle to the tastes of "boors."[46] But Howells was drawn more to the sense of community implied by Heine's poems of sorrowful *Sehnsucht*—the notion that concentration on self might greatly benefit others. Howells hoped for a national airing of his Heinesque poems in the *Atlantic Monthly* or in the New York *Saturday Press*. Occasional publication in these journals, while it would not pay his way in the world, might sustain his sense of usefulness. So long as he was cast-iron enough to be both a political journalist and a poet, he would not have to depend entirely on the faceless mass audience.

Yet Howells still aspired to have his being wholly in literature. Despite his effort to purge himself of Dick Dowdy, he began to experiment with ways he might please him or, more importantly, please his female equivalent. Feminized Dick Dowdy had served as a stand-in for the female reader. The mass audience was impersonal, but it was definitely female. "It is the women," admitted the highly successful sketch writer Nathaniel Willis, "who give or withhold a literary reputation." The sense of dependency on female readers even extended to Howells's masculine sphere of journalism, for his publisher, Cooke, had reproved him for a paragraph he considered "too graphic." In his early *State Journal* itemizing, Howells had not shied away from scandalous reports. In the instance of "A Seducer Shot," he pointed out the "unromantic fact" that the seduced woman had "offered to take eight hundred dollars, and put up with her ruin." "Never, *never*," Cooke admonished, "write anything you would be ashamed to read to a woman." In respectable literature this rule was ironclad.[47]

Even if he succeeded with the refined *Atlantic* audience, Howells knew he would have to please female readers and that in wooing them he would chance the fate of sentimental writers, who were generally regarded as womanly men. Representing the sole reader of the *Atlantic*'s fiction and poetry as a "fair young lady" in one of his reviews, Howells slipped into a posture of obeisance, gently coaxing her to consider the current offering of Oliver Wendell Holmes's series "The Autocrat of the Breakfast Table": "You that stand at the parlor window looking out upon the sloppy streets, and thinking of last night's party and of Charles,—take the book, and sit down at the Autocrat's table. When the cloth is off, and the company gone, you will doubtless find other things to entertain you." But it seems that all the *Atlantic* articles are not for her. Howells urged that she show the one of metaphysics to her brother and the political essays to her father. Mother is not included among these readers. Perhaps Howells imagined that she could be found in a comfortable corner reading sentimental stories in the *Ledger*. But the gender differentiation in his review is absolute: Women are the only readers of the literature that he aspired to write.[48]

During his initial months in Columbus, Howells worked long, hard, and secretly over his Heinesque poems while he published lesser efforts—experimental prose sketches—geared to a larger female audience. These sketches reveal Howells's ambivalence. In some he lapsed into sentimental postures little different than those in the *Ledger*, while in others he became a sayer of "disagreeable truths" who skillfully mocked the sentimental expectations of his imagined audience.[49]

Howells felt ambivalent even toward the most blatant forms of sentimentalism. In a *Ledger* parody Howells entitled "An Incident," the narrator is winding his way to his hotel when he encounters a drunk asleep before the magnificent State House. The scene becomes the backdrop for a grandiloquent sentimental oration, touching on the expression of father's hopes and mother's tears that had greeted the birth of this now-sorry lad. These musings abruptly end when the narrator consigns the remainder of the sketch to the *Ledger* stable of writers.[50] Howells offered no surprises in a similar sketch. In "The Lost Child—A Street Scene," he tried to evoke the tearful sentimental response, surrounding his lost child with a sympathetic community of "sturdy mechanics, whose hearts were as soft as their hands were hard" and tender-hearted women with "gentle pitying eyes."[51]

In his most original sketches, however, Howells broke entirely free from *Ledger* posturings and asserted his "masculine" independence. His most devious undermining of sentimental expectation occurs in "Not a Love Story," a sketch that opens with a yawn to announce the boring nature of all "melting tales of love." Howells presented his anti–love story in three scenes, each ending with a deflationary point. In the first scene, an expectant Fanny is on a porch with an impassive Arthur. Fanny is growing impatient, for Arthur is having trouble summoning a sentimental mood that would allow the stock occurrences of a love story to proceed. His inability to be the hero in a love story is perplexing because he has eaten his breakfast, and, as everyone knows, "one is always more sentimental immediately after meals than at any other time."[52]

When Arthur yawns, he infuriates Fanny. She is about to slap him for his insolence when he grabs and kisses her. Confused by this precipitous denouement, Fanny flees to her room in tears. She diligently prepares herself for a grandly sentimental reconciliation, but when she returns she finds that Arthur is simply gone. The second scene, an interlude, continues the bafflement of sentimental expectation. Fanny's family has invited Arthur to dinner. While everyone eats heartily of peas and potatoes, table talk focuses on a young man who died of consumption because he was disappointed in love. In the final scene, absurdity again dominates sentiment. Arthur has finally overcome his lethargy, worked himself into a sentimental mood, and is about to confess his love to Fanny. But as Arthur begins to speak, his ardent expressions are drowned by the shrieking accompaniment of a train whistle. In an afterword, Howells pictured Fanny grown old and fat. She has married a dull grocer and slaps her children. No doubt they, like Arthur, have violated her sentimental expectations. The fate of Arthur is more serene. He has abandoned sentimental lovemaking and now collects geological specimens.

Humorous sketches like "Not a Love Story" probably won Howells his following among the literary women of Columbus society. Many were sophisticated readers who appreciated his witty, ironical style. These women were not a faceless crowd. Their immediate presence and flattering remarks provided a verifying context for his identity as a writer, allowing him to feel a sense of consequence and authenticity. Howells's anti–love stories had opened a vein of writing that continued to win him a following throughout his novelistic career. A basic tactic of his realism was the subversion of extravagant, self-focused desires and expectations, beginning with those expressed in the conventions of sentimental love and deepening as he extended his view to all human relations.[53]

But the gratification he obtained from a small coterie of sophisticated women readers in Columbus did not fully satisfy Howells, for it verified his usefulness narrowly. Howells was drawn to the mass audience of female readers, who represented a greater but more abstract realm of usefulness. Addressing this audience of faceless readers, he lost his ironical detachment and fell back upon a tradition of successful sentimental appeal—sketch writing after the manner of Washington Irving by inheritors like Ik Marvel, George Curtis, and Nathaniel Willis. Howells had experimented with Ik Marvel's manner in Jefferson, presenting his column "You and I" as a "quiet corner" apart from the tumultuous world. He had also followed the sketches that Curtis had written before his turn to politics. Sketches by male sentimentalists typically presented the meditations of a self-deprecatory observer, a dreamy "idler," including accounts of his sensitive sufferings and descriptions of scenes colored by his genial but melancholic temperament. The sentimental, idealized intimacy between writer and reader that these sketches presumed was often reinforced by settings emphasizing a home-like atmosphere: The narrator muses near the hearth, on the porch, or in the village store.[54]

While this style of sentimentalism appealed to the mass audience of journals like the *Ledger*, it opened male writers to ridicule. A reviewer of the time complained that male writers of sentimental sketches had been unmanned by the commercial success of their female competitors: "The magnetism produced by her outgiven heart-throbs has warmed into vitality a vast number of womanly men, who, without manly force or manly vigor of intellect, have given way to unmanly mawkishness and morbid complainings . . . prettiness and sentimentalisms."[55] Sentimental sketch writing was a hazardous psychological undertaking for literary men, especially for young men like Howells who were trying to affirm absolutely that they were "true" men.

The idler figure enters a number of sketches Howells wrote in Columbus and emerged fully in a sketch he called "A Summer Sunday in a Country Village: As Experienced by an Ennuyé." The premise of the sketch—that it is difficult even to be idle on the enervating day of Sunday—suggests a humorous *reductio ad absurdum.* But little in Howells's sketch confirms that he had this debunking intention. The narrator gives a detailed account of his claustrophobic surroundings, describes the languishing aspect of nature, and imagines scenes in the dull lives of his fellow villagers. He trivializes literature by identifying reading as an idle habit, while he defensively maintains that his books have given him many thrilling adventures. In other sketches of this kind, Howells employed similar tactics and attitudes of the idle man: He strove for overt literary allusion and verbal glitter, he concentrated on touching effects, he made familiar, self-deprecating asides, and he apologized whenever his moralizing became too "earnest."[56]

The accommodating poses of the idler figure diminished the serious, moral intentions Howells identified with literature. Sentimental sketch writing brought back the sense of passivity and ineffectualness he had felt in Jefferson. The scene in "A Summer Sunday in a Country Village" is a thinly disguised Jefferson, the aspect of the village that was the habitat of his defeated aspirations. In a series of sketches he wrote while visiting home, Howells claimed dislike for cultivated indolence, pointing out that "contentment is not an art, and will not be achieved by idle people." But in his next sketch he was discoursing on "nothing," just as any sentimental sufferer from ennui was apt to do.[57] In a letter to Victoria, he brought together the feelings of stifling entrapment he expressed in his sentimental sketches:

When I was home, it seemed to me that all of the time I had been absent was merely a dream, and all that had happened to me here [in Columbus] was as unsubstantial and unreal as the essence of a dream. The people I had known, the things I had done, the events that had occurred, seemed to me, while I spoke to you of them, even fictional, and that impression was sometimes so strong and vivid that it annoyed me excessively. When evening came on, and the utter desolation of that dreary little village closed around me, I would think of myself still the hapless wretch I used to be there—so useless to others, and disagreeable to myself.[58]

The persona of the idler expressed Howells's despairing feelings. While this mode of writing broadened his perspective to the mass audience, it accentuated the image of literature as a womanly and therefore trivial concern. The idler represented another reaction of psychological reversal, momentarily restoring a feeling of autonomy and control. As an effort to merge with readers on some idealized "home" ground, however, it could deepen the writer's immersion in a sense of dependency and passivity. Beneath the quiet musings of the idler lay a dire sense of impotence. The attitudes of the idler expressed a longing for wholeness, but they could ultimately paralyze the writer's capacity for moral engagement.

The idler was one of several masks Howells donned in Columbus to establish his sense of literary vocation. Paired with his stance as an ironist of sentimental love, it reflected his ambivalence toward the sentimental postures the mass audience seemed to demand. Howells debunked sentimentalism in some forms while he embraced it in others. The ironist in Howells was sustained by an immediate, knowable circle of readers, but the sentimentalist appeared when he lifted his eyes to the remote, impersonal mass audience. As long as he sought influence with the mass audience but despaired of this possibility, the sentimental idler remained his nagging double, appearing in his later work in several guises— particularly as the mere "aesthetic observer," the man whose perception of reality is distorted by literary visions. The return of the idler figure suggests that Howells had not escaped his feeling that literature confined him to a passive, ineffectual, womanly role.

During Howells's youth, when his experiments with literary personae had formative effects on his sense of vocation, the idler figure was the persistent double of Howells's Heinesque persona. In some ways, the sentimental idler and the Heinesque poet were kin. The sorrowful, vain yearning of Heine's poems could be taken as enervating sentimentality. Insofar as the poet accepted a vision of the world as desultory and sought no other alternative, he languished in passivity. Many of Heine's poems conveyed this attitude, particularly the early poems of *Buch der Lieder*. But Heine both languished in sentimentalism and condemned it out-of-hand as "gall and wormwood." In *Buch der Lieder* as a whole, the poet-persona transcends his sorrows and gains a positive sense of the poet's power and strength.[59] By following Heine's example, Howells could believe he might eventually escape the idler figure. He could continue to concentrate on his subjective moods, he could seek to be "dreamy" just as Heine often was, and still he could believe that he would eventually speak with the highest moral authority.

At the same time that he indicted Dick Dowdy for his farcical masquerade, Howells was sensitive to his own varied performances. During his time in Columbus, he was the family hope, the devoted son and brother who would alleviate the sufferings of his family. Sometimes he was also the psychologically fragile home boy, unable to cope with difficulties that seemed illusory. He was publicly the heir of his father's and his village's political radicalism, the manly and acerbic journalist who gave no quarter to the defenders of slavery. More privately he was the enthusiast of literature, whose interests tied him to feminine concerns. He was the sincere, engaging confidant of Columbus's literary women, but he sometimes seemed to be no more than a feminized poseur, a self-suffering, trivial idler, especially when he looked to the new mass literary audience. Opposing the idler figure was his ideal self, the passionate Heinesque poet, a manly being of cast-iron resolve who embraced sorrowful contradictions. The character Howells would try to keep would be hedged by all of these divergent selves. But through his experimentation he needed to forge a character he could afford to keep. He needed to become, above all else, someone whose commitment to usefulness was entirely free of selfishness.

CHAPTER 7

The Laying On of Hands

I arrived in Boston . . . when all talents had more or less a literary coloring, and when the greatest talents were literary. These expressed with ripened fulness a civilization conceived in faith and brought forth in good works; but that moment of maturity was the beginning of a decadence which could only show itself much later. New England has ceased to be a nation in itself.

HOWELLS, 1893

One of Howells's acquaintances in Columbus, William T. Coggeshall, was an ardent admirer of local scenes and a perennial defender of local literature. He advocated a "protective policy in literature," an embargo designed to end "servile dependence upon the Atlantic States." He argued that the best literature had always been "local," written and published near the source of its inspiration, read and admired by local citizens. While he devised ambitious schemes for restoring Western literature to the prominence that he believed it enjoyed before the advent of national competition—when cities like Cincinnati were thriving cultural centers—Coggeshall complained that Western readers had become indifferent to homegrown talent and enamored of Eastern journals.[1]

Coggeshall was not alone in his longings. Increased geographical

mobility and rampant speculation in overnight towns sped a dizzying demise of social and cultural bearings anchored in distinct
localities. As place lost causal connection with everyday economic
affairs, antebellum Americans like Coggeshall adhered more firmly
to the moral meanings represented by localities. Some idealized a
pastoral countryside of villages and homesteads; others merged
country and city values in a new vision of pastoral suburbanism;
still others found solace in an urban scene of stately neighbor-
hoods, restful parks, and expansive boulevards. Antebellum Americans also became more sensitive to the moral meanings that survived in the communal patterns of villages, towns, and cities.
When Joshua Giddings yearned for the "sweet[-]natured silence"
of a Jefferson Sabbath, he expressed an arcadian conception of
village life, yet his description was strongly reinforced by experience he had previously taken for granted.[2]

In 1857 when Howells came to Columbus to do legislative
reporting, Coggeshall, as state librarian, had become Howells's
literary companion. But Howells had grown wary of his friend's
enthusiasm for local literature. He privately described Coggeshall
as "a prodigious man, with a fine faculty for feeding the public on
sawdust."[3] Howells had no wish to become another proof in Coggeshall's lament that Western writers had become strangers in their
own land. During his later years in Columbus, Howells began to
draw away from the local literary scene. He began to wonder how
he would fare in the literary society of New York or Boston, cities
that seemed to offer a greater strength of place.

Publication in the *State Journal* or in other local outlets no longer
satisfied Howells. He anticipated that local publication of his best
efforts—his Heinesque poems—would fail to win a sympathetic
response from the "predatory press." He disliked allowing his
writing to become fodder in the exchanges, "tossed upon a newspaper sea, a helmless boat, with no clearance papers aboard." The
State Journal was not his "finality" he told Victoria. Boston and
New York had become the "courts" where "canons of criticism"

set literary tastes for the nation. To further his career, Howells looked to the most "honored Eastern periodicals," Boston's *Atlantic Monthly* and New York's *Saturday Press*.[4]

Although Howells later observed that it was "nearly as well for one to be accepted by the *Press* as to be accepted by the *Atlantic*," his qualification "nearly" counted enormously during his youth. The *Atlantic* possessed the imprimatur of better Boston, a sphere of established literary refinement with an unrivaled constellation of recognized poet-scholars, including Lowell, Longfellow, Holmes, Emerson, and Whittier. Modeled on the English reviews, the *Atlantic* represented an assertion of secular intellectual authority. This authority was posed against waning Calvinist orthodoxy and popular forms of evangelicalism. The *Atlantic*, as Holmes's breakfast-table monologues in the magazine made clear, favored the cultural leadership of an enlightened elite. The *Press*, on the other hand, mirrored New York's parvenu competitiveness. Its editors were fond of iconoclastic poses and disdainful manifestoes set against Boston's presumption of literary leadership. The *Press*, Howells noted from his remove in Columbus, displayed a "perfectly independent-and-don't-care" attitude; its *raison d'être* was to defy "usage."[5]

The *Press* claimed Howells's allegiance by its appeal to the naturally rebellious young. Its defiant tone satisfied a youthful need to protest traditional conformities and assert prerogatives of the present, however vaguely these might be defined. "We cannot describe [the *Press*] better," Howells wrote in admiration, "than by saying it is *spicy*. . . . There is a dash of French sprightliness in it, that its heavier contemporaries lack." The *Press* was hospitable to literary fashions in vogue among the young. Poets like Longfellow preached moderation and restraint; the *Press* encouraged experiment and excess. Its pages were filled with romantic prose and poetry resembling Heine's most "passionate" writing. Its poems evinced moods of brooding subjectivity consistent with the Heinesque manner that Howells was cultivating as his truest self-expression. When he sent his poems to the *Press*, therefore, Howells was competing with his generational peers and demonstrating sympathy with their self-conscious moods.[6]

The editor of the *Press*, Henry Clapp, had augmented its rebellious image by associating it with the Bohemian life-style he remembered from Paris. Like Parisian Bohemianism, however, this rebellion did not go very deep. Bohemian celebration of personal expression was continuous with the ethos of autonomous individualism, and the Bohemians who gathered at Pfaff's saloon were just as concerned with "sincerity" as were the arbiters of "good society." "The Bohemian," claimed Ada Clare, the acknowledged "queen" of New York Bohemia, "is not, like the creature of society, a victim of rules and customs; he steps over them all with an easy, graceful joyous unconsciousness, guided by the principles of good taste and feeling." Still, as the presence of Ada Clare attested, New York Bohemia had some legitimate claims to unconventionality and, by its association with Paris, an attractive hint of wickedness.[7]

The *Press* most nearly mirrored a Bohemian life-style by existing on the brink of financial ruin. The editors were said to hide whenever contributors sought their pay. Bohemianism made necessity a virtue, giving an aura of romance to poverty in the name of art. Howells had never been enamored of threadbare clothes and cheap boardinghouses. The atmosphere of the *Press* suggested that serious literary life in New York—hedged in by sensational journalism and popular story weeklies like the *Ledger*—involved the sort of precariousness Howells had vowed to avoid. The success he envisioned did not accord with a life of stringent necessity. Columbus society, where he was encouraged and sometimes feted by the well-to-do, better represented his aspirations.[8]

"Good society" in Columbus had more affinity with Boston Brahmins than with New York Bohemians. By the time Howells arrived in Boston on his literary pilgrimage, he had assented to the idealized image of the city favored by its intellectual elite. He imagined that Boston was the one place in America where serious literature was held in high esteem and given unstinting support. This image had a certain foundation in reality, for literary refinement in Boston was closely allied with solid middle-class respectability. Boston's merchant elite had molded an institutional matrix

that included Harvard College, the Boston Athenaeum, and the
Lowell Institute. The *Atlantic Monthly* was aligned with a strategy
emphasizing cultural rather than political control. In practical terms,
literary men in Boston enjoyed the advantage of business patronage. Publishers like Ticknor and Fields encouraged serious poetry
and other literary forms that sold poorly with the mass reading
audience. Other businessmen joined in projects of cultural betterment. The Saturday Club, founded for the entertainment and
edification of men of letters, admitted John Murray Forbes and
other entrepreneurs, along with Longfellow, Lowell, Holmes, and
Emerson. The finer intricacies of the Boston establishment—such
as its extensive cousinship—were beyond Howells's knowledge,
but what he knew confirmed his belief that literary men in Boston,
though many worked as editors and educators, were granted a
dignity that was denied elsewhere. To be accepted by the *Atlantic*,
therefore, was to be given an approval that eclipsed all others.[9]

Early in 1859, probably by late February, Howells completed a
Heinesque poem that he considered worthy of *Atlantic* publication,
an ambitious effort of six parts and twenty-nine quatrains. The
poem's title, "Andenken" (Memories), reflected its Germanic derivation and its inspiration as a summa of sensibility. Howells evoked
romantic *Sehnsucht* through a reverie concentrating on images of
death, disillusion, and disappointed love. He identified the poet-
persona's brooding, longing soul with "languid" and "gloomy"
nature. But he also employed less obvious devices such as the
Stimmungsbrechung or abrupt break of voice often represented in
Heine's poetry. Like Heine, he also presented stark contrasts of
death-in-life and life-in-death, such as a dead chestnut tree "blos-
somed" into life by an engulfing fire. The whole poem displayed
Howells's fidelity to Heine in image, mood, diction, meter, and
rhyme.[10]

Howells did his work too well. Lowell, who was chief editor of
the *Atlantic*, later told Howells that he hesitated over the poem
because it appeared to be a translation. Intending to check "Andenken" against Heine's works, Lowell put the poem aside. In June,
the *Press* published a single Heinesque lyric by Howells, but appar-

16. Howells in Columbus, ca. 1861. A few years later Howells described
his Heinesque sensibility. It came from awareness of the "contradictions"
of modern life, "the sad base of doubt, the ineffable yearning that stretches
one arm up imploring to the future, and one of passionate regret to the
past, and all this interfused with mocking derision, with sardonic gayety."

ently this acceptance by his generational peers at the *Press* did not
merit great rejoicing. In contrast, when the *Atlantic* finally broke
its dispiriting silence in late July and accepted "Andenken" for
publication, Howells traveled the two hundred miles to Jefferson,
burst in upon his family, and exclaimed the "wonderful news [that]
was too precious to trust to the mail." Howells considered Lowell's
letter of acceptance "the potentiality of immeasurable success." He
placed the letter in the pocket next to his heart where he could feel
for it to make sure of its reality.[11]

Lowell's letter had the effect of a talisman. It momentarily
delivered Howells from a deepening depression. Beginning in April,
he had felt touches of his "hypo," at times suffering a "regular
turn" of his "familiar devil." Without verification of his literary
ambitions from the paramount authority of Boston, Howells had
to make do with the praise of literary women in Columbus and the
prospect of becoming a New York free lance. The anxiety of
waiting for the *Atlantic*'s response also reawakened his "dormant
homesickness." "It seems to me," he wrote Victoria, "I'm drifting
away from you all the time, and I want to hear often from home."
The phrase "drifting away," with its evocation of the nautical
metaphor, provided the germ of a poem that Howells wrote in
early July for the *Press*. The poet-persona describes life as a tumultuous ocean to be braved by a "frail shallop without sail or oar."
As the shallop is lost in "dark gulfs" and "unknown deeps," his
"old beliefs" fade like faint lights along the shore. He reaches out
to embrace what remains to his vision but finds nothing to grasp.[12]

Even after the *Atlantic*'s acceptance finally came, Howells could
not overcome his hypochondria. Haunted by his fear of dying, he
sought relief from a fatherly doctor, Samuel M. Smith, the patri-
arch of a literary house he frequented. It was probably at this time
that Dr. Smith told him he would not sicken and die merely in
twenty-four hours. Words of kindly irony were supportive because
Howells needed alleviation beyond what he was accomplishing in
his poems.[13]

In early August, Howells began to bear another burden when
trouble in the counting room at the *State Journal* forced Cooke to

suspend his salary. Howells could no longer pay his room and board, much less send money home to his family. He wrote his father that he was convinced the newspaper would fail, but to stave off any suggestion that he return to Jefferson, he added assuredly, "I shall take care of myself."[14]

The financial crisis at the *State Journal* may have been the blow that crumbled Howells's cast-iron facade. By the end of August he was "thoroughly knocked down," as he reported to his mother, by a serious illness he described as diphtheria. Diphtheria—a devastating disease of childhood—was congenial to his death-focused thoughts, but it is unlikely that he could have recovered from diphtheria, as he claimed, in merely a week. Like his other illnesses, this break was partly a plea for release from his anxieties. Writing his mother, he admitted to an "intolerable gnawing and longing for home."[15]

Howells aided himself by concentrating on his literary work. Beginning a more active correspondence with his friend and fellow poet John J. Piatt in early September, he listed his recent reading —Tennyson's *Idylls of the King*, a book on Montaigne, Arthur Meissner's memoir of Heine, De Quincey's *Klosterheim*, all of Thackeray's lesser works, and George Eliot's *Adam Bede*. He reported that he had "scribbled much" and added nonchalantly that the *Atlantic* had accepted his poem, "to appear when there is room."[16]

By the end of the month, Howells's claim to poetic equality with Piatt had become tenuous. Howells began to read rumors in the exchanges that Phillips, Sampson and Company, publishers of the *Atlantic*, had suspended payments to creditors. To counteract this distressing news, he proposed a joint book with Piatt, offering to take a subordinate role. When the "confounded Atlantic people" failed to publish his poem in the October number, he more boldly suggested that they play equal parts. After Piatt consented, Howells concentrated on this new project. Writing home, he cast himself in a dramatic, grandiose light: "I am working very hard— reading, studying, and scribbling constantly—aside from the drudgery I perform on the Journal," he told Victoria. "So that I grudge myself even the time it will take to go home. O, it's such a long way up! But I have my eye on the temple that 'shines afar,' and I will fall uphill, if I must succumb." [17]

Howells's resolve was put to the test. On a "dreary Saturday" in mid-October, he read news that convinced him that the *Atlantic* would go to its doom without publishing his poem. "It is probable," he reported in his column, "that the second attempt to establish a good magazine in this country, has proven more disastrous than the first." He quoted a report that predicted the *Atlantic* would go the way of *Putnam's*. After being sold on the open market, it would "degenerate into a mere receptacle of pictorialism and twa[dd]le." With his vision of himself as a Boston man of letters fading, Howells turned to a poem by Piatt, so beautiful, he stated, that it transforms "cobwebs" in the October heart to "shining gossamers." Placed at the head of his column, the poem was a reminder of the "poetical firm" he had established with his friend —a firm that he hoped would never go bankrupt. [18]

Rumors soon began to circulate that the Boston publishers Ticknor and Fields would rescue the *Atlantic*. On 21 October, Howells reported that the transaction had occurred. "The magazine is now in the best of hands," he stated, "and its admirers may look confidently to its continuance and success." Until "Andenken" appeared, Howells could not share in this success. The November *Atlantic* arrived without his poem; the magazine contained two that he considered "tolerably good" and one he considered quite bad. "I am heartsick with waiting and disappointment," he wrote his father. "The 'Atlantic' has not published my poem yet. I don't know what to think. I'm afraid it won[']t at all." In his present situation, Howells did not see how he could help out "mon[e]ywise" at home. He expected no return from his book of poems, and Cooke probably would never pay him the ten-weeks' salary he was due. [19]

Howells had reason to doubt the augury of the crumpled letter he carried next to his heart. Instead of acceptance in Boston, it seemed he was destined for torturous rejection. Although he would soon make his literary debut in a book of poems, his venture with Piatt identified him as a "local" poet in the nomenclature of Coggeshall, whose manifestoes were issued by the same Columbus publisher, Follett and Foster.

While immersed in difficulties that threatened his sense of literary vocation, Howells was growing more assertive in the one sphere of his life where issues were defined absolutely. He began to emphasize his role as a radical antislavery agitator, describing himself as purer in his radicalism than those who would compromise moral absolutes for political gain. "The returns from the State came in gloriously," he wrote Victoria when Republicans swept the state elections; "but you know I'm too radical to rejoice much in half-worn Republican triumphs." Howells's urge toward self-justification found greater opportunity when news arrived of John Brown's raid on the Federal Arsenal at Harper's Ferry, Virginia, in the late night hours of 16 October 1859. At first Howells followed Reed, treating the event as "laughable" and "absurd." Aspects of the affair, Reed observed, were "droll enough to make a dog laugh." Howells chimed in with the suggestion that the raid was simply "poor crazy" Brown's attempt to gather unwilling listeners for an incendiary "harangue."[20]

Within a few weeks, Howells's attitude toward Brown had shifted from ridicule to adoration. Expressing his new feeling in a letter to his father, he exclaimed, "If I were not your son, I would desire to be Old John Brown's—God bless him!" In the interval between his parody and praise, Howells had watched Brown undergo a "sea change into something rich and strange." Brown had found an oracular voice that excited admiration even from his Virginia captors. But the transformation of Brown's image had been aided immeasurably by a chorus of adulation from Northern men of letters. It was extremely important for Howells that during the crisis literary men stepped forward to assume prophetic roles. Emerson and Thoreau spoke from Boston. They portrayed Brown as a man who had carried his ideals into action. The problem of the scholar's relation to society vanished in their enthusiastic en-

dorsements. If Brown were a "transcendentalist," as Thoreau insisted, there was no need to defend the literary life with creeds of
solitude.[21]

Such praise swept up Howells completely. His fascination for
Brown crystallized into a sense of personal involvement when he
read Wendell Phillips's speech "The Lesson of the Hour." Phillips
was extremely gratified that Brown had acted on principles Phillips
had been preaching for thirty years. Brown seemed to prove that
antislavery ideals had gained widespread acceptance among Americans, affecting men who were willing to use the bowie knife and
pistol. Still, Phillips argued, the age was one of ideas, and men of
ideas were rightfully in command. He proposed that John Brown
had become an idea, one that had already brought slavery under
greater popular censure. "Do you suppose that these things mean
nothing?" Phillips asked. "What the tender and poetic youth, as
Emerson says, dreams today, and conjures up with inarticulate
speech, is tomorrow the vociferated result of public opinion, and
the day after is the charter of nations."[22]

The lesson of the hour that Howells grasped most eagerly was
Phillips's unapologetic affirmation of men of ideas, not forgetting
the "tender and poetic youth." Phillips's vigorous endorsement and
the continuing illustration of the role of ideas in John Brown's
miraculous transformation supported Howells's need for self-affirmation. He saw himself in Phillips's grandiose image—as the
champion of absolute right, the man whose ideas were actions.
From this vantage point, he towered over those who were concerned merely with political issues, even over such a commanding
figure as Joshua Giddings. When Giddings remarked that Harper's
Ferry would occupy only a "brief page" in historical annals, Thoreau replied, "If this is true, how long will be the paragraph that
records the history of the Republican party?" Reporting this "hit"
by a "Boston man" to his father, Howells asserted, "Brown has
become an idea—a thousand times purer and better and loftier
than the Republican idea, which I'm afraid is not an idea at all."[23]

Howells's statement was more than casually self-justifying. As
Phillips and others embraced the idea of John Brown, Republican

publicists like Reed and William Cooper Howells held aloof, fearing that the clamor would identify Republicans with violence. They worked out a compromise, admitting that Brown was insane but insisting that slavery had made him a "monomaniac." While William Cooper Howells maintained the party line, his son pressed his advantage, writing home that he was disappointed that nothing "violent" on Harper's Ferry had appeared in the *Sentinel*. Later when his father described Brown as a Swedenborgian hero—someone whose deeds were "unalloyed by a single motive of selfish ambition"—while still reciting the party line, Howells chided his father in print. He stated that it was surprising that a newspaper from the abolitionist "hot-bed" of Ashtabula County should not have "a more decided smack of righteousness."[24]

In his own writing, Howells supplied the righteousness he found wanting in his father's editorials. In a fervent poem, he portrayed Brown as an animating idea and predicted that a vine of liberty would ripen around his gallows tree. In his most radical column, he compared slaves to genies imprisoned in a vase: Slaves were similarly confined to the woodpile that supported the American nation. Those who try to ignore their anguished cries do so in vain, for "in their dreams they are haunted by frightful visions of the Woodpile in a blaze, and the maddened geni[es] making havoc by the light of the bloody flame." John Brown had illustrated that retribution was imminent. "There are six million in the Woodpile," Howells concluded, " 'and God is just.' " By his righteous pronouncements, Howells claimed a Swedenborgian usefulness surpassing his father's. He intimated his rebellion when he declared that if he were not his father's son, he would be the son of John Brown. But his rebellion actually revealed his yearning for the moral world of his father, the world of absolute right and wrong.[25]

For the moment, Howells's enthusiasm for John Brown chased away his doubts concerning the manliness of the literary vocation. In his columns and letters, Howells cited numerous literary men who had responded to the present crisis or who had been moral leaders in the past. An important example was the German poet and dramatist Robert Blum. Blum's support of the 1848 revolutions and his martyr's death demonstrated that "tender sweetness" and "manly heroism" were complementary rather than antagonistic qualities. But the lesson of the hour taught that the poet did not have to take up arms like Robert Blum. Strictly as a poet, he was no lesser kind of man. Ideas, his powerful weapons, were instruments of truth and liberty, now and for all time.[26]

In the midst of the Brown fervor, the December *Atlantic* arrived without "Andenken," but a few weeks later Howells's fortunes turned. The *Atlantic* announced his poem for the January issue, nearly coinciding with the publication of *Poems of Two Friends* (1860), his modestly titled venture with Piatt.[27] For the first time in a long while, Howells had the opportunity to draw from a reserve of cumulative success.

Uppermost in Howells's mind after the publication of *Poems of Two Friends* was how the public would respond to his poems. In the book's preface, he wondered whether it would have been better to "leave these poor Children of the Heart to generous Oblivion." Follett and Foster tried valiantly to make the book a popular success, printing it on "blush" paper and binding it in gilt covers. But Howells declared to a friend in Cincinnati that it was "disgustingly probable that every copy sent to your city, will rot upon the booksellers' shelves." At the very least, he wanted a critical success. While waiting anxiously for reviews from the East, he suppressed a burlesque notice by Reed. He failed to collar the local reporter Harris, who declared in his column that his proximity to a shining poet had made him "luminous." To ensure that the book received a proper assessment in the *State Journal*, Howells wrote one himself, concentrating entirely on Piatt's contributions. Wanting to avoid "even the shadow of advertising," he said of his own poems only that he hoped "some will be found not so bad as others."[28]

Howells's apologetic approach to his potential readers verged on the defensive manner of the sentimental idler. But the first Eastern review from the *Saturday Press* granted him a more positive identity. Since he had appeared eight times in its pages, the *Press* claimed him as one of its own "don't-care" poets and a true "genius" besides. Possibly because he had not yet been seen among the coterie at Pfaff's saloon, it added that his genius was not of the "highest order." Nevertheless, the *Press* recognized the Heinesque persona that was Howells's most cherished ideal, seriously describing his poetry in the terms parodied by Harris. Howells's passionate poems, the *Press* observed, "illumine the dark places of the human heart."[29]

While his peers at the *Press* accepted him on his own terms, another Eastern reviewer, Gail Hamilton, the gifted, acerbic essayist, discerned his vulnerabilities and exploited them mercilessly. Writing in the *National Era*, she suggested that the book was slightly feminized, tripping "with daintiest tread to softest melodies," and that its theme of sorrowful longing was a pose. She speculated that the two friends probably did not pace "desolate chambers, bewailing buried hopes, sorrowing over broken hearts, and defying a cold, unfeeling world." Instead, they were undoubtedly "a pair of stout-limbed, ruddy-cheeked, corn-fed country boys." Stung by her lampoon, Howells sent off a hot reply. Later he regretted showing his wounds, but he continued to burn from Hamilton's "patronizing manner."[30]

The key review was Lowell's in the *Atlantic*. Having complained in previous notices that "genius" seemed to spring up "like mullein, wherever the soil is thin enough," Lowell emphasized Howells's capacity for "higher achievement." "The poems," he suggested, "give more than glimpses of a faculty not so common that the world can afford to do without it." Less assurance that his poems promised a "richer maturity" would have satisfied Howells immensely. Lowell's judgment—the voice of Boston authority—was reinforced on the *Atlantic*'s other pages where two new Heinesque poems by Howells appeared. A less ambitious effort had been printed in the February 1860 number, so that Howells could now claim to be the most substantial *Atlantic* contributor in the West.[31]

Feeling supported in his sense of literary vocation, Howells gained some relief from his self-recriminations and fears of death. He momentarily embraced a positive notion of death, describing it

as kindly and fatherly. Hawthorne's *Marble Faun* inspired Howells
to write a litany that disassociated death from punishment:

Not that ghastly thing which triumphs over our joy, and shows itself
grinning and hideous at our feasts—but Death, the old attendant of our
race, inevitable, and universal, standing in wait for us at the end of the
journey, and embracing the beggar and the prince with wide arms that
know no difference. Death the moss-bearded,—death the vague but not
the terribly mysterious,—death the rest but not the punishment,—death
the inexorable but not unkind—venerable, serene.[32]

Imagining the achievement of "poetic pre-eminence" that would
grandly demonstrate his usefulness, Howells began to feel cramped
in the incommensurate world of Columbus literary society. "As
Columbus grows old to me," he wrote home in mid-April, "it
seems to contract, and I begin to feel here the gnawing discontent
that I felt in Jefferson." If he could not immediately obtain a place
in Boston, he might find a stepping-stone in New York, where the
Press had already assented to his "genius." "Father need not be
afraid that I should be seduced by Bohemianism in New York," he
continued. "I confess that a life which defies usage has its charm
for me; but I chiefly long now for change from a comparatively
narrow to a wider field of action."[33]

The prospect of going East was nevertheless daunting, for it
would take Howells further away from his family and the securi-
ties he had established in Columbus. His anticipation may have
brought on the slight recurrence of "hypo" that he suffered toward
the end of April. "As the summer approaches, I begin to feel
touches of hypochondria," he wrote home, "but I hope not to go
crazy."[34] Preparing his defense, he appealed to his brother Joseph
for affirmation:

It seems to me that I am growing away from whatever was gentle and
good in the influences of my life. Sometimes I shudder to think how
nearly beyond them I am; and I believe if I can be with you all a few
weeks, I shall renew and better myself. I *do* nothing bad, I hope, but my
habit of thought is harsh and skeptical, and I am the victim of an *ennui*
which I cannot escape. While I work, I am comparatively content, but
the moment I throw off the harness, I am languid, weary of myself and

everything else. How it is all to result, I do not know. I have ceased to look forward with much comfort. . . . I know well enough that if I live, I shall succeed in the ambition of my life, but that I shall be a happy man I do not believe. Religion seems such a fabulous far-off thing; and if I should taste all the pleasures of the world, I should be tired of them all, and then—what? To die at bay entering the future backwards.—I suppose this bores a married man like you, with his child at his knee, and his dear wife to love and live for; and it is not the custom for one to make one's brother the confid[a]nt of dyspeptic wretchedness. Yet I let what I have written, remain—for it speaks my mind more than half my time.[35]

Howells had more reason to feel wretched after a change in the management of the *State Journal* left him out. Being "unhorsed" in this manner was humiliating and left the doubt whether he would ever see the twenty-weeks' salary he was by now owed by Cooke. But Howells soon found another position editing manuscripts for Follett and Foster. He continued to supply the *State Journal* with columns of "Literary Gossip" while his new employer, Frank Foster, was involving him in schemes to exploit his talents.[36] One project was a subscription book on manufacturing in New York and New England. While this project went against his literary instincts, Howells was anxious to head East. Foster had ambitious plans, but he would not finance the trip himself. Then, on 18 May 1860, Abraham Lincoln received the Republican nomination for president, and Foster jumped into the competition for a campaign biography. He assigned the task to Howells, providing him with the chance to earn the money necessary for his Eastern trip. Howells set to work, forming a biography out of hastily gathered materials, including notes from an interviewer whom Foster had dispatched to Springfield. Howells wrote the book and saw it through publication in eighteen days.[37]

The writing came easily because Howells found his subject appealing. Lincoln appeared to be a man of "restless ambition" who had overcome prejudices and adversities in pursuing his studies. Discounting the popular myths that railsplitting and flatboating had been essential preparation for the candidate, Howells contended that they were important only because Lincoln had risen above them. This tack evoked the success ethos, but it was more elitist than the approach taken by most Republican publicists, who were anxious to identify their candidate with the common voter. Seeing a Lincoln who mirrored his own struggles, Howells gave his development a scholarly turn. He intimated that the most significant ingredient in Lincoln's success had been his "insatiable appetite" for books. Before the end of June, as his contribution to the Lincoln legend was being distributed to bookstores, Howells was on his way home, beginning an Eastern pilgrimage that he hoped would help him follow Lincoln's example and "triumph over all the obstacles of fortune."[38]

Howells's pilgrimage got off to a false start. He tarried in Jefferson to renew the "gentle and good" influences in his life, but a week in his village brought back his sense of entrapment and uselessness. In the first of the letters he wrote for the *State Journal* describing his journey, he lapsed into the persona of the idler. His letter from "Anywhere, Nowhere, Ohio," as he dubbed Jefferson, recounts the minor difficulties of arising to catch the early morning train. The narrator is a "most obliging creature," easily put upon by women who ask him to watch their baggage. Although most of his traveling companions are women, one turns out to be a "sun-bronzed youth," whose striking countenance is "sharply and decisively cut" by lines of wisdom. Howells revealed in the last line of his letter that this youth was Barclay Coppac, a raider who had escaped capture at Harper's Ferry. Confronted with this young man of action, Howells reversed the priority he had given the man of ideas during the John Brown fervor. The narrator provides comfort as the raider slumps against his shoulder and sleeps. When the "taciturn" youth wakes, he pays the narrator a high compliment: "He was . . . so good," wrote Howells, "as to smile at a joke which is not new to these columns nor to the friends of this writer." Challenged by the presence of the man of action, Howells assumed the guise of a trifling jokester with no more to offer than a well-worn jest.[39]

Being an idle observer had served Howells on his earlier river trip to St. Louis, but since that time the stakes had been raised.

He had planned an ambitious itinerary, bringing him to New England along the St. Lawrence River through the French cities of Canada. According to canons of the romantic picturesque, the grandeur of nature and the living presence of the past would suggest morals to the sensitive literary observer. Howells had "schooled [him]self for great impressions," making his journey another test of his literary mettle.[40] From the beginning, however, he found that he could not assent to sublime emotions. Howells's travel sketches anticipate later writings in which he sharply defined a distaste for "sentimental" literary postures, undercutting what he saw as their emotional exaggeration by various maneuvers of irony. This protorealist impulse is present in his earlier travel sketches as well, but at the same time Howells tried to express the sublime emotions he satirized.

Howells's ambivalence appears in one of his very first attempts to evoke associations appropriate to sensitive literary observation. Anxious to reach Niagara Falls, the supreme example of the sublime in nature, he could not resist a prefiguring gesture. He transformed the familiar sight of Lake Erie into a vision of the sea where "the soul feels oppressively the mystery of life." After a few lines in this manner, he made an awkward retreat, attributing the thoughts to other passengers and admitting that his images were not original, that he had lifted them from Tennyson's "Sea Dreams." He ended by offering noisy hackmen clamoring for passengers as a figurative alternative to the spiritual associations of breaking waves. Howells's undercutting offered neither the bitterness of Heine's "devastating last lines" nor the tension of Heine's attitude of vain yearning. Howells's sense of the Heinesque fell away as he resorted to his apologetic idle-man persona, portraying himself as a "nervous person" who finds ordinary tasks, like securing a hack, very formidable.[41]

Although Howells expected a turnabout at Niagara Falls, one of his first responses to the falls was terror. Encountering the rapids at the base of American Falls, he reexperienced his "inveterate vertigo," and throughout his stay he battled his old nemesis. When he recorded his initial impressions in his sketches, he suppressed his feeling of dread and described his "vague disappointment." "One always approaches the sublime with a pre-disposition to be glorified," he wrote. "It is the conventional habit of thought, which on a second glance at Niagara falls from you, and leaves you free to be affected naturally." The fact of Niagara, he pointed out, unburdens the mind of "all old lumber of expectation, which you have stored away from pictures, and travels, and foolish poems— for all poems about Niagara are ridiculously inadequate." This liberation from literary poses did not prevent him from writing his own poems about the falls. If he could not abide the more preten- tious apostrophes to the falls, he did not believe that all transcen- dent associations were inauthentic.[42]

In his sketches on Niagara, Howells presented a mixture of attitudes. In some instances he attached sublime meaning to the falls, pointing out "how it cries aloud with the strong voice of its agony to the Everlasting." In other instances he parodied similar statements. Observing that one is "alive to the inadequacy of hu- man life and human affairs" before the great tumult of the falls, he illustrated his point facetiously: "One cannot bear to see a battered tin cup or an old castaway boot, when the voice of Niagara thun- ders to him." Unable to establish his own authority, he sought the authority of others. He described the falls in painterly terms, citing the expertise of Godfrey Frankenstein, a Cincinnati artist he met at the falls who had made Niagara his special subject. In one of his travel letters, Howells claimed that Frankenstein taught him "to see some of the beautiful tints of the water and mists—delicious purples, and greens and crimsons—that escape the greedy, com- mon eye, which gulps and bolts the whole thing, as it were, untasted." In later life, Howells remembered that he never did see the finely varying colors that Frankenstein pointed out: "I looked very hard, and as I was not going to be outdone in the perception of beauty, I said I did see them, and I tried to believe that I saw them, but, Heaven knows, I never did."[43]

Howells's experience of the falls left him feeling inadequate. Despite his disdain for the "greedy, common eye," he was keenly aware that his own descriptions did not rise very far above the prose of ordinary guidebooks. Breaking off a sketch, he confessed, "I have no doubt that [my] most decorative expressions are borrowed from the book which I paid too much for on the cars." It seemed to him that he was "doing" the falls like the ordinary tourist. Rather than demonstrating his depth of perception and understanding, he was being a kind of Dick Dowdy, a collector of sensations. Howells's apologetic idle-man persona, therefore, flits throughout his Niagara sketches, appearing when he undercuts serious statements, when he strives for an undemanding light touch, and when he portrays his literary purposes as "utterly idle."[44]

During the remainder of his journey through Canada, Howells had less difficulty assuming the picturesque manner. But his experiences at Niagara stayed with him, reinforcing his feeling that his real subject was not outward things. He seemed to be primarily a poet of Heinesque perception whose most authoritative subject was himself. When he reached Portland, Maine, Howells searched out Longfellow's beginnings and found Deering's Woods, the scene of Longfellow's mildly lamenting poem, "My Lost Youth." On this ground, Howells experienced an upsurge of inspiration and regained faith in his Heinesque persona:

The comrade of my walk and I had been talking of the poet's mission, and how he should be the great teacher and preacher; but when we stood within the shadow and whisper of those trees, I forgot the fine scheme of poethood that my philosophy had spun, and would have the poet be only as he had been, in all the world full of sorrowful glances, sublime yearning, inscrutable power—yet the equal of every man in human weakness and human passion, as much a teacher in his helplessness as in his great strength.[45]

Drawing inspiration from a poet who actually believed Heine possessed "a morbid, ill-regulated mind," Howells sanctioned the attitude of sorrowful *Sehnsucht* before following the path Longfellow had traveled to Boston.[46] He expected to receive further confirmation of his poetic faith from Longfellow's Brahmin peers.

Recounting his Boston experiences in later life, Howells described himself as a pilgrim and Boston men of letters as priests who had

been willing to accept him into their order.[47] Howells's early association with these men helped him overcome doubts about his
usefulness. Their example disputed charges that the literary vocation was impractical and feminine. Boston men of letters were
embedded in a social matrix that strengthened their assumption of
moral authority and fortified their belief that order and justice
were fundamental properties of the universe. Aided primarily by
Lowell, Howells discovered a foundation for integrated belief and
self-affirmation in Boston. His Celestial City promised to free him
forever from his anxieties.

When he first arrived in Boston, Howells was disappointed to
learn that its literary notables were not clustered around Tremont
Street near the offices of the *Atlantic*. Instead, they were scattered
about in Boston, Cambridge, and Concord. He finally decided that
he could properly present himself to Lowell at his home in Cambridge, since their letters concerning his poems were a kind of
personal correspondence. After floundering in the unfamiliar city,
he finally found himself in Lowell's study, feeling like "an obscure
subaltern . . . before his general."[48]

As Howells remembered their first meeting, Lowell's welcome
was given with "a certain frosty shyness, a smiling cold." Lowell
established his authority by sitting back and assessing whether
Howells could begin a conversation. Howells's first offering proved
false. Comparing his search for Lowell to Heine's effort to find
Börne in Frankfort—another instance of a disciple seeking a master—Howells stated that he had asked several times for directions.
Lowell was disturbed by this remark, Howells later surmised,
because Lowell liked to think he was well known in his *"patria"* of
Cambridge. Howells followed with expressions of his sympathy
for Heine, and Lowell responded negatively, criticizing Heine's
manner and informing Howells that his first poem had been held
back because it appeared to be a translation. Howells then described his pleasure in thinking that he might be a literary descen-
dant of Sir James Howells, the Welsh writer, but Lowell corrected
him by pointing out that the name was spelled "Howels." Rising
from his chair, he brought forth the rare volume that substantiated

the point. By this time, Howells had become Lowell's "captive," always a necessary preliminary, as Howells recalled from their long association, to more comfortable discussions.[49]

From his very first meeting with Lowell, Howells glimpsed that the cost of acquiring Bostonian authority was the sacrifice of individual autonomy. He later observed that a "defect" he had discovered in Lowell and other Boston literary men was that "wittingly or unwittingly, they propose themselves to you as an example, or if not quite this, that they surround themselves with a subtle ether of potential disapprobation in which, at the first sign of unworthiness in you, they helplessly suffer you to gasp and perish."[50] At first, however, the stultifying effect of this ether was not so great. Howells was intoxicated to be in the presence of Lowell. After he had bowed to Lowell, he was rewarded beyond his imagining with an invitation to dine at Parker House, where he would meet Oliver Wendell Holmes and James T. Fields, who had succeeded Lowell as editor of the *Atlantic*.

At Parker House, no frost remained to chill Howells's enjoyment. Lowell and Holmes were brilliantly loquacious, while Fields proved adept at lively caricature. The talk ranged far but concentrated on literary matters. Learning that Howells wrote for the *Saturday Press*, Holmes informed him that the Bohemians were considered upstarts in Boston. But Howells was not chagrined, for he was an *Atlantic* contributor as well. He delighted in all of his hosts' "delicious wit and wisdom and drollery." Holmes realized the significance of the evening for Howells by observing to Lowell, "Well, James, this is something like the apostolic succession; this is the laying on of hands." As the dinner closed, Fields asked Howells to breakfast the next morning, Holmes said he must come to tea in the evening, and Lowell offered to give him a note of introduction to Hawthorne, if he planned to go to Concord.[51]

The next evening when he visited Holmes, Howells confessed "the effects that had lingered so long" from "a time of broken health and troubled spirit." The physician-author suggested that these matters were part of their shared humanity. Howells met Holmes's son, the future Justice Oliver Wendell Holmes, Jr., who was about to begin his senior year at Harvard. As they roamed Boston Common past midnight, talking "psychics"—spiritual forces and things of the soul—Howells tried to make out an affinity between a Bostonian, whose life had been "deeply schooled and definitely regulated," and himself, whose way had been "desultory and self-found."[52]

Before visiting Hawthorne in Concord, Howells glanced at Lowell's note of introduction and discovered that it complimented his poetry. Although Hawthorne was shy and meditative in their talk, he gave Howells a note to Emerson that read, "I find this young man worthy." With Emerson and Thoreau, however, Howells met unexpected resistance. Thoreau seated Howells at an unfriendly distance and confounded his attempts to speak of John Brown and Walden Pond. Emerson was formally cordial but dismissive of other writers' reputations. He called Hawthorne's *Marble Faun* "a mere mush" and Poe "the jingle-man." When he learned Howells was a poet, Emerson pulled the *Atlantic* from the shelf and looked over Howells's poems without a word. As Howells was leaving, Emerson suggested that now and then one might "give a pleasant hour" to poetry. Feeling diminished by Thoreau's aloofness and Emerson's comments, Howells wandered back to his hotel and lost himself in a fit of self-accusation. He focused on a minor breach of social ceremony with Emerson and plotted wild schemes of restitution.[53]

When he returned to Boston, Howells unburdened his tale to Fields. The publisher responded with uproarious laughter. Within the year Emerson had been added to Fields's list of most-favored authors, but he was no advocate of Emerson's philosophy. He had once written in caricature, "But what have we here, a fool swinging on a clothes line?—No!—Mr. Emerson swinging himself on an inverted rainbow." Secret ridicule of Emerson and his followers was not uncommon among the intellectual elite of Cambridge and Boston. Recently Lowell and Thoreau had come into open conflict over Thoreau's celebration of the lone individual. Emerson and Thoreau may have been frosty to Howells because he appeared to be Lowell's devotee. Whatever the mix of motive and circumstance, Howells's experiences had distanced him from Concord and drawn him closer to Boston. He had fortified his sympathy with those intellectuals who shared his need to fulfill a literary vocation within rather than apart from society.[54]

Howells's allegiance to Boston easily survived the taunts of his peers at the *Saturday Press.* Arriving in New York, Howells found the Bohemians less serious and far tamer than he had expected. They mainly tried to deflate his enthusiasm for Boston and make gibes at his expense. The exception was Walt Whitman, who was more their idol than their compatriot. Although the *Press* had recently printed Howells's dissenting opinion on the 1860 edition of *Leaves of Grass*, Whitman shook Howells's hand with genuine friendliness. Apart from Whitman, the Bohemians appeared to be groupish. Lowell and Holmes shared many convictions, but they were distinctly different personalities. In contrast, it seemed to Howells that the Bohemians' rebellious style "absorb[ed] identity." When he returned to Columbus, Howells wrote Fields a letter disparaging New York and praising Boston, saying that he looked forward to living in Boston someday—"being possibly the linchpin in the hub." "I know that the pen is a feeble instrument with which to keep the wolf from the door," he stated, "but then, what will not youth dare—to hope?"[55]

Remembering his literary pilgrimage to Boston, Howells retained his youthful wonder. What could Lowell, Holmes, and Fields have seen in someone who was "the mere response, the hollow echo" of their incisive commentary and wit? Their graciousness was not entirely exceptional. Lowell frequently held out a welcoming hand to beginning writers, and the dinner at Parker House was part of Fields's effort to recruit new talent. As men imbued with a high ideal of civility, the Brahmins felt obliged to be agreeable on public occasions, and they were all irrepressibly entertaining talkers. Yet, while Fields's home was a noted showplace, Lowell and Holmes usually protected their privacy. When they admitted Howells to their homes, they granted a rare privilege. They disregarded their usual separation of public and private spheres because they considered Howells a special phenomenon.[56]

Later, in his review of *Venetian Life* (1866), the book that established Howells's credentials in Boston, Lowell recalled his initial acquaintance with his protégé. He had regarded Howells's poems as one of the "favorable omens of our literature." From the moment Lowell discovered that Howells was thoroughly Western and wholly untutored, the delicacy and finish of his poetry took on significant meaning:

This delicacy, it appeared, was a product of the rough-and-ready West, this finish the natural gift of a young man with no advantage of college-training, who, passing from the compositor's desk to the editorship of a local newspaper, had been his own faculty of the humanities. . . . A singular fruit, we thought, of our shaggy democracy,—as interesting a phenomenon in that regard as it has been our fortune to encounter. Where is the rudeness of a new community, the pushing vulgarity of an imperfect civilization, the licentious contempt of forms that marks our unchartered freedom, and all the other terrible things which have so long been the bugaboos of European refinement? Here was a natural product, as perfectly natural as the deliberate attempt of "Walt Whitman" to answer the demand of native and foreign misconception was perfectly artificial. Our institutions do not, then, irretrievably doom us to coarseness and to impatience of that restraining precedent which alone makes true culture possible and true art attainable. Unless we are mistaken, there is something in such an example as that of Mr. Howells which is a better argument for the American social and political system than any empirical theories that can be constructed against it.[57]

To the "modest preludings" of his young literary friend, Lowell had attached a weight of ideological meaning. A feeling of crisis existed among Brahmin intellectuals, focusing on "democracy misunderstood." Mass politics had opened the way for vulgar men with vulgar methods. Lowell was disturbed by the rising tide of Irish immigrants and looked nostalgically to the past when his patria Cambridge had contained only the "foreign admixture" of two Scotch gardeners. Lowell had idealized democracy as the extension of the best of thought and feeling to greater numbers of men and women, but by the 1850s, as Howells later summarized his attitude, Lowell no longer had "faith in insubordination as a means of grace." Instead, Lowell stressed the leadership of culti-vated men and respect for tradition—those things he shared with his Brahmin peers—to safeguard sacred ideals. Holmes, too, wor-ried whether natural leaders from the "privileged order"—the "Brahmin caste of New England"—would continue to guide the "great multitude."[58]

Lowell's assessment of Howells renewed his faith in democracy. If Howells were a typical product of "shaggy" American society, the dangers associated with democracy might be exaggerations. For Holmes, Howells probably was not so salutary an omen. He appeared to fit Holmes's description of the single exception to the Brahmin's natural superiority—the rare outlander, the "uncombed youth," whose vigor surpasses that of the hereditary scholars. Howells found it surprising that none of his hosts questioned him about politics, since he was the campaign biographer of Abraham Lincoln and the writer of an antislavery poem, "The Pilot's Story," recently accepted by the *Atlantic*. But the Brahmins believed they could discern the shape of events from individual character. How-ells offered reassuring signs that the West—as the realm of demo-cratic man—did not necessarily foster a "contempt of forms" and an impatience of "restraining precedent."[59]

Howells was not immediately up to Brahmin standards. A few years later, Lowell reiterated his initial advice: "You have enough in you to do honor to our literature," he told Howells. "Keep on cultivating yourself. You know what I thought. You must sweat the Heine out of you as men do mercury. You are as good as Heine —remember that." At their first meeting, Lowell had described the Heinesque as a "leeshore" to be avoided by constant dili-gence.[60]

During the period when he became involved with Howells as a mentor, Lowell was reconsidering the poetic imagination and de-fining, more absolutely than before, a position that identified the Heinesque—along with similar forms of "sentimentalism"—as the "cant of modern literature." The subjective, self-reflective ten-

17. James Russell Lowell at age forty, in 1859, the year before he met Howells. Howells recalled that Lowell was "reluctant to part with [his own] youth, and was willing to cling to it wherever he found it." Lowell sometimes tried to sustain a feeling of youthfulness in physical competition with his protégés. During their first meeting, Lowell took Howells on a backyard route through Cambridge. Lowell failed to bound over a fence. After succeeding on the third attempt, he said, "I commonly do that the first time."

dency of modern poetry, the effort of poets like Heine to be concerned minutely with their own feelings, the sorrowful *Sehnsucht* that they saw as a possible means of redemption—all this Lowell viewed as "vanity" and "disease." In his critical essays, he excoriated this kind of sentimentalism in crescendos of derisive epitaphs: Such poetry was "degenerate," "sickly," and "feminine." Poets who accepted its premises were "idlers" and "*dilettanti.*" They were "feeble," "insincere," and "weak in the knees."[61]

According to Lowell, sentimental egoism destroyed the poet's natural sympathy with "universal nature." Looking into the "narrow well of self," the sentimentalist saw only the distorted reflection of his own image and mistook it for poetic truth. Instead of presenting "the thing itself," the preexistent ideal of perfection, "the eternal harmony which we call God," the sentimentalist offered merely a "fidgety assertion of selfhood." Lowell condemned the idea that the poet's vision was necessarily fragmentary and limited; he believed nothing of significance existed within one's "vast interior." The most the sentimentalist could portray was a passing mood, a thing harmless in itself, like "a fit of mental indigestion," but a sure sign of "disease" if indulged in for long. The habitual sentimentalist was seeking "to justify personal failings by generalizing them into universal laws." The poet's duty lay elsewhere. His office, Lowell asserted, was to reveal in "ideal portraitures" the universal qualities that emanate from God—"grace and goodness, the fair, the noble, and the true."[62]

Lowell identified sentimental, self-referential poetry with the disintegration of "authoritative limitations of thought" that had followed in the wake of the French Revolution.[63] In the realm of the social as well as the spiritual, he was preoccupied with the need for restraint, proportion, control, all subsumed in subordination to tradition and "just" authority.[64] Lowell distrusted internalized self-control; he idealized a time when controls were established from above and followed from below.

A personal source of Lowell's attitude was the Job-like despair he suffered during the late 1840s and early 1850s, when he lost three children and his wife. He lay awake at night thinking of his razors and his throat. Finally he subdued his grief by halting the free flow of his emotions. From this time, he remained chastened toward what could be known by self-exploration and humbled in relation to the mysterious workings of the universe. Howells came into Lowell's life when he was formulating the lessons of his experience. Lowell had been forced back to first principles, and for him the most important of these principles was the belief that a moral order reigned despite contrary appearances.[65]

Lowell and Howells formed a relationship that was mutually affirming. For Lowell, Howells appeared to be a young man who promised the durability of Lowell's beliefs among the common people of the "shaggy" American democracy. For Howells, Lowell offered all he had hoped to find in the sphere of Boston: authoritative sanction for his sense of literary vocation, a "laying on of hands" that carried the strength of place, association with a realm where literature appeared to be woven into the fabric of life. By his authority, furthermore, Lowell posed the possibility of integrated belief in a moral universe. Not only that, Lowell's advice strongly implied that devotion to this ideal was necessary for admittance to Boston.

CHAPTER 8

The Province of Reason

We see nothing whole, neither life nor art. We are so made, in soul and in sense, that we can deal only with parts, with points, with degrees; and the endeavor to compass any entirety must involve a discomfort and a danger very threatening to our intellectual integrity.

HOWELLS, 1895

Confirmed in his reverence for Boston, Howells believed a consecrated path had opened before him. He realized, however, that following it would demand his utmost devotion. "A man may have ever so much in him," Lowell had told him, "but ever so much depends on how he gets it out." Once he returned to Columbus, Howells organized his affairs to the single end of getting out whatever it was in him that Lowell might consider ever so much. His first step was to buttress Lowell's fatherly regard. "I find myself willing and able to work," he wrote Lowell, "which [is] only another locution for willingness and ability to be happy." He added that for the time being the "little immediate applause" he received from his Columbus readers would be enough to satisfy "the young poet." To free his time for study and writing, Howells limited his evening calls to the minimum and announced to his family that he would not be visiting home. Neither would it be wise for any of the family to come to Columbus, he pointed out, since his financial situation was still very shaky. Fearing a more disturbing distraction, he declared to Victoria, "But as my only selfish aim is to suc[c]eed in literature, I will help with my money all of you as fast as I get it."[1]

Howells was determined to reserve his evenings exclusively for literature because his days were again consumed by journalism. Finding that Foster could offer nothing to occupy him at the publishing house, he had regained a position on the *State Journal.* Cooke had resumed command of the newspaper and hired Howells to replace Reed, who had moved on, as Howells phrased it, to the "Cimmerian darkness of the Cincinnati *Gazette.*" While Howells assumed the main editorial duties, he shared some of the responsibility for political commentary with a newcomer more his own age named Samuel Price. Reed's sarcastic style remained the tradition of the office. Since Howells had editorial charge of the newspaper, he expanded his literary reviews, providing an outlet for his evening labors. With Lowell's words for inspiration—"more power to your elbow!"—he aimed for an authoritative critical voice to complement his poetry and fiction.[2]

As often as he could find occasion, Howells reported his progress to Lowell. He let Lowell know that he had listened carefully to his suggestions and picked up their finer nuances. Lowell had warned him to avoid printing "too much & too soon." A preliminary to becoming a man of "genius," he had observed, was becoming a man of "sense." Howells replied that he was striving for "definiteness" in his poetry, eliminating poems that failed to survive a sober second reading. Nevertheless, he continued to draw inspiration for his poetry from "curious revelations of self," retaining the Heinesque mode of perception that Lowell disliked. Howells told Lowell that he had prepared a lecture celebrating "the genius of Heinrich Heine" for an Atheneum series in Columbus. He let this statement have its own effect but later defended his Heinesque sensibility more directly and apologetically. "I try to write always outside of my affection for [Heine]," he told Lowell. "But what with the German blood I have, and my intense love for

German poetry, it is hard for me to avoid the German manner."
Howells did not mention that he had shifted the subject of his
lecture to the aesthetic, political, and civil character of Boston.[3]

In his letters to Lowell, Howells was jockeying to retain his
autonomy. Like other antebellum Americans, he felt this natural
need in an exaggerated way. As communal orientations of belief
eroded, individuals were forced more upon themselves to determine what was real and what was false. Transparent public hoaxes
like those invented by P. T. Barnum played to a widespread desire
to unmask deceptive appearances and ground belief in immediate
experience.[4] Some individuals found safety in moral platitudes or
secular gods; others sought verification through the senses—in the
ecstasies of camp-meeting conversions, the voices of spiritualist
séances, or the revelations of dreams. But for young people like
Howells, the most intensely felt reality seemed the reality of self.
Within the diffuse atmosphere of doubt, they looked within themselves to establish a basis of belief.[5]

While Howells sought to affirm belief on the basis of his own
experience, his mentor had retreated to spiritual givens. "The
eternal harmony which we call God," Lowell believed, was manifested in a "fire-proof" moral universe that would endure all incendiary passions of the present. For Howells, however, the passions
of the present could very well be revelations of the soul, illumined
more deeply by "the secret lightning of feeling." The method he
derived from Heine was to understand the moral universe in a
fragmentary way through intense explorations of self. Despite the
warnings of Lowell, Howells retained the Heinesque mode of
perception that promised to draw the world of his experience into
cohesive order. "Creeds are good," he declared in a review, "but
thoughts are better."[6]

Because he feared Lowell would never accept his Heinesque inclinations, Howells was unsure how he should ready himself for
Boston. He had found a promising stand-in for Lowell, however,
in the companion of his midnight walk on the Boston Common. In
correspondence with Oliver Wendell Holmes, Jr., he measured his

development against a Bostonian who was more his peer, despite their differences of place, family, and schooling. Howells portrayed himself as Holmes's intellectual equal: "I have been doing a little French Revolution, Milton, Leigh Hunt's Autobiography, Italian Poets, and Faust," Howells wrote. "Politics and criticism not counted."[7]

Holmes had as much to gain as Howells from their "pen-and-paper" friendship. No doubt Holmes had read his father's description of the Brahmin with deep chagrin, for his father had raised an alarm over "lowered vitality" in Brahmins of successive generations. Holmes replied to his father's implicit gibe in an essay he sent Howells. He claimed that someone "bred in the midst of riches, and educated from his earliest youth" possessed an advantage over any "self-made man" that "can never be annulled, whatever may be his inferiority in natural parts." Howells's reputation as a type of Western vigor gave Holmes the chance to demonstrate that he was not proof of his father's thesis.[8]

Howells and Holmes shared an allegiance they both acknowledged—the bond of youth. Holmes had defined their generation of young men as among the first "who have been brought up in an atmosphere of investigation, instead of having every doubt answered." Howells had felt the same generational urge to question authority. "I am going largely into skepticism at present," he reported. "Cultivating my incredulity on a course of Voltaire and the Westminster Review." He later reported—only partly in jest—that he had dropped Voltaire: "I thought it idle to read a man who was not disposed to question anything more than I."[9]

On the basis of their shared skepticism, Howells cautiously gauged Holmes's attitude toward Heinesque perception. Because Holmes specialized in aesthetics, Howells expressed enthusiasm for portraits of Christ's passion he had observed in Catholic shop windows. Quoting Heine's analysis, Howells suggested that the representations of "abnegation and self-sacrifice" were subjective renderings of the artists' "martyrdom." "I don't quote Heine on any subject anymore, if I can help it," he added. "I have wearied a little of his brilliance and subtlety—both partly false."[10]

The essays Holmes sent in exchange for Howells's subjective poems showed that Holmes's skepticism departed very little from his elders' perspectives. Holmes shared his elders' distrust of self-exploration as a means of revelation. Completed during the summer of Howells's pilgrimage, "Notes on Albert Durer" and "Plato" contain seeds of Holmes's later empiricism. "I do not feel sure," Holmes stated in his Plato essay, "that each man's own experience is not always to be that which must ultimately settle his belief." His hedging was appropriate, for he still adhered to his father's philosophical positions. "Experience" more potent than Holmes had gained at Harvard College would speed his departure from the philosophical world of his father. Holmes later associated this break with his four years of Civil War combat.[11]

Although he had allowed that "every vagary of the human mind" was subject to investigation, Holmes contended in his Dürer essay that "personal and individual" experience was not the ultimate ground of truth. "The presumption is always in favor of that picture being greatest," Holmes wrote, "in which the lower truth of the individual is made subservient . . . to the profounder truth of the idea. Knowledge of the stains of the earth, and of the decay that accompanies all earthly life, doubtless the painter needs, but higher than this is the sight which beholds the type disguised beneath the wasting form, and higher than anything connected with the individual is the conception of the harmonious whole of a great work, and this again is great, just as its idea partakes of what is eternal."[12] Nothing in Holmes's Dürer essay would have disturbed James Russell Lowell.

Holmes's judgment against "personal and individual" experience implicitly rebuked Howells's fascination for Heine. According to Heine, "whole" poets of the past had penetrated easily to eternal meanings, but the presumption of wholeness among modern artists was "a lie which every sound eye penetrates; and which cannot escape scorn." Howells replied to Holmes's Dürer essay by pointing to the "analytical tendency" of modern thought: Unlike whole artists of the past, divided moderns were "critical" and "uncreative"; their characteristic expressions in literature were "the philo-

sophical speculation, the subjective poem, and the analytical fiction
—the fiction as written by Hawthorne, Thackeray and Bulwer,
and 'The Autocrat.' " Howells associated the subjective poem with
Holmes's own taste for speculative philosophy and his father's
novel "The Professor's Story," then running serially in the *Atlantic*. Howells revealed that he too was writing an extended story
that was growing "frightfully analytical." [13]

Holmes failed to take the bait. "I should like to talk about what
you said of the analytic tendency of our time," he replied after a
two-month wait. "My tendencies natural[l]y rather run that way
and not a small part of my analysis is as is too often now the case
applied to the unprofitable subject—of self." [14] Though Holmes
said no more, his slight acknowledgment may have encouraged
Howells to ignore the word *unprofitable* and continue his pursuit.
Although he had been accomplishing a great deal in his evening
study, he told Holmes, "I have been writing nothing, reading
nothing, thinking nothing for the last two months." Enlarging on
his sense of inertia, he raised an issue that had triggered his Jefferson breakdown: "I always shiver with the doubt: Is this indolence
a pause in the scheme of my development? Have I come to the
end?" Holmes's mention of a classmate's death allowed Howells to
ask further, "Are you like myself, in leaving death altogether out
of the scheme of life? I have a small salary, on which I live with
the splendor of a lord, and the generosity of a vagabond.—Recklessly I squander my mortality in the same way. I think from the
nature of things that I cannot be long-lived, but yet I live as if no
night lay between this and eternity. I take my eternity at once, in
fact—and if there *should* happen to be nothing after death—why,
I have had my eternity, you know." [15]

Expanding on his associations, Howells combined the ideas of
inertia and death in a story. "Some lives seem to be perfectly
accomplished before existence ceases—," he began, "that is, no
fortuity can suggest new possibilities for them." Howells claimed
that his didactic story was a true relation, the authentic experience
of a "young girl" who had worked in his father's printing office.
He endowed her with an exceptional sensibility, one as steeped in

the Heinesque as his own. She had a strange, almost spectral beauty; her eyes revealed a "divine languor," an "ineffable" richness and warmth. In addition, she "had intelligence, taste, culture —she had read a great deal, with the deep inner sense of the beautiful, belonging to so few readers." Howells elaborated her character to prepare for the dramatic lesson of his homily: "And now behold one of the contradictions that tempt one to atheism!" Despite her literary sensitivities, the girl "could not write well enough, or would not write ill enough to achieve that doubtful splendor and distinction of female authorship." Nothing was in store for her but "a monotonous drudgery through life at the trade she detested, or a domestic round of tasks and stupid little duties." She was saved from this fate, however, by "good death." "It seems a hard and cruel thing to say that the only thing one can do is to die," Howells reflected. "But for her, what else remained?"

"Only death," Howells repeated, had allowed the girl to escape an existence contrary to her nature. "Have I made this idea clear to you," he asked Holmes, "or does my long story go for nothing?" Holmes may have had difficulty understanding this profusion of analysis from someone he had met briefly in Boston and known through an occasional exchange of letters. Howells had pushed his justification of the Heinesque into a confessional mode. Ostensibly a look into another life, illustrating the analytical tendency of modern thought, Howells's story was an exercise in self-exploration, concentrating on tensions he had been trying to control for several years. There is good reason to believe that the girl in his story was apocryphal, that she was Howells's creation of an alter ego, representing the worst that he imagined for himself—confinement to "woman's sphere," arrested development, and death-in-life.[16] Howells's story was a last resort, a plea for understanding set against the unsympathetic messages he had received from Holmes.

Letters to Brahmins required too much concealment for the kind of speculation on faith and experience that had become Howells's dominant concern. His reviews for the *State Journal* allowed him more freedom. In his reviews, his tensions with Brahmin expectations could recede beneath the surface. Following his return from Boston, the *State Journal's* columns sometimes displayed the character of leading controversial magazines like the *Westminster Review*, becoming similarly "opulent in paragraphic mention and analysis."[17] Howells plunged ahead whenever he sensed an occasion for reflection, not passing opportunities even when they appeared in arcane medical journals and dreary theological treatises.

Darwin had not yet entered the scene. For Howells and his generational peers, religious and philosophical controversies were still framed in Enlightenment terms of *reason* versus *revelation*. Partly to align himself with Holmes's philosophical interests, Howells dipped into the metaphysical discourses of Sir William Hamilton and his disciples, heirs of the Scottish "Common Sense" philosophy, who claimed that the "Infinite" was excluded from the "province of reason." According to Hamilton, the gulf between man and God could not be bridged. He elaborately demonstrated that man was conditioned by time, space, and degree, while God was "unconditioned" and "absolute." Consequently, Hamiltonians stressed, spiritual belief depended solely on faith in God's revelation.[18]

Though he was impressed by Hamilton's reputation as "the master philosophical mind of the age," Howells did not read very far in his philosophy, probably because he found the Hamiltonians' limitation of reason uncongenial. Hamilton appealed most to Americans like Francis Bowen, professor of moral philosophy at Harvard, whose efforts to shore up orthodoxy and contain the intellectual energies of his students made him Holmes's nemesis. Howells was content to bemuse himself with the "marvellous spectacle" afforded by Hamilton's contrast to Oxford clergy who were currently questioning revelation in the name of reason. Modern life, as Heine suggested, had become "topsy-turvy." Divines provoked skepticism while philosophers defended faith. Howells soon recovered from his "touch of metaphysics." He had taken the first escape he found in his philosophical reading, detouring to his literary ideal when he came across a reference to Heine's *Zur*

Geschichte der Religion und Philosophie in Deutchland, a survey of philosophy geared to the sensibilities of poets.[19]

Heine had already specified the "province of reason" Howells found most compelling. What Howells required, in his own phrase, was "experimental knowledge," evidences clothed in the attire of everyday life, resembling his own experience. The modern tendency, defined by Heine as the "intensest self-consciousness" and the "feeling of personality," seemed to permeate all forms of significant literature. Even novelists of the previous generation had become "subjective" and "analytical" in their current works. Counting them for Holmes, Howells had listed Hawthorne, Thackeray, Bulwer, and Holmes's father, "The Autocrat." By dissecting passions and examining the wayward impulses of the human heart, the novel was becoming "the modern poem." When Dickens's *Great Expectations* began to appear serially in *Harper's Monthly*, Howells enthusiastically added Dickens's name to his roll of analytical novelists. Howells believed Dickens penetrated "the strange inner world of man's consciousness, about which so little is known." Dickens showed how the random association of thoughts revealed "your instinctive self." This method provided a "magic lens by which your infusorial ideas become visible—formless, as they are, but inhabiting your unconsciousness by myriads."[20]

From his nervous sufferings, Howells knew that the association of thoughts and other avenues of self-exploration might lead to irrational fears and self-accusations. He had read "Last Words," a poem by Owen Meredith that voiced a warning "from the subjective deep." Advising poets to "cull the latest effect, leave the cause," Meredith cautioned that nothing but "black death" lurked within the self.[21] Although he fully appreciated Meredith's meaning and believed he was among the few who did, Howells was intrigued by the mastery of the inner life demonstrated by his analytical novelists. Though it penetrated the instinctive self, Dickens's novel did not lose its way in a flood of confusion. "The ideas," Howells pointed out, "rise and float down its strong, profound current, that never breaks from the channel." Another brac-ing example was "The Professor's Story" by the elder Holmes. In this arresting novel, it appeared that the physician-author "had studied the anatomy of the soul." His characters, Howells enthused, go about "with windows in their brains, through which you look, and behold the subtle processes of thought before they outwardly declare themselves in action.—'Causes, causes, and again causes.' "[22]

Narrowing his appreciation of Dickens and Holmes to what he identified as the subjective elements of their stories, Howells constructed a supportive tradition for the analytical novel. The sporadic theme of Holmes's novel "The Professor's Story" was individual responsibility for evil. Holmes offered the bizarre example of a young girl whose mother had been bitten by a snake before the girl's birth, communicating a venomous influence that drove the girl to violence. Using chorus figures to debate the meaning of her affliction, Holmes proselytized his brand of liberalized Christianity. While asserting the rule of a moral universe, he urged leniency toward exceptional cases of individuals who had been robbed of their will. Holmes's exploration of a personal symptom leading to broad philosophical speculation precisely suited Howells's needs, offering a type of the analytical novel, the kind that Howells wished to write himself.[23]

Holmes's example encouraged Howells to make his own connections between personal symptoms and questions of belief. While Holmes's novel was progressing in the *Atlantic*, Howells found an instance comparable to the serpentine heroine, one that was drawn indisputably from life. He had come across a medical discussion of Edgar Allan Poe by Dr. Henry Maudsley, the famous English theorist of mental disorder. Even more than the case imagined by Holmes, Maudsley's evidence supported the idea of limited individual responsibility for evil. Everyone would agree, Howells observed, that Poe was the "ultimate bad man of this time": "He was weak, drunken, ungrateful, mendacious, vindictive and cowardly—capricious beyond caprice, impulsively an angel, and very deliberately a devil." It was impossible, Howells suggested, "to love the character of such a man." It was difficult "even to compassionate his sufferings."[24]

Yet Maudsley's evidence appeared to demonstrate that Poe had been "born and fostered amid influences calculated to destroy the balances of self-control, and render him irresponsible for the sins of his career." Unlike Holmes, Howells could not rest comfortably with the idea that the exception proved the rule. When he considered Poe's tortured life, Howells brought forward the insights of his own desultory experience. He speculated on the anomaly of frustrated and unfulfilled lives, the kind of contradictions that tempted him to atheism:

Poe's education [Howells began in his final evaluation of Maudsley's evidence] was of the kind to exaggerate every defect of his character, and to do little for the development of its latent good. Throughout life he seems to have suffered in his own individuality, the results of causes, many of which were wholly anterior to himself. To every man there is a compensation in kind: good for good, evil for evil, is the stern law of nature, which has no Bible. But here was a man who was compensated, not alone for his own wrongdoing, but for the errors of those who went before him—the errors which became a part of his spiritual organism, and weakened all his purposes for good—the very errors out of which his own sprang. The instance is not singular, and questions result from it all, that are not pleasant ones to answer. Does the ultimate bad man of this time, represent anything but a sum of follies, shames, passions, sins, which had their root in his own race, when its blood warmed the hearts of ancestors long since dead, and now flourish in him with a growth and strength beyond his control? This seems to be the scientific view of the case. If it be correct, does divine justice consist with the pangs suffered for the indulgence of inherited frailties? And how much individuality is there left us, when the dead so possess and torment us?[25]

Howells quickly ended his hazardous speculations. Although he had stated that Poe's example was not "singular," he abruptly ended his discussion by asserting that Poe was "crazed—a madman," an aberrant occurrence in the ultimate scheme of things.[26] Poe's career, he implied, was not disproof of a moral universe, a hasty conclusion that lacked the comfortable assurance Holmes displayed in his treatment of the serpentine girl.

When the issue was presented in the guise of fiction or literary debate, Howells was better able to confront the darker implications of his speculations. One means he had found for self-expression was a conception of "destiny" derived from Greek tragedy. His understanding was based on his earlier reading of A. W. Schlegel's *Lectures on Dramatic Art and Poetry*. While Schlegel contended that tragedy reached its apogee in the plays of Aeschylus and Sophocles, where "destiny" carried a sense of man's moral freedom within a providential universe, Howells had responded more to Schlegel's discussion of Euripides. Euripides, Schlegel argued, had been responsible for the degeneracy of tragedy among the Greeks. In his plays, destiny became the mere "caprice of chance," losing its tie to the "moral liberty of man." "[Euripides'] characters," Schlegel observed, "generally suffer because they must, and not because they will." [27]

Howells had first referred to the Greek conception of destiny while defending Hawthorne against a critic writing for the *North British Review*. The critic had charged that Hawthorne possessed a second-rate imagination because he exaggerated everything he touched. In his review, Howells asserted that nothing could be further from the truth: "No one presides more like destiny over the career of his characters—and it is this impressive fatality which the author represents, that makes his books so powerful and unique in their effect." Because Hawthorne had mastered the inner influences that lead to action—"the psychal cause and its results"—Howells believed Hawthorne could speak with the authority of destiny. Nevertheless, the working out of destiny in his novels left the moral universe in doubt, for it illustrated the contagion of evil from the guilty to the innocent, much like the transfer of misery to Poe from the indulgences of his parents. Hawthorne, Howells observed, taught "the truth that Sin acts not so directly upon the sinner as indirectly, and becomes ultimate calamity afflicting the innocent with the guilty—this is the most exalted reach of the imagination—this is the destiny of the Greek tragedy." [28]

In terms of Schlegel's definitions, it was more specifically the destiny of Euripides, for when the innocent suffered with the guilty, neither moral freedom nor moral order reigned. Howells invested "destiny" with the most despairing insights, finding occasion for elaboration in the sermon of an orthodox minister who argued for divine retribution by analogy to human vindictiveness. The minister had claimed that retribution was the essence of Greek tragedy, but Howells countered that it was "pure Destiny": "In the Greek tragedy—that sublimest conception of the Night-side of human life—the innocent suffer with the guilty, a common ruin involves good and bad, and inexorable Destiny broods over the affairs of men. It is not justice, nor retribution. It is Destiny, ignorant of both." Delivering his negative epiphany with the emphasis of a debater clinching his point, Howells ended by citing "the Dantesque conception of human misery—the most logical idea of hell ever formed, beginning, continuing and ending in hideous injustice and wrong." [29] Howells betrayed none of the hesitancy that had marked his essay on Poe. His feeling of mastering his thoughts helped him command his fears.

With growing conviction, Howells was deciding that analytical fiction was best suited for confronting troublesome issues. By its means, final answers were to be discovered rather than presumed. "Every fiction of course ought to have its chief idea," he observed, "about which the forms of thought and character may crystallize, leaving it perfectly visible. But a theory is fatal to the interest of a fiction." [30] Allowing a more deliberate inquiry into the "contradictions that tempt one to atheism," analytical fiction buffered Howells's personal despair and preserved his hope for unqualified belief.

At the same time, analytical fiction appeared to be acceptable in Boston. Howells had identified The Autocrat himself as an able practitioner. Because it treated other lives—or at least the self shaded into other lives—analytical fiction eased away from the overt egoism of the subjective poem, avoiding the hazard Lowell had identified as Howells's "Heine-leeshore." In analytical fiction, individual consciousness gave way to the outer world, the only terrain, according to Lowell, where the workings of a moral universe could be discerned. Inspired by his reading and reviewing,

Howells turned to his "frightfully analytical" novel as a way to quell his doubts and prove himself worthy.

By late November 1860, Howells had begun his novel. His writing tested not only his ability to speak with the moral authority of the analytical novelist but also the viability of his Heinesque sensibility. Titling his story "Geoffrey Winter" after his Heinesque protagonist, Howells presented a reprise of his home-leaving experiences and his umbrella-man fantasy of transformation. Having failed in the great world, Geoffrey Winter has returned to his home village of "Dulldale" to work out his salvation.[31]

When he arrives in Dulldale, no one grants Geoffrey Winter "the whole sidewalk." Contrary to Howells's umbrella-man fantasy, villagers regard Geoffrey with "hard antipathetic eyes." Howells returned the favor: Farm life is drudgery, village culture is stifling. Men consider whether certain colts were "horsey-looking colts," women hungry for gossip scan the streets. Sentimental village culture takes center stage, characterized by the "grim parlor" that dominates every house. Cluttered with tasteless bric-a-brac and suffused with a "gloomy, oppressive odor," the parlor epitomizes Dulldale. Drawing from the Jefferson he associated with imprisonment, Howells offered a humorless portrait of Geoffrey Winter's home village.[32]

Humorless self-involvement colored Howells's characterization of his protagonist as well. "When I contemplate Geoffrey in his relation to the commonplace facts of life," the narrator observes, "I confess the effect is to loosen my hold upon his shadowy and elusive identity. His nature was so wholly introverted, that the attempt to bring his real character in contact with the world would be a useless violence." Geoffrey cannot be characterized truly by the "motives which actuate other men" because he is specifically Heinesque, someone whose habitual mode of thought is subjective and brooding.[33]

After seven years, Geoffrey has returned as a prodigal to his village because of a disappointment, presumably in a literary career: "In his youth he did some things that gave belief in his power to achieve grander results; but it seemed that these things were the effect of youthful heat and force; rather than of genius. When he found out the truth, and the belief in his own powers passed away, his ambition faltered, and his activity ceased." But Howells allowed his protagonist "one last great effort." Geoffrey marries a lost love who had remained in the village and becomes editor of the Dulldale *Chronicle*. At first, newspaper work broadens his sympathies. He is drawn to the odd, conversing with spirit rappers, water curists, and "wild-eyed" abolitionists, an "endless number of public benefactors, and all the courageous and plausible children of humbug." As his observation of others takes him out of himself, Geoffrey becomes more "objective[,] positive and healthful."[34]

Geoffrey is adept at writing "charming little paragraphs," but his journalism does not fire him to greater ambition. The abolitionists he befriends lament "the languid temper that was content with praising a cause—that rested at thinking right, and left the deed undone." Geoffrey is nevertheless swept into the "whirling currents" of politics. He is nominated and runs for office. As in "The Independent Candidate," however, the campaign becomes an "absurd melée," a "scuffle with lies, detraction, malice and ignorance." Defeated in the huckstering election, Geoffrey returns to his introverted ways.[35]

This result comes as no surprise. Throughout his novel, Howells had difficulty separating the positive features of his Heinesque character from the traits of his enervating double, the idler. In Howells's "frightfully analytical" novel, the man of Heinesque sensibility is subsumed in self-suffering sentimentalism. Because his self-concern does not expand to larger meanings, Geoffrey slides into utter, desolate passivity. Geoffrey suffers from "ennui," he is "fond of [his] sorrows," he is "an idle man." No catharsis results from his "narcotic melancholy"; his thought bruises "itself incessantly against the narrow close" of his life. In sum, Geoffrey Winter represents Howells's despairing feeling that the Heinesque was a languishing sensibility, with no transcendent possibilities.[36]

Howells completed his negative portrait of his Heinesque sensibility by creating a feminine alter ego for Geoffrey in the character

Jane Grove, a sewing girl who lives in Geoffrey's household. Jane is similar to the young girl Howells had described in his letter to Holmes, someone of "intelligence, taste, culture," a reader who appreciates the "deep inner sense of the beautiful." Jane Grove shares all of Geoffrey's better traits. They are "alike," the narrator points out, "in many things—in the sweetness and goodness of their natures, in their spiritual delicacy, and [in] their rare instincts of beauty and purity." But Geoffrey reacts with "instinctive repugnance" toward Jane Grove, for "pain and renunciation" are part of the "occult alliance" that binds them. When someone suggests that he and Jane are very much alike, Geoffrey denies it petulantly.[37]

Jane Grove represents Howells's fear that his literary ambitions would confine him to "woman's sphere," a realm of diminished expectations and abject passivity. Meditating his own anxieties in the character of Geoffrey Winter, Howells found no possibility for synthesis, wholeness, or inner peace. Mired in passivity, confined to sentimental surroundings, Geoffrey has reached the end of his development. He lapses from the "highest intellectuality" and hides himself in "apathetic seclusion."[38] Considering what remained, Howells broached the question he had put to Holmes, whether in such a situation only "good death" provided a remedy. Howells deflected this speculation from Geoffrey by discussing Geoffrey's wife, Clara, who has become miserable trying to rouse Geoffrey from his estranged condition:

Is it a cruelty to say that one has no longer any business to live? Destiny seems sometimes to have perfectly accomplished the ends of an existence, before the existence ceases, removing the possibilities that make life a better thing than death, that make life a different thing to annihilation.

It may be that our happiness is only a system of deceptions more or less harmless—a sum of absurd delusions, into which we cheat ourselves and are willing to be cheated by our friends. Yet when the hope of this is forever taken away, the truth is such an intolerable thing, that it seems better for us not to be.[39]

Howells generalized Geoffrey's condition to all humanity. "Doubtless," the narrator says, "men do not radically change in anything, and the seeming transformations of their lives are but the development of the principles that existed in the uncreate[d] atoms of their being before the beginning." This speculation was fearful. If Geoffrey's fate represented the shared "destiny" of humanity, his story refuted belief in a moral universe. "I am sad for the defeated existences," Howells wrote. "They seem somehow a defeat of eternal purposes, and one hardly knows whether to doubt or trust."[40]

Writing "Geoffrey Winter" was more grief-work than synthesis as Howells confronted an aspect of his being that seemed confined to an unlovely death-in-life. He could assume a degree of detachment because he was present in his novel as both author and protagonist. As author, he was trying to brood like destiny over the careers of his characters, establishing the kind of control over dangerous materials of self that he identified with the novels of Hawthorne and Holmes. If he could not affirm his Heinesque sensibility directly in the character of Geoffrey Winter, he might do so indirectly, expressing the subjective tendency of modern thought in the guise of the analytical novelist.

While he tried valiantly to brood like destiny over his characters' fate, Howells was impeded by his feeling that he was vying for control of his novel with a force outside himself. Like his character Geoffrey Winter, Howells as author-narrator could not escape the sentimental ethos. The expectations of the mass reading audience intruded on his writing, pushing him in directions he wished to avoid. Finding that his description of a minor character fell back upon the conventional village gossip, he blamed his readers' limited appreciation: "If I portrayed her with the modification of a conscientious justice," he asserted, "you would refuse to believe in her, and I should be untrue to art." Producing sentimental art was not Howells's primary intention, but the tastes of his imagined readers, "skilled in fiction," continually intervened as he reverted to sentimental diction and melodramatic incidents. Knowing his sentimental readers would dislike Geoffrey's dismal domestic life, he testily asserted that someone who mistakenly marries his first love was "agreeable to the usages of many fictions." "It is hardly

my fault," he told his imagined readers, "if these people are not
entirely happy, nor exactly entertaining."[41]

Although he had meant to confound the expectations of his
sentimental readers, Howells could not muster the ironical distance that had sustained this motive in sketches like "Not a Love
Story." He was determined, however, that he would not resort to
a "catastrophe" to tie up loose ends of his novel neatly and agreeably. He was against the "good Providence" that watched over
many sentimental novels and diverted the true course of individual
destiny. Rather than conclude with the usual "calamities of fiction," he portrayed ends that seemed consistent with the "causes"
that determined his characters' individual destinies. He did not
jerk his characters into contrary resolutions by means of sentimental bargains.[42]

Despite his recognition of flaws that frustrated his best intentions, Howells believed his portrayal of Geoffrey Winter approximated "an accurate print of the human heart." He had concentrated on the mysterious influences that produce character, showing
how subtle, unconscious impulses—"mere infusorial ideas, little
different from dreams"—issued in action. He had torn away the
veil of appearances and had found "wretched shapes of deformity
and pain, that miserably emulate the ways of health, and grimly
mock the harmony of the whole." By delving into the inner world
of the self, he had not established a conclusive basis for autonomy
and coherent belief. But he had grasped a degree of self-control by
indulging the most dire insights of his desultory experience. Although he had "struggle[d] continually against impulses of disgust,"
novel writing had proved to be a way he could battle, if not
subdue, his conflicts.[43]

While Howells was contemplating the sorry fate of Geoffrey Winter, the country was moving steadily toward war. The outer reality
of sectional tension and threat of war had supported the negative
tendency of Howells's inward-turning novel. As the war came, the
assumption of individual control over the forces of destiny became
more and more untenable. The rush to war also rekindled How-

ells's feelings of selfishness. Once the war began, the antislavery volunteer replaced the political agitator as the worthiest representative of manly usefulness.

In the fall of 1860 after he had returned to the *State Journal*, Howells made sure that all of his editorials carried a "smack of righteousness." As rumors of secession began to fly, he scoffed at the Southern "bluster" but advocated force if rebellion actually occurred. Nothing would discourage secession more, he observed, than "the burning of a little gunpowder and a judicious use of hemp." At other times, he proposed letting the "wretched little oligarchy of South Carolina" have its way: "They have been an element of discord and panic—and now, we say, let us cast them forth though they enter all the swine of Cincinnati and run into the sea." Contempt for slavery was the simple consistency for which Howells strove in the shifting circumstances of the crisis.[44]

Writing his editorials, Howells assumed the stance of the "true man." In the atmosphere of conflict, the principal keepers of his conscience reverted to an assertive rhetoric of manliness. "Let it be known at once," William Cooper Howells observed on the eve of secession, "that the freemen of Ashtabula have no more compromises to make with crime—they will compound no more felonies—they will surrender no more rights. They have yielded all but *manhood* for peace. *That they will maintain.*" Lowell was inspired by a similar aggressive spirit. He pointed out that during the Revolutionary War "blood was as freely shed to secure our national existence as milk-and-water is now to destroy it."[45]

Though he matched his father and Lowell in his public pronouncements, Howells was far from belligerent. He and a philosophical friend had concluded that slavery would endure another two hundred years. In one of his literary essays, Howells searched for an illustration of how lies acquire credence when enlarged. He hit on the analogy of war, in which "throat-cutting on a vast scale becomes battle and glory."[46] Concealing his true face behind his agitator's mask had been a psychological necessity, but it became increasingly difficult as the secession crisis intensified.

Howells found relief from his struggles in a surfeit of parties and dances. Emerging from his "intellectual solitude," he was surprised to learn that penance was necessary before Columbus society would accept him on its old terms. He reestablished good graces in time to meet an intriguing visitor from Vermont named Elinor Mead. She was vivacious, witty, and interested in the arts, an assertive "American girl" of the type Howells would later celebrate in his novels. Though he concealed his infatuation with Elinor from his father, he admitted to his sisters that he had become involved in "a violent flirtation."[47]

Elinor Mead had been surprised and impressed when told Howells was an *Atlantic* contributor, but since the retirement of Lowell, the magazine had begun to disfavor Howells's Heinesque poems. Fields, Lowell's replacement, wanted narrative poems on American subjects similar to Howells's antislavery poem, "The Pilot's Story." Hoping that prose might win his way to Boston, Howells concentrated on his analytical novel. The alternative of free-lancing in New York had lost more of its appeal with the demise of the *Saturday Press*. In the fall, Howells noted that the *Press* was "slightly suspensory," and it soon fell victim to the capricious literary marketplace. Howells was attracted to another alternative. He had been wondering whether his campaign biography might gain him the post of consul to Munich. While sensitive to the Republican charge that political appointees were "partisan hacks," Howells believed that in Munich, on Heinesque ground, he might truly become a poet. In early March he obtained a letter on his behalf, signed—for the sake of conscience as well as influence—by "all the office-holding virtue" of Ohio from the governor on down.[48]

The tenuousness of Howells's vocational prospects revived his old anxieties. In late March he sent a letter home representing himself in the self-deprecatory guise of Geoffrey Winter, and Victoria in the sympathizing guise of Jane Grove. "Dear Vic," he wrote, "after I began to see thoroughly the meanness and hollowness of that wretched little village-life, and narrowed the circle of my days to the limits of home, you made me many a dreary Sunday evening pleasant. You were always kind and full of sympathy, and believed in me, often when I could not believe in myself." Because Victoria had shared his literary ambitions, but was now imprisoned in Jefferson, caring for their retarded brother, Henry, Howells felt an unspoken rebuke in her self-sacrifice. "I am sure," he said, "when I think of the good, unselfish life you live, devoting yourself to poor little Henry, I am quite ashamed of myself, and want to do something better than achieve reputation, and be admired of young ladies who read the 'Atlantic.' I take myself quite sharply to task, and go on being just as 'languid and base' as before."[49]

Bouts of self-recrimination made Howells vulnerable to the rush of events that followed the firing on Fort Sumter in the early morning hours of 12 April 1861. To spread the electrifying news, the *State Journal* put out a special Sunday edition, and a crowd hungry for details gathered at the newspaper office to read the telegraphic dispatches. Within a few days, President Lincoln had issued a call for 75,000 ninety-day men to put down the Southern rebellion. Soon Columbus, like other state capitals, was an armed camp. All through his life, Howells retained a vivid image of the volunteers who descended upon the city in "a tidal wave of youth." Most of the "transfigured" young men were under twenty-five. Singing and shouting with "wild hilarity," they marched down the sidewalks with interlinked arms.[50]

As an agitator, Howells was expected to mobilize minds. He supported the radical cause as it had been transformed by war by drawing from the traditional republican theme of self-sacrifice. Citizens had become "too sluggish, too secure, too selfish," he observed, but the war had imbued them with purpose: "They say that the deaf can hear in a great uproar. Thank God! amid the thunders of the cannon at Charleston, the voice of honor and of patriotism has at last reached the dull sense of the people. This blaze of battle lights up the path of duty with its glare." Howells's voice matched his father's. "This is our war, our cause," William Cooper Howells declared to antislavery Republicans in Ashtabula County. He observed that the young volunteers had answered a holy summons—they all wore the beautiful "air of crusaders."[51]

While keeping in step with his father and other radical agitators,

Howells teemed with dissent. His true feelings soon overflowed in a letter to Victoria:

> Everything is in an uproar here, and the war feeling is on the increase, if possible. There has been a sort of calm to-day in the city, but down at the camp the carpenters were busy building barracks, and the troops were drilling and the mad and blind devil of war was spreading himself generally. The volunteers seemed to be in very good spirits, and to look upon campaigning as something of a frolic. A good many of them are young boys—not over eighteen. . . . Poor fellows! I pitied them but being at work on a patriotic paper, I tried to see some sense in the business they had undertaken, but couldn't. . . . I don't see that the war could have been avoided, but it is not the less a stupid and foolish war on that account. War is always stupid and foolish.[52]

As new waves of youth arrived in Columbus, Howells became more distressed. Many of those who joined Columbus companies were friends and acquaintances. Some had shared rooms at the College or frequented the literary houses of Columbus society. One of the earliest to volunteer was Howells's closest friend, Comly. The companies that arrived from Ashtabula County, including the Giddings Zouaves and the Jefferson Guards, were filled with fa-miliar faces. Though many of the volunteers were young boys, "manliness" was the lesson of the hour. The volunteers exerted themselves in pugilistic displays and in constant marching. "The whole state resounds with the 'left! left!' of the monotonous and ubiquitous drill sergeant—," Howells observed, "a sentiment that may be tortured into a reproach by such conscience[-]stricken people as have not yet volunteered."[53]

He would not volunteer, Howells told Victoria, "so long as there are people more eager to go." But the waves of volunteers only intensified the claim on his conscience.[54] Hearing that his philosophical correspondent, Holmes, had volunteered, Howells shot off an anxious letter:

Is that true? If so,—how? why? when? For myself, I have not yet gone in. But who knows himself now-a-days? I seriously contemplate a Zouave company now forming here of my young men friends, who offer me a privacy, on favorable terms. But as I said, who knows himself? The hot weather comes on. The drill will be very hot and oppressive. And whatever valor I have had in earlier years, has been pretty well metaphysicked out of me, since I came of thought.

Your New England fellows, by Jove! are glorious. And you've heard how Ohio has done? It *is* a great country, isn't it? And what a magnificent age—for throat-cutting. Bon dieu! how sad was the error of the people that died last year! [55]

The mixture of astonishment, flippancy, pride, and bitter irony reflects Howells's ambivalence. His most poignant note was his refrain, "who knows himself." In the sudden shift of circumstances, Howells had lost the moment when it appeared that he might answer this question once and for all.

Howells feared that volunteering would delay and possibly derail his literary career. Though he felt that he had chosen the higher cause, his decision tortured him throughout his life. Marching with interlinked arms, the youthful volunteers represented the "manly" solidarity of his generation, one that left him out. In a recurrent dream, one that he first had in his youth, his volunteering peers came back to claim him. Howells envisioned "shapes of armed men, who, sometimes heralded by martial noises, sometimes approaching with awful, silent tread, passed in procession to the house where I was concealed, prone upon the floor or crouched cowering in corners, in the frenzied endeavor to keep out of the range of sight of the windows through which the death shot was to strike me." [56] The image of marching men and the sound of martial noises tie this dream to the days following the firing on Fort Sumter when Howells heard the monotonous call of the drill sergeant as a voice of conscience.

Though Howells remained steadfast to literature, literature succumbed to the war. He complained that "literary newspapers have all suffered a war change and reek of gunpowder and blood." He was disappointed to see that even the *Atlantic* had gone "gunpowderfully" into the war, filling itself with "cartridge papers." With his literary plans in disarray and his generation's sacrifice to the war beginning, Howells began to reveal his disaffection in his *State Journal* writing. On 12 June news arrived of a skirmish at

Great Bethel, in which twenty-five volunteers had been lost, largely through the bungling of the Union general Pierce. Among the dead was the *Atlantic* contributor Theodore Winthrop, whose articles had celebrated his regiment's progress from New York to Washington. "He fell at Great Bethel," Howells remarked bitterly, "an offering to Freedom and General Pierce's 'absence of mind.' "[57]

The massive clash of arms at Manassas on 21 July compelled Howells to subdue his dissent. Though the reported ante of lives had been upped from twenty-five to three thousand, defeat at Manassas, he asserted, would not discourage "true men." Returning to the republican theme of self-sacrifice, he added that defeat would have the beneficial effect of rousing the "easy going, confident North" to employ its "whole strength."[58]

The requirement that he wring meaning from battles he considered senseless epitomized the dissolution of autonomy Howells had felt from the beginning of the war. The coming of war had deranged his literary plans, roused his latent sense of selfishness, and taken command of his voice. Howells had left the intensely subjective Geoffrey Winter immured in inertia and longing for repose. Now the obscure causes felt within the self that determined character and directed individual destiny seemed allied with more powerful, external forces beyond individual comprehension and control.

In mid-August, Howells was finally released from his painful position when another change at the *State Journal* left him out. He had already begun to concentrate on office seeking, finally securing his second choice—the consulship at Venice. He needed a fresh start, for in late July the *Atlantic* editors rejected "Geoffrey Winter." When Howells visited Cambridge after arranging his consular appointment in Washington, Lowell gave him new incentive. Lowell jested that Howells should be poisoned for taking the Venice post away from the painter William Stillman. Howells understood Lowell's pointed allusion to the fabled Venetian means of redress. Stillman had intended to write a book that would supersede John Ruskin's *The Stones of Venice*. Lowell expected Howells to make his opportunity in Venice count just as much. This expectation was flattering and fortifying. With great anticipation, Howells returned to Jefferson to await his departure. On the day he said his good-byes and left his family, beginning his longest and most distant separation from home, he jotted in his diary, "Mihi cura futuri"— "My care is for the future."[59]

CHAPTER 9

Desperate Leisure

To make one live in others, this is the highest effect of religion as
well as of art, and possibly it will be the highest bliss we shall ever
know.

HOWELLS, 1895

Howells viewed his four years in Venice as "a great part, a vital
part" of his youth. He stated that he would never feel "exiled"
from Venice. He believed that the city altered "the whole course
of [his] literary life." In Venice, Howells became a "gentleman,"
by his own definition someone "who has trained himself in morals
or religion, in letters, and in the world." Given the "measureless"
leisure of his consular post, he expanded his knowledge of literature, history, and art, extended his facility in languages, and honed
his powers of observation. The result of these labors was *Venetian
Life* (1866), the book that made "friends with fortune" and gained
his entrée to Boston.[1]

The personal achievement of Howells's Venetian years is expressed in his idea that the "gentleman" is someone who has disciplined his impulses so that his manner grows "naturally out of
habits of self-command and consequent habitual self-respect."[2]
While in Venice, Howells maintained an edge of self-control against
his feelings of uselessness and despair. He took Lowell's advice

deeply to heart, steering clear of his "Heine-leeshore," sweating out Heine's influence "as men do mercury." Lowell's strenuous images precisely convey Howells's determined effort. Although Howells found that the leisure of his consular post was measureless, he also found that it was "desperate."[3] Adhering to Lowell's vision of a moral universe required a drastic turn of mind, one that denied the insights Howells derived from his desultory experience. Consequently, the identity he formed in Venice was one of compromise rather than true synthesis. Believing that he could fail no more, Howells made healthy-mindedness his desperate necessity. But the feeling persisted that he had concluded too hastily. Later in life, Howells returned to the problems he had determinedly put aside in Venice.

On 15 December 1861, eight days after his arrival by night in Venice, Howells recorded his initial impressions in his diary. He had been dazzled by the city's spectacular beauty as he glided by gondola to a hotel resting at the water's edge. Nevertheless, he had felt an "intolerable despondency of spirit." Intense sadness before decayed magnificence was a conventional aesthetic posture, but his feeling genuinely expressed the burdens he had carried with him from America. "The emptiness of my life, the vagueness of my purposes—were before me," he reflected, "and it seemed all so hopeless and insane. I did not know why I had wandered hither, nor what I should do in after years (to be spent, please God! amid the hard and earnest struggle of my native land)—with the experience to be garnered in the indolent desolation of Venice."[4]

Utterly alone for the first time in his life, Howells saw his problems writ large in contrasts between Venice and America. Although he had longed for release from daily toil in Columbus, he now missed the "hard and earnest struggle" of American life. America seemed a world he had "died from," but he could not lay the ideals of his native land to rest. "Go-ahead" excitement now appeared essential for "incentive." "Our people are manlier and purer than any in Europe," he wrote Victoria; "and though I hope to stay here my full four years, and know I shall profit by my experience and enjoy it, I still hope to go back and engage in the strife and combat, which makes America so glorious a land for individuals."[5]

Howells's homage to strenuous individualism was set against his fascination for Venice's "indolent desolation." As he recalled in *Venetian Life*, he had come "in some unconscious way to regard her fate as [his] own." Melancholy Venice seemed the outward representation of his negative, idle-man persona. Clothed in "feminine" Catholic mysticism, her sadness was suffusive and beguiling. She threatened to drown the unwary in a wash of impotent sentimentalism. Writing to his friend Piatt, Howells reflected that Venice is "so beautiful, so sad—and I could be unlimitedly sentimental here, and melancholy and wretched."[6]

Little in his beautiful and sad surroundings helped Howells resist his feeling that he was an idle man whose desires were useless and damning. Indolence seemed the prevailing standard of good living. Only the street beggars demonstrated any "industry" and "energy." On his first day in the city, Howells had put himself in sympathy with the fashionable ease of Venetian life. The approved style for young men of his class was "lodgings near the Piazza di San Marco," "meals at the restaurant Capello Nero," and "coffee thrice a day at Florian's Cafe." Florian's was a noted gathering place for "young idlers," the resort of "tranquil, indolent, Italian loafers," men who carried canes, wore gloves, and stared at passing women.[7]

Because his consular duties interfered very little with his inclinations, Howells set aside a part of each day to "loaf" at Florian's. In these small doses, the cafe's indolent atmosphere was pleasant and diverting, but Howells's enjoyment was soon tarnished by an "inscrutable feeling of shame," a self-loathing he could not understand. "As I sat in the caffè last night, talking to the Russian gentleman whose acquaintance I have made," he confided in his diary, "I began to feel stealing upon me a sense of the deepest humiliation, and when he had shaken my hand, and gone to the opera, I sat brooding over this fantastic sentiment of shame, and came home at last, a disgraced and ruined man."[8]

18. Howells, dressed in the style of the "idlers" at Florian's Cafe, probably in early 1862. He described his initial impressions of Venice for his friend John J. Piatt: "The gondolas are more black swanlike than you could have thought, San Marco and the Doge's Palace are more glorious, the Bridge of Sighs more impressive, and the Titians and Tintorettos more gorgeous and magnificent than your gayest dreams of them. Each morning the golden angel on the crest of the Campanile looks in my drowsy eyes and makes me glad and proud to be here, and it is only when I remember how utterly alone I am that I feel at all downcast."

Prompted by his conscience, Howells plunged immediately into his literary study. While considering his moment of self-accusation at Florian's, he pondered his sensitivity to "influences, often the vaguest and remotest," but he set aside this Heinesque sense of self when he began his work. The previous fall, he regretted writing "The Pilot's Story" when Fields cited it as an achievement beyond his Heinesque poems. Now he tried to write Fields's kind of poem, a narrative in hexameters recreating a Western camp meeting. But even with an objective story Howells could not resist subjective intrusions. He framed "Louis LeBeau's Conversion" with a description of its motive: This "story of free, wild life in Ohio," he stated, had suddenly come to him as he moved "unwilled," gazing with "idle" eyes on desolate Venetian splendors. Although he tried to exclude all that was "unnatural, extravagant or improbable" from his poem, Howells included his doleful identification with Venice. He hit the *Atlantic* mark but felt no sense of accomplishment. He recalled that after completing "Louis LeBeau's Conversion" in early February 1862, he "idled away" the rest of the year in "homesick despair." More accurately, he put away thoughts of immediate literary success and began to concentrate on his unresolved problems.[9]

As he struggled with his old malady of homesickness, Howells found little relief in Venetian society. He felt Venice lacked the natural freedom he had enjoyed in Columbus. Italians seemed to place little trust in sincerity. Chaperones strictly guarded young women from male predators. Social gatherings were dull and uninspiring, all "whist and dowagers." Few Italians indulged Howells's wish to use his beginner's knowledge of Italian. He formed friendships with Italians, but most seemed to hold themselves aloof. He made acquaintances more easily in the international community and gained partial relief from his homesickness by accepting the welcome of the American consul at Trieste, the historian Richard Hildreth. But his contact with Hildreth and his family was sporadic. He relieved his loneliness by writing lengthy letters home and by living for the future in his diary, especially for the moment —sealed by an exchange of letters—when he would marry Elinor

Mead and bring her to Venice. Displaying the playfulness and wit that had won him a following in Columbus society, he made his diary a long love letter to Elinor. He recounted their courting days in Columbus, and knowing she would later read his entries, he teased her with his attraction to Venetian beauties and charming American tourists. He was careful to add frequent laments for her absence: "O, E. G. M., why *aren't* you here!"[10]

While he expected Elinor to lighten his burdens, Howells knew he must face one formidable difficulty alone. His recurrent sense of shame and his persistent homesickness contributed to his dread of the coming spring when he expected another bout with his devil, hypochondria. Writing in his diary in early January, he prepared himself for the confrontation:

I have been oppressed for the last few days with a gloom that I cannot shake off, and which will rather increase, as I know from the terrible experiences of the past, with the approach of spring and summer. It is the cruel fatality of my life, that the season which makes others so glad, only makes me wretched, and that the summer brings pleasant thoughts and associations to them, while it raises a devil for my torment. God keep me through the coming summer! At home, I had father to counsel and sustain me; at Columbus the gentlest hearted of men was my physician and kindest friend; but here I am utterly alone, with none to speak my thoughts, or reveal my forebodings to, and if my hypochondria does not turn into madness, it will be through God's mercy, and those strong efforts of the will which I have taught myself to make. I must learn to fix my mind firmly upon this point: that no great evil has happened to me yet, and that I have either exaggerated or created all the calamities with which I have threatened myself.[11]

A test of will came sooner than Howells imagined, in late February before the Venetian spring. Finding a German translation of Euripides' *Medea*, he read late into the night, undoubtedly fascinated by its portrayal of an inexorable destiny neither just nor vengeful. He wrote the single word, "Terrible!" in his diary beside his notation of the tragedy. When he finished his reading, he rose "with aching shoulders, dull brain, and a cold shuddering from the heart out." The next ten days he suffered a fever that made him yearn, he told his father, "for voices, for steps, for touches, for

tenderness that made sickness an empire when I was with you."
Howells avoided overstudy that would "tax [his] brain," and a
fatherly Italian named Tortorini, a retired pharmacist, prescribed
and administered medicines. Soon he was "on the high turnpike
road to recovery." "I think," he concluded in his report home, "it
was only my determination to not give up that saved me from a
very long illness."[12]

For Howells, seeing his recovery as a triumph of will was
important because it steeled him against the "hints of hypochondria" that began with warm weather. At the beginning of the
summer, he reiterated his determination: "Now's the time, if ever,
to encounter the dragon and overcome it." He added the water-
cure remedy to his routine for "insurance benefits," bathing three
times a week in the Lido. Following this disciplined regimen,
Howells survived the summer and was able to pronounce it the
"least oppressive" he could remember.[13]

"Strong efforts of the will" were important, but another defense
was more significant. Preparing for his struggle in January, Howells had written in his diary, "I must interest myself deeply in
study." When he informed his father of his recovery from fever,
he added a report on his work: "I write a good deal, here, and after
the first confusion of ideas, consequent upon the novelty, begin to
think somewhat—which is better than writing. I take it that if I
do nothing in literature publicly until the war is over, it will be
just as well."[14] The key to his developing strength was the direction of his study and writing. Howells began to work himself out
of his confusion of ideas by turning against his Heinesque sensibility. He began to purge himself of all that seemed "sentimental" in
his reactions, particularly his urge to make vagaries of self his
predominant concern.

Having left Geoffrey Winter languishing in the banal desolation
of Dulldale, Howells feared he might lose himself in the exquisite
ruin of Venice. Later in *Venetian Life*, he recalled his change of
mind. Though alone in an alien land, he felt "curiously at home,"
drawn to the city's aura of indolence and hopelessness. He "rioted
sentimentally" over Venice's picturesque displays of mournful de-

cay and pathetic charm. But in his writing he reacted against this passive, sentimental response. His self-referential vision of Venice seemed a "luxurious dishonesty" that detracted from "the whole hard truth of things." "One's conscience, more or less uncomfortably vigilant elsewhere, drowses here," he wrote, "and it is difficult to remember that fact is more virtuous than fiction."[15]

In a diary passage slightly elaborated in *Venetian Life*, Howells described a moment when he had asserted the priority of fact:

It had snowed overnight, and in the morning when I woke it was still snowing. The flakes fell softly and vertically through the motionless air, and all the senses were full of languor and repose. It was rapture to lie still, and after a faint glimpse of the golden-winged angel on the bell-tower of St. Mark's, to give indolent eyes solely to the contemplation of the roof opposite, where the snow lay half an inch deep upon the brown tiles. The little scene—a few square yards of roof, a chimney-pot, and a dormer-window—was all that the most covetous spirit could demand; and I lazily lorded it over that domain of pleasure, while the lingering mists of a dream of new-world events blent themselves with the luxurious humor of the moment and the calm of the snowfall, and made my reverie one of the perfectest things in the world. When I was lost the deepest in it, I was inexpressibly touched and gratified by the appearance of a black cat at the dormer-window. In Venice, roofs commanding pleasant exposures seem to be chiefly devoted to the cultivation of this animal, and there are many cats in Venice. My black cat looked wonderingly upon the snow for a moment, and then ran across the roof. Nothing could have been better. Any creature less silent, or in point of movement less soothing to the eye than a cat, would have been torture of the spirit. As it was, this little piece of action contented me so well, that I left every thing else out of my reverie, and could only think how deliciously the cat harmonized with the snow-covered tiles, the chimney-pot, and the dormer-window. I began to long for her reappearance, but when she did come forth and repeat her maneuver, I ceased to have the slightest interest in the matter, and experienced only the disgust of satiety. I had felt *ennui*— nothing remained but to get up and change my relations with the world.[16]

Howells's rooftop reverie represents the kind of passive brooding he had begun to challenge. He emphasized the narrowness of his self-referential perspective in numerous ways. His vision is constricted by the window and offered in the Heinesque manner with aspiration toward wholeness excised. Lacking a concern for larger meaning, his vision reverts to indulgence: It is an exercise of "indolent eyes," it occurs "lazily," it draws upon a "luxurious humor." It ends not in satisfaction, but in satiety and *ennui*, the bane of all idlers. In his *Venetian Life* version, Howells concluded with his intention "to get up and change [his] relations to the world." He expressed an urge that had become more and more imperative in Venice. He desired to escape the "luxurious dishonesty" encouraged by Venetian desolation and engage "the whole hard truth of things," to free himself from passivity by plunging actively into the surrounding reality, to seek the Venice of fact rather than the Venice of fiction.

The day before he recorded his rooftop reverie, Howells had seen an arresting allegorical engraving of "Luxury" that seemed to him the work of genius. The figure, he wrote in his diary, "was represented, naked, swathed in spiked bands of wire, and with paps not only on the chest, but down the side, to the number of half a dozen—a monster, that turned my stomach, notwithstanding the symmetry and beauty of her form otherwise. The effect was ineffably disgusting—such as I could not have thought would be produced in that way. It looked vile—filthy—sowish." Howells meant to return to the street stall where he had seen the engraving to study it more carefully.[17] While there is a hint of sexual ambivalence in Howells's reaction, his fascination derived primarily from the allegorical meaning of the engraved female figure. Swathed in spikes, the figure represented the horror of entrapment in luxurious, passive, "feminine" self-indulgence.

Howells ceased reading Heine. Instead, he studied Italian, trying, as Lowell had suggested, to sympathize with Dante's vision of wholeness. After doing the churches "in the most stupid guidebook-in-hand manner," he retreated to prepare for a more knowledgeable and independent perspective on Venetian art and architecture. Unlike other Protestant Americans, he resisted the appeal of Catholic art that idealized an all-forgiving maternal being. He allowed himself only small doses of idealization in the midst of St. Mark's powerful symbolism, where he felt "the spirit oppressed with the heaviest load of sin might creep nearest to forgiveness, hiding the anguish of its repentance in the temple's dim cavernous recesses."[18]

Howells soon discovered that he was becoming more and more fascinated with the life outside cathedrals and art museums. As a committed republican, he admired the Venetians' steadfast "demonstration" against their Austrian rulers, but he was most intrigued with scenes of common life—the hardy beggars, the argumentative gondoliers, the everyday dramas he could observe in the streets and on the canals. In early spring, Howells began reading the plays of the eighteenth-century Venetian dramatist Carlo Goldoni and discovered the Venice that was opening before his eyes. Goldoni, Howells recalled, "had the power of taking me out of my life, and putting me into the lives of others."[19]

Although he still considered himself a poet, Howells had acquired an alternative interest in Venetian society that expanded as he continued to cultivate his reporter's eye and instinct. During the summer of 1862, he started the sketches that later made up *Venetian Life*. By his own estimation, the "living human interest" in his sketches predominated over their "sentimental and historical relish." He wrote his sketches to please Lowell, skirting the emotions that pervaded his brooding, subjective poems. He emphasized moderation and self-control, the marks, he said, of the gentleman. Instead of strenuous encounters with deathly things, he presented "average," everyday realities. The truth he sought was available to all, not only to the fragmented vision of the Heinesque poet.[20]

By the end of his Venetian consulship, Howells had disowned his Heinesque sensibility, expressing his dislike of "personality and consciousness" in poetry. His reading of Italian poets and his study of painting and sculpture, he suggested, had weaned him from his "excessive admiration" of subjectivity in literature. But he admitted that he was also "insensibly moulded to this shape by other influences which [he] could not so readily specify."[21] Heinesque subjectivity had seemed a dead end, a form of indulgent "feminine" passivity. Howells had turned from his "Heine-leeshore" toward the example of Lowell. Attention to outward things had promised to release Howells from his feelings of uselessness and his disbelief in a moral universe.

This critical turn of mind did not happen at once. Howells required Lowell's recognition as well as his own assent, and word from Lowell came only after "a long series of defeats." Meanwhile, Howells's identity conflicts remained intense. He was aware that when he left the languid eddy of Venice, he would sink or swim in the stronger currents of American life. His friendship with Richard Hildreth revived his awareness of the hazards of the American scene. When Howells visited the historian in Trieste, he found Hildreth humorously distracted. When asked to say farewell as Howells was about to return to Venice, Hildreth turned absently and recited a line from *Paradise Lost*. Later Hildreth's wife confided that he had not been delivering a witticism. Neither was he merely eccentric. During his newspaper days, he had been afflicted by "overwork of the brain." Now he was suffering the consequences. After recording this revelation in his diary, Howells wrote Victoria that he was working with "a new access of earnestness." He was determined to avoid Hildreth's fate. He wanted something "better and higher" than newspaper life.[22]

Other painful reminders of his past difficulties troubled Howells. Writing long letters to his family and waiting impatiently for replies, he was sensitive to the slightest pressure from home. He had promised Joseph part of his earnings for the family debt, but he found he had nothing to send. He pleaded for understanding of "unavoidable delays," but soon he was suffering more bouts of shame and guilt. Placating his mother was also stressful. Accompanied by his sisters' laments for his absence, her siren call intensified Howells's homesickness. "We want you to come back unchanged[,]," his mother had written on his departure. "Come just as you went for we could never Love you more th[a]n we do and we want you to come the same dear boy that you always were and you will find full warm heart[s] only to[o] happy to receive [you]." Howells wanted to stay in Venice until he could return to America a new person. Relying on his mother's sympathy, he told her that he had dreamed of being home again, just as she wished, but in his dream he was oppressed by the thought of opportunities lost in Venice.[23]

When questions arose over his engagement to Elinor, Howells defended his autonomy more forcefully. He scoffed at his mother's and sisters' anxiety that Elinor might be "violently intellectual," an austere New England bluestocking. "She's good as well as smart—," he chided, "and in fine I love her very much, which may remotely account for my intending to marry her." His father's reaction, apparently suggesting that marriage might interfere with his literary accomplishments, was more unsettling, requiring a more convoluted self-defense. "I quite comprehend your feeling in regard to me," he replied to his father, "and it is a matter of grief to me that I may not realize all your expectations. Here I shall not, I know; for the climate is decidedly against me. What little vitality I have is kept at so low an ebb; that I can scarcely more than exist, and work of any kind is almost impossible."[24] Confronted with his father's expectation that he fulfill his role as the family hope, Howells gestured toward his psychological fragility and his strange susceptibility to frustrating maladies. He suggested to his father that now, as always, he was battling against the odds.

Enduring the summer of 1862 without a return of his "hypo" was a considerable accomplishment for Howells. In addition to the emotional pressures exerted from home, other aspects of his situation might have thrown him into guilty despair. The war news was extremely disconcerting, a constant refrain of Northern defeats, from Shiloh in April to Antietam in September. The massive number of deaths deprived the war of moral purpose, reducing it to a "bloody farce." Howells was nonetheless vulnerable to guilt concerning his duty. His single act for antislavery Republicanism was to demand his *carte de visite* returned from a Mississippi "rebel" who misrepresented himself as a citizen of Maine. When news arrived of fearful clashes near Richmond, he became "dreadfully anxious" about the war's outcome: "I'm afraid that even proclamations of abolition won't help us out," he wrote his father. "In fact, in the case of my run-off, the breeching broke long ago, and having lost consequently my trust in Providence, I don't know where *to* put it." Howells resisted the guilt he felt for his "run-off" with the bitter thought that no one was responsible in a desultory world.[25]

Howells's anxieties concerning the war increased as the war threatened to strike near home. In mid-September his brothers Sam and Johnny were among the "Squirrel Hunters" who converged on Cincinnati to save the city from Confederate attack. While no attack actually occurred, the possibility that the Howells family would be spared actual fighting became less likely with the draft. Howells offered his "every cent" to buy a substitute for Joe, who was the mainstay of the *Sentinel*. If the draft took Sam, Howells hoped he would go, though he finally made his offer of money stand for Sam as well.[26]

While brisk volunteering in Jefferson Township eliminated the draft, the threat to his brothers drove Howells back to Heinesque expression. In a poem he entitled "The Mulberries," he described his poet-persona as "listless dust by fortune blown / To alien lands." The poem was a personal statement, he told Victoria: "We pay too much for pride and ambition. I have given home, and peace and almost hope for them; and now I feel that if I died to-day my name would perish to-morrow. And I would hardly care. —So little it comes to, after all, this world." Although he had initiated his "sanative" turn toward Lowell, Howells still had much further to go.[27]

On Christmas Eve 1862, Howells married Elinor in Paris, and by the first week of January they had set up housekeeping in Venice. They found an apartment in an old palace named Casa Falier, with a balcony overlooking the Grand Canal. "We're very near the iron bridge, and just opposite the Academy," Howells wrote a friend. "Our house-keeping is the funniest and delightfullest thing in the world. The house was furnished with an absolutely irreproachable servant . . . and she takes care of us as tenderly and jealously as if we were children." Venice acquired new meaning through Elinor's artistic gaze. Their talk became a "jargon . . . of Titians and

Tintorettos, of paintings and sculptures and mosaics, of schools and of manners." As Elinor sketched paintings by the masters of Italian art, Will sat to the side, reading the masters of Italian literature. He believed his interest in Elinor's artistic pursuits provided "objective" correctives for his tendency toward "personality and consciousness." Elinor, he frequently found, also possessed the wit to tease "Pokey" out of his gloomy reveries. "It is hard to understand," Howells wrote his father, "that the world has not just been made for us to enjoy ourselves in."[28]

With Elinor's happy alteration of his life, Howells disclaimed the Heinesque more unequivocally. When his father noticed a reprinting of a Heinesque poem in which Howells's poet-persona, enclosed in a well, stares at the uncomprehending stars in the noonday sky, Howells replied that he no longer identified with the poem. "I have got out of the well sometime since," he observed, "and have so little prospect of unhappiness before me that I think I shall probably give up seeing the stars by day in the forlorn manner indicated by the poem."[29]

Howells was strengthened further when he and Elinor began anticipating the birth of their first child. "I suppose I have always been old and grave enough," Howells wrote his father following the birth of their daughter, Winifred, in December 1863, "but the new relation put upon me, has made me more thoughtful than ever, and has awakened new desires to be good for the little one's sake, if I cannot for my own."[30]

Another change that diminished his anxieties was the success of a new family enterprise. The printing of soldiers' songbooks had proven profitable and promised to pay off the family debt. "I suppose you girls remember that pride is sinful," Howells teased his sisters, "although father *is* prospering so splendidly in business. Do you wear silk dresses when you're scrubbing and white-washing? I suppose Vic has a satin Iron-holder, and mother a silver hook for taking off stove covers, and Annie a brocade dish-cloth."[31]

His new responsibilities urged Howells to look more definitely toward his future. "I am trying gradually," he wrote home, "to carve myself out a place." Hoping most of all for a place in Boston,

19. Casa Falier. "[We lived]," Howells wrote of the apartment to which he brought Elinor in December 1862, "in one corner of an old palace on the Grand Canal, and the window of the little parlor looked down upon the water, which had made friends with its painted ceiling, and bestowed tremulous, golden smiles upon it when the sun shone. . . . Through this window, also, we could see the quaint, picturesque life of the canal; and from another room we could reach a little terrace above the water."

he sent his best efforts to the *Atlantic*. By the end of January 1863 he was awaiting the editors' verdict on a number of poems, an article, a story, and a batch of Venetian sketches. Through Charles Hale, a friend of Elinor's family, he had opened another line of communication with Boston by agreeing to write a periodic letter on Italy for Hale's Boston *Advertiser*. He also had begun to seek a publisher in England for a book of poems.[32]

Besides efforts to publish his best work, Howells began to toy with the strategy of pursuing a number of lesser projects geared to success with sentimental readers. In May 1863 he elaborated a plan to his former publisher, Frank Foster, who had moved his business to New York. He offered a "pretty little volume," a longish poem in hexameters modeled on *Evangeline*, to be illustrated by Elinor.

Howells outlined a plot that mildly parodied the conventions of sentimental love. He proposed that the book, which he titled in the proper diminutive, "Disillusion: A Little Venetian Story," would end agreeably in "comic farce—in marriage, of course." Prepared for the Christmas trade, it could be sold for twenty-five cents. Putting aside his disdain of self-promotion, Howells concluded, "So cheap a book could be sent to nearly every journal in the country, and could be thoroughly advertised."[33]

Foster agreed to the project but then began to beg off, citing a host of publication problems. It soon appeared that the poem would never be ready for the Christmas trade. By early fall, Howells's other literary projects were also floundering. No publisher in England would risk a book of poems. The *Atlantic* remained silent. Hearing nothing from that "purgatory," Howells concluded the worst and offered his Venetian sketches to Hale. This alternative made his sketches a species of journalism rather than literature, but publication in Boston, he reasoned, would "reach just the public I wish to please." Before Hale accepted his offer, Howells received a comprehensive note of rejection from the *Atlantic*, summarized in the statement, "Not one of the MSS. you have sent us swims our sea." Howells's literary prospects had dwindled to his sentimental story-poem "Disillusion," his lesser, more commercial effort. "My heart is half sick with working and hoping," he lamented in his diary, "to no visible effect."[34]

Just when his literary prospects narrowed to the project he had described to a correspondent as something "to amuse the least worthy of your half hours," Howells received a letter from home that revived his feelings of selfishness. His family had tried to withhold the news, but Johnny revealed that Sam had enlisted in an Ohio regiment. The antislavery Howells family now had an antislavery volunteer, the brother from whom least was expected. The "sudden shock" chased away Howells's other thoughts. "Poor Sam!" he exclaimed. "He puts us all to shame, and I pray God will keep him safe through the war." He later puzzled over Sam's character, suggesting that he may have volunteered because of his failure to "grapple with life." This reduction of Sam's motivation

20. Elinor Mead Howells, ca. 1865, in Venice. Elinor kept a diary of calls, domestic happenings, and "excitements." She enjoyed bathing at the Lido and breakfasts of muskmelon and cheese in the "Venetian way." Visiting Americans included Henry Ward Beecher. While sightseeing in Rome, Elinor recorded a "blunder." At the top of Saint Peter's, she declared, "The Pope is a murderer to let men risk their lives in illuminating the dome."

did not remove Howells's self-blame. "There is a sting of remorse at the bottom of my anxiety for [Sam]," he admitted, "for I have not always been so patient with him, nor so mindful of him, as I ought to have been. But, indeed, of whom have I ever been thoughtful, but of myself?"[35]

While Howells celebrated his new life with Elinor, the war news lost its accusatory resonance. But Sam's enlistment brought the war home. As the eldest brother not essentially needed in the family business, Howells, more than Sam, was the obvious volunteer. Howells had offered all of his savings to buy Joseph a substitute, but he had hesitated over Sam. With his least-worthy literary effort as his surest thing, Howells had no literary success to counter his self-accusations.

To supply this need, Howells began a new poem, "greater," he wrote Joseph, "than any I have yet written." The poem he called "Ordeals" concerned the war and love between two brothers. One brother is killed, and the other carries the news to their parents, who lose all awareness of their second son: "My father talked as if he had no son / My mother forgot to name me in her prayer." Feeling that he should have died in his brother's place, the second brother volunteers even though he sees the war as purposeless. The two brothers are spiritually reunited when the second brother dies on the battlefield. The doubting brother is proclaimed worthy because his death has worked for the unseen good of all. Howells spoke truly when he told Joseph that his new poem had "a great deal of heart and real feeling in it," for his tale of two brothers was an attempt to lessen his guilt. He completed the poem in January 1864 and sent it to the *Atlantic*, where it was lost in silence.[36]

Before Howells finished his poem, Winifred was born. Cherishing this "trust," he found some relief from his self-accusations. He proposed a more modest account of himself: "I've grown doubtful of great success—at least sudden success," he told Joseph. "I've been chasing celebrity all my life, with only a glimpse of it now and then, and now I shall try to be content, if I can tell some truth and do some good."[37]

For Howells, literature continued to be a source of both pain

21. William Cooper Howells in July 1863 during his successful campaign for the Ohio Senate. William Cooper Howells opposed the wartime fusion of political parties because he feared fusion would compromise antislavery principles. But in 1863, after President Lincoln issued his Emancipation Proclamation, he joined the Union ticket made up of Republicans and war Democrats. He was given a role of honor in the official ending of slavery. In February 1864, he offered the joint resolution in the Ohio legislature ratifying the Thirteenth Amendment to the Constitution.

and solace. While literature raised the specter of selfish ambition, it seemed to offer atonement. Howells found his ambivalent feelings mirrored in George Eliot's *Romola*. He strongly identified with the character Tito Mellema. "[He] was not only a lesson," Howells recalled, "he was a revelation, and I trembled before him as in the presence of a warning and a message from the only veritable perdition." Howells was especially struck by the mixture of worthy and damnable inclinations in Tito, "how near the best and worst were to each other, and how they sometimes touched without absolute division in texture and color." [38]

Although he had not freed his literary ambitions from the charge of selfishness, Howells believed they permitted the greatest good. He thought it strange that at the same time he was reading *Romola*, he was fascinated by a series of melodramatic novels by Caroline Wigley Clive that were "full of unwholesome force." While seeing his fate as Tito's, he sympathized with Clive's hero, Paul Ferroll, a murderer who escapes all punishment. Howells was willing to evade Eliot's entangled world of salvation and damnation by imagining a world where there was no retribution for sins, even though this world was presented with the tawdry melodramatic devices he usually despised. [39]

Howells began the new year restored. Though Sam remained in danger, he was still alive, wintering with Grant's army near Chattanooga. Life with Elinor continued pleasantly, and Winifred grew more endearing every day. "Though I am not dead yet (except in a literary sense)," Howells confided to the poet Edmund Stedman, "I venture to pronounce myself happy." Things were not altogether bleak. Hale had accepted his Venetian sketches, and Howells was polishing them for their Boston debut, hoping to impress Lowell with his intellectual growth. Feeling he had finally skirted his "Heine-leeshore," he told Stedman that by shifting from subjectivity to objectivity he had grasped the "purer ideal." [40]

A new ideal did not ensure a living. Losing faith that his commercial venture with Foster would succeed, Howells considered comparable projects, laying plans for a lavishly illustrated study of the "Out-Door Beauty of Florence." When he offered the idea to *Harper's*, he retained a slight hold on his literary integrity, citing his "unsentimental liking for the Italian civilization" as a point in his favor. But to sell the project with the greatest possible force, he abandoned all pretense. "I do not know if I have given you the idea," he concluded his letter, "that while this would be a book 'without which no gentleman's library would be complete,' it would also 'form an elegant ornament to the centre-table,' etc." Returning to America the author of a sumptuous, heavily advertised book destined for the parlor table was not Howells's idea of worthy success.[41]

Soon afterward, Howells turned to another project, one that promised to avoid all compromises, redress past defeat, and establish his sense of literary vocation on the very highest ground. Lowell had returned to editing, taking over the *North American Review* with Charles Eliot Norton. With a direct line open to his mentor, Howells prepared another assault on Boston. He planned a scholarly article to combine his everyday observation of the Italian people with commentary on their current literature. He had decided that Italian comedy captured the essence of Italian character at a time when Italians were struggling for national unity and political independence. Howells knew this thesis would attract Boston's Italianate scholars. He meant to rise to Boston standards and consider all of Italian comedy, past and present.[42]

Howells set to work in late February 1865. "At present," Elinor wrote his sister Annie, "the head of this house is devoted to the Italian Comedies—reading them in the soberest manner possible from morning till night. . . . We breakfast, dine & sup on comedy, and go to the theater in the evening to see the charming comedies of Goldoni played." Until late May, Howells concentrated on this single project.[43]

The result of Howells's labors, "Recent Italian Comedy," was a carefully crafted message to Lowell. Howells announced that he possessed credentials—scholarship and correct ideas—that made him acceptable among Brahmins. Presenting himself as a "sojourner and student of human nature in Italy," he demonstrated his assumption of a healthy-minded perspective that disclaimed the Heinesque. He used the words *dreamful* and *subjective* pejoratively. He showed no sympathy for a mysterious and fragmentary reality. Italian civilization, he asserted, was "transparent," and any clear-eyed observer could see the workings of human impulses beneath its thin veneer. Howells implied that Italian comedy depicted human impulses in true proportion by avoiding morbid self-analysis. He turned his former conception of "modern doubt" completely around, contending that the phrase supported "faith and virtue" against cynical assessments of human nature. Modern doubt was doubt of all that questioned the "dignity of man," the "purity of woman," and the "sanctity of all family ties." Howells concluded that Italian comedy sought the ideal, "a loftier code of morality for the whole conduct of life." Corresponding to his emphasis in his Venetian sketches, with their concern with outer rather than inner realities, "Recent Italian Comedy" bowed gracefully to Lowell's authority.[44]

Howells later described Lowell's acceptance of "Recent Italian Comedy" as the turning point of his life. In his letter, Lowell reiterated his belief in Howells's "genius," intimating that he expected its full realization. He repeated that Howells must purge himself of Heine, once and for all. And to Howells's immense delight, he expressed his liking for the Venetian sketches that had begun to appear in the Boston *Advertiser*. "They are admirable, and fill a gap," Lowell wrote. "They make the most careful and picturesque *study* I have ever seen on any part of Italy. They are the thing itself." Lowell's recognition consoled Howells for all his defeat and made him feel worthy to have suffered and survived. Set against Howells's dark imaginings, Lowell's letter was "a dawn, a sunburst, a full day!"[45]

Lowell's recognition gave Howells the start he desired in literature and validated his turn away from the Heinesque. This recognition was all the more powerful because it came in the nick of time. While working on his article and then waiting for word from Lowell, Howells endured experiences similar to those that had brought on the full force of his self-accusations and the torments of his hypochondria. Because he placed all of his hopes on his article, he worked to near exhaustion, fending off attacks of nervousness. Then, in the midst of his work, word arrived from home that raised the whole question of his "run-off." Jim Williams, the boon companion of his earlier youth, had been killed in the war. Feeling his friend's death the "keenest loss" of his life, Howells pushed on with his article, completing it on 20 May. He announced to his family that he was sick from the strain. The next day, all possibility of relief vanished when he learned that his brother Johnny had died of "spotted fever" while attending school in Cleveland. William Cooper Howells had written Elinor, so that she might break the news gently to Will.[46]

Instead of celebrating the completion of his article, Howells threw himself into writing an elegy for his brother. For days he anxiously awoke at daybreak, the hour of Johnny's death. He had reason to blame himself for his brother's fate. Through his insistence Johnny had been given the opportunity to attend school in Cleveland. Howells had pleaded that at least one family member deserved "the stamp of the schools." He had invested Johnny with his own earlier hopes, urging his brother to cherish an opportunity he had been denied when he was seventeen. Howells may well have thought that were it not for his own ambitions, Johnny might have never left home and might still be alive. Howells lamented to his sister Annie, "I wish I were as fit to die as he was. But I am not, and never was since I was a little child."[47]

Amid much desperation and grief, Howells completed an article that signaled his turn to healthy-mindedness. Sending his article to Lowell on 24 May with an urgent request to know its fate immediately, he waited until 21 August for a reply. Through the summer he turned doggedly to other projects. The uglier turn of the war in midsummer when Grant began his methodical approach to Richmond left him depressed. In the cool of his Venetian apartment, Howells contrasted himself with "the poor souls fighting for us in the steaming swamps of Virginia." He was dismayed to learn that Sam had exposed himself to rifle fire to claim the experience of battle. The war seemed bloody and absurd, but it still exerted a claim on his conscience: "I begin to lose any faith in our triumph," he wrote home, "though it may be I am guilty to despair; when hope is the sole duty I can fulfill."[48]

When Lowell's letter finally arrived and cleared the skies, Howells immediately wrote a long reply full of his devotion and his literary plans. Once more, however, his elation was short-lived. Four days later, he received an "extremely distressing" letter from his father. The news from home concerned another draft and the possibility that Jefferson Township would not clear itself by volunteering. If Joe were taken, Will was expected to take his place in the printing office.[49] Arriving just when his literary future seemed assured, his father's letter threatened to bring back the anxieties of the past.

The letter Howells immediately wrote his father oscillated between his wish to satisfy family claims and his desire to assert his independence. With open acquiescence, he stated, "Your wish must be law with me . . . I cannot think of anything more unworthy than my shrinking from a duty of the kind." Howells told his father that he would come "cheerfully and gladly" to assume Joe's work on the newspaper. "If poor Joe must be taken from you, and it appears desirable to you," he assured him, "you have only to say come, and I come."[50]

Howells clearly understood the antagonists in his inner struggle and paid homage to that part of himself that desired to play the dutiful son. Along with his several statements submitting to family authority, however, he offered an argument that none in his family would wish to refute. Early in his letter, he emphasized his incompetence in managing the business side of the newspaper and printing shop. He pointed out that the new venture in soldiers' songbooks would tax him even more. A more powerful and conclusive representation of his unfitness was his allusion to his psychological fragility, his unfathomable illnesses, and his terrible breakdown in Jefferson: "I do not conceal from you that I have not yet in the three years shaken off my old morbid horror of going back to live in a place where I have been so wretched. If you did not live in J. and my dear Johnny did not lie buried there, I never should enter the town again. It cannot change so much but I shall always hate it." If his family wished to overthrow his long years of restoration, particularly the time in Venice when he had defeated his "hypo," seemingly for good, all they had to do, Howells implied, was to say, "come."[51]

Along with his suggestion that he would become a dismal, suffering failure—a kind of Geoffrey Winter—if his father called him home, Howells portrayed himself in a positive light. Literature, he suggested, was the only way he could fulfill the Swedenborgian admonition to live a worthy life: "My only usefulness," he said, "is in that direction." Before Lowell's letter, he could not have made this claim convincing to himself, but now he had a credible success backed by a great name. He quoted all the pertinent parts of Lowell's letter and enumerated the many literary tasks he would have to complete before he came home.[52]

Although he strongly asserted his commitment to literature, Howells made another reference to his defense of last resort. He told his family that he could never stay a long period in the West, for a literary career was possible only in the "great literary centres" of the East. Even three months in Ohio seemed impossible. It would "dissipate" his chance to profit from the "éclat" he had finally gained in Europe, and this waste would weigh him down: "[These difficulties] would not be altogether in other men, but [a] great part in myself. I should be dispirited and discouraged. Many subjects that I could write up at once in New York or Boston, and thus open place to me, would pass from my mind, and the struggle for position would be twice as hard."[53]

After Howells sent the letter off to his father, he began battling his self-accusations. He scattered references to his "selfishness" in his next letters home. A month passed before a "long, kind letter" finally arrived from his father, alleviating his conflict between his duties and his desires. The threat of the draft taking Joe had come to nothing, as Jefferson Township filled its quota with volunteers.[54]

This news provided Howells with a significant emotional victory. He was not to be tested by returning to Jefferson, but surviving this final personal crisis in Venice demonstrated his self-control. His seven-month effort to sustain his healthy turn of mind had steeled him against doubt and desperation, and his father's blessing had sanctioned his continued effort to make literature, and literature only, the means of his atonement. In the wake of his emotional victory, Howells's sense of a desultory world receded, becoming an undercurrent of his thought and feeling. He expressed his new, more positive sense of life to his sister Annie, stating that his share of the family grief had done him good: "I have little fear, now, knowing how bad the worst is, and I think I have won a kind of faith out of the want of hope."[55] Sustaining faith while confronting the sad contradictions of life became the moral perspective Howells tried to maintain throughout his life.

The day finally came in Italy when Howells felt that he could bid farewell to his youth. Before returning to America, he made a tour of Italian cities, gathering impressions for future writing. While in Rome, he passed the Protestant Burial Ground, and knowing Keats was buried within, he stopped to offer his homage:

When I came to the grave of Keats, [he wrote soon afterward,] it was with a pang of personal grief that I read how "in the bitterness of his heart," he had asked that it might be written there, "Here lies one whose name was writ on water." The world has long ago written his name in the brass of its endless praise; but how vain and empty is the compensation! As I stood by this saddest spot on earth, it seemed now to be Johnny lying there, and now my own earlier youth, on which "the malice of my enemies" has had power even to death,—my enemies of my own house, my restless ambition, my evil thoughts, my scornful hopes, my sinful deeds. What if the world shall some day wake to applaud what I do? I fear my name will still be writ on water.[56]

Gesturing to his past, Howells tried to write an end to his troubles. Despite his reservations, he felt he had risen above his Heinesque sense of life. He trusted that along with his earlier youth, he had forever buried all the self-defeating enemies of his own house and all the difficulties that had frustrated him for so long.

22. Howells in Venice, 1 May 1865.

PART III

Later Life and the Return to Youth

CHAPTER 10

Bound to the Highest
and the Lowest

Every life is a fragment; it is broken off always and never rounded
to a close; something in it is still left unfinished.

HOWELLS, 1890

Returning to America in August 1865 with an edge of self-control
and a literary success that opened opportunities in the East, Howells gained a position in New York as a writer for the *Nation*. After
a period of seasoning, he was called to Boston to become the
assistant editor of the *Atlantic Monthly*. When Howells assumed his
place in his Celestial City, he followed Lowell's advice to "work in
entire subordination," even to "*écraser*" himself. Helped by his
fluent Italian and his dogged editorial work, Howells slowly eased
into Brahmin graces, eventually succeeding to the *Atlantic* editorship. Although twice blackballed by unknown Brahmins in the
Saturday Club, he finally gained the imprimatur that came with
admission. Before long, Oliver Wendell Holmes pronounced that
Howells had become so assimilated to Boston that he seemed to
have "cheated some native Esau out of his birthright."[1]

Nevertheless, Howells felt that he was living in false comfort,
that he had found no home of his own in Boston. To gain his

independence, he began to devote more time to his writing apart from his editorial duties. In his fictionalized *Suburban Sketches* (1871), he brought the style of wandering ruminations he had developed in Venice to the consideration of life in Cambridge. He described common, everyday scenes but often satirized his sentimental, "aesthetic" perspective. He also introduced jarring references to his sense of homelessness: "We wander away and away," he wrote in one instance; "the dust of the road-side gathers upon us; and when some strange shelter receives us, we lie down to our sleep, inarticulate, and haunted with dreams of memory, or the memories of dreams, knowing scarcely more of the past than of the future."[2] By the time Howells wrote *Their Wedding Journey* (1872), he had gained more control over the idler figure and expressions of anxiety in his writing. He had settled on the novel—abandoned since "Geoffrey Winter"—as his life's work. Begun as an extension of his travel writing, Howells's novel writing eventually carried him back to the full range of problems he had put away in Venice.

In his article "Recent Italian Comedy," Howells had defined the domain of the novel, contending that it "must bear the causes which produce character, and reveal all the feelings and explain the circumstances which influence men to action."[3] This urge toward absolute understanding was tempered by the strategy he had tested while writing "Geoffrey Winter." Each novel, much like a Heinesque poem, could be seen as a fragment of the whole, providing a limited perspective to be enlarged by successive efforts. Howells began his novel writing in the 1870s with a surge of faith, believing that successive confirmations of a moral universe were possible in closely observed segments of everyday life. Each of his novels focused on a few characters whose thoughts and actions he could examine thoroughly. "I see clear before me a path in literature which no one else has trod," he wrote his father, "and which I believe I can make most distinctly and entirely my own."[4]

Howells's optimism corresponded to the optimism of the middle class in the decade immediately following the war. With the troubles of war and reconstruction fading from their minds, Northern middle-class Americans were anxious to renew belief in inevitable progress. Henry Ward Beecher hit the highest pitch of celebration: "There is not on the face of the globe," he declared, "another forty millions that have such amplitude of sphere, such strength of purpose, such instruments to their hand, such capital for them, such opportunity, such happiness."[5] Few middle-class Northerners matched Beecher's gift for hyperbole, but many, including Howells, shared Beecher's expectation of expanded possibilities. Howells committed himself to writing about the "commonplace" lives of average Americans, whom he took to be people risen from relatively humble beginnings to respectable, middle-class status.

Howells intended a fine-tuning of middle-class civilized morality. While he disdained the role of preacher, he confessed that he would be "ashamed and sorry" if his novels "did not unmistakably teach a lenient, generous, and liberal life."[6] In the novels he wrote during the 1870s, his targets were the minor ailments of middle-class life, such deviations from self-control as those caused by sentimental infatuation and snobbish intolerance. He understood that his main readers would be a small number of middle-class women, but he assumed that they would be the "best sort," like the literary women of Columbus society. The domestic ideal suggested that reaching these women would be critical, for their influence was the heart of family life and the basis of morality.

Novel writing became Howells's way to claim moral importance for the literary vocation. Increasingly, however, he confounded his own ends by representing the impulses and motives of his characters as profoundly complex and nearly inscrutable. His novels subverted his wish to believe that people were free to choose the civilized, humane courses of action. In *The Undiscovered Country* (1880), his narrator observes, "The origin of all our impulses is obscure, and every motive from which we act is mixed. Even when it is simplest we like to feign that it is different from what it really is, and often we do not know what it is."[7] In *The Undiscovered Country*, Howells had shifted from the minor ailments of middle-class life to one of the troubling questions he had confronted during his youth. He asked once again how religious and moral belief could be confirmed in what appeared to be a desultory world.

The Undiscovered Country, Howells reported to his father, was no "mere love-story," but treated "serious matters."[8] He presented the tortured spiritualist seeker Dr. Boynton, whose self-obsessed quest for proof of an afterlife distinguishes him from the relatively calm characters of Howells's previous novels. Boynton is unconsciously possessive of his daughter Egeria. Using his parental authority and his mesmeristic powers, he forces her to act as his spiritualist medium. He has suppressed Egeria's "warm, happy, and loving" nature, making her "purely the passive instrument of [his] will."[9] Boynton's control over his daughter represents a subversion of moral nurture.

Howells intimated Boynton's ambivalence toward his daughter's sexuality, but he suggested that these feelings were part of a more pervasive distrust of the next generation. "Those who doubt were bred in the morality of those who believed," Boynton observes. "But how shall it be with the new generation, with the children of those who feel that it may be better to eat, drink, and make merry, for to-morrow they die forever? Will they be restrained by the morality which, ceasing to be a guest of the mind in us, remains master of the nerves?"[10] Howells cautioned parents to trust moral nurture and the next generation's capacity for self-control. When Boynton's mesmeristic spell loses its power, Egeria regains her autonomy. Understanding that he has "played the vampire," Boynton is repentant. He dies comforted but not fully at ease in his doubts.[11]

Although ending "in full sunshine" with most of its dark speculations dissipated, *The Undiscovered Country* looked forward to the severe crisis of faith Howells suffered the next year while writing *A Modern Instance* (1882).[12] To a greater degree than in *The Undiscovered Country*, he broke with his strategy of fragmentary vision and returned to tensions he had experienced during his youth. In January 1881, Howells resigned as editor of the *Atlantic*, feeling that his "nerves [had] given way under the fifteen years' fret and substantial unsuccess." *A Modern Instance* was the first novel he wrote after deciding to "throw [him]self upon the market." [13] Howells could no longer depend on his editorial position to sustain his sense of literary vocation. He required a success far exceeding his previous novels. This novel would stand alone as a symbol of his Swedenborgian usefulness.

As he began his novel, Howells was immersed in other troubling reminders of his youthful trials. Winifred had started to experience vertigo and other nervous symptoms he had suffered at the same age. In early 1880, Howells expressed confidence that Winifred was "growing up a strong, tranquil nature." But during his writing of *A Modern Instance*, her ailments were diagnosed as "nervous prostration." James Jackson Putnam recommended the "rest cure" developed by S. Weir Mitchell. But Winifred remained "morbid and hypochondriacal." "I see these days of her beautiful youth slipping away, in this sort of dull painful dream," Howells wrote, "and I grieve over her." [14]

Despite his return to past tensions, Howells pushed on with *A Modern Instance*. He had armed himself with a theme of unquestionable seriousness. His novel treated divorce, a subject he thought "only less intense and pathetic than slavery." Divorce raised critical issues for middle-class Americans. Guardians of civilized morality idealized marriage as the way to refine self-control, subordinate passion to reason, and anticipate divine love through self-renunciation. Struck by the disparity between these high ideals and the apparent prevalence of divorce, Howells offered a cautionary tale about a couple whose "love marriage" is broken by their "undisciplined character[s]." He promised his publisher that he would not "let the moral slip through [his] fingers." [15]

Proposing to treat his theme "tragically," Howells brought forward the concept of "destiny" he had formulated during his youth. Giving his novel the working title of "The New Medea," he meant to test whether a common case of divorce would demonstrate the moral liberty of men and women or the mere caprice of chance. Would his characters suffer because they will or because they must? Would he be able to preside like destiny over their careers, showing the workings of a moral universe? He approached these questions with his deepened understanding that often "interests and passions are complex and divided against themselves."[16]

The protagonists of *A Modern Instance*, Marcia Gaylord and Bartley Hubbard, possess little of the self-control admired by middle-class moralists. Squire Gaylord, a lawyer and the chief resident of Equity, Maine, brought up Marcia without the aid of his wife, who abandoned her responsibility for moral nurture when the Squire would not budge from his religious skepticism. The Squire "spoiled" Marcia. "What resulted," the narrator notes, "was a great proficiency in the things that pleased her, and ignorance of the other things."[17] Howells implied that parental indulgence fostered Marcia's passionate and jealous attachment to her father and later to Bartley Hubbard.

Bartley Hubbard's past is more obscure. He is an orphan "pitied" and "petted" by his benefactor, but he appears in the novel somewhat like the "stranger" of uncertain origins and intentions, the force of evil that bedeviled middle-class advice writers. Bartley is "smart" rather than sincere. He wins the editorship of the *Equity Free Press* and espouses the cause of the village with burlesque ardor. He cynically attends all the churches to cultivate universal favor. Some villagers are duped by Bartley's "hunger for sympathy." "If his sarcasm proved that he was quick and smart, his recourse to those who had suffered from it proved that he did not mean anything by what he said; it showed that he was a man of warm feelings and that his heart was in the right place."[18]

Bartley enjoys basking in Marcia's admiration while remaining "free as air." But his parody of sincerity, playing upon the middle-class ideal of "influence," entangles him with Marcia against his inclinations: " 'Of all the women I have known, Marcia,' he said, 'I believe you have had the strongest influence upon me. I believe you could make me do anything; but you have always influenced me for good; your influence upon me has been ennobling and elevating.' "[19] Later, desiring sympathy for a chain of discomfort that begins with indigestion from a midnight snack of mince pie and toasted cheese, Bartley inadvertently tells Marcia he loves her and seals their engagement.

Begun on this fragile basis, their engagement does not last. During a quarrel, Bartley injures his assistant on the *Free Press*. When Bartley seeks legal counsel from Marcia's father, the Squire brings out Bartley's flirtatious past. Marcia breaks their engagement but soon wants Bartley back. "Don't you see," the Squire urges, "that the trouble is in what the fellow *is;* and not in any particular thing he's done? He's a scamp, through and through; and he's all the more a scamp when he doesn't know it. He hasn't got the first idea of anything but selfishness."[20] Despite her father's pleas, Marcia marries Bartley. As they begin life anew in Boston, they resolve to be good and patient with each other.

In the Boston phase of his story, Howells concentrated on Bartley's damning selfishness. Consistent with the Swedenborgian notion of "ruling love," he allowed glimpses of Bartley's latent good. Had Bartley heeded the promptings of his conscience and worked to change his disposition, Howells suggested, he might have received "mercy and reprieve from the only source out of which these could come." Earlier, for instance, Bartley is walking in the forest when, the narrator observes, "a curious feeling possessed him: sickness of himself as of some one else; a longing, consciously helpless, to be something different; a sense of captivity to habits and thoughts and hopes that centered in himself, and served him alone."[21]

Although Bartley has moments of self-disgust, his reveries invariably end in self-justification and hasten his decline. His fellow journalists consider him "smart as chain-lightning and bound to rise," but his disregard of ethics in journalism reveals his moral decay. Another sign of his lapse is his fondness for Tivoli beer. The more he consumes, the more bulk he acquires—"a corky, buoyant tissue," thinks his colleague Ricker, "materially responsive to some sort of moral dry-rot." Bartley begins to "deal savagely" with Marcia, becoming verbally abusive in their quarrels. He disputes the middle-class ideal, asserting that nothing "sacred" exists in their marriage. After losing steady work as a journalist, he takes money borrowed from his college friend Ben Halleck and gambles on mining stock. He uses more of the money to bet on the presidential election of 1876, backing the Democrat Tilden rather than the Republican Hayes. Finally, after a vicious quarrel with Marcia, he flees west. His "good instincts" revive in Cleveland. He tries to buy a return ticket to Boston but discovers someone has stolen the remainder of Ben Halleck's money. Emphasizing the notion of ruling love, the narrator concludes, "Now he could not return; nothing remained for him but the ruin he had chosen."[22]

As Howells rushed Bartley to judgment, Howells's trust in a moral universe wavered. His pairing of Bartley's *chosen* ruin with the *chance* theft of money expressed his ambivalence. Howells was not always content to allow Bartley choices; he sometimes forced the issue by pronouncing Bartley damned.[23] While he was deciding Bartley's fate, Howells broke off his work on the novel. Before stranding Bartley in Cleveland, he fell sick with a fever that sent him to bed for "seven endless weeks." Elinor reported that he had become "very, very nervous." During his convalescence, Howells recalled, he "could not read anything of a dramatic cast, whether in the form of plays or of novels. The mere sight of the printed page, broken up in dialogue, was anguish." He was not bothered by narratives of travel, which he read in great number. He was disturbed only by "fiction."[24]

Howells's revulsion from "fiction" was a symptom of his vocational crisis. He had proposed adjusting the moral perspectives of his readers when he lacked a sure sense of moral order himself. How responsible was Bartley for his sins if he lacked a rudimentary foundation for self-control? How much autonomy did Bartley possess when, in the Squire's words, he was "all the more a scamp when he [didn't] know it"? Could Bartley, like Poe, an earlier "ultimate bad man," be dominated by "inherited frailties"? Howells raised this possibility when he returned to his novel. Considering the fate of the Hubbards, the lawyer Eustace Atherton reflects, "somehow the effects follow their causes. In some sort they chose misery for themselves,—we make our own hell in this life and the next,—or it was chosen for them by undisciplined wills that they inherited."[25]

By portraying the impoverishment of religious and moral traditions, Howells further diminished the degree of individual responsibility he could attribute to the Hubbards. In *Equity*, church socials have replaced the means of salvation, and the solitary moral watchman, the Squire, is a sarcastic unbeliever. Ben Halleck's parents represent the "simple and good" traditions of early village migrants to Boston, but cloistered in their high-walled garden they have lost touch with the city. By investing all their hopes in Ben, furthermore, the Hallecks have made him morbidly sensitive. Lacking self-confidence, Ben has not found a "useful" vocation.[26]

As he described a defeated family hope in Ben, Howells renewed his own self-accusations. Doubt of his authority to pass judgment on Bartley eroded Howells's sense of moral usefulness, raising the specter of his own selfishness. These feelings forged an identification with his chief sinner, causing a shift in his novel. When Howells began writing after his illness, he merged the fate of his characters with the fate of civilized morality in the modern world. The last chapters of *A Modern Instance* represent Howells's failed effort to free himself from the grip of his self-accusations. He tried to disarm the principles of civilized morality in debates between a moral prig, Eustace Atherton, and a moral cripple, Ben Halleck. The debates focus on emotional issues raised when Howells lost his affirmative sense of literary vocation. As the voice of civilized morality, Atherton argues that Ben has no right to desire Marcia, a married woman, even though she has been abused by her husband and is wretchedly unhappy.

In terms directly out of middle-class advice books, Atherton contends that Ben represents the perfection of civilized morality, the ideal of self-control grown from "implanted goodness that saves,—the seed of righteousness treasured from generation to generation, and carefully watched and tended by disciplined fathers and mothers in the hearts where they had dropped it." But Ben is an exceedingly reluctant exemplar. He considers himself "a miserable fraud." He argues that Atherton's reasons for denying him Marcia—the need to provide a moral example and preserve the institution of marriage—are mere abstractions. Atherton nevertheless persuades Ben to flee to South America and to stay

there for years rather than tarnish the ideal. This absurd proposal
—the suggestion that ideals can be maintained only if they are
never tested—reduces Atherton's authority, as does Howells's representation of Atherton's cushioned existence. "Natural goodness
doesn't count," Atherton exclaims while defending the notion of
implanted goodness. "The natural man is a wild beast, and his
natural goodness is the amiability of a beast basking in the sun
when his stomach is full." Atherton speaks these words in his
luxurious dining room suffused with sunlight, while sipping delicately flavored souchong tea from expensive translucent china.[27]

Howells closed *A Modern Instance* with Atherton's first admission
of self-doubt. Bartley has been killed in retaliation for a scandal-
mongering newspaper article, and Ben has asked Atherton if he
must continue to renounce Marcia even though her husband is
dead. Howells summed up the crisis of civilized morality in Atherton's last words, "Ah, I don't know! I don't know!" Despite this
final note of bewilderment, however, Atherton's less extreme assertions defined Swedenborgian notions Howells could never finally abandon—the idea that "every day is Judgment Day" and
the idea that everyone is morally responsible, no matter how perplexing motive and action may appear.[28] Still, Howells raised the
doubt whether judgment were possible when individuals had no
charge of their fate and when the moral universe seemed in desperate disarray. Perhaps, he suggested, no one is responsible in a
desultory world.

In *A Modern Instance*, Howells narrowed his focus to issues impli-
cated in his own sense of selfishness, but he proposed a way to
reach beyond his individual suffering and moral confusion to a
larger community. He described an idea he would later call "complicity," drawing inspiration from the Pauline text, "Remember
them that are in bonds as bound with them." "We're all bound
together," Atherton declares. "No one sins or suffers to himself in
a civilized state, or religious state—it's the same thing. Every link
in the chain feels the effect of the violence more or less intimately.
We rise or fall together in Christian society. It's strange that it

should be so hard to realize a thing that every experience of life teaches. We keep on thinking of offenses against the common good as if they were abstractions!"[29]

With his idea of complicity, Howells brought forward a host of meanings from his childhood and youth. The biblical admonition to remember those in bonds as if you were bound with them was a common refrain of antislavery rhetoric. The image of bondage also evoked Howells's personal image of dancing in chains, a phrase that suggested both his aspiration to moral usefulness and his sense of confinement and diminished autonomy. Complicity promised release from subjection to mysterious forces. It brought to consciousness communal and Swedenborgian notions of mutual responsibility essential for Howells's atonement. Complicity expressed faith in a dominant moral order that compelled active engagement with others. Being bound to others was the inescapable condition of humanity. "No one for good or for evil, for sorrow or joy, for sickness or health, stood apart from his fellows," a Howells spokesman asserts in a novel, "but each was bound to the highest and the lowest by ties that centered in the hand of God."[30]

In the years that followed *A Modern Instance*, Howells attempted to renew a sense of complicity throughout American society. He assumed a more public stance by advocating clemency for the Haymarket anarchists. He believed the anarchists had been tried "for socialism and not for murder." Similar hysterical proceedings, he pointed out, "would have sent every ardent antislavery man to the gallows," men like Giddings and Wade, Wendell Phillips and Thoreau.[31] Howells strengthened his communal commitment by recalling his youthful radicalism and by reading Tolstoy's "heart-searching books." Tolstoy taught that the sole source of happiness was "never-ceasing care" for others, especially for the "vast masses" sunk in poverty and misery. Inspired by the imperatives of his own past and by Tolstoy's moral example, Howells declared, "It is a day of anxiety to be saved from the curse that is on selfishness."[32]

Howells's sensitivity to economic inequalities intensified his feelings of selfishness and gave greater urgency to his effort to make the literary vocation a force for class reconciliation and communal betterment. In *The Rise of Silas Lapham* (1885) and *The Minister's Charge* (1887), he parodied the myth of success, dismantling the middle-class ideal of the autonomous individual, while showing in intricate ways how business imperatives had penetrated American life. Figures like the newly risen paint king Silas Lapham and the poor country boy Lemuel Barker were strange to respectable fiction, but Howells was undeterred by reviewers' charges that he had introduced readers to "low" characters. After visiting the cotton and carpet mills at Lowell, he wrote *Annie Kilburn* (1889), assessing whether the plight of workers could ever move the hearts of the comfortable middle class. His pessimistic conclusion propelled him toward a more ambitious effort. Feeling he should accomplish something "for humanity's sake," he planned a novel that would fully express his ethic of complicity. "Words, words, words!" Howells exclaimed as he began writing *A Hazard of New Fortunes* (1890). "How to make them things, deeds."[33]

With renewed faith, Howells believed that the moment for translating words into deeds had arrived and that the literary vocation was essential for revitalizing the nation. Changes in the literary marketplace reinforced his sense that the time was critical. In a later essay, "The Man of Letters as a Man of Business," Howells expressed apprehensions he began to feel acutely in the late 1880s. He considered it "false and vulgar" to treat literature as a commodity; putting a price on words was "a truly odious method of computing literary value." But literature was increasingly tied to "huckstering." Abject dependence on the literary marketplace threatened the literary artist's moral autonomy. Howells believed that if the literary artist were lost, all others were lost. He feared that business was "the only human solidarity," that everyone was "bound together with that chain."[34] He hoped *A Hazard of New Fortunes* would force Americans to recognize the human solidarity of mutual responsibility, the solidarity sustained by ties of complicity.

To achieve a Tolstoyan sweep of vision, Howells set *A Hazard of New Fortunes* in the vast urban landscape of modern New York

City. As his principal theme he portrayed Basil March's education in complicity. Howells's portrait of Basil, his most transparent fictional persona, was deepened by Howells's own recent break with Boston and his plunge into the "vast, gay, shapeless life" of New York. Basil has been persuaded by his ebullient friend Fulkerson, a newspaper syndicator and "born advertiser," to leave the insurance business in Boston to become editor of a literary and artistic magazine Fulkerson is starting in New York. At first, Basil and his wife Isabel are reluctant to leave Boston, "the only safe place on the planet." But becoming editor of the magazine Fulkerson has christened *Every Other Week* would fulfill Basil's youthful dream of a literary career. Despite his humdrum insurance job, Basil has continued to write poetry and cultivate an intellectual life of "inner elegance." Basil and Isabel also believe New York would offer a refreshing change of pace, a chance to satisfy their inclination, formed during earlier days of European travel, to "divine the poetry of the commonplace." Still, New York is immense and daunting. "I'm terribly limited," says Isabel, expressing hesitations she shares with Basil, "I couldn't make my sympathies go round two million people; I should be wretched."[35]

Howells revived the vernacular device of confrontation to challenge the habitual views of the Marches. In place of the leveling vernacular character, he represented New York itself. "There seems to be some solvent in New York life that reduces all men to a common level," his narrator observes, "that touches everybody with its potent magic and brings to the surface the deeply underlying nobody."[36] While evoking a sense of personal estrangement and loss of identity, Howells's "nobody" also represents the realization of vernacular potential, the emergence of a being in its essential democratic state, stripped of the false sense of individuality promoted by emblems of respectable middle-class status.

Leaving their sequestered middle-class existence in Boston, Basil and Isabel are dismayed by the leveling solvent of New York life. The "picturesque raggedness" they find in the teeming tenement sections of the city once seemed to exist for their pleasure. But their confrontation with modern New York has undone their distanced, "purely aesthetic view" of impoverishment. When Isabel asserts that no "*real* suffering" exists among the poor because they have learned to endure their difficulties, Basil slightly qualifies her assertion. Suddenly they come upon a "decently dressed" man who is searching through garbage for food. Basil pursues the man, presses a coin in his hand, but comes away ashamed and confused. To escape their distress from this encounter, Basil suggests that he and Isabel retreat to the theater.[37]

The city not only obstructs the Marches' distanced enjoyment of the streets but also frustrates Basil's inclination to "philosophize" his experiences. An admirer of Basil's "striking phrases," Fulkerson has asked Basil to write sketches of New York life for the magazine. Testing his views with Isabel, Basil observes that no child could grow up in tenement housing with a middle-class conception of "home" because poor people lack means to give "character" to their dwellings. Basil then lapses into a discourse on the middle-class flat. He attacks the flat for having drawing rooms instead of living rooms, for fostering social pretense at the expense of family life. "Why, those tenements are better and humaner than these flats!" Basil exclaims. "There the whole family lives in the kitchen, and has its consciousness of being; but the flat abolishes the family consciousness." Basil escapes this line of reasoning by contrasting the middle-class house with the flat, but his philosophizing has already negated his initial proposition that nothing like the middle-class "home" could exist in a tenement. Isabel perplexes him further by taking him at his word. If a house is better than a flat, she declares, they will naturally seek a house, no matter the expense. "[Basil] had been denouncing the flat in the abstract," the narrator adds, "and he had not expected this concrete result."[38]

Basil's philosophizing is ad hoc, confined to abstract speculation and supported by no perspective that transcends his middle-class biases. He admits that his proposed sketches will probably be "very desultory." Since walking the city streets leads to unexpected, painful encounters with "sad and ugly things," Basil begins to limit his observations to scenes glimpsed from elevated railroad cars.[39] Flashing in and out of his mind, these scenes pose no danger of prolonged, disorienting confrontation. Distanced observation from the el, like the voyeurism of the theater, is narrow and escapist. From his high, comfortable perspective, Basil sees a kaleidoscope of nationalities and urban rot. The daze of shifting scenes, each too brief for analysis, lessens his anxiety over how to assess his experiences. But Basil continues to feel "vague discomfort." The narrator portrays Basil's "half recognition" that underlying forces exist in the "frantic panorama" he is witnessing:

Accident and then exigency seemed the forces at work to this extraordinary effect [of frantic panorama]; the play of energies as free and planless as those that force the forest from the soil to the sky; and then the fierce struggle for survival, with the stronger life persisting over the deformity, the mutilation, the destruction, the decay of the weaker. The whole at moments seemed to him lawless, Godless; the absence of intelligent, comprehensive purpose in the huge disorder, and the violent struggle to subordinate the result to the greater good, penetrated with its dumb appeal the consciousness of a man who had always been too self-enwrapt to perceive the chaos to which the individual selfishness must always lead.[40]

Behind this allusion to incessant Darwinian struggle are forces Howells discerned in different terms during his youth. His sense of a desultory world is suggested by the whole prospect of New York seeming "lawless, Godless," and without "intelligent, comprehensive purpose." This vision of life appears as a powerful force against faith in a moral universe, which can be confirmed only through "violent struggle." Howells's strenuous terms revive Swedenborgian admonitions. Moral action requires subordinating self to the "greater good" and resisting acts of selfishness that are the source of chaos.

Achievement of this greater good, Howells stressed in *A Hazard of New Fortunes*, required an essential first step—personal realization of complicity. The solvent of the city leaves Basil on the verge of this realization. His escape to the el is ultimately unsuccessful. He cannot "release himself from a sense of complicity with [life in the city], no matter what whimsical, or alien, or critical attitude he took."[41]

Yet the solvent of the city is not enough. Basil requires a more thorough education. Although the city reduces his middle-class defenses, he is more decisively challenged to give up his "self-enwrapt" habits by his relationships with others, particularly with a figure from his youthful past, the German radical Berthold Lindau. As the friend and teacher who had introduced Basil to the German language and the writings of Heinrich Heine during his youth in Indianapolis, Lindau represents a composite of Howells's youthful literary and political ideals, his current critique of capitalism, and his public defense of the Haymarket anarchists. Modeled on Otto Limbeck and refugees of the 1848 revolutions Howells had known in Columbus, Lindau speaks with the moral absolutism of radical Republican agitators like Giddings and Wade.[42] Lindau expresses Howells's most despairing view of the state of American civilization while offering Howells's utopian hope for a change to communal socialism. Appearing in his first scene as biblical and fatherly, Lindau is the very embodiment of conscience.

Meeting a tattered old man with a missing hand at a cheap Italian restaurant, Basil is surprised to recognize the friend of his youth. Lindau has lost his hand fighting in the Civil War for his antislavery principles, but Basil is saddened to learn Lindau is embittered toward his adopted country. Thinking he should pay Lindau back for his many past kindnesses, Basil considers various possibilities, but he forgets his old teacher until Fulkerson proposes that Lindau translate selections from foreign journals for publication in *Every Other Week*. When Basil conveys the offer to Lindau at his room near Mott Street, he learns that Lindau has chosen to live among the poor so that he will never forget their sufferings.

Lindau is no longer the "cheery, poetic, hopeful idealist" Basil had known during his youth. He has become a caustic and bitter opponent of capitalism. He angrily asserts that capitalists who presume to "give work" to the poor have already gathered their millions "from the hunger and cold and nakedness and ruin and despair of hundreds of thousands of other men." Unprepared by his "life of comfortable revery" to accept this view of capitalist enterprise, Basil thinks Lindau must have drawn his "curious" and "lamentable" ideas from his reading. Although he fails to tell Lindau, Basil considers it "droll" that as translator for *Every Other Week*, Lindau will be working for Dryfoos, the natural gas millionaire who is backing the magazine to push his idealistic son Conrad into a business career as a publisher.[43]

Although he sometimes feels guilty for neglecting the subject of Dryfoos, Basil settles into the comfortable role of provider for his old teacher. At a publicity dinner for the magazine, however, Lindau learns not only that Dryfoos is a rich speculator in gas fields but also that he has a past of vicious union breaking. Despite Basil's efforts to silence him, Lindau denounces Dryfoos and leaves the dinner after impassionedly advocating a society of brotherhood where everyone would have work and where all the people would own the mills and mines. Calling Lindau "a red-mouthed labor-agitator," Dryfoos orders Basil to fire him from the magazine.[44] Without considering the consequences for himself and his family, Basil replies that he will resign as editor rather than persecute Lindau. Basil soon regrets his words, but he is never forced to back them up. Wanting nothing to do with Dryfoos, Lindau quits the magazine and returns pay that he says is covered with blood. When Basil tries to dissuade him, they argue and part in anger.

Basil is troubled by a "fantastic sense of shame," but he consoles himself by thinking that he never imagined Lindau was serious in his "preposterous attitude" toward self-made millionaires like Dryfoos, "men who embody half the prosperity of the country."[45] After this slight bout with guilt, Lindau fades from Basil's mind. Much later, Basil is wandering the city streets, trying to draw closer to the atmosphere of a streetcar strike that he intends to work into his sketches. Encountering a struggle between police and strikers, he hears a shot and is shocked to see Lindau fall under the blows of a policeman's club. When he reaches Lindau, he discovers Conrad Dryfoos, who had tried to prevent the beating, dead beside him. Lindau survives for a time but dies after the amputation of his arm. A welter of talk follows as Basil and Isabel try to sort out the meaning of Lindau's and Conrad's deaths.

Until this time, Basil had steadfastly resisted the sense of com-

plicity represented by Lindau. Howells emphasized Basil's penchant to forget. After first meeting Lindau at the restaurant, Basil
had forgotten his teacher until reminded of him by Fulkerson. He
had forgotten him again after their quarrel.[46] Basil had also distanced himself from Lindau by allowing others to dismiss him
with epithets. He had not dissented when they called Lindau a
"crank" and an "old dynamiter." And Basil himself had described
Lindau as "a fraternity and equality crank." These lapses jarred
with Basil's admiration of Lindau's kind, high-minded, unselfish
nature. Basil had defended his friend when Dryfoos ordered his
firing, but Basil had been incensed in part because Dryfoos had
treated Basil like the "foreman of a shop."[47] Furthermore, Basil
himself had tried to silence Lindau, first at the dinner and then
when he urged him to keep Dryfoos's money, a course that would
have compromised the moral integrity that gave power to Lindau's
words.

Basil begins to take Lindau's words seriously only after Lindau
is gone. Lindau's descriptions color Basil's lament that American
civilization is an "economic chance-world" that pits each against
all:

It ought to be law as inflexible in human affairs as the order of day and
night in the physical world, that if a man will work he shall both rest and
eat, and shall not be harassed with any question as to how his repose and
his provision shall come. Nothing less ideal than this satisfies the reason.
But in our state of things no one is secure of this. No one is sure of
finding work; no one is sure of not losing it. I may have my work taken
away from me at any moment by the caprice, the mood, the indigestion
of a man who has not the qualification for knowing whether I do it well
or ill. At my time of life—at every time of life—a man ought to feel that
if he will keep on doing his duty he shall not suffer in himself or in those
who are dear to him, except through natural causes. But no man can feel
this as things are now; and so we go on, pushing and pulling, climbing
and crawling, thrusting aside and trampling underfoot; lying, cheating,
stealing; and when we get to the end, covered with blood and dirt and sin
and shame, and look back over the way we've come to a palace of our
own, or the poorhouse, which is about the only possession we can claim
in common with our brother-men, I don't think the retrospect can be
pleasing.[48]

Recognizing his past failings, Basil asserts everyone knows this vision of modern American life is true but anyone who says so is labeled "a fraud and a crank."[49] At long last, Basil realizes a kind of complicity with the poor in a shared sense of insecurity. But Howells showed that Basil's revelation is insufficient, for the basis of Basil's sympathy is narrow and self-referential. Fretting that *Every Other Week* will fail now that Conrad is dead, Basil jokes that he will beg coins on the street. He suggests that the man he and Isabel had seen searching for food when they first came to New York had been working a similar fraud. Just when he is remembering the poor, Basil is beginning to forget.

Basil's fleeting recognition of shared oppression leads nowhere. He proposes no goals, utopian or otherwise, for changing conditions. Margaret Vance, the young society woman whose "romantic conception of duty" has led her to actual work among the poor, recognizes that the Marches suffer the "nervous woes of comfortable people." These woes, Howells suggested in the final pages of his novel, usually issue in talk rather than action. When Dryfoos sells *Every Other Week* to Basil and Fulkerson, Basil is relieved of his anxieties. Forgetting his indictment of the economic chance world, he follows the motto that "business is business." He turns out one employee and reduces payments to contributors. *A Hazard of New Fortunes* ends ironically in talk, with the Marches questioning the sincerity of Margaret Vance.[50]

Twenty years after writing *A Hazard of New Fortunes*, Howells declared that he retained hope for "truer and better conditions" in American society, though these conditions had not achieved "the fulfillment" he would have "prophesied for them" in 1889. Returning to his theme of forgetting, he observed, "They who were then mindful of the poor have not forgotten them, and what is better the poor have not often forgotten themselves in violences such as offered me the material of tragedy and pathos in my story."[51] Howells had not expressed as much sympathy for strikes and similar agitations in his novel. He had been inspired by a Tolstoyan "light so clear and strong" that "being and doing had a new meaning and a new motive."[52] But this light, premised on a fully realized sense of complicity among Americans, had faded by the end of the novel. Howells had stalled on the obdurate insularities of his middle-class representative Basil March, who proved too "self-enwrapt" to escape the chains of his old habits. Nevertheless, Howells had provided a modest basis for hoping that his middle-class readers would recognize their frailties in Basil March and want to change. In this way "a righteous public" would evolve, as a Howells spokesman in an earlier novel had predicted, out of the "slow process of having righteous men and women."[53]

Still, *A Hazard of New Fortunes* was skewed toward conclusions that overturned Howells's original intentions. His sense of a desultory world pervades the last pages of his novel. Considering the deaths of Lindau and Conrad, Basil asserts, "That belonged to God; and no doubt it was law, though it seems chance."[54] This remark reflects not only renewed tensions from Howells's youth but also his immediate personal suffering. In the midst of writing the novel that was to be the testament of his Tolstoyan faith, Howells experienced a catastrophe that seemed to mock a purposeful moral universe. Winifred's nervous condition had grown more severe throughout the 1880s, but she regained strength when she submitted to another trial of S. Weir Mitchell's "rest cure." Then, as Howells set to work on his novel, she suddenly died, taking with her, he lamented, "most of the meaning and all the dignity of life." His grief was intense. "It is heavy—crushing—," he wrote, "and it does not avail to remember that all must not only die, but must writhe in the anguish of bereavement till the law of death is fulfilled in the last of our poor, bewildered race, for which truly there seems no reason." With poignant reference to his image of dancing in chains, he added, "All the feet that dance must drag bleeding over the way that we are now going."[55] When Howells returned to his novel, the seeming verification of a desultory world in Winifred's death gave conviction to Basil March's feeling that the whole of life appeared empty of "intelligent, comprehensive purpose."

Howells's struggle with the meaning of suffering and death did not end with his completion of *A Hazard of New Fortunes*. Finishing the novel that presented his largest cast of characters and longest engagement with the problems of the outer world, he wrote his most compressed and intensely inward novel, *The Shadow of a Dream* (1890). The Marches reappear as observers, but they are utterly unable to fathom the meaning of the dire events they witness. Suffering from a fatal illness, Douglas Faulkner is beset by a recurring dream in which his friend Nevil desires him dead so that he might marry his wife, Hermia. With this theme, Howells returned to the psychological complexities he had explored at the end of *A Modern Instance*, touching again on emotions that left him vulnerable to harsh self-accusation. After Faulkner dies, Nevil and Hermia are drawn together and desire to marry, but they cannot escape their horror of Faulkner's dream. Basil finally convinces Nevil to discount the irrational dream, but as Nevil steps from the train where their conversation has occurred, he is crushed against a concrete tunnel.

This calamity confirms the suspicion entertained earlier by Basil that "existence [is] all a miserable chance, a series of stupid, blundering accidents." When this thought first crossed Basil's mind, he negated it at once. "We could not believe that, for our very souls' sake," he told himself; "and for our own sanity we must not." But nothing in the course of the novel, climaxing with Nevil's hideous death, encourages him to believe otherwise.[56] In *The Shadow of a Dream*, Howells returned to the threatening sense of life that had plagued him during his youth. Confining the questions raised by his "panoramic" novel to the interactions of a few characters, Howells tried to control his dark thoughts by giving them full expression.

Never again did Howells attempt to draw all of his tensions together and settle issues once and for all. In the succeeding years, he sustained his concern for social justice, even though his message of self-renunciation was uncongenial to an American public increasingly drawn to therapeutic messages celebrating the self and to self-referential escapes from the pain and suffering of others.[57] To recall a sense of mutual concern, Howells sought to revitalize the language of complicity in essays on liberty, equality, and fraternity. His utopian novels provided another forum for this task and gave him the mask of a traveler from a better, more equitable world he called Altruria. The traveler expressed Howells's trust that the sense of complicity would endure against all forms of selfishness because forgetting the poor required an impossible suppression of memory: "In your pleasures you must forget the deprivation which your indulgence implies; if you feast, you must shut out the thought of them that famish; when you lie down in your bed, you cannot sleep if you remember the houseless who have nowhere to lay their heads. You are everywhere beleaguered by the armies of want and woe, and in the still watches of the night you can hear their invisible sentinels calling to one another, 'All is ill! All is ill!' "[58]

Howells continued to act as a sentinel himself, and he encouraged younger writers, such as Hamlin Garland, Stephen Crane, Frank Norris, Abraham Cahan, Edward Harrigan, and Paul Laurence Dunbar, to go beyond his own accomplishment and tell the stories of the poor.[59] To be a warning voice preserving hope for complicity was an ethic Howells upheld against his sense of a desultory world. While he continued to question the existence of a moral universe, he bowed before the uncertainty of his speculations: "Such reason as [life] has is often crossed and obscured by perverse events which in our brief perspective give it the aspect of a helpless craze," he stated in *The Son of Royal Langbrith* (1904). "Obvious effect does not follow obvious cause; there is sometimes no perceptible cause for the effects we see. The law that we find at work in the natural world is apparently absent from the moral world, not imaginably because it is without law, but because the law is of such cosmical vastness in its operation, that it is only once or twice sensible to any man's experience."[60]

Although a moral universe appeared a mystery beyond positive knowledge, Howells felt bound by his conscience to fulfill the greatest possible use. He resisted his impulse to escape his feelings of responsibility to others. He endured his doubts by trusting the "logic of his self-knowledge." "The only proof I have that I ought to do right," he wrote his father shortly after completing *A Hazard of New Fortunes*, "is that I suffer for my selfishness; and perhaps this is enough."[61]

23. William Dean Howells at age sixty-two in 1899.

Epilogue

After he had reached age seventy-nine, Howells explored his youth for the last time. In two stories—"The Pearl" (1916) and "A Tale Untold" (1917)—he recalled the spring of 1858 and the river journey he had taken on his uncle's sternwheeler, the *Cambridge*.[1] In his persona, "dreamy-eyed" Stephen West, Howells re-created his youthful self: "He was intensely, almost bitterly, literary; he was going to be an author, and above all he was going to be a poet." Tales of steamboats and youth compelled comparison with his close friend and fellow realist Mark Twain. In "A Tale Untold," a small retinue of Twain characters accompanies Stephen West on his river journey, including a practical-minded pilot, resembling Horace Bixby of "Old Times on the Mississippi" (1875), and two confidence men, resembling the Duke and the Dauphin of *Adventures of Huckleberry Finn* (1885).

Stephen himself is a version of the uninitiated Twain, who at the beginning of "Old Times" boards a river steamboat, hoping to learn the romantic vocation of piloting. In "Old Times," Horace Bixby's gruff but benevolent instruction teaches Twain to read the river according to the signs of experience rather than the illusions of romance.[2] By casting himself in circumstances like Twain's in "Old Times," Howells was asking why he had missed a similar rite of passage. Why, despite the Western background he shared with Twain, had he committed himself to an aesthetic mode of perception that hindered his development as a vernacular writer?

Although Stephen has accepted a vision of the world from literature, he is open to revision, for "he liked to verify [what he has learned] from the experience of a practical man like the pilot, and he had the habit of talking with him about life." But Stephen is dismayed when the pilot propounds the "abominable doctrine" that Negroes have no souls. The pilot's bigotry prevents any further talk on the nature of life. Although Stephen feels hurt and angry, he learns that the pilot would not have proved a useful guide in any case. One of the confidence men sells the pilot a gold watch chain, and Stephen follows the pilot's example and buys one for himself. Not long afterward, Stephen sees the confidence men fleeing the steamboat, laughing and jeering as they escape. He realizes that he and the pilot had fallen for a ruse. The incident suggests Howells's feeling that his pilots—the potential teachers and guides of his youth—possessed no superior way of separating the real from the sham; no less than himself, they were victims of their illusions.

After ruling out an enlightening apprenticeship, Howells considered whether he could have reached a vernacular perspective on his own, following the course of self-teaching he had pursued during his youth. Though he has lost self-respect, Stephen has gained insight. He has ceased his literary reveries and has begun to look at the life immediately at hand. Tossing his watch chain away, he sees a loafer pick it up "in the delusion that he was stealing value." This irony stimulates Stephen to consider whether his experience with the confidence men has value, whether he could use it in a story, perhaps in the comic, picaresque mode he admires in Cervantes. He wonders, however, whether readers of polite literature would accept so crude a tale. Then, in a transition that approximates Twain's literary development from *Tom Sawyer* to *Adventures of Huckleberry Finn*,[3] Stephen sees how the comic and the tragic are mixed in the scenario he is imagining:

The field of his rascals' adventures narrowed every year; always haunting the rivers, they must often take the same boat at such short intervals that the officers would come to know them; they must often escape at the same landing, where they would be recognized with welcome more and more ironical; their game would often be spoiled from the start; their dupes would know them and their lives would never be safe; they would be in constant danger of violence. He followed them from one squalid event to another, through the mud or the dust of the brutal little riverside towns, where they were tarred and feathered and ridden on rails by the hooting mob, or stabbed or shot.

When the law . . . saved them from the mob and sent them to prison, he saw them come out white and weak and bewildered in a world where they could find nothing but harm to do. They grew old on his hands and became each other's foes in the lapse of the black arts which had kept them friends. At last, one of them would sicken and die, after weeks, or months, or years. . . . The one who was left would wander back to the village where he had been a worthless boy and end there a friendless pauper.

"In the hands of a master," Stephen reflects, "it would be one of the most powerful [stories], because the elements were the dust of the earth which all men were made from." Despite this realization, however, he decides to postpone writing the story himself, at least until he has gained the necessary mastery. His decision proves fateful: "As he did not write the comedy of those evil lives, because he rejected it," the narrator concludes, "so he did not write the tragedy of them, because it rejected him."

"A Tale Untold" ended with Howells's painful regret that he had not developed his potential as a vernacular writer. He believed he had turned from this opportunity as a youth. Probably he was considering his humiliation with "The Independent Candidate." Unlike Twain and unlike his later protégés, he had not chosen "the bitter and burning dust, the foul and trampled slush of the common avenues of life."[4] Howells had remained within the narrower, more respectable way established by the dominant literary practice, representing middle-class lives for middle-class readers. He had introduced his refined audience to rough characters like the newly risen Silas Lapham, and he had become a penetrating critic of the middle class, an analyst of their maladies, evasions, and saving aspirations. But these accomplishments did not satisfy the demands of his Swedenborgian conscience. To the end of his life, Howells blamed himself for falling short of Twain.

While this harsh judgment remained, Howells had sketched an alleviating perspective in his earlier river story "The Pearl," where he confronted for the last time the mystery of his severe conscience. In this tale, Stephen West is traveling with his two cousins aboard a steamboat like the one that had taken Howells from Pittsburgh to St. Louis in the spring of 1858. Distracted by his literary dreams, Stephen hardly notices his cousins' busy activities until one cries out that he has lost his gold scarfpin. After a hurried search, the pin is found in Stephen's satchel. His cousins accept Stephen's innocence completely, suspecting that the cabin boy hid the pin in Stephen's satchel when he could not safely steal it. Nevertheless, Stephen feels at fault and worries over the incident. During the entire trip, "the nightmare thing that had happened lurked in his consciousness and haunted him through all that was passing." Throughout his life, Stephen retains the "sore place in [his] soul." It causes him deep pain whenever he touches it in memory. Finally, late in life, he confesses his feelings of guilt to one of his cousins, who tells him that his irrational irritation has produced a pearl. Although it has cost him his peace, this "pearl of great price" has sustained his conscience, making him merciful to others.

In his two river stories turning upon true and false gold, Howells examined the elements most precious in his vocational life. And in "The Pearl" he may have reached a self-understanding that transcended the vain regret he expressed in "A Tale Untold." In "The Pearl," he connected the most enduring heritage of his troubled youth, his tendency to severe self-accusation, with the real achievements of his life. He had not rested in his effort to make the literary vocation a force for moral usefulness and social transformation. He had left Boston rather than remain in protective Brahmin surroundings, and he had faced the challenges posed by poverty and inequality in American life. He had pressed himself as far as he could go, urging a sense of complicity that would turn his middle-class readers away from their self-referential escapes. And he had encouraged other writers to go further. The vision of the literary life that finally sustained Howells united his Swedenborgian conscience with Tolstoyan imperatives. "[Tolstoy] teaches such of us as will hear him," Howells had written, "that the Right is the sum of all men's poor little personal effort to do right, and that the success of this effort means daily, hourly self-renunciation, self-abasement, the sinking of one's pride in absolute squalor before duty. This is not pleasant . . . but is this not the truth? Let any one try, and see!"[5]

Notes

The following abbreviations are used throughout the notes:

Alfred   Herrick Memorial Library, Alfred University
AS   *Ashtabula Sentinel*
CG   Cincinnati *Gazette*
DT   Dayton *Transcript*
Harvard   Houghton Library, Harvard University
Hayes   Rutherford B. Hayes Presidential Center
HI   Hamilton *Intelligencer*
MHS   Massachusetts Historical Society
OHS   Ohio Historical Society
OSJ   *Ohio State Journal*
WCH   William Cooper Howells
WDH   William Dean Howells

Acting for heirs of the Howells Estate, William White Howells has kindly granted permission to quote from unpublished letters and papers by Howells. Further publication of material drawn from these letters and papers requires this same permission.

Epigraph: W. D. Howells, "Calvary," *Stops of Various Quills* (New York: Harper and Brothers, 1895), [22].

Preface

1. For appreciative accounts of Howells, see esp. Edwin H. Cady, *The Road to Realism: The Early Years, 1837–1885, of William Dean Howells* (Syracuse, N.Y.:

Syracuse Univ. Press, 1956); Edwin H. Cady, *The Realist at War: The Mature Years, 1885–1920, of William Dean Howells* (Syracuse, N.Y.: Syracuse Univ. Press, 1958); Kermit Vanderbilt, *The Achievement of William Dean Howells: A Reinterpretation* (Princeton: Princeton Univ. Press, 1968); Kenneth S. Lynn, *William Dean Howells: An American Life* (New York: Harcourt Brace Jovanovich, 1971).

2. Erikson's concept of the identity crisis provides the framework and several key assumptions of my study. I accept Erikson's conception of identity as a merger of private and public selves, personal imperatives and cultural values. Study of identity in these terms requires sensitivity to psychic residues of early experiences, formative influences of later life stages, and pervasive constraints of culture. During the identity crisis of youth, the tensions of an individual's past development coalesce, forcing delimiting "choices" that determine his ideological and vocational commitments. The individual must form a viable bond with his or her society by means of integrative beliefs and a life task. But aspiration for the synthesis or "wholeness" promised by such a bond is a motivating force in identity formation, not a guarantee of success. Struggle for identity inevitably partakes of the dread as well as the hopefulness that dominates any era.

The best introduction to Erikson's understanding of "identity" and the "identity crisis" is Erik H. Erikson, *Identity: Youth and Crisis* (New York: W. W. Norton, 1968). Cushing Strout, "Ego Psychology and the Historian," *History and Theory*, 7 (1968): 281–97, remains an excellent consideration of the identity crisis as a focus for historical analysis. Model applications of Erikson's perspectives are Cushing Strout, "William James and the Twice-Born Sick Soul," *Daedalus*, 97 (1968): 1062–82; Richard L. Bushman, "Jonathan Edwards as Great Man: Identity, Conversion, and Leadership in the Great Awakening," *Soundings*, 52 (1969): 15–46.

Erikson's discussions of "ideology" and "vocation" occur at various points in his writings. He defines "ideology" broadly as "a coherent body of shared images, ideas, and ideals which whether based on a formulated dogma, an implicit *Weltanschauung*, a highly structured world image, a political creed . . . , or a 'way of life,' provides for participants a coherent, if systematically simplified, over-all orientation in space and time, in means and ends." Ideas in any form, therefore, if they tend toward systematic expression and locate an individual in a larger companionship can fulfill the "developmental necessity" Erikson attributes to ideology. Although stated in ideal terms, this conception of ideology allows for discontinuities, divided loyalties, and other incoherencies that may frustrate a complete synthesis of identity. For statements concerning ideology, see Erikson, *Identity: Youth and Crisis*, 27, 31, 128–34, 187–91, 247, long quotation on 189–90; Erik H. Erikson, *Young Man Luther: A Study in Psychoanalysis and History* (New York: W. W. Norton, 1958), 22, 41, 42, 110; Erik H. Erikson, *Insight and Responsibility: Lectures on the Ethical Implication of Psychoanalytic Insight* (New York: W. W. Norton, 1964), 90–91; Erik H. Erikson, *Life History and the Historical Moment* (New York: W. W. Norton, 1975), 204–7. For an explication and extension of Erikson's notion of ideology, see Kenneth Kenniston, "Youth and Its Ideology," *American Handbook of Psychiatry*, 2d ed., ed. Silvano Arieti (New York: Basic Books, 1974), 1, esp. 411–16.

Erikson gives less exposition to "vocation," but he asserts that "work mastery is in any culture the backbone of identity formation." He contends that to establish his identity an individual "must acquire a 'conflict free,' habitual use of a dominant faculty, to be elaborated in an occupation; [this becomes] a limitless resource, a feedback, as it were, from the immediate exercise of this occupation, from the companionship it provides, and from its tradition." Vocation implies not only the task itself but also the ideological meaning of the task. For statements concerning vocation, see Erikson, *Identity: Youth and Crisis*, 127–28, long quotation on 150; Erik H. Erikson, *Identity and the Life Cycle: Selected Papers* (New York: International Universities Press, 1959), 163n. On "wholeness" and some of its vicissitudes, see Erikson, *Identity: Youth and Crisis*, 53–54, 80–82, 88, 89.

3. Treating Howells's life history in broad social and cultural context, my study differs from biographical approaches that stress Howells's idiosyncratic "neuroticism" or "neurotic history." See Edwin Harrison Cady, "The Neuroticism of William Dean Howells," *Publications of the Modern Language Association*, 61 (1946): 229–38; Cady, *The Road to Realism*, esp. 22–24, 54–60; Lynn, *William Dean Howells*, passim. Recently, John W. Crowley, *The Black Heart's Truth: The Early Career of W. D. Howells* (Chapel Hill: Univ. of North Carolina Press, 1986), has extended the view of Howells's "neuroticism" suggested by Cady and Lynn as a prologue to his Freudian exploration of sexual themes in Howells's fiction. My contrasting approach does not dispose of Howells's fears and irrational anxieties, including those potentially neurotic. In accord with Eriksonian perspectives, I see Howells's psychic difficulties as part of a developmental process of individual adaptation and synthesis in which his struggle for literary vocation played a decisive role. Howells's sense of literary vocation, especially his belief that it permitted the greatest usefulness to others, provided him with a way to resist and master potentially neurotic conflict.

On the distinction between neurotic potential and actual neurosis, see Peter Blos, "The Epigenesis of Adult Neurosis," *Psychoanalytic Study of the Child*, 27 (1972): 106–35. Blos points out that "the irruption of a neurotic illness can be averted, despite the existence of a neurotic potential, whenever the growing individual is able to draw on constitutional resources, object relations, and environmental conditions so as to work out a serviceable adaptation to life. Such a favorable outcome is often helped along by the fact that possession of a special propensity—called gift, talent, 'knack' or 'bent'—facilitates the resolution of internal disharmonies. The individual's neurotic potential, however, continues to exist throughout his life; indeed, it may serve as both incentive and activator, or, on the other hand, constitute a unique vulnerability. Both conditions, however, lend direction to the individual's adaptive tendencies and evoke his adaptive inventiveness: the mastery of early trauma, which is generally cumulative in nature, has become, under these conditions, a 'life task.' " (p. 109).

4. Howells to Victoria M. Howells, 18 Sept. 1860, MS at Harvard. On ambivalence toward "ambition," see Ann Douglas Wood, "The 'Scribbling Women' and Fanny Fern: Why Women Wrote," *American Quarterly*, 23 (1971): 3–24; Burton J. Bledstein, *The Culture of Professionalism: The Middle Class and the Develop-*

ment of Higher Education in America (New York: W. W. Norton, 1976); George B. Forgie, *Patricide in the House Divided: A Psychological Interpretation of Lincoln and His Age* (New York: W. W. Norton, 1979), esp. 55–88.

5. Studies that recognize connections between the disruption of traditional life and nineteenth-century skepticism include Thomas L. Haskell, *The Emergence of Professional Social Science: The American Social Science Association and the Nineteenth-Century Crisis of Authority* (Urbana: Univ. of Illinois Press, 1977), esp. 24–47; T. J. Jackson Lears, *No Place of Grace: Antimodernism and the Transformation of American Culture, 1880–1920* (New York: Pantheon, 1981); James Turner, *Without God, Without Creed: The Origins of Unbelief in America* (Baltimore: Johns Hopkins Univ. Press, 1985), 114–40.

6. Erikson, *Identity: Youth and Crisis*, 155.

7. Howells to Hamlin Garland, 15 Jan. 1888, *Selected Letters of W. D. Howells*, ed. Robert C. Leitz III, Richard H. Ballinger, and Christoph K. Lohmann (Boston: Twayne, 1980), 3: 215. Permission to quote from volumes of *Selected Letters of W. D. Howells* was granted by Twayne Publishers. For treatments of Howells's growing social concerns in the late 1880s and early 1890s, see Cady, *The Realist at War*; Lynn, *William Dean Howells*, esp. 282–311; William Alexander, *William Dean Howells: The Realist as Humanist* (New York: Burt Franklin, 1981). Lears, *No Place of Grace*, has illuminated how most middle-class elites tried to escape their nervousness in self-referential ways, seeking personal authenticity rather than the realization of communal potentialities.

1. A Selfish Ideal of Glory

Epigraph: WDH, "Sphinx," *Stops of Various Quills*, [69].

1. W. D. Howells, *Years of My Youth and Three Essays*, ed. David J. Nordloh (Bloomington: Indiana Univ. Press, 1975), 18–19.

2. Ibid., 20. Though he interprets this episode differently, concentrating on its "psychosexual" aspects, Crowley, *Black Heart's Truth*, 26, is sensitive to its place in an "associative context."

3. W. D. Howells, *The Flight of Pony Baker: A Boy's Town Story* (New York: Harper and Brothers, 1902), 141.

4. In this paragraph and the one following, I draw my descriptions of developmental difficulties and their importance for the origins of conscience from Erikson's "psychosocial" elaborations of Freudian theory. I use the pronoun "he" because I am concerned with male development. Erikson suggests that children at about age three to six are engaged in a variety of similarly "intrusive" behaviors and fantasies that allow them to anticipate adult roles and gain confidence in their capacities. He observes that the key tension of this stage of life is "initiative versus guilt." Guilt partly arises from what he describes as the "sexual core" of the child's exuberant behavior. A male child's identification with his father helps to mitigate the child's tendency to dictatorial conscience, yet other contingencies may encourage an obedience far beyond what his parents expect. Inhibitions and severe self-criticism may affect any area of a child's life, but a critical one is his

anticipation of roles, including those inclinations that later form his sense of vocation. See Erik H. Erikson, *Childhood and Society*, 2d ed. (New York: W. W. Norton, 1963), 85–91, 255–58 (quotation on 256); Erikson, *Identity: Youth and Crisis*, 115–22. The importance of the child's acceptance of separation from his mother is elaborated by Christopher Lasch in his synthetic presentation of recent psychoanalytic theory, *The Minimal Self: Psychic Survival in Troubled Times* (New York: W. W. Norton, 1984), 163–96.

5. See note 4.

6. The pertinent section of Howells's story is *Flight of Pony Baker*, 141–64.

7. On "glory," see text.

8. W. D. Howells, *A Boy's Town* (New York: Harper and Brothers, 1890), 15.

9. WDH, *Years of My Youth*, 21.

10. Ibid.

11. Ibid.

12. Ibid., 69–70, 79–81; WDH, *A Boy's Town*, 15, 16–18, 25–26, 55–56, 99, 198, 200, 202, 204.

13. WDH, *Years of My Youth*, 26–27.

14. Ibid., 27–28.

15. Ibid., 29, 30–31.

16. Ibid., 27.

17. WDH, *A Boy's Town*, 247.

18. William Cooper Howells, *Recollections of Life in Ohio, From 1813 to 1840* (Cincinnati: Robert Clarke, 1895), 4, 6–20, 47–48.

19. Ibid., 47, 50, 57–60, 62–63, 81, 82–83, 95, passim; Joseph Howells and Anne T. Howells to William C. Howells, 22 Feb. 1852, MS at Alfred; Joseph Howells to William C. Howells, 20 Apr. 1852, MS at Alfred; Anne T. Howells and Joseph Howells to William C. Howells, 14 Nov. 1852, MS at Alfred; Anne T. Howells to William C. Howells, 29 Aug. 1854, MS at Alfred.

20. WCH, *Recollections of Life in Ohio*, 95, 96–97, 160–61, 163, 164, 165–71.

21. Ibid., 169, 171–72.

22. WDH, *Years of My Youth*, 101; W. D. Howells, *New Leaf Mills: A Chronicle* (New York: Harper and Brothers, 1913), 30.

23. The general outlines of the transition to a national market are presented in George Rogers Taylor, *The Transportation Revolution, 1815–1860* (New York: Holt, Rinehart and Winston, 1951); Douglas C. North, *The Economic Growth of the United States, 1790–1860* (Englewood Cliffs, N.J.: Prentice Hall, 1961); Stuart Bruchey, *The Roots of American Economic Growth, 1607–1861: An Essay in Social Causation* (London: Hutchinson Univ. Library, 1965), esp. 79–94, 151–57; Clarence H. Danhof, *Change in Agriculture: The Northern United States, 1820–1870* (Cambridge: Harvard Univ. Press, 1969); Alan R. Pred, *Urban Growth and the Circulation of Information: The United States System of Cities, 1790–1840* (Cambridge: Harvard Univ. Press, 1973).

Recent studies examine the emergence of the national market and specify forms of accommodation and resistance. See esp. Michael Merrill, "Cash is Good to Eat: Self-Sufficiency and Exchange in the Rural Economy of the United

States," *Radical History Review*, 4 (1977): 42–71; James A. Henretta, "Families and Farms: *Mentalité* in Pre-Industrial America," *William and Mary Quarterly*, 35 (1978): 3–32; Christopher Clark, "The Household Economy, Market Exchange and the Rise of Capitalism in the Connecticut Valley, 1800–1860," *Journal of Social History*, 13 (1979): 169–89; Richard L. Bushman, "Family Security in the Transition from Farm to City, 1750–1850," *Journal of Family History*, 6 (1981): 238–56; Mary P. Ryan, *Cradle of the Middle Class: The Family in Oneida County, New York, 1790–1865* (Cambridge: Cambridge Univ. Press, 1981), esp. 18–59; Robert A. Gross, "Culture and Cultivation: Agriculture and Society in Thoreau's Concord," *Journal of American History*, 69 (1982): 42–61; Jonathan Prude, *The Coming of Industrial Order: Town and Factory Life in Rural Massachusetts, 1810–1860* (Cambridge: Cambridge Univ. Press, 1983); Steven Hahn and Jonathan Prude, eds., *The Countryside in the Age of Capitalist Transformation: Essays in the Social History of Rural America* (Chapel Hill: Univ. of North Carolina Press, 1985); John Mack Faragher, *Sugar Creek: Life on the Illinois Prairie* (New Haven: Yale Univ. Press, 1986).

24. For the pervasive sense of widespread economic opportunity among antebellum Northerners, see Eric Foner, *Free Soil, Free Labor, Free Men: The Ideology of the Republican Party before the Civil War* (New York: Oxford Univ. Press, 1970), 11–19. Andrew Jackson, "Second Annual Message," 6 Dec. 1830, *A Compilation of the Messages and Papers of the Presidents, 1789–1897*, ed. James D. Richardson (Washington, D.C.: Government Printing Office, 1896), 2: 521. On Andrew Jackson as the embodiment of the ethos of autonomous individualism, see John William Ward, *Andrew Jackson: Symbol of an Age* (1955; reprint, New York: Oxford Univ. Press, 1962), esp. 166–80; Michael Paul Rogin, *Fathers and Children: Andrew Jackson and the Subjugation of the American Indian* (New York: Alfred A. Knopf, 1975). For other expressions of the ethos of autonomous individualism, see Lears, *No Place of Grace*, 12–18, passim. Communal potentialities of the faith in expanding opportunities are discussed by Arthur Bestor, *Backwoods Utopias: The Sectarian Origins and the Owenite Phase of Communitarian Socialism in America, 1663–1829*, 2d ed. (Philadelphia: Univ. of Pennsylvania Press, 1960).

25. For John Jacob Astor, see Washington Irving, *Astoria, or Anecdotes of an Enterprise Beyond the Rocky Mountains*, 2 vols. (Philadelphia: Carey, Lea and Blanchard, 1836); *The Life of P. T. Barnum Written by Himself* (New York: Redfield, 1855); Barnum's popular lecture, "The Art of Money-Getting" (1858), reprinted in Moses Rischin, ed., *The American Gospel of Success: Individualism and Beyond* (Chicago: Quadrangle, 1968), 47–66. Antebellum entrepreneurial success literature is critically discussed by Irvin G. Wyllie, *The Self-Made Man in America: The Myth of Rags to Riches* (1954; reprint, New York: Free Press, 1966), 16–20; John G. Cawelti, *Apostles of the Self-Made Man* (Chicago: Univ. of Chicago Press, 1965), 39–75.

26. Recent studies have exploded the myth that market opportunities were readily available to all. See Edward Pessen, "The Egalitarian Myth and the American Social Reality: Wealth, Mobility, and Equality in the 'Era of the Common Man,'" *American Historical Review*, 76 (1971): 989–1034; Edward Pessen, *Riches, Class, and Power Before the Civil War* (Lexington, Mass.: D. C. Heath,

1973). Alexis de Tocqueville, *Democracy in America*, ed. Phillips Bradley (New York: Alfred A. Knopf, 1945), 2: 144–47.

27. See the studies cited in note 23, esp. those by Henretta and Ryan. Among the many studies of earlier corporate life, see John Demos, *A Little Commonwealth: Family Life in Plymouth Colony* (New York: Oxford Univ. Press, 1970); Michael Zuckerman, *Peaceable Kingdoms: New England Towns in the Eighteenth Century* (New York: Alfred A. Knopf, 1970); Robert A. Gross, *The Minutemen and Their World* (New York: Hill and Wang, 1976). For overall perspective and discussion of dynamics of change, see Darrett R. Rutman, "The Social Web: A Prospectus for the Study of the Early American Community," *Insights and Parallels: Problems and Issues of American Social History*, ed. William L. O'Neill (Minneapolis: Burgess, 1973), 57–88; Robert A. Gross, "Lonesome in Eden: Dickinson, Thoreau, and the Problem of Community in Nineteenth-Century New England," *Canadian Review of American Studies*, 14 (1983): 1–17.

28. Thomas Bender, *Community and Social Change in America* (New Brunswick, N.J.: Rutgers Univ. Press, 1978), has provided a theoretical framework for assessing this dilemma of community life. He has explored the emergence of "bifurcated" social experience as a consequence of national market development and noted its crucial importance for understanding the lives of nineteenth-century Americans. Bender stresses interplay between communal and noncommunal ways of living as well as tensions between local and translocal loyalties.

29. The formation of a definable middle class from the "middling sort" is the subject of a growing body of scholarship. See esp. Daniel Walker Howe, "Victorian Culture in America," *Victorian America*, ed. Daniel Walker Howe (Philadelphia: Univ. Pennsylvania Press, 1976), 3–28; Bledstein, *The Culture of Professionalism;* Joseph F. Kett, *Rites of Passage: Adolescence in America, 1790 to the Present* (New York: Basic Books, 1977); Paul E. Johnson, *A Shopkeeper's Millennium: Society and Revivals in Rochester, New York, 1815–1837* (New York: Hill and Wang, 1978); Paul Boyer, *Urban Masses and Moral Order in America, 1820–1920* (Cambridge: Harvard Univ. Press, 1978), esp. 1–120; Introductions to David Brion Davis, ed., *Antebellum American Culture: An Interpretive Anthology* (Lexington, Mass.: D. C. Heath, 1979); Daniel Walker Howe, *The Political Culture of the American Whigs* (Chicago: Univ. of Chicago Press, 1979); Ryan, *Cradle of the Middle Class;* Karen Halttunen, *Confidence Men and Painted Women: A Study of Middle-Class Culture in America, 1830–1870* (New Haven: Yale Univ. Press, 1982); Gross, "Lonesome in Eden"; Steven Mintz, *A Prison of Expectations: The Family in Victorian Culture* (New York: New York Univ. Press, 1983); Stuart M. Blumin, "The Hypothesis of Middle-Class Formation in Nineteenth-Century America: A Critique and Some Proposals," *American Historical Review*, 90 (1985): 299–338.

30. The effects of market interdependence on common understandings of social reality, individual autonomy, and moral belief are incisively analyzed and related to the development of professions by Haskell, *The Emergence of Professional Social Science*, esp. 24–47. Lears, *No Place of Grace*, subtly interprets the responses of nineteenth-century Americans to the unease of living in a national market society, which along with other influences contributed to individual and collective quests for revitalization in intense experience.

31. For the beginnings of age-graded schooling and professional training, see Kett, *Rites of Passage;* Carl F. Kaestle, *Pillars of the Republic: Common Schools and American Society, 1780–1860* (New York: Hill and Wang, 1983); Haskell, *Emergence of Professional Social Science;* Bledstein, *Culture of Professionalism.* WCH, *Recollections of Life in Ohio,* 89–91.

32. For changes in child-rearing advice during the early nineteenth century, I have relied primarily on Mintz, *A Prison of Expectations,* 27–39; Nancy F. Cott, "Notes Toward an Interpretation of Antebellum Childrearing," *Psychohistory Review,* 6 (1978): 4–20. For long-term changes, see Philippe Ariès, *Centuries of Childhood: A Social History of Family Life* (New York: Vintage, 1962); Lawrence Stone, *The Family, Sex and Marriage in England, 1500–1800* (New York: Harper and Row, 1977), 105–14, 159–95, 405–80. The general unsettling of cultural forms by the spread of market capitalism is illuminated by Jean-Christophe Agnew, *Worlds Apart: The Market and the Theater in Anglo-American Thought, 1550–1750* (Cambridge: Cambridge Univ. Press, 1986). On American child rearing, see also Bernard Wishy, *The Child and the Republic: The Dawn of Modern American Child Nurture* (Philadelphia: Univ. of Pennsylvania Press, 1968); Demos, *A Little Commonwealth,* esp. 100–106, 131–70; Edwin G. Burrows and Michael Wallace, "The American Revolution: The Ideology and Psychology of National Liberation," *Perspectives in American History,* 6 (1972): 255–67; Peter Gregg Slater, *Children in the New England Mind: In Death and in Life* (Hamden, Conn.: Archon, 1977); Philip Greven, *The Protestant Temperament: Patterns of Childrearing, Religious Experience, and the Self in Early America* (New York: Alfred A. Knopf, 1977); Jay Fliegelman, *Prodigals and Pilgrims: The American Revolution against Patriarchal Authority, 1750–1800* (Cambridge: Cambridge Univ. Press, 1982); Carl N. Degler, *At Odds: Women and the Family in America from the Revolution to the Present* (New York: Oxford Univ. Press, 1980), 66–110; Mary P. Ryan, *The Empire of the Mother: American Writing about Domesticity, 1830–1860* (New York: Harrington Park Press, 1985), 45f. For family tensions and family support for the self-made man, see Nancy F. Cott, *The Bonds of Womanhood: "Woman's Sphere" in New England, 1780–1835* (New Haven: Yale Univ. Press, 1977), 84–98; Ryan, *Cradle of the Middle Class,* 145–85; Mintz, *A Prison of Expectations,* 18–20, 27–28, passim.

33. Theodore Dwight, Jr., *The Father's Book; or, Suggestions for the Government and Instruction of Young Children on Principles Appropriate to a Christian Country,* 2d ed. (Springfield, Mass.: G. and C. Merriam, 1835), 36–39, 123–24, quoted in Cott, "Notes Toward an Interpretation of Antebellum Childrearing," 14; L. H. Sigourney, *Letters to Mothers,* 6th ed. (New York: Harper and Brothers, 1838), 56.

34. I have followed Thomas R. Cole's suggestion of *civilized morality* as a covering term for the emergent middle-class ethos of self-control. See Thomas R. Cole, "Past Meridian: Aging and the Northern Middle Class, 1830–1930" (Ph.D. diss., Univ. of Rochester, 1980). The term derives from Freud's essay " 'Civilized' Sexual Morality and Modern Nervous Illness," *The Standard Edition of the Complete Works of Sigmund Freud,* ed. James Strachey (London: Hogarth, 1959), 9: 181–204. Applying the term to American society, Nathan G. Hale, Jr., has observed, " 'Civilized' morality operated as a coherent system of related economic, social, and religious norms. It defined not only correct behavior, but correct models of

the manly man and the womanly woman, and prescribed a unique regime of sexual hygiene. . . . 'Civilized' morality was, above all, an ideal of conduct, not a description of reality. In many respects this moral system was a heroic attempt to coerce a recalcitrant and hostile actuality." *Freud and the Americans: The Beginnings of Psychoanalysis in the United States, 1876–1917* (New York: Oxford Univ. Press, 1971), 24–46, quotation on 25.

The historical literature discussing civilized morality in its many dimensions is vast. For long-term perspective, see Norbert Elias, *The Civilizing Process: The History of Manners* (New York: Pantheon, 1978) and *The Civilizing Process: Power and Civility* (New York: Pantheon, 1982), 229–333. For American developments, see esp. Lears, *No Place of Grace*. Other pertinent studies include those concerning the family and child rearing cited in note 32. For studies demonstrating the effects of ideals of self-control in individual life history, see Lewis Perry, *Childhood, Marriage, and Reform: Henry Clarke Wright, 1797–1870* (Chicago: Univ. of Chicago Press, 1980); Robert H. Abzug, *Passionate Liberator: Theodore Dwight Weld and the Dilemma of Reform* (New York: Oxford Univ. Press, 1980).

Considering forms of culture that became available to middling families like the Howells family, historians have stressed the accommodation to market capitalism promoted by the ideal of self-control. Regulating the "passions" through self-control, for instance, furthered the middle-class rationalization of self, helping to prepare individuals for modes of work that required reserves of energy and devotion to time-oriented discipline. See for example Peter T. Cominos, "Late Victorian Sexual Respectability and the Social System," *International Review of Social History*, 8 (1963): 18–48, 216–50; G. J. Baker-Benfield, "The Spermatic Economy: A Nineteenth-Century View of Sexuality," *Feminist Studies*, 1 (1972): 45–74; Martin Cornelius Van Buren, "The Indispensable God of Health: A Study of Republican Hygiene and Ideology of William Alcott" (Ph.D. diss., Univ. of California, Los Angeles, 1977); Stephen Nissenbaum, *Sex, Diet, and Debility in Jacksonian America: Sylvester Graham and Health Reform* (Westport, Conn.: Greenwood, 1980), 136–37, passim. Nissenbaum observes that Grahamite dietary restrictions, especially insistence upon home-produced bread, were expressly set against inroads of market capitalism even though the Grahamite regimen ultimately promoted the new rationalization of self. Other historians have pointed out the coercive uses of civilized morality in overturning the habits of an industrial labor force oriented to the rhythms of a traditional agrarian economy. See for example Paul Faler, "Cultural Aspects of the Industrial Revolution: Lynn, Massachusetts, Shoemakers and Industrial Morality, 1826–1860," *Labor History*, 15 (1974): 367–94; Barbara M. Tucker, "The Family and Industrial Discipline in Ante-Bellum New England," *Labor History*, 21 (1979–80): 55–74. Faler observes that some shoemakers turned civilized morality to their own purposes.

35. The ideal of self-control responded to a wide range of anxieties experienced by antebellum Americans, including fears that individual self-assertion would destroy all commitment to traditional communal obligations. Carroll Smith-Rosenberg emphasizes various symbolic and expressive dimensions of sexual self-control, including the effort to protect communal values by containing individual

desire. See "Sex as Symbol in Victorian Purity: An Ethnohistorical Analysis of Jacksonian America," *Turning Points: Historical and Sociological Essays on the Family*, ed. John Demos and Sarane Spence Boocock (Chicago: Univ. of Chicago Press, 1978), 212–47; and "Davey Crockett as Trickster: Pornography, Liminality and Symbolic Inversion in Victorian America," *Journal of Contemporary History*, 17 (1982): 325–50.

T. J. Jackson Lears, "The Concept of Cultural Hegemony: Problems and Possibilities," *American Historical Review*, 90 (1985): 567–93, proposes a flexible approach to understanding the formation of hegemonic values such as self-control, an approach that allows for the interplay of contradictory elements, contested meanings, and oppositional potentialities. In addition, see Raymond Williams, "Base and Superstructure in Marxist Cultural Theory," in *Problems in Materialism and Culture* (London: Verso, 1980), 31–49.

36. WDH, *A Boy's Town*, 7; WCH, *Recollections of Life in Ohio*, 43, 44; William Dean Howells, Introduction to *Recollections of Life in Ohio*, by WCH, vi–vii. "Moral universe" was commonly used in the nineteenth century for a providentially ordered universe, guaranteeing moral purpose and allowing voluntary action for salvation. See D. H. Meyer, *The Instructed Conscience: The Shaping of the American National Ethic* (Philadelphia: Univ. of Pennsylvania Press, 1972), esp. 89–97; W. D. Howells, "Lyof N. Tolstoy," *North American Review*, 188 (1908): 851.

37. [WCH], "Universalism," *Retina*, 26 Apr. 1844. William Cooper Howells's published discussions of Swedenborgianism include *Retina*, 1 July 1843 to 5 July 1844; Wm. C. Howells, *Science of Correspondences: Or the Relation of Spirit to Matter, Considered as a Means of Scriptural Interpretation* (Toronto: R. Carswell, 1879); W. C. Howells, *The Freewill of Man and the Origin of Evil: A Lecture* (London: James Speirs, 1881); [WCH], "Creation," *New Jerusalem Magazine*, 6 (1882): 425–39. For Swedenborgianism in America, see Marguerite Beck Block, *The New Church in the New World: A Study of Swedenborgianism in America* (New York: Henry Holt, 1932); Scott Trego Swank, "The Unfettered Conscience: A Study of Sectarianism, Spiritualism, and Social Reform in the New Jerusalem Church, 1840–1870" (Ph.D. diss., Univ. of Pennsylvania, 1970).

38. [WCH], "Universalism," *Retina*, 25 Nov. 1843; WCH, *The Freewill of Man and the Origins of Evil*, 5–6. I draw from William Cooper Howells's later statements for vividness of expression. His later statements are wholly consonant with the ideas he expressed earlier in the *Retina*.

39. Emanuel Swedenborg, *Heaven and its Wonders and Hell: From Things Heard and Seen* (New York: Swedenborg Foundation, 1970), 224; [WCH], Untitled essay on "Character," 3–4, MS at Alfred. The phrases "ideal of glory" and "ideal of usefulness" recur in various forms throughout Swedenborgian writings: "One who rules from the love of self," wrote Swedenborg, "wills good to no one except himself; the uses he performs are for the sake of his own honor and glory, which to him are the only uses; his end in loving others is that he may himself be served, honored, and permitted to rule." Swedenborg, *Heaven and Hell*, 407. For other representative statements, see 37, 400–401.

40. [WCH], "Youth's Department," *Retina*, 7 Oct. 1843. On "ruling love," see Swedenborg, *Heaven and Hell*, 336, 337, 380. WDH, *A Boy's Town*, 12.

41. WDH, *My Literary Passions*, 8; WDH, *A Boy's Town*, 20–21.

42. Henry Ward Beecher, *Lectures to Young Men, on Various Important Subjects*, 3d ed. (Salem, Mass.: John P. Jewett, 1846), [15]. For other examples of the word "usefulness" in the vocabulary of the middle class, see Bledstein, *Culture of Professionalism*, 159, 165, 167, 169; Daniel T. Rogers, *The Work Ethic in Industrial America, 1850–1920* (Chicago: Univ. of Chicago Press, 1978), 9–14; Ruth Miller Elson, *Guardians of Tradition: American Schoolbooks of the Nineteenth Century* (Lincoln: Univ. of Nebraska Press, 1964), 222–23. On secularization, see Lears, *No Place of Grace*, 40–47, passim; Joseph Haroutunian, *Piety Versus Moralism: The Passing of the New England Theology* (New York: Henry Holt, 1932); Turner, *Without God, Without Creed*.

43. See the studies cited in note 32. Heman Humphrey, *Domestic Education* (Amherst, Mass.: J. S. and C. Adams, 1840), 45–48, quoted Mintz, *A Prison of Expectations*, 33.

44. Quotation from "Parental Fault-Finding," *Retina*, 25 Nov. 1843. For additional examples, see T. E. W., "A Walk with Father," *Retina*, 15 Sept. 1843; M. C., "Frank Hale," *Retina*, 14 June 1844; "Duties to Parents," *Retina*, 9 Feb. 1844; "Interesting Anecdote," *Retina*, 14 June 1844; "The Neglected Boy," *Retina*, 5 July 1844.

45. William C. Howells to Anne Howells Fréchette, 23 Aug. 1882, MS at Alfred.

46. WCH, *Recollections of Life in Ohio*, 2–3, 21–25, 27, 28, 29–30, 33–34, 38, 42–43, 89–94; William Cooper Howells, "Camp Meetings in the West Fifty Years Ago," *Lippincott's*, 10 (1872): 203–12; Richard T. Vann, "Nurture and Conversion in the Early Quaker Family," *Journal of Marriage and the Family*, 31 (1969): 642–43; [WCH], "Youth's Department," *Retina*, 7 Oct. 1843.

47. WDH, *A Boy's Town*, 13.

48. Ibid., 15.

49. The phrases are from Anne Howells Fréchette, 2d draft of an untitled speech concerning William Dean Howells, 4, MS at Alfred. On conscience, see Cott, "Notes Toward an Interpretation of Antebellum Childrearing," 14.

50. WDH, *Flight of Pony Baker*, 142.

51. Howells to William C. Howells, 21 Aug. 1881, MS at Harvard. For discussion of Winifred Howells's illness and death, see Cady, *Realist at War*, 96–99; Lynn, *William Dean Howells*, 252, 297–98; John W. Crowley, "Winifred Howells and the Economy of Pain," *Old Northwest*, 10 (1984): 41–75. The study that treats nineteenth-century "nervousness" in broadest cultural perspective is Lears, *No Place of Grace*, esp. 47–58.

52. WDH, *Years of My Youth*, 10, 14, 22, 84; WDH, *A Boy's Town*, 202; Alexander Dean to William C. Howells, 15 Oct. 1868, MS at Alfred; List of the Children of Elizabeth (Dock) Dean, MS at MHS. For the difficulties of separation experienced by women in the new circumstances of a national market society, see Ryan, *Cradle of the Middle Class*, 193–95, passim; Mintz, *A Prison of Expectations*,

118; Cott, *Bonds of Womanhood*, 80–83; Carroll Smith-Rosenberg, "The Female World of Love and Ritual: Relations Between Women in Nineteenth-Century America," *Signs*, 1 (1975): 11–18, 22; Degler, *At Odds*, 104–10; Ellen K. Rothman, *Hands and Hearts: A History of Courtship in America* (1984; reprint, Cambridge: Harvard Univ. Press, 1987), 67–71.

53. WCH, *Recollections of Life in Ohio*, 190–91, passim; [WCH], "Memoranda of Incidents of My Life and Various Other Matters Jotted Down for My Dear Children," 276–77, MS at Alfred; John Dean to William C. Howells, 20 Sept. 1835, MS at Alfred; "Veteran Newspaper Man and Former Resident Writes Interestingly of Days When Martin's Ferry was Martinsville," Martin's Ferry *Evening News*, 30 Mar. 1905, Clipping of article based on a letter from Howells's brother Joseph, at Alfred; WDH, *Years of My Youth*, 8–9, 10, 34; Mary D. Howells to Howells, 14 Mar. 1864, MS at MHS.

54. WCH, *Recollections of Life in Ohio*, 191–94; WCH, "Memoranda of Incidents of My Life," 282, MS at Alfred.

55. WDH, *A Boy's Town*, 11, 12, 13, 202; WDH, *Years of My Youth*, 14, 22; [WCH], "Mrs. Caroline Matilda Thayer," *Retina*, 17 May 1844. A canceled passage in the typescript for *A Boy's Town* ties Joseph Howells's lament over his grandchildren to the "dismay" he felt for their "lost condition." WDH, "A Boy's Town," (9-20), TS at Harvard.

56. Calvin Dill Wilson and David Bruce Fitzgerald, "A Day in Howells's 'Boy's Town,' " *New England Magazine*, 36 (1907): 295; Leonard L. Richards, *"Gentlemen of Property and Standing": Anti-Abolitionist Mobs in Jacksonian America* (New York: Oxford Univ. Press, 1970); [WCH], "The Dayton Riot," *HI*, 5 Feb. 1841; [WCH], "Dayton Again," *HI*, 12 Feb. 1841; [WCH], "The Dayton Transcript," *HI*, 19 Feb. 1841; [WCH], "The Dayton Transcript," *HI*, 5 Mar. 1841; Joseph A. Howells to W. H. Venable, 27 July 1909, Dolores Venable Memorial Collection, MSS 127, TS at OHS; WDH, *A Boy's Town*, 11; WDH, *Years of My Youth*, 10–11.

57. WDH, *Years of My Youth*, 25.

58. WDH, *A Boy's Town*, 19. Melanie Klein, among other psychoanalysts, suggested that "splitting" is a way a child handles ambivalent feelings. A child projects his own aggressive fantasies and fears of punishment onto a "bad" mother figure while reserving unspoiled love and affection for a "good" mother figure. See Klein, *Contributions to Psycho-Analysis, 1921–1945* (London: Hogarth, 1950), esp. 219–21, 346–49, 365, 379.

59. WDH, *Years of My Youth*, 20.

60. WDH, "Sphinx," *Stops of Various Quills*, [69].

2. A Kind of Double Life

Epigraph: WDH, *A Boy's Town*, 171.

1. Ibid., 185.

2. For the family strategies described in this and the next paragraph, see esp. Ryan, *Cradle of the Middle Class*, 145–85. See also Mintz, *A Prison of Expectations,*

16, 18–19, 35; Daniel Scott Smith, "Family Limitation, Sexual Control, and Domestic Feminism in Victorian America," *Clio's Consciousness Raised: New Perspectives on the History of Women*, ed. Mary Hartman and Lois W. Banner (New York: Harper and Row, 1974), 119–36; Clifford E. Clark, Jr., "Domestic Architecture as an Index to Social History: The Romantic Revival and the Cult of Domesticity in America," *Journal of Interdisciplinary History*, 7 (1976): 49–53.

3. For these traditional family strategies, see esp. Ryan, *Cradle of the Middle Class*, 25–31, 43–51; Henretta, "Families and Farms," esp. 25–32.

4. For the differentiation of middle-class and working-class family styles, see Ryan, *Cradle of the Middle Class*, 167–68, 171; Mintz, *A Prison of Expectations*, 14–15, 18–19; Kett, *Rites of Passage*, 168–70; Michael B. Katz and Ian E. Davey, "Youth and Early Industrialization in a Canadian City," *Turning Points*, ed. Demos and Boocock, 87–92; John Modell and Tamara K. Hareven, "Urbanization and the Malleable Household: An Examination of Boarding and Lodging in American Families," *Journal of Marriage and the Family*, 35 (1973): 467–78.

5. Some spokesmen for civilized morality assumed parental control would cease altogether after early childhood. Horace Greeley, "Counsels to the Young," reprinted in *HI*, 10 Nov. 1842, identified the precocious age of six as the time when a child passed beyond parental influence and began his or her "self-culture." In actual experience, children's autonomy was usually hedged in a variety of ways. See Kett, *Rites of Passage*, 29, 45–46, passim; Ryan, *Cradle of the Middle Class*, 165–79; Mintz, *A Prison of Expectations*, esp. 59–101.

6. WDH, *A Boy's Town*, 184.

7. WDH, *Years of My Youth*, 18.

8. Ibid., 17–18, 26; WDH, *My Literary Passions*, 6–7, 11; WDH, *A Boy's Town*, 21, 177–79. For discussion of the child's earliest anticipation of vocational roles, see Erikson, *Identity: Youth and Crisis*, 115–22.

9. [WCH], Untitled essay on "Character," 34, MS at Alfred. For the traditional devotional practice of the husband and father reading aloud to his family, see David D. Hall, "The Uses of Literacy in New England, 1600–1850," *Printing and Society in Early America*, ed. William L. Joyce, et al. (Worcester, Mass.: American Antiquarian Society, 1983), 21–26. For the antebellum valuation of literature as a spiritual means, see Mintz, *A Prison of Expectations*, 22–27, 57–58; Ann Douglas, *The Feminization of American Culture* (New York: Alfred A. Knopf, 1977).

10. See the items selected for "Youth's Department," beginning in *Retina*, 7 Oct. 1843. WDH, *Years of My Youth*, 50; WDH, *My Literary Passions*, 5.

11. WDH, *Years of My Youth*, 18; WDH, *A Boy's Town*, 11–12.

12. Quotations in this and following paragraphs are from WDH, *A Boy's Town*, 61–62.

13. For discussion of Swedenborg's conception of heaven, see Colleen McDannell and Bernhard Lang, *Heaven: A History* (New Haven: Yale Univ. Press, 1988), 181–227. William Cooper Howells corrected poems submitted to the *Retina* when they contained "Old Church" beliefs. See "The Female Missionary," *Retina*, 11 Nov. 1843. His distinction between heaven as a *place* and as a *state* reflected his quarrel with Universalists concerning the voluntary nature of salvation. "[Uni-

versalists]," he wrote, "rest all their reasoning on the hypothesis that Heaven is a place, into which men come by Divine favor—that any one can be brought into it, without reference to his will or affections—that the Lord wills the salvation of all, and to save them will control their wills, and oblige them to enter that holy place—when the truth is, that Heaven is a state of the affections voluntarily induced by man himself. God gives, but man receives or rejects." "Universalism," *Retina*, 25 Nov. 1843. When his father wrote this defense of individual moral responsibility, Howells was six years old.

14. WDH, *My Literary Passions*, 8; WDH, *Years of My Youth*, 15, 16; WDH, *A Boy's Town*, 20, 126–27, 131, 238–39; [WDH], canceled passage in "A Boy's Town," (11-20), TS at Harvard; Joseph A. Howells to William H. Venable, 15 Apr. 1909, Dolores Venable Memorial Collection, MSS 127, TS at OHS; Joseph A. Howells to William H. Venable, 27 July 1909, Dolores Venable Memorial Collection, MSS 127, TS at OHS; Waldon Fawcett, "Mr. Howells and his Brother," *Critic*, 35 (1889): 1027.

15. WCH, *Recollections of Life in Ohio*, 97; WDH, Introduction to *Recollections of Life in Ohio*, by WCH, iv–v; WDH, *Years of My Youth*, 24, 32, 60; WDH, *My Literary Passions*, 5–6; WDH, *A Boy's Town*, 22; [WCH], "We might mention, by the way . . . ," *Retina*, 3 May 1844; W. C. Howells, "To the Readers of the Hamilton Intelligencer," *HI*, 19 Sept. 1844; W. C. Howells, "The 'Intelligencer,' " *HI*, 29 May 1845.

16. WDH, *Years of My Youth*, 60, 83; WCH, "Memoranda of Incidents of My Life," 277, MS at Alfred.

17. WDH, *Years of My Youth*, 82.

18. WDH, *A Boy's Town*, 22.

19. WDH, *My Literary Passions*, 70.

20. William C. Howells to ?, 2 May 1862, quoted in Cady, *Road to Realism*, 45. For psychoanalytic consideration of the communication of unfulfilled desire from father to son, see Erikson, *Young Man Luther*, 65, passim. The relationship of Henry James, Sr., and his son William is the classic American example. See Strout, "William James and the Twice-Born Sick Soul"; Howard M. Feinstein, *Becoming William James* (Ithaca, N.Y.: Cornell Univ. Press, 1984).

21. W. D. Howells, "The Country Printer," *Impressions and Experiences* (New York: Harper and Brothers, 1896), 28–29, 32, 33, 34–35, 43, 44; Lewis Atherton, *Main Street on the Middle Border* (Bloomington: Indiana Univ. Press, 1954), 161–65.

22. WDH, "Country Printer," 10.

23. The children in order of birth were Joseph Alexander (b. 1832), William Dean (b. 1837), Victoria Mellor (b. 1838), Samuel Dean (b. 1840), Aurelia Harriet (b. 1842), Anne Thomas (b. 1844), John Butler (b. 1846), and Henry Israel (b. 1852).

24. WDH, *Years of My Youth*, 87–88; WDH, *A Boy's Town*, 146–47, 242; Joseph A. Howells, "Notes by the Editor, From Turks Island, West Indies: 1853 —Fifty-five Years in Jefferson—1908," *AS*, ca. 2 Jan. 1908, Clipping at Alfred; Harvey Greene to William C. Howells, 26 Dec. 1854, MS at Alfred.

25. See the studies cited in note 4.

26. WDH, *Years of My Youth*, 36, 78, 83, 107; WDH, *A Boy's Town*, 23; Joseph A. Howells to William H. Venable, 15 Apr. 1909, Dolores Venable Memorial Collection, MSS 127, TS at OHS; WDH, *My Literary Passions*, 31, 56, 62–63, 68, 109, 114, passim; [WDH], " 'The Real Diary of a Boy': Howells in Ohio, 1852–1853," ed. Thomas Wortham, *Old Northwest*, 10 (1984): 21–22, 23.

27. WDH, "Real Diary of a Boy," 38–39 n. 58.

28. WDH, *A Boy's Town*, 171, 184.

29. WDH, *Years of My Youth*, 31.

30. WDH, *A Boy's Town*, 130–31, 237–38; W. D. Howells, Conclusion to *Recollections of Life in Ohio*, by WCH, 197–98, 199; [WCH], "What We Should Do?" *HI*, 22 June 1848; [WCH], "Our Vote," *HI*, 9 Nov. 1848; [WCH], "Valedictory," *HI*, 16 Nov. 1848.

31. WDH, *Years of My Youth*, 31; WDH, *A Boy's Town*, 237–38; WDH, Conclusion to *Recollections of Life in Ohio*, by WCH, 200; [WCH], "Let's Reason the Matter," *DT*, 10 Apr. 1850; [WCH], "Out at Last," *DT*, 12 Apr. 1850; [WCH], "The Cha[m]pions—Where are They[?]" *DT*, 20 July 1850.

32. WDH, *Years of My Youth*, 31, 35–36; [WCH], "The Cha[m]pions—Where are They[?]" *DT*, 20 July 1850. [WCH], "Fair Typesetting," *DT*, 15 June 1850, praised his son publicly for setting 9,500 ems of type, from six in the morning until six at night, after Howells had delivered papers around the city. Howells stayed up until eleven to receive the telegraph dispatches and set them in type.

The relation between "delight" and "ruling love" is suggested throughout Swedenborg's writings. "All the delights that a man has," he wrote, "are the delights of his ruling love, for he feels nothing to be delightful except what he loves, thus especially that which he loves above all things." *Heaven and Hell*, 263, 336 (quotation), 337.

33. WDH, *My Literary Passions*, 28–29, 31, 33; WDH, *Years of My Youth*, 31–32; [WCH], "Mysterious Knockings," *DT*, 15 June 1850, suspended judgment on the knockings, saying that if one believed in spiritual existence, it was rational to believe spiritual existence could be manifested.

34. WDH, *Years of My Youth*, 33, 265; WDH, *A Boy's Town*, 242–43; Charles E. Rosenberg, *The Cholera Years: The United States in 1832, 1849, and 1866* (Chicago: Univ. of Chicago Press, 1962), 40–54, 120, 121–22.

35. For Mary Howells's recourse to "providence," see Mary D. Howells to Victoria M. Howells, ca. 29 Oct. [1864]; Mary D. Howells to Anne T. Howells, n.d., "It is now a week tomorrow since you and dear Joe left us," MSS at Alfred. Mary Howells expressed her sense of the fragility of life by habitually attaching "poor" to the names she mentioned in letters. See Mary D. Howells to Anne T. Howells and Aurelia H. Howells, 27 Feb. [1864], MS at Alfred, where "poor" precedes a reference to herself and the names of her husband, three children, and one family friend. Lewis O. Saum, *The Popular Mood of Pre–Civil War America* (Westport, Conn.: Greenwood, 1980?), esp. 3–26, notes frequent recourse to "providence" in the writings of "common" people to account for hazard, illness, and death, a tendency that reveals their dissent from the progressive optimism asserted in public rhetoric.

36. WDH, *Years of My Youth*, 33–35. In the federal census of 1850, two

printers, Ebeneser Allcott (age 20) and Alfred Carter (age 18), are listed as part of the Howells household. See *Seventh Census of the United States: 1850. Original Returns of the Assistant Marshalls. First Series: White and Free Colored Population. Schedule I, Free Inhabitants, 3rd Ward, Dayton, Montgomery County, Ohio*, 2 October 1850.

37. William Cooper Howells had opposed discussion of "Fourierism" in the *Retina*, contending that "the New Church can lead us to the philosophy of Association much sooner than Fourier." "To day we publish the article of John White . . . ," *Retina*, 9 Feb. 1844. See also [WCH], "Fourierism," *Retina*, 19 Jan. 1844; [WCH], "Fourierism &c," *Retina*, 15 Mar. 1844. For William Cooper Howells's radical critique of the national market, see [WCH], "Land Reform," *DT*, 16 Jan. 1850; [WCH], "Radicalism," *DT*, 9 Apr. 1850; [WCH], "Radicalism —Land Absorption," *DT*, 10 Apr. 1850; [WCH], "Labor and Capital," *DT*, 11 Apr. 1850; [WCH], "Organization of Labor," *DT*, 11 Apr. 1850; [WCH], "Land Absorption," *DT*, 12 Apr. 1850; [WCH], "Interest upon Loans," *DT*, 13 Apr. 1850; [WCH], "Homestead Exemption," *DT*, 22 Apr. 1850. For working-class movements in 1850, see Sean Wilentz, *Chants Democratic: New York City and the Rise of the American Working Class, 1788–1850* (New York: Oxford Univ. Press, 1984), 363–89.

38. [WCH], "Homestead Exemption," *DT*, 22 Apr. 1850.

39. WDH, *New Leaf Mills*, 50.

40. WDH, *Years of My Youth*, 36–37.

41. Ibid., 36. For discussion of middle-class conceptions of sexuality in these terms, see Charles Rosenberg, "Sexuality, Class, and Role," in *No Other Gods: On Science and American Social Thought* (Baltimore: Johns Hopkins Univ. Press, 1976), 71–88.

42. WDH, *Years of My Youth*, 36.

43. Ibid., 37–38, 351; WDH, *My Literary Passions*, 30; WDH, Conclusion to *Recollections of Life in Ohio*, by WCH, 200–201; [WCH], "No Discussions," *DT*, 30 Jan. 1850; [WCH], "Mr. Webster's Speech," *DT*, 9 Mar. 1850; Cady, *Road to Realism*, 32.

44. WDH, *Years of My Youth*, 38, 70, 351; WDH, *My Literary Passions*, 30; WDH, Conclusion to *Recollections of Life in Ohio*, by WCH, 200–201; Israel Felix Howells to William C. Howells, 13 Jan. 1851, MS at Alfred; Joseph Howells to William C. Howells, 22 Jan. 1851, MS at Alfred.

45. WDH, *Years of My Youth*, 40–41, 43–48, 49, 50–51, 53; WDH, *My Literary Passions*, 21, 28, 31–35.

46. WDH, *Years of My Youth*, 39–40, 42–43, 45, 46, 48, 50, 51, 55–56, 356, 357, 359, 360, passim; Anne T. Howells to William C. Howells, 2 May 1851, MS at Alfred; Alexander Dean to William C. Howells and Mary D. Howells, 3 Nov. 1851, MS at Alfred.

47. WDH, *Years of My Youth*, 53–54, 362. For the traditional practice of sending children away from home for occasional work, see Kett, *Rites of Passage*, 17–18, 21–23, 29.

48. WDH, *Years of My Youth*, 53–54.

49. Ibid., 54–55, 362.

50. Howells recalled that his homesickness in childhood and youth was always linked to a longing for his mother: "Whenever I went away from home, it was with the foreboding and realization of homesickness which was merely longing for her." Howells to Harriet T. Upton, 9 Mar. 1910, *Selected Letters of W. D. Howells*, ed. William C. Fischer and Christoph K. Lohmann (Boston: Twayne, 1983), 5: 312. Writers on "domesticity" offered idealized images of home and mother as shields against the hazards of the outside world. Regretful glances homeward were to remind home-leaving youth of domestic sentiments and moral duties. See Cott, *Bonds of Womanhood*, 63–100; Ryan, *Cradle of the Middle Class*, 175.

51. WDH, *A Boy's Town*, 236.

52. WDH, *Years of My Youth*, 55, 56, 59–60, 70, 362; WDH, *My Literary Passions*, 36; Joseph A. Howells to William H. Venable, 15 Apr. 1909, Dolores Venable Memorial Collection, MSS 127, TS at OHS; Joseph A. Howells to Anne Howells Fréchette, 29 Mar. 1911, TS at Alfred; Howells's description of his brother's life as a "succession of sacrifices" appears in a canceled passage in "A Boy's Town," 349, TS at Harvard.

53. WDH, *Years of My Youth*, 60–67, 68, 69; WDH, *My Literary Passions*, 44–45; WDH, "Real Diary of a Boy," 16, passim.

54. WDH, *My Literary Passions*, 36.

55. Ibid., 37; WDH, *Years of My Youth*, 64–65; [WDH], "Old Winter loose thy hold on us," *OSJ*, 23 Mar. 1852; WDH, "Real Diary of a Boy," 20, 21–22, 23.

56. Joseph Howells to William C. Howells, 20 Apr. 1852, MS at Alfred; WDH, *Years of My Youth*, 11; Joseph A. Howells to William H. Venable, 27 July 1909, Dolores Venable Memorial Collection, MSS 127, TS at OHS.

57. WDH, *Years of My Youth*, 65–67, 68; WDH, *My Literary Passions*, 39–41, 46–47, 48; William Dean Howells, "The Turning Point of My Life," *Harper's Bazaar*, 44 (1910): 165; George Sherburn, *The Early Career of Alexander Pope* (Oxford, Eng.: Oxford Univ. Press, 1934), chaps. 1–4.

58. WDH, *My Literary Passions*, 41.

59. WDH, "Real Diary of a Boy," 7–8.

3. An Instance of Nervous Prostration

Epigraph: Howells to Thomas B. Aldrich, 3 July 1902, *Selected Letters*, 5: 32.

1. WDH, *Years of My Youth*, 67–68, 70; WDH, "Country Printer," 5; J. A. Howells, "Ashtabula Fifty Years Ago," Ashtabula *Beacon Record*, 28 June 1902, TS copy of clipping at Hayes; "Notes by J. A. Howells," *AS*, ca. 8 Oct. 1909, Clipping at Hayes; Eugene H. Roseboom, *The Civil War Era: 1850–1873*, vol. 4 of *The History of the State of Ohio*, ed. Carl Wittke (Columbus: Ohio State Archaeological and Historical Society, 1944), 203.

2. WDH, *Years of My Youth*, 70; WDH, "Country Printer," 11; "Notes by J. A. Howells," *AS*, ca. 8 Oct. 1909, Clipping at Hayes; William A. Williams, *History of Ashtabula County, Ohio, with Illustrations and Biographical Sketches of Its*

Pioneers and Most Prominent Men (Philadelphia: Williams Brothers, 1878), 40, 41, 121; James Brewer Stewart, *Joshua R. Giddings and the Tactics of Radical Politics* (Cleveland: Press of Case Western Reserve Univ., 1970), 16–17, 95, 158–59, 214–15; H. L. Trefousse, *Benjamin Franklin Wade: Radical Republican from Ohio* (New York: Twayne, 1963), 56–59, 68, 70; Joshua R. Giddings to Joseph A. Giddings, 8 Feb. 1840, Joshua R. Giddings Papers, MIC 7, MS at OHS; Joshua R. Giddings to Joseph A. Giddings, 11 Jan. 1853, Joshua R. Giddings Papers, MIC 7, MS at OHS.

3. WDH, *Years of My Youth*, 70; WDH, "Country Printer," 7–8; [Joseph A. Howells], "Notes by the Editor," *AS*, 19 Sept. 1907, Clipping at Alfred; "Notes by J. A. Howells," *AS*, ca. 8 Oct. 1909, Clipping at Hayes; Williams, *Ashtabula County*, 121. The land contract for the two town lots on which the Howells family established its residence is dated 1 Sept. 1853, MS at Alfred. The Howells family house is named Saints' Rest on a photographic print located at Hayes.

4. WDH, *Years of My Youth*, 73, 78, 83; WDH, *My Literary Passions*, 25, 62, 68–70, 114.

5. WDH, *Years of My Youth*, 79–81. The probable time of Howells's breakdown has been established by John Crowley, "Dating Howells' Adolescent Breakdown," *Old Northwest*, 8 (1982): 13–22. Compare my Eriksonian interpretation of Howells's breakdown in the following pages with the Freudian interpretation in Crowley, *Black Heart's Truth*, 21–32.

6. WDH, *Years of My Youth*, 80–81.

7. Nineteenth-century "nervousness" has drawn considerable attention from historians. See Hale, *Freud and the Americans*, 47–68; Charles E. Rosenberg, "The Place of George M. Beard in Nineteenth-Century Psychiatry," *Bulletin of the History of Medicine*, 36 (1962): 245–59; Rosenberg, *No Other Gods*, 4–8, 54–62f, 98–108; Carroll Smith-Rosenberg, "The Hysterical Woman: Sex Roles and Role Conflict in Nineteenth-Century America," *Social Research*, 39 (1972): 652–78; John S. Haller, Jr., and Robin M. Haller, *The Physician and Sexuality in Victorian America* (Urbana: Univ. of Illinois Press, 1974), 5–43; Barbara Sicherman, "The Paradox of Prudence: Mental Health in the Gilded Age," *Journal of American History*, 62 (1976): 890–912; Lears, *No Place of Grace*, 47–58; Harvey Green, *Fit for America: Health, Fitness, Sport, and American Society* (New York: Pantheon, 1986), 137–66; F. G. Gosling, *Before Freud: Neurasthenia and the American Medical Community, 1870–1910* (Urbana: Univ. of Illinois Press, 1987).

8. For Winifred Howells's illness and death, see the studies cited in chap. 1, note 51.

9. Lears, *No Place of Grace*, 47–58, passim, offers the most acute analysis of the cultural meaning of nineteenth-century "nervousness" while demonstrating its relationship to the emerging therapeutic ethos.

10. For pertinent biographical detail on Jacobi and Beard, see Sicherman, "Paradox of Prudence, " 891–92, 901–9.

11. The major study of nineteenth-century adolescence is Kett, *Rites of Passage*, 3–211. Harvey J. Graff, "Early Adolescence in Antebellum America: The Remaking of Growing Up," *Journal of Early Adolescence*, 5 (1985): 411–27, notes that while Kett stresses the emergence of adolescence as a concept in the late nine-

teenth century, the foundation in experience for the concept derived from the early nineteenth century. In addition, see Ryan, *Cradle of the Middle Class*, 145–85; Katz and Davey, "Youth and Early Industrialization in a Canadian City," 81–119; Harvey J. Graff, "Patterns of Adolescence and Child Dependency in the Mid-Nineteenth Century City: A Sample from Boston, 1860," *History of Education Quarterly*, 13 (1973): 129–43; John Demos, "The Rise and Fall of Adolescence," *Past, Present and Personal: The Family and the Life Course in American History* (New York: Oxford Univ. Press, 1986), 92–113. For comparison with European patterns, see John R. Gillis, *Youth and History: Tradition and Change in European Age Relations, 1770–Present*, 2d ed. (New York: Academic Press, 1981).

12. For a general discussion of the shift in belief toward voluntary salvation, see William G. McLoughlin, *Revivals, Awakenings, and Reform: An Essay on Religion and Social Change in America, 1607–1977* (Chicago: Univ. of Chicago Press, 1978), 98–140.

13. Joshua R. Giddings to Joseph A. Giddings, 21 May 1835, MS at OHS; Joshua R. Giddings to Benjamin F. Wade, 22 May 1835, MS at OHS; Joshua R. Giddings to Laura W. Giddings, 28 June 1836, MS at OHS; Joshua R. Giddings to Laura W. Giddings, 11 Mar. 1836, MS at OHS; Joshua R. Giddings to Laura W. Giddings, 14 July 1837, MS at OHS; Joshua R. Giddings to Laura W. Giddings, 9 Dec. 1838, MS at OHS (all Giddings letters are in the Joshua R. Giddings Papers, MIC 7, OHS). Stewart, *Giddings*, 11, 15, 31.

14. WDH, *A Boy's Town*, 204; Aurelia H. Howells to Howells, 14 June 1915, MS at Alfred.

15. Howells's fears were appropriately expressed in terms of time—reaching his sixteenth year, waiting for the death knell. Like other antebellum Americans, he was becoming oriented to a rationalized conception of life stages that was replacing the more flexible divisions between childhood, adolescence, and adulthood that prevailed in the earlier traditional world. See Kett, *Rites of Passage*.

16. WDH, *Years of My Youth*, 78, 82, 102; WDH, *My Literary Passions*, 109; WDH, "Country Printer," 30.

17. WDH, *Years of My Youth*, 95; WDH, *My Literary Passions*, 69–70, 84–85, 113; WDH, "Country Printer," 30.

18. Howells to Joseph A. Howells, n.d., *Life in Letters of William Dean Howells*, ed. Mildred Howells (Garden City, N.Y.: Doubleday, Doran, 1923), 1: 73; Howells to John B. Howells, 2 Sept. 1863, *Selected Letters of W. D. Howells*, ed. George Arms, Richard H. Ballinger, Christoph K. Lohmann, John K. Reeves, et al. (Boston: Twayne, 1979), 1: 156; Howells to Aurelia H. Howells, 21 July 1915, *Selected Letters of W. D. Howells*, ed. William M. Gibson and Christoph K. Lohmann (Boston: Twayne, 1983), 6: 82; Aurelia H. Howells to Howells, 8 Aug. 1915, MS at Alfred; WDH, *Years of My Youth*, 97–98; Williams, *Ashtabula County*, 190.

19. WDH, *Years of My Youth*, 97–98; Kett, *Rites of Passage*, 19, 20; Announcement, Grand River Institute, *AS*, 21 Apr. 1853; "A Statement," Letter from William P. Brown, *AS*, 26 Jan. 1854.

20. WDH, *Years of My Youth*, 15, 87–88, 98–101; WDH, "Country Printer," 11–14; Howells to Harriet T. Upton, 9 Mar. 1910, *Selected Letters*, 5: 313; Howells

to Victoria M. Howells, 10 Oct. 1874, MS at Harvard; Howells to Joseph A. Howells, 11 Dec. 1910, *Selected Letters*, 5: 338; Howells to Joseph A. Howells, 9 Jan. 1911, MS at Harvard.

21. WDH, *My Literary Passions*, 56, 104–6, 109.

22. Ibid., 104; WDH, *Years of My Youth*, 85, 98.

23. WDH, *Years of My Youth*, 107; WDH, *My Literary Passions*, 63; [WDH], "Jefferson Lyceum Legislature," *AS*, 24 Nov. 1853; [WDH], "Lyceum Legislature," *AS*, 1 Dec. 1853; [WDH], "Jefferson Legislature," *AS*, 5 Jan. 1854.

24. WDH, *Years of My Youth*, 88, 92; WDH, *My Literary Passions*, 55–56.

25. WDH, *Years of My Youth*, 83, 91–92; WDH, *My Literary Passions*, 72–73, 77–78, 79–80, 86–88; Howells to Thomas W. Higginson, 9 Aug. 1888, *Selected Letters*, 3: 228.

26. WDH, *Years of My Youth*, 86–89, 91, 102; WDH, *My Literary Passions*, 56–57, 61–62; WDH, "Country Printer," 22–23, 30–31.

27. WDH, *Years of My Youth*, 92–93; WDH, *My Literary Passions*, 104–5; Joseph A. Howells to William H. Venable, 27 July 1909, Dolores Venable Memorial Collection, MSS 127, TS at OHS.

28. For examples of the writings of Celestia R. Colby, see "The Daughter's Appeal," *AS*, 15 June 1854; "Clara Vinlay," *AS*, 6 July 1854; "A Requiem," *AS*, 3 Aug. 1854; "The Deserted Dwelling," *AS*, 14 Sept. 1854. Howells's distaste for the sentimental writing sent to the *Sentinel* is evident in " 'Original Poetry,' " *AS*, 12 Oct. 1854; "Obituary Poetry," *AS*, 2 Nov. 1854. For the clash of reading interests between Will and Joseph, see Fawcett, "Mr. Howells and his Brother," 1027. Howells referred to "blood-puddings" in [WDH], "The Independent Candidate: A Story of To Day," *AS*, 7 Dec. 1854.

29. On lyceums, see Donald M. Scott, "The Popular Lecture and the Creation of a Public in Mid-Nineteenth-Century America," *Journal of American History*, 66 (1980): 791–809. On academies, see Kett, *Rites of Passage*, 18–20. WDH, *My Literary Passions*, 55–56, 95; Mary Land, " 'Bluff' Ben Wade's New England Background," *New England Quarterly*, 27 (1954): 491; Aurelia H. Howells, "Paper on William Dean Howells," n.d., TS at Harvard.

30. Joshua R. Giddings to Comfort P. Giddings, 26 Apr. 1840, Joshua R. Giddings Papers, MIC 7, MS at OHS; Aurelia H. Howells to Howells, 27 Aug. 1916, MS at Alfred.

31. Joshua R. Giddings to Comfort P. Giddings, 26 Apr. 1840, Joshua R. Giddings Papers, MIC 7, MS at OHS.

32. Antilawyer sentiment and the social relations of village lawyers are discussed in Lawrence M. Friedman, *A History of American Law* (New York: Simon and Schuster, 1973), 265–78; William R. Johnson, "Education and Professional Life Styles: Law and Medicine in the Nineteenth Century," *History of Education Quarterly*, 14 (1974): 185–207. The status of Jefferson lawyers can be gleaned from Williams, *Ashtabula County*, 67–85, 91, 93, 105–6, 151–52; [Cornelius Udell], *Condensed History of Jefferson, Ashtabula County, Ohio* (Jefferson: J. A. Howells, 1877), 46, 88–89, 90, 92, 93; George W. Julian, *The Life of Joshua R. Giddings* (Chicago: A. C. McClurg, 1892), 399. Jefferson lawyers were among the most wealthy holders of property reported in the federal census returns. The wealthiest

person in the 1860 census was a lawyer, N. L. Chaffe, whose real and personal property totaled $38,000. Six and perhaps seven of the thirteen most wealthy property holders were lawyers or members of lawyers' families. William Cooper Howells reported $2,900 in total property in 1860, ranking forty-fifth in the village. See *Seventh Census of the United States: 1850. Original Returns of the Assistant Marshalls. First Series: White and Free Colored Population. Schedule I, Free Inhabitants, District No. 8, Jefferson Borough, Ashtabula County, Ohio, 28 June 1850;* and *Eighth Census of the United States: 1860. Original Returns of the Assistant Marshalls. First Series: White and Free Colored Population. Schedule I, Free Inhabitants, Jefferson Village, Ashtabula County, Ohio, 18 June 1860.*

33. WDH, "The Turning Point of My Life," 165; WDH, "Country Printer," 30.

34. For discussion of antislavery enclaves, see Lawrence J. Friedman, *Gregarious Saints: Self and Community in American Abolitionism, 1830–1870* (Cambridge, Eng.: Cambridge Univ. Press, 1982). On the idea of a "slave power" conspiracy, with references to Giddings's pronouncements, see Eric Foner, *Free Soil, Free Labor, Free Men,* 73–102. [WCH], "Let Us Be Up and Doing," *AS,* 5 Jan. 1854; [WCH], "Anti-Slavery Doctrines," *AS,* 12 Jan. 1854.

35. [Joshua R. Giddings], "The Church—Its Relations to Freedom: A Letter from Joshua R. Giddings," Clipping from *National Anti-Slavery Standard,* ca. 1857, in Giddings Scrapbook, 1853–1859, Joshua R. Giddings Papers, MIC 7, OHS; Joshua R. Giddings to Laura W. Giddings, 19 Jan. 1845, Joshua R. Giddings Papers, MIC 7, MS at OHS. [Joshua R. Giddings], "This errant infidelity . . . ," *AS,* 9 July 1857; [Joshua R. Giddings], "Washington Correspondent," *AS,* 4 Mar. 1858; [WCH], "American Infidelity," *AS,* 25 Mar. 1858; [WCH], "To the Voters of Ashtabula County," *AS,* 19 Sept. 1861.

36. [WCH], "Let Us Be Up and Doing," *AS,* 5 Jan. 1854. The urge to assert individual autonomy as an impulse in antislavery agitation has received intricate treatment by historians. See, in particular, Ronald G. Walters, *The Antislavery Appeal: American Abolitionism after 1830* (Baltimore: Johns Hopkins Univ. Press, 1976), 54–87; Peter Walker, *Moral Choices: Memory, Desire and Imagination in Nineteenth-Century Abolition* (Baton Rouge: Louisiana State Univ. Press, 1978); Abzug, *Passionate Liberator;* Perry, *Henry Clarke Wright.*

37. Allan Nevins, *Ordeal of the Union: A House Dividing, 1852–1857* (New York: Charles Scribner's Sons, 1947), 2: 88f; Roseboom, *Civil War Era,* 279–86; Stewart, *Giddings,* 223–30; [WCH], "People's Meeting," *AS,* 2 Feb. 1854.

38. Ibid.; Trefousse, *Wade,* 84–93; [WCH], "People's Meeting," *AS,* 23 Feb. 1854; [WCH], "Progress of Freedom," *AS,* 2 Mar. 1854; [WCH], "B. F. Wade," *AS,* 9 Mar. 1854; [WCH], "The Fourth," *AS,* 29 June 1854; [WCH], " 'What of the Night?' " *AS,* 24 Aug. 1854.

39. [WCH], "Let Us Be Up and Doing," *AS,* 5 Jan. 1854.

40. WDH, *Years of My Youth,* 78–79.

41. WDH, *My Literary Passions,* 71, 114–15.

42. Anne T. Howells to William C. Howells, 5 Mar. 1854, MS at Alfred; Anne T. Howells to William C. Howells, 25 Apr. 1854, MS at Alfred; Henry Howells to William C. Howells, 14 May 1854, MS at Alfred; Anne T. Howells

to William C. Howells, 27 May 1854, MS at Alfred; Joshua R. Giddings to Grotius R. Giddings, 16 July 1854, Joshua R. Giddings Papers, MIC 7, MS at OHS; Joshua R. Giddings to Laura W. Giddings, 16 July 1854, Joshua R. Giddings Papers, MIC 7, MS at OHS; [WCH], "Dogs—Dogs," AS, 29 June 1854; [WCH], "Cholera prevails . . . ," AS, 3 Aug. 1854.

43. WDH, Years of My Youth, 19, 79; [WCH], "Hydrophobia," HI, 30 July 1841; [WCH], "Hydrophobia," HI, 13 Aug. 1841; [Isaac T. Saunders], "Horrible Death by Hydrophobia," HI, 13 Aug. 1841.

44. WDH, Years of My Youth, 79.

45. Ibid., 80–81; WCH, Recollections of Life in Ohio, 188–89, 190–91; Joseph A. Howells to William C. Howells, 16 Sept. 1877, MS at Alfred.

46. Aurelia H. Howells to Howells, 14 June 1915, MS at Alfred.

47. WDH, Years of My Youth, 81.

48. For studies treating expressive dimensions of "nervous prostration," see note 7. Feinstein, Becoming William James, esp. 182–205, analyzes the covert language of illness in the James family. The most thorough discussion of the psychoanalytic concept of the active reversal of passive experience or "reversal of voice" is George S. Klein, Psychoanalytic Theory: An Exploration of Essentials (New York: International Universities Press, 1976), 259–79. Klein explains "reversal of voice" as the individual's unconscious effort to master feelings of helplessness and to restore a sense of continuity and control: "There is a tendency to recreate in an active mode an event that has been passively experienced as in some respect unacceptable, unrelated, or alien to the self. Such events can be experienced as meaningless, hence anxiety evoking, unfamiliar, and even as profoundly traumatic and alienating blows. The response in such circumstances is of the nature: 'What I have experienced as being done to me, I must make happen.' " (p. 261).

49. On water-cure establishments, see Green, Fit for America, 54–67. Advertisement for Austinburg Water Cure Establishment, William A. Baldwin, Physician and Proprietor, AS, 1 June 1854; Joseph Howells, Jr., to William C. Howells, 10 Aug. 1854, MS at Alfred.

50. Joseph Howells, Jr., to William C. Howells, 10 Aug. 1854, MS at Alfred; Howells, My Literary Passions, 71; [WDH], "The Exodus of Dickens," AS, 10 Aug. 1854.

51. [WDH], review of The Potiphar Papers, by George William Curtis, AS, 31 Aug. 1854.

52. [WDH], " 'Original Poetry,' " AS, 12 Oct. 1854; [WDH], "Obituary Poetry," AS, 2 Nov. 1854.

53. [WDH], "You and I," AS, 12 Oct. 1854; WDH, My Literary Passions, 64–66.

54. [WDH], "Goldsmith," AS, 3 Aug. 1854; [WDH], "You and I," AS, 12 Oct. 1854; WDH, My Literary Passions, 97–98.

55. [WCH], "Ohio Redeemed!" AS, 12 Oct. 1854; [WCH], "The Elections," AS, 19 Oct. 1854; [WCH], "The Victory," AS, 26 Oct. 1854.

56. [WDH], "Nightly Rain," AS, 5 Oct. 1854.

57. Howells to Mary D. Howells, 13 July 1868, Selected Letters, 1: 296; WDH, Years of My Youth, 81.

58. WDH, Introduction to *Recollections of Life in Ohio*, by WCH, vi.
59. WDH, *My Literary Passions*, 69.
60. Ibid., 75.
61. Ibid.

4. The Umbrella Man

Epigraph: WDH, *My Literary Passions*, 74.

1. Joshua R. Giddings to Laura W. Giddings, 22 and 23 Apr. 1837, Joshua R. Giddings Papers, MIC 7, MS at OHS; Joshua R. Giddings to Laura W. Giddings, 16 Dec. 1838, Joshua R. Giddings Papers, MIC 7, MS at OHS; Stewart, *Giddings*, 89–90, 146–47.

2. Stewart, *Giddings*, 69–76; Joshua R. Giddings to Laura W. Giddings, 16 Dec. 1838, Joshua R. Giddings Papers, MIC 7, MS at OHS.

3. The force of "locality" in the thought and feeling of antebellum Americans is emphasized in Bender, *Community and Social Change in America*, esp. 86–108. In addition, see his "The Cultures of Intellectual Life: The City and the Professions," *New Directions in American Intellectual History*, ed. John Higham and Paul K. Conklin (Baltimore: Johns Hopkins Univ. Press, 1979), 181–95. On the ideas of "free labor" and "slave power," see Foner, *Free Soil, Free Labor, Free Men*, passim.

4. WDH, "Country Printer," 10, 11–14; Joseph A. Howells to Howells, 24 Sept. 1911, TS at Alfred; [WCH], "Mechanics," *AS*, 9 June 1853.

5. [WDH], "The Independent Candidate: A Story of To Day," *AS*, 23, 30 Nov., 7, 21, 28 Dec. 1854, 4, 11, 18 Jan. 1855. All quotations in the following paragraphs are from these installments.

6. WDH, *My Literary Passions*, 66–67; Fawcett, "Mr. Howells and his Brother," 1028.

7. Howells lifted "Old Smith" from a sketch he had written earlier, where the character voices the author's detached musings much in the manner of the sentimental "Ik Marvel." Like Howells's author-narrator in "The Independent Candidate," this earlier "Old Smith" is sensitive to the fickleness of his imagined audience. "How shall I, when you have read my article," he asks, "become again the rusty old fellow whom nobody knows!" [WDH], "What I Saw at the Circus: Old Smith's Experience," *AS*, 7 Sept. 1854.

8. Stewart, *Giddings*, 224–25.

9. Ibid., 95; Joshua R. Giddings to Joseph A. Giddings, 30 June 1852, Joshua R. Giddings Papers, MIC 7, MS at OHS; [WCH], "The Conneaut Reporter," *AS*, 2 Nov. 1854; Williams, *History of Ashtabula County*, 41.

10. For an overview of vernacular humor, see Walter Blair, *Native American Humor (1800–1900)* (New York: American Book, 1937). Kenneth S. Lynn, *Mark Twain and Southwestern Humor* (Boston: Little, Brown, 1960), treats vernacular humor as a subversive element in the tales of humorists oriented to the Whig party and the plantation tradition. Although he observes that the typical narrator in these tales was a "self-controlled Gentleman" who ambivalently allowed ver-

nacular characters a voice, he does not point out the specifically middle-class values represented by the narrators. Lynn discusses how the "frame" of the self-controlled narrator failed to contain the vitality of vernacular language in confrontations of narrators and vernacular characters. The device of confrontation is further discussed in Henry Nash Smith, *Mark Twain: The Development of a Writer* (New York: Harvard Univ. Press, 1962), esp. 1–22. Ivan Illich traces the origin of the word *vernacular* and defines it as designating "the activities of people when they are not motivated by thoughts of exchange, a word that denotes autonomous, non-market-related actions through which people satisfy everyday needs." Following Illich, I use the word to refer broadly to language and action that fostered communal values associated with the traditional world of household production. See Illich, *Shadow Work* (Boston: Marion Boyars, 1981), esp. 29–74.

11. WDH, *My Literary Passions*, 71–73, 97–98, 100–101; [WDH], "The Exodus of Dickens," *AS*, 10 Aug. 1854.

12. On the sentimental landscape aesthetic, see Smith, *Mark Twain*, 77–81; Leo Marx, "The Pilot and the Passenger: Landscape Conventions in the Style of *Huckleberry Finn*," *American Literature*, 28 (1956): 129–46.

13. In his analysis of Mark Twain's development as a vernacular writer, Henry Nash Smith observes that Twain worked through a "middle style" before he arrived at a fully developed vernacular style. This middle style included concern for the "world of commonplace things," with the assumption "that the reader lives in the same world," and the use of "homely images introduced without self-consciousness." Smith, *Mark Twain*, 81.

14. WDH, *Years of My Youth*, 84; WDH, *My Literary Passions*, 67.

15. The lectures as they appeared in the Boston *Advertiser* are reprinted in James Russell Lowell, *Lectures on English Poets* (Cleveland: Rowfant Club, 1897).

16. Ibid., 11, 18, 92, 162–63, 164, 170, 200, 203, 206, 209–10; WDH, *My Literary Passions*, 81.

17. Lowell, *Lectures on English Poets*, 203, 209–10, passim.

18. On the romantic strategy of withdrawal to an ideal realm of value, see Raymond Williams, *Culture and Society, 1780–1950* (New York: Columbia Univ. Press, 1960), 30–48. For reactions of American romantic writers to the marketplace, see Michael T. Gilmore, *American Romanticism and the Marketplace* (Chicago: Univ. of Chicago Press, 1985). The broad cultural significance of patterns of engagement and withdrawal is discussed by Lears, *No Place of Grace*, 218f.

19. [WDH], "Spring," *National Era*, 3 May 1855, reprinted in [W. D. Howells and J. J. Piatt], *Poems of Two Friends* (Columbus: Follett, Foster, [1860]), 118; [WDH], "The Death of May," *National Era*, 21 June 1855, reprinted in Howells and Piatt, *Poems of Two Friends*, 111–12; [WDH], "James R. Lowell, in one of his Boston lectures . . . ," *AS*, 22 Feb. 1855; [WDH], "The 'Reviews,' " *AS*, 4 Jan. 1855; [WDH], "The Westminster Review," *AS*, 22 Feb. 1855; [WDH], "Magazines and Notices," *AS*, 14 June 1855; WDH, *My Literary Passions*, 91–92.

20. [WDH], "The Exodus of Dickens," *AS*, 10 Aug. 1854.

21. WDH, *Years of My Youth*, 83, 98; WDH, "The Wreath in Heaven—A Fancy," *Ohio Farmer*, 26 May 1855, reprinted in Howells and Piatt, *Poems of Two Friends*, 106.

22. WDH, *My Literary Passions*, 92; WDH, "Real Diary of a Boy," 34.

23. WDH, *My Literary Passions*, 93–96; WDH, *Years of My Youth*, 93, 94–95.

24. WDH, *My Literary Passions*, 94–95; WDH, *Years of My Youth*, 94–95; Hans L. Trefousse, *The Radical Republicans: Lincoln's Vanguard for Racial Justice* (Baton Rouge: Louisiana State Univ. Press, 1968), 8; "Stays True to Its Traditions," Cleveland *Plain Dealer*, Story on Jefferson politics with Joseph A. Howells interview, n.d., Clipping at Alfred.

25. WDH, *My Literary Passions*, 95–96.

26. [WDH], "Notices of Magazines, etc.," *AS*, 28 June 1855; WDH, "Country Printer," 26–27, 32; [WCH], "Female Compositors," *AS*, 9 June 1853; W. J. Rorabaugh, *The Craft Apprentice: From Franklin to the Machine Age in America* (New York: Oxford Univ. Press, 1986), 76–96.

27. WDH, *My Literary Passions*, 106–8; [WDH], Translation of chapter from *Lazarillo de Tormes*, *AS*, 15 Nov. 1855; Michael Alpert, trans., *Two Spanish Picaresque Novels* (Baltimore: Penguin Books, 1969), 23–79.

28. WDH, *My Literary Passions*, 106–8. The *Sentinel* had reprinted an article describing J. P. Jewett and Company's great success with *Uncle Tom's Cabin*, pointing out that the Cleveland branch alone had sold over one hundred thousand copies. "The Book Trade," *AS*, 8 Sept. 1853.

29. WDH, *My Literary Passions*, 115; "Song," Excerpt from *Maud*, *AS*, 30 Aug. 1855; [George W. Curtis], "Editor's Easy Chair," *Harper's Monthly*, 65 (1855): 705; Alfred Tennyson, *Maud, and Other Poems* (Boston: Ticknor and Fields, 1855), 7–106.

30. WDH, *My Literary Passions*, 116–19, 122.

31. Lowell, *Lectures on English Poetry*, 203.

32. WDH, *My Literary Passions*, 118; WDH, *Years of My Youth*, 85.

33. WDH, *Years of My Youth*, 106–9. Victoria's ultimately unfulfilled literary desires are reflected in Journal of Victoria M. Howells, 30 Mar. 1871 to 30 Apr. 1871, entries for 5, 18, 19, 20 Apr. 1871, MS at Alfred; Victoria M. Howells to Howells, 2 Dec. 1875, MS at Alfred; Victoria M. Howells to Howells, 14 Dec. 1875, MS at Alfred. For discussion of how sibling ties in nineteenth-century families took on symbolic meanings relating to family duty and personal identity, see Mintz, *A Prison of Expectations*, 147–87. Lears, *No Place of Grace*, 218–25, 241–43, 244–45, 248–50, 278–79, passim, specifies complex ways in which an idealized feminine principle, partly derived from the cult of domesticity, attracted nineteenth-century males who sought a revitalized sense of self.

34. WDH, *Years of My Youth*, 85.

35. Ibid., 103; [WCH], "The Election," *AS*, 11 Oct. 1855; Roseboom, *Civil War Era*, 309–12. See William Cooper Howells's political reports from Columbus, beginning with "Letters from the Capitol," *AS*, 10 Jan. 1856.

36. Howells to William C. Howells, 10 Jan. 1856, MS at Alfred; [WDH], "Ohio, the first Democracy . . . ," *AS*, 24 Jan. 1856; [WDH], "Culpa Nostra!" *AS*, 21 Feb. 1856; [WDH], "Mr. Giddings," *AS*, 21 Feb. 1856.

37. [WDH], "The Pittsburgh Convention," *AS*, 14 Feb. 1856.

38. WDH, *My Literary Passions*, 120; WDH, *Years of My Youth*, 110–11.

39. [WCH], "Brutality in Congress," *AS*, 29 May 1856; [WCH], "Destruction

of Lawrence," *AS*, 29 May 1856; [WCH], "Indignation Meeting," *AS*, 29 May 1856; [WCH], "Friends of Freedom," *AS*, 5 June 1856; [WCH], "From Kansas," Introduces letter from Harvey Greene, *AS*, 5 June 1856; [WCH], "Indignation Meetings," *AS*, 12 June 1856; [WCH], "Subscription for Kansas," *AS*, 12 June 1856; "The Kansas Herald of Freedom," Letter from Harvey Greene, *AS*, 12 June 1856; "Late Kansas Letter," Letter from Harvey Greene, *AS*, 11 Sept. 1856; "Terrible Butchery," *AS*, 18 Sept. 1856.

40. [WCH], "Kansas," *AS*, 17 July 1856; [WDH], "Kansas Song," *AS*, 7 Aug. 1856, MS at Harvard; [WCH], "Rally, Rally," *AS*, 23 Oct. 1856; [WCH], "What Does It Mean?" *AS*, 23 Oct. 1856; [WCH], "To the Battle," *AS*, 30 Oct. 1856; [WCH], "The Coming Struggle," *AS*, 30 Oct. 1856.

41. [WCH], "4, 163!!!," *AS*, 6 Nov. 1856; [WCH], "Glorious Old Ashtabula," *AS*, 6 Nov. 1856; Nevins, *Ordeal of the Union: A House Dividing*, 2: 510–11, 514; Roseboom, *Civil War Era*, 322–23.

42. Howells used the phrase "Holy Cause" in his campaign lyric, "Kansas Song," *AS*, 7 Aug. 1856. Charles Eliot Norton, ed., *Orations and Addresses of George William Curtis* (New York: Harper and Brothers, 1894), 1: [1]–35; W. D. Howells, *Literary Friends and Acquaintance*, ed. David F. Hiatt and Edwin H. Cady (Bloomington: Indiana Univ. Press, 1968), 95.

5. Striving away from Home

Epigraph: [WDH], "Editor's Study," *Harper's Monthly*, 83 (1891): 155.

1. WDH, *My Literary Passions*, 122; WDH, *Years of My Youth*, 25–26; Anne T. and Joseph Howells to William C. Howells, 13 Nov. 1853, MS at Alfred; Anne T. Howells to William C. Howells, 18 Jan. 1857, MS at Alfred; Joseph Howells to William C. Howells, 24 Feb. 1857, MS at Alfred.

2. [WDH], "A Tale of Love and Politics: Adventures of a Printer Boy," *AS*, 1 Sept. 1853. Howells's contemporary Horatio Alger (b. 1832) has been credited with adding the element of chance to the success tale as he began writing in the genre after the Civil War. See Wyllie, *The Self-Made Man in America*, 60; R. Richard Wohl, "The 'Country Boy' Myth and Its Place in American Urban Culture: The Nineteenth-Century Contribution," ed. Moses Rischin, *Perspectives in American History*, 3 (1969): 124–25. Cawelti, however, points out earlier instances of "chance" in success stories of the 1840s and 1850s. *Apostles of the Self-Made Man*, 106–7, 109, 115–16.

3. "Without [self-reliance and self-government]," wrote Artemas Muzzey, "we can never trust a child in the world; but with them, filled with a personal piety, a deep-rooted benevolence, and a calm moral independence, he is armed at all points." A. B. Muzzey, *The Fireside: An Aid to Parents* (Boston: Crosby, Nichols, 1854), 110. The specter of home leaving informs the advice literature as a whole, and the idea of self-control was predicated on the inevitability of separation from home. For specific references to home leaving, see Muzzey, *The Fireside*, 20–21; John Angell James, *The Young Man From Home* (New York: D. Appleton, 1840), v–viii, 9–14, passim. The home-leaving anxieties of young women were

often compounded by difficult adjustments to marriage. See the studies cited in chap. 1, note 52. Smith-Rosenberg discusses home-leaving young men as "liminal" figures, persons in transition, suspended between worlds, whose uncontained energies raised the threats of disorder and instability. "Sex as Symbol in Victorian Purity," 121–47; "Davey Crockett as Trickster," 325–50. The concept of liminality is also applied to antebellum youth by Halttunen, *Confidence Men and Painted Women*, 27. Agnew, *Worlds Apart*, 24–27, passim, analyzes more generally how the spread of market exchange generated liminal or liminoid forms of cultural expression.

4. The phrase "nautical metaphor" is employed by Kett to describe the sea or voyage imagery used by the advice books to portray the passage from home. *Rites of Passage*, 95. The exaggeration of youthful depravity is addressed by Ryan, who sets moral reformers' notions that "thousands" in antebellum Utica, New York, had fallen victim to sexual vice against the very few recorded arrests for prostitution or cases of illegitimacy. Young men themselves resisted the charge of impurity by issuing resolutions asserting their uprightness. *Cradle of the Middle Class*, 116–27. The dangers that advice writers saw besetting home-leaving youth are well described in Halttunen, *Confidence Men and Painted Women*, esp. 1–55; Ryan, *Empire of Mother*, 6of. "Early departure from the homestead . . . ," quoted in Kett, *Rites of Passage*, 127; "juvenile depravity" and "Reformation . . . ," Muzzey, *The Fireside*, 296–97.

5. In my understanding of separation anxiety, I am indebted to the synthesis of psychoanalytic studies presented by Lasch, *Minimal Self*, 163–96. The principal theorist of the response to separation anxiety and consequent feelings of self-disintegration in fantasies of grandiosity and idealization is Heinz Kohut. For clarity, I use "grandiosity" to describe Kohut's fantasy of "mirroring." See *The Analysis of the Self: A Systematic Approach to the Psychoanalytic Treatment of Narcissistic Personality Disorders* (New York: International Universities Press, 1971); *The Restoration of the Self* (New York: International Universities Press, 1977). Lasch has pioneered application of Kohut's perspectives along with other theorists of narcissism to the analysis of culture in *The Culture of Narcissism: American Life in an Age of Diminishing Expectation* (New York: W. W. Norton, 1979), esp. 31–51. Though he uses different terms, Lears, *No Place of Grace*, analyzes nineteenth-century psychic and cultural expressions of separation anxiety with exceptional sensitivity.

6. For the idealization of home and mother, see Barbara Welter, "The Cult of True Womanhood, 1820–1860," *American Quarterly*, 18 (1966): 151–74; Cott, *Bonds of Womanhood*, esp. 63–100; Ryan, *Empire of Mother*, passim; Colleen McDannell, *The Christian Home in Victorian America, 1840–1900* (Bloomington: Indiana Univ. Press, 1986). For the ideology of autonomous individualism, see the studies cited in chap. 1, notes 24 and 25. Discussions of antebellum death consciousness and funereal imagery include David E. Stannard, *The Puritan Way of Death: A Study in Religion, Culture, and Social Change* (New York: Oxford Univ. Press, 1977), 167–88; Lewis O. Saum, "Death in the Popular Mind of Pre–Civil War America"; Ann Douglas, "Heaven Our Home: Consolation Literature in the Northern United States, 1830–1880"; and Stanley French, "The Cemetery as

Cultural Institution: The Establishment of Mount Auburn and the 'Rural Cemetery' Movement," in David E. Stannard, ed., *Death in America* (Philadelphia: Univ. of Pennsylvania Press, 1975), 30–91; Halttunen, *Confidence Men and Painted Women*, 124–52; Martha V. Pike and Janice Gray Armstrong, eds., *A Time to Mourn: Expressions of Grief in Nineteenth Century America* (Stony Brook, N.Y.: Museums at Stony Brook, 1980).

7. WDH, *Years of My Youth*, 110.

8. The quotation is from a canceled passage in [WDH], ["Luke Beazeley"], MS at Harvard, 7.

9. WDH, *Years of My Youth*, 114–15; WDH, *My Literary Passions*, 120–21.

10. WDH, *Years of My Youth*, 108, 110–11, 112–13, 114, 115; WDH, *My Literary Passions*, 121.

11. WDH, *Years of My Youth*, 107, 111–12, 113, 114, 374.

12. Ibid., 114, 115, 119.

13. Ibid., 124; Howells to Martin D. Potter, 9 Oct. 1858, *Selected Letters*, 1: 19; Foner, *Free Soil, Free Labor, Free Men*, 49; Roseboom, *Civil War Era*, 335–36; [WDH], "Letter from Columbus," *CG*, 2 Feb. 1857.

14. Foner, *Free Soil, Free Labor, Free Men*, 138–40; [WDH], "Letter from Columbus," *CG*, 10 Jan. 1857; [WDH], "Letter from Columbus," *CG*, 4 Feb. 1857; [WDH], "Letter from Columbus," *CG*, 23 Mar. 1857.

15. [WDH], "Letter from Columbus," *CG*, 24 Jan. 1857; [WDH], "Letter from Columbus," *CG*, 28 Jan. 1857; [WDH], "Letter from Columbus," *CG*, 29 Jan. 1857; [WDH], "Letter from Columbus," *CG*, 18 Mar. 1857.

16. [WDH], "Letter from Columbus," *CG*, 15 Jan. 1857; [WDH], "Columbus Correspondence," *CG*, 16 Jan. 1857; [WDH], "Letter from Columbus," *CG*, 19 Jan. 1857; "Slough Re-nominated and Rowdyism Indorsed—The Democratic Party—An Opposition Candidate," *CG*, 9 Feb. 1857.

17. [WDH], "Letter from Columbus," *CG*, 30 Jan. 1857; [WDH], "Letter from Columbus," *CG*, 2 Feb. 1857; [WDH], "Letter from Columbus," *CG*, 9 Feb. 1857; [WDH], "The Slough Case Again," *CG*, 9 Feb. 1857; "The Late Case of Expulsion," *CG*, 4 Feb. 1857; "Slough Re-nominated and Rowdyism Indorsed—The Democratic Party—An Opposition Candidate," *CG*, 9 Feb. 1857; "The Approaching Election—The Proper Course," *CG*, 10 Feb. 1857; "The Full-Stomached Party," *CG*, 11 Feb. 1857; "The Slough Case," *CG*, 13 Feb. 1857. The election's final result is given in *CG*, 20 Feb. 1857.

18. WDH, *Years of My Youth*, 121; WDH, *My Literary Passions*, 124, 125; Howells to Joseph A. Howells, 10 Apr. 1857, *Selected Letters*, 1: 8.

19. Howells to William C. Howells, 19 Apr. 1857, MS at Harvard. In a letter to his sister Victoria, Howells stated that he would be home "within a few weeks." Howells to Victoria M. Howells, 20 Apr. 1857, *Selected Letters*, 1: 9. In *My Literary Passions*, 124–25, Howells recalled that his total time in Cincinnati was "a few weeks."

20. Howells to Joseph A. Howells, 10 Apr. 1857, *Selected Letters*, 1: 8; "City Intelligence," *CG*, 24 Mar.–1 Apr. 1857; WDH, *My Literary Passions*, 124; WDH, *Years of My Youth*, 123.

21. WDH, *Years of My Youth*, 122; "City Intelligence," *CG*, 24 Mar.–1 Apr. 1857.

22. WDH, *My Literary Passions*, 125; WDH, *Years of My Youth*, 121, 122, 123. Moncure D. Conway, who lived in Cincinnati at this time, described it as "the most cultivated of western cities." See his fondly remembered catalogue of cultural activities. *Autobiography, Memories and Experiences of Moncure Daniel Conway* (London: Cassell, 1904), 1: 226–27.

23. Howells to Victoria M. Howells, 20 Apr. 1857, *Selected Letters*, 1: 9; WDH, *My Literary Passions*, 125.

24. WDH, *My Literary Passions*, 125; WDH, *Years of My Youth*, 124; Mary D. Howells to Victoria M. Howells, 29 Oct. [1857], MS at Alfred; Mary D. Howells to Anne T. and Aurelia H. Howells, 3 Mar. [1864], MS at Alfred.

25. WDH, *My Literary Passions*, 125; WDH, *Years of My Youth*, 124; Howells to Dune Dean, 9 and 11 Sept. 1857, *Selected Letters*, 1: 11.

26. [WDH], "Local and Other Matters," *AS*, 25 June 1857; [WDH], "Local and Other Matters," *AS*, 2 July 1857; [WDH], "Local and Other Matters," *AS*, 9 July 1857; [WDH], "Local and Other Matters," *AS*, 16 July 1857; [WDH], "Local and Other Matters," *AS*, 30 July 1857.

27. WDH, *My Literary Passions*, 125–27; [WDH], "Gossip," *AS*, 13 Mar. 1856; Howells to Dune Dean, 9 and 11 Sept. 1857, *Selected Letters*, 1: 10. Howells's translations from the German include "The Walpurgis-night: From the German of H. Zschokke," *AS*, 6, 13, 20 Aug. 1857; "The Prince's Book: From the German of H. [Z]schokke," *AS*, 15, 22, 29 Oct. 1857; "Measure for Measure: From the German of C. Weisflog," *AS*, 5, 12, 19 Nov. 1857; "Massacre of the Jews at Lisbon: From the German of John Frederic Jacobs," *AS*, 26 Nov., 2, 10, 24 Dec. 1857, 7 Jan. 1858.

28. WDH, *My Literary Passions*, 129; "Henry Heine, the German poet . . . ," *AS*, 9 Mar. 1854.

29. Howells to Dune Dean, 9 and 11 Sept. 1857, MS at Harvard. My reading of Howells's translation of Heine's motto from Ludwig Börne differs from the editors' reading in *Selected Letters*, 1: 10. I read *time* while the editors read *times*.

30. Heinrich Heine, *Travel-Pictures: Including "The Tour in the Harz," "Norderney," and "Book of Ideas," Together with "The Romantic School,"* trans. Francis Storr, 2d ed. (London: George Bell and Sons, 1895), 2–78. For treatment of *Die Harzreise* in terms of the poet-persona, see Jeffrey L. Sammons, *Heinrich Heine: The Elusive Poet* (New Haven: Yale Univ. Press, 1969), 103–15.

31. [WDH], "Editor's Easy Chair," *Harper's Monthly*, 107 (1903): 483; WDH, *My Literary Passions*, 126. Sammons suggests that Heine had a "hard time in overcoming what today we should call his adolescence." He argues that Heine's early writings allowed him to gain "control over the management of his self-image": "It would not be misleading to say that the creation of a surrogate persona, achieved with such energy in the years of *Buch der Lieder* and the *Reisebilder*, became a habit with Heine throughout most of the rest of his public and private life." *Heinrich Heine: The Elusive Poet*, 17, 21, 122, passim. In addition,

see Jeffrey L. Sammons, *Heinrich Heine: A Modern Biography* (Princeton: Princeton Univ. Press, 1979).

32. WDH, *My Literary Passions*, 130, 141; [WDH], "Editor's Easy Chair," *Harper's Monthly*, 107 (1903): 480–81.

33. WDH, *My Literary Passions*, 128–29, 130; Howells to George Bainton, 8 Jan. 1888, *Selected Letters*, 3: 213.

34. WDH, *My Literary Passions*, 46–47; [WDH], review of *Scintillations from the Prose Works of Heinrich Heine*, trans. Simon Adler Stern, *Atlantic Monthly*, 32 (1873): 237; Howells to Oliver W. Holmes, Jr., 1 Sept. 1860, *Selected Letters*, 1: 62.

35. W. D. Howells, "Professor Cross's Life of Sterne," *North American Review*, 191 (1910): 275. On Heine and dancing, see Sammons, *Heinrich Heine: The Elusive Poet*, 330–31, 335f; Barker Fairley, *Heinrich Heine: An Interpretation* (Oxford: Clarendon, 1954), 34–46; A. I. Sandor, *The Exile of Gods: Interpretation of a Theme, a Theory and a Technique in the Work of Heinrich Heine* (The Hague: Mouton, 1967), 172–74. The translation of the phrases from *Florentinische Nächte* is by Michael Hamburger, *Contraries: Studies in German Literature* (New York: E. P. Dutton, 1970), 166–67. Heinrich Heine, "Das Sklavenschiff," *Lyric Poems and Ballads*, trans. Ernst Feise (New York: McGraw-Hill, 1961), 36–45.

36. Swedenborg's phrase "ends, causes, and effects in an indissoluble connection" is quoted in Block, *New Church in the New World*, 40. Much of Swedenborg's appeal to Americans, according to John Humphrey Noyes, was that he appeared to be "a man of science" who "seemed to reduce the universe to scientific order." Quoted in Whitney R. Cross, *The Burned-Over District: The Social and Intellectual History of Enthusiastic Religion in Western New York, 1800–1850* (Ithaca, N.Y.: Cornell Univ. Press, 1950), 343.

37. "Life," Heine wrote, "is so comically sweet, and the world is so delightfully topsy-turvy, the dream of some half-tipsy god, who has taken French leave of the Olympian carousal, has lain down to sleep on a solitary star, and knows not that while he dreams he is creating; and the dreams themselves are a jumble of motley madness and harmonious design. The Iliad, Plato, the Battle of Marathon, Moses, the Venus de' Medici, the Strasburg Cathedral, the French Revolution, Hegel, steamboats, &c., are some of the happy thoughts in the sleeping god's dream; but it won't be long before the god awakes and rubs his drowsy eyes and smiles—and our world, like a dream, has melted into nothing—nay, it *was* nothing." Heine continued, however, by asserting his bitter persistence: "No matter, I live. If I am only the shadow of a dream, even this is better than the cold black empty nothingness of death. Life is the highest good, and the worst evil is death." *Travel-Pictures*, 122.

38. WDH, *My Literary Passions*, 128, 129.

39. Stephen E. Whicher, ed., *Selections from Ralph Waldo Emerson: An Organic Anthology* (Boston: Houghton Mifflin, 1957), 24, 139, passim; Bledstein, *Culture of Professionalism*, 259–62.

40. WDH, *Literary Friends and Acquaintance*, 14, 56.

41. [WDH], "Gossip," *AS*, 13 Mar. 1856.

42. In *Die Romantische Schule*, Heine proposed, "In the heart of a nation's

writers there lies the image of a nation's future, and if a critic with a sufficiently sharp knife could dissect a modern poet, he might, as an old augur by inspection of the entrails, predict with certainty the features of Germany in the future." Heine's attitude toward the poet's role in universal history was ambivalent; a tension between belief in the efficacy of the poet's efforts and despair over their impertinence best expresses his position. Claiming that poetry could be "a consecrated means whereby to attain a heavenly end," Heine added that poetry might be instead "only a holy plaything." René Welleck identifies "an evolutionary view of history that is Hegelian and Schlegelian in derivation" as the coherence in Heine's thought but suggests that there is "barely hope" in his writings for an end of division. Heine, *Travel-Pictures*, 308; Charles Godfrey Leland, trans., *The Prose and Poetical Works of Heinrich Heine* (New York: Crosup and Sterling, [1900]), 5: 114; René Welleck, *A History of Modern Criticism, 1750–1950* (New Haven: Yale Univ. Press, 1955, 1965), 3: 195–97; Sammons, *Heinrich Heine: A Modern Biography*, 78–81. On the general background of German romanticism and the context of universal history, see Welleck, *History of Modern Criticism*, 1: 227, 228, 232f; 2: 11–16, 58–59, 318–20; 3: 192–201. See also Lawrence Ryan, "Romanticism," *Periods in German Literature*, ed. J. M. Ritchie (London: Oswald Wolff, 1968), 123–43; D. C. Muecke, *The Compass of Irony* (London: Methuen, 1969), 119–29, 180–205, 214–15.

43. On Emerson and the problem of "society," see George M. Frederickson, *The Inner Civil War: Northern Intellectuals and the Crisis of the Union* (New York: Harper and Row, 1965), 10–12; R. Jackson Wilson, *In Quest of Community: Social Philosophy in the United States, 1860–1920* (New York: John Wiley and Sons, 1968), 3–13. Heine's sense of the poet's engagement with society appears throughout his writings. "The roar of the revolution begins to echo in human hearts and heads," he wrote in one instance; "and what the age feels and thinks, what it needs and will have, it gives expression to, and this is the material of modern literature." Heinrich Heine, *Religion and Philosophy in Germany: A Fragment*, trans. John Snodgrass (Boston: Houghton, Mifflin, 1882), 172. Sammons, *Heinrich Heine: A Modern Biography*, 159–68, passim, discusses Heine's ambivalent political involvements, including his flirtation with Saint-Simonianism. For Heine's sense of the poet as a god and his theme of the debasement of gods, see Sander, *Exile of Gods*, 14–42, 131–33, passim. Heine's representation of the Greek gods taking plebeian jobs appears in his essay *Die Götter im Exil*. See Havelock Ellis, ed., *The Prose Writings of Heinrich Heine* (London: Walter Scott, n.d.), 269, passim.

44. WDH, *My Literary Passions*, 111; Welleck, *History of Modern Criticism*, 2: 58–59; August Wilhelm Schlegel, *Lectures on Dramatic Art and Literature*, trans. John Black, 2d ed. (London: George Bell and Sons, 1892), 26–27, 342–43.

45. WDH, *My Literary Passions*, 111. The full passage where Heine's description occurs is as follows: "The universal characteristic of modern literature is the predominance in it of individuality and of scepticism. The authorities are dethroned; reason is now the only lamp to illumine the steps of man; conscience his only guiding-staff in the dark labyrinth of this life. Man now stands face to face alone with his creator and sings to him his lay. Thus our modern literature begins with spiritual songs. Later on, however, as literature becomes secular, the inten-

sest self-consciousness, the feeling of personality, predominates. Poetry is no longer objective, epic, and naïf; it is subjective, lyrical, and reflective." Heine, *Religion and Philosophy*, 172–73. [WDH], "Literary," *OSJ*, 20 Feb. 1861.

46. On Heine's characteristic technique of *Stimmungsbrechung* or "break of voice," see Sammons, *Heinrich Heine: The Elusive Poet*, 49.

47. [Henry Wadsworth Longfellow], "Defense of Poetry," *North American Review*, 34 (1832): 76.

48. Howells to Dune Dean, 9 and 11 Sept. 1857, *Selected Letters*, 1: 11.

49. Ibid., 11, 12–13.

50. [WDH], "A Fragment," *AS*, 26 Nov. 1857; Heine, *Travel-Pictures*, 73–74; [WDH], "The Autumn Land," *Ohio Farmer*, 6 (21 Nov. 1857): 188, reprinted in Howells and Piatt, *Poems of Two Friends*, 95–96.

51. Howells to Victoria M. Howells, 27 Oct. 1857, *Selected Letters*, 1: 13–14.

52. Howells had signed his poem "The Autumn Land" with the pseudonym "Geoffrey Constant." WDH, *Years of My Youth*, 124; Howells to Joseph A. Howells, 11 Dec. 1910, *Selected Letters*, 5: 338; Howells to Harvey and Jane Greene, 30 Nov. 1857, *Selected Letters*, 1: 15–17; Samuel Dean to Howells, 30 Aug. 1857, MS at Alfred.

53. WDH, *My Literary Passions*, 32, 132–33; Howells to William C. Howells, 28 Nov. 1880, MS at Harvard; Howells to William C. Howells, 21 Aug. 1881, MS at Harvard.

54. WDH, *My Literary Passions*, 134; Howells to Ellen Smith, 3 Apr. 1858, TS copy at Harvard.

55. The relation between vertigo and the disequilibrium experienced by infants is suggested by Charles Rycroft, "Some Observations on a Case of Vertigo," *Imagination and Reality* (New York: International Universities Press, 1968), 14–28.

56. Heine, *Travel-Pictures*, 72–73.

57. WDH, *Years of My Youth*, 117–18, 187; WDH, *My Literary Passions*, 131–32, 133, 140–41; [WDH], "Literary Gossip," *OSJ*, 17 Jan. 1860; La Vern J. Rippley, *The Columbus Germans* (Columbus, Ohio: Columbus Mannerchor, 1968).

58. WDH, *Years of My Youth*, 118–19, 124; [WCH], "Letters from Columbus," *AS*, 24 Dec. 1857.

59. Allan Nevins, *The Emergence of Lincoln: Douglas, Buchanan, and Party Chaos 1857–1859* (New York: Charles Scribner's Sons, 1950), 104–6, 254, passim; Roseboom, *Civil War Era*, 326–29; Emmett D. Preston, "The Fugitive Slave Acts in Ohio," *Journal of Negro History*, 28 (1943): 472–73.

60. On Howells's reporting, see, for instance, [WDH], "Letter from Columbus," *CG*, 4 Jan. 1858; [WDH], "Letter from Columbus," *CG*, 7 Jan. 1858; [WDH], "Letter from Columbus," *CG*, 15 Jan. 1858. WDH, *My Literary Passions*, 133.

61. Howells's description of Safford is in [WDH], "Letter from Columbus," *CG*, 19 Feb. 1858, quoted in Louis J. Budd, "Howells' 'Blistering and Cauterizing,'" *Ohio State Archaeological and Historical Quarterly*, 62 (1953): 340. [WDH], "From Columbus," *CG*, 19 Feb. 1858; [WDH], "Letter from Columbus," *CG*, 24 Feb. 1858; [WDH], "Letter from Columbus," *CG*, 26 Feb. 1858.

62. Howells's remark concerning Brooke is in [WDH], "Letter from Colum-

bus," *CG*, 27 Feb. 1858, quoted in Budd, "Howells' 'Blistering and Cauterizing,' " 340. [WDH], "Letter from Columbus," *CG*, 1 Mar. 1858; [WDH], "Letter from Columbus," *CG*, 3 Mar. 1858.

63. WDH, *Years of My Youth*, 115; [WCH], "Editorial Correspondence," *AS*, 11 Feb. 1858.

64. Howells to Aurelia H. and Anne T. Howells, 21 Feb. 1858, MS at Harvard; Howells to Ellen Smith, 3 Apr. 1858, TS copy at Harvard; WDH, *My Literary Passions*, 134.

65. "Literary Pursuits," *AS*, 8 Apr. 1858; Will D. Howells, Handbook for 1857 and 1858, entries for 9, 10, 11 Apr. 1858, MS at Harvard; WDH, *My Literary Passions*, 134; Howells to Ellen Smith, 3 Apr. 1858, TS copy at Harvard.

66. [WDH], "Correspondence: Down 'La Belle Rivière,' " *AS*, 20 May 1858. I thank David J. Nordloh of the Howells Edition Center, Indiana University, for bringing these letters to my attention.

67. [WDH], "Correspondence: Down 'La Belle Rivière,' " *AS*, 27 May 1858; [WDH], "Correspondence: 'Father of Waters,' " *AS*, 3 June 1858.

68. [WDH], "Correspondence: Down 'La Belle Rivière,' " *AS*, 3 June 1858; [WDH], "Correspondence: Down the Mississippi," *AS*, 10 June 1858. For one of the most prominent descriptions of the "strange woman" in the advice literature, see Beecher, *Lectures to Young Men*, 170–214.

69. [WDH], "Correspondence: Down the Mississippi," *AS*, 10 June 1858.

70. [WDH], "Correspondence: Up the Ohio, May 27," *AS*, 10 June 1858.

71. [WDH], "Correspondence: Cincinnati, May 31," *AS*, 10 June 1858; [WDH], "Correspondence: Wheeling, June 3d," *AS*, 10 June 1858; Howells to Aurelia H. Howells, 19 May 1858, TS copy at Harvard.

72. WDH, *Years of My Youth*, 124; J. A. Harris to Howells, 3 Sept. 1858, MS at Harvard; Howells to Martin D. Potter, 9 Oct. 1858, *Selected Letters*, 1: 19; Howells to Gamaliel Bailey, 21 Sept. 1858, *Selected Letters*, 1: 18; Advertisement for *AS*, 28 Oct. 1858; Howells to William C. Howells, 25 Aug. 1864, *Selected Letters*, 1: 196.

73. WDH, *My Literary Passions*, 135–37; WDH, *Years of My Youth*, 125.

74. [WDH], "The Mysteries," *Ohio Farmer*, 7 (2 Oct. 1858): 320, reprinted in Howells and Piatt, *Poems of Two Friends*, 101.

6. *Woman's Sphere*

Epigraph: W. D. Howells, "Novel-Writing and Novel-Reading: An Impersonal Explanation," *Howells and James: A Double Billing*, ed. William M. Gibson (New York: New York Public Library, 1958), 19–20.

1. Aurelia H. Howells, "Paper on William Dean Howells," n.d., TS at Harvard; [WCH], "The Ohio State Journal," *AS*, 25 Nov. 1858.

2. For the ideal concept of "woman's sphere," see Welter, "The Cult of True Womanhood"; Cott, *Bonds of Womanhood*, esp. 63–100; Ryan, *Empire of Mother*; McDannell, *The Christian Home in Victorian America*. Cf. Ryan's discussion of practice, *Cradle of the Middle Class*, 186–229. For male gender ideals, see Smith-

Rosenberg, "Sex as Symbol in Victorian Purity"; Smith-Rosenberg, "Davey Crockett as Trickster"; Rosenberg, "Sexuality, Class, and Role"; E. Anthony Rotundo, "Body and Soul: Changing Ideals of American Middle-Class Manhood, 1770–1920," *Journal of Social History*, 16 (1983): 23–38; Peter N. Stearns, *Be A Man!: Males in Modern Society* (New York: Holmes and Meier, 1979), 39–58, 79–112. Cf. Ryan's discussion of practice, *Cradle of the Middle Class*, 145–85.

3. [WCH], "Women's Sphere &c," *DT*, 17 Jan. 1850.

4. WDH, *A Boy's Town*, 74, 76, 179.

5. On the identification of literature as part of the realm of women, see Douglas, *Feminization of American Culture*.

6. WDH, *My Literary Passions*, 146.

7. Roseboom, *Civil War Era*, 338; [WCH], "The Ohio State Journal," *AS*, 25 Nov. 1858; "To our editorial brethren . . . ," *OSJ*, 6 Dec. 1858; [Harris], "Local Affairs: An Article Discursive upon Local Matters," *OSJ*, 20 Jan. 1860; WDH, *Years of My Youth*, 125, 126, 127, 128.

8. [WDH], "Local Affairs: Changes in the State Journal," *OSJ*, 20 July 1861; WDH, *Years of My Youth*, 126–27, 128, 130, 137; WDH, *My Literary Passions*, 143–44. I have attributed unsigned writing in the *Ohio State Journal* to Howells using the following criteria: the distribution of duties at the newspaper; comparisons of Howells with his associates; his self-references; his writing style, including pet words, turns of phrase, and literary allusions; his recurrence to subjects and themes; his mention of items in letters and later writings.

9. WDH, *Years of My Youth*, 127–31; WDH, *My Literary Passions*, 143–44.

10. For the movement of young men into urban employment as clerks and professionals, see Kett, *Rites of Passage*, 93–108, passim; Ryan, *Cradle of the Middle Class*, 125–30; Smith-Rosenberg, "Sex as Symbol in Victorian Purity"; Allan Stanley Horlick, *Country Boys and Merchant Princes: The Social Control of Young Men in New York* (Lewisburg, Pa.: Bucknell Univ. Press, 1975). WDH, *Years of My Youth*, 157–58, 160–61; Howells to Victoria M. Howells, 26 Dec. 1858, *Selected Letters*, 1: 19–20.

11. WDH, *Years of My Youth*, 158–59, 389; WDH, *My Literary Passions*, 141–42; WDH, *Literary Friends and Acquaintance*, 8; Howells to Victoria M. Howells, 2 Jan. 1859, *Selected Letters*, 1: 22.

12. WDH, *Years of My Youth*, 156, 160, 182–83, 196–97; Howells to Victoria M. Howells, 18–24 Apr. 1859, *Selected Letters*, 1: 30.

13. WDH, *Years of My Youth*, 159, 196; [WDH], "The Poet's Friends," *Atlantic Monthly*, 5 (1860): 185.

14. WDH, *Years of My Youth*, 64, 196, 399, 401; WDH, *My Literary Passions*, 45; Howells to John J. Piatt, 4 Mar. 1859, *Selected Letters*, 1: 26–27; Howells to John J. Piatt, 10 Sept. 1859, *Selected Letters*, 1: 40–41; Howells to John J. Piatt, 5 Oct. 1859, *Selected Letters*, 1: 46. For typical "puffs," see [WDH], "News and Humor of the Mails," *OSJ*, 10 Oct. 1859; [WDH], "News and Humor of the Mails," *OSJ*, 15 Nov. 1859. On Piatt, see Clare Dowler, "John James Piatt, Representative Figure in a Momentous Period," *Ohio State Archaeological and Historical Quarterly*, 45 (1936): 1–26.

15. WDH, *Years of My Youth*, 141–42, 145–46, 150; Howells to John J. Piatt, 10 Sept. 1859, *Selected Letters*, 1: 41.

16. L[ida] R. McCabe, "Literary and Social Recollections of W. D. Howells," *Lippincott's*, 40 (1887): 551; WDH, *Years of My Youth*, 141, 142.

17. WDH, *Years of My Youth*, 107, 132–34, 141, 156; Howells to Victoria M. Howells, 2 Jan. 1859, *Selected Letters*, 1: 22.

18. On middle-class parlor behavior, see Halttunen, *Confidence Men and Painted Women*, 59–61, 101–12, 174–75, 184–85. WDH, *Years of My Youth*, 133–34; Howells to Victoria M. Howells, 25 Apr. and 1 May 1859, *Selected Letters*, 1: 34.

19. WDH, *Years of My Youth*, 141–42, 150–51, 156–57; WDH, *My Literary Passions*, 137–38; WDH, *Literary Friends and Acquaintance*, 7, 9; Howells to Victoria M. Howells, 13 Mar. 1859, *Selected Letters*, 1: 28–29; Howells to Victoria M. Howells, 18–24 Apr. 1859, *Selected Letters*, 1: 30–31; Howells to Victoria M. Howells, 25 Apr. and 1 May 1859, *Selected Letters*, 1: 33–34; Howells to John J. Piatt, 10 Sept. 1859, *Selected Letters*, 1: 41.

20. WDH, *Years of My Youth*, 131, 137–38, 140–41, 157; WDH, *Literary Friends and Acquaintance*, 7.

21. Howells to Victoria M. Howells, 2 Jan. 1859, *Selected Letters*, 1: 21–22.

22. Howells to Victoria M. Howells, 2 Jan. 1859, MS at Harvard. My reading of the first quoted passage in this paragraph differs from the editors' reading in *Selected Letters*, 1: 22. I read *expand* while the editors read *expend*. Howells to Victoria M. Howells, 23 Jan. 1859, *Selected Letters*, 1: 23.

23. WDH, *Years of My Youth*, 131.

24. W[illiam] D[ean] H[owells], "Bobby, Study of a Boy," *OSJ*, 14 Dec. 1858.

25. WDH, *Years of My Youth*, 106, 107–9, 111; Howells to Victoria M. Howells, 2 Jan. 1859, *Selected Letters*, 1: 21; Howells to Aurelia H. Howells, 22 Jan. 1860, TS copy at Harvard; Aurelia H. Howells to Howells, ca. June 1914, MS at Alfred.

26. Howells to Victoria M. Howells and John B. Howells, 15 Feb. 1859, *Selected Letters*, 1: 24–25.

27. WDH, *Years of My Youth*, 155; Howells to Victoria M. Howells, 26 Dec. 1858, *Selected Letters*, 1: 20; Howells to Victoria M. Howells and John B. Howells, 15 Feb. 1859, *Selected Letters*, 1: 25; Howells to Victoria M. Howells, 13 Mar. 1859, *Selected Letters*, 1: 29; Howells to Victoria M. Howells, 16–22 May 1859, *Selected Letters*, 1: 35–37; Howells to Victoria M. Howells, 3 July 1859, TS copy at Harvard; Howells to William C. Howells, 21 Apr. 1860, *Selected Letters*, 1: 55; Howells to Anne T. Howells, 12 Sept. 1860, *Selected Letters*, 1: 63.

28. WDH, *Years of My Youth*, 130, 155–56; Howells to Victoria M. Howells, 25 Apr. and 1 May 1859, *Selected Letters*, 1: 33–34.

29. Howells to Mary D. Howells, 24 May 1859, *Selected Letters*, 1: 38–39.

30. WDH, *Years of My Youth*, 149.

31. Ibid., 144–45.

32. Ibid., 118, 132, 133, 187; Howells to Victoria M. Howells, 18–24 Apr. 1859, *Selected Letters*, 1: 31; Howells to Victoria M. Howells, 25 Apr. and 1 May 1859, *Selected Letters*, 1: 33, 34.

33. [WDH], "Literary Matters," *OSJ*, 20 Nov. 1858.

34. On "sentimental" women writers, see Douglas, *Feminization of American Culture;* Mary Kelly, *Private Woman, Public Stage: Literary Domesticity in Nineteenth-Century America* (New York: Oxford Univ. Press, 1984); Nina Baym, *Woman's Fiction: A Guide to Novels by and about Women in America, 1820–1870* (Ithaca, N.Y.: Cornell Univ. Press, 1978).

35. William Charvat, *Literary Publishing in America, 1790–1850* (Philadelphia: Univ. of Pennsylvania Press, 1959), 55–56, passim; William Charvat, "The People's Patronage," *The Profession of Authorship in America, 1800–1870,* ed. Matthew J. Bruccoli (Columbus: Ohio State Univ. Press, 1968), 298–316; Susan Geary, "The Domestic Novel as a Commercial Commodity: Making a Best Seller in the 1850s," *Papers of the Bibliographical Society of America,* 70 (1976): 365–93; Ronald J. Zboray, "The Transportation Revolution and Antebellum Book Distribution Reconsidered," *American Quarterly,* 38 (1986): 53–71.

36. Douglas, *Feminization of American Culture,* emphasizes the enervating effects of female "influence," while Cott, *Bonds of Womanhood,* demonstrates how women used the ideology of domesticity to expand their sphere. Cf. Ryan, *Cradle of the Middle Class,* passim. Baym points out that domestic novels sought a reformed world based on an "affectional model of human relationships." *Woman's Fiction,* 20, 22–50.

37. See chap. 5, note 5.

38. [WDH], "New Publications," review of *Say and Seal,* by Susan Warner, *OSJ,* 29 Mar. 1860; [WDH], "Literary: New Publications," review of *Hopes and Fears; or Scenes from the Life of a Spinster,* by ?, *OSJ,* 7 Mar. 1861. On the contrary and subversive impulses in domestic novels, see Wood, " 'Scribbling Women' and Fanny Fern"; Kelly, *Private Woman, Public Stage;* Baym, *Woman's Fiction;* Jane Tompkins, *Sensational Designs: The Cultural Work of American Fiction, 1770–1860* (New York: Oxford Univ. Press, 1985); Cathy N. Davidson, *Revolution and the Word: The Rise of the Novel in America* (New York: Oxford University Press, 1986).

39. Mary Noel, *Villains Galore: The Heyday of the Popular Story Weekly* (New York: Macmillan, 1954); Carl Bode, *Antebellum Culture* (Carbondale and Edwardsville: Southern Illinois Univ. Press, 1970), 257–58; Frank Luther Mott, *A History of American Magazines, 1850–1865* (1938; reprint, Cambridge: Harvard Univ. Press, 1967), 2: 15–16, 23–24, 356–63.

40. [WDH], "News and Humors of the Mail," *OSJ,* 1 Dec. 1858; [WDH], "A Terrible Suspicion," *OSJ,* 24 Mar. 1859.

41. [WDH], "John G. Saxe," *OSJ,* 30 Nov. 1858; WDH, "A Terrible Suspicion."

42. WDH, "John G. Saxe."

43. Quotations in this and the following paragraphs are from [WDH], "Local Affairs: Dick Dowdy: Study of a First-rate Fellow," *OSJ,* 6 Dec. 1858.

44. Howells to James M. Comly, 7 July 1868, *Selected Letters,* 1: 294–95; Howells to James M. Comly, 9 Aug. 1868, *Selected Letters,* 1: 295 n. 1; W. D. Howells, *Their Wedding Journey,* ed. John K. Reeves (Bloomington: Indiana Univ. Press, 1968), 42. The full sentence illustrates how far Howells had to go in his

appreciation of ordinary people: "Ah! poor Real Life, which I love, can I make others share the delight I find in thy foolish and insipid face?"

45. See Williams, *Culture and Society*, 30–48. Williams uses the phrase "guiding light[s] of the common life." (p. 36). The contrast between "individual and local" truths and "general and operative" truths is from William Wordsworth's 1800 preface to the *Lyrical Ballads*. (Quoted on p. 41). See also Gilmore, *American Romanticism and the Marketplace*.

46. Quoted in [WDH], "Bitters," *OSJ*, 18 Nov. 1859.

47. WDH, *Years of My Youth*, 126; [WDH], "News and Humors of the Mails," *OSJ*, 6 Jan. 1859. Willis is quoted in Douglas, *Feminization of American Culture*, 103.

48. [WDH], "The Autocrat sits down with his friends . . . ," *OSJ*, 24 Nov. 1858.

49. [WDH], "Unworthy Mr. Thackeray," *OSJ*, 17 May 1859.

50. [WDH], "An Incident," *OSJ*, 28 Dec. 1858. Howells was parodying Bonner's practice of running "teasers" in other magazines. Bonner would pay to print several chapters of a serial in another magazine, breaking it off at a thrilling point with the message that the serial would continue in the *Ledger*. See Mott, *History of American Magazines, 1850–1865*, 2: 16.

51. [WDH], "The Lost Child—A Street Scene," *OSJ*, 4 Mar. 1859.

52. Quotations in this and the following paragraphs are from [WDH], "Not a Love Story," *Odd Fellows' Casket and Review*, 1 (1859): 222–24. Other sketches in this vein are [WDH], " 'A Perfect Goose,' " *Odd Fellows' Casket and Review*, 1 (1859): 379–80; [WDH], "Romance of the Crossing," *Odd Fellows' Casket and Review*, 1 (1859): 443–44.

53. Alfred Habegger, *Gender, Fantasy, and Realism in American Literature* (New York: Columbia Univ. Press, 1982), argues that ambivalent resistance to sentimental readers was *the* decisive influence in the development of the literary realism of Howells and Henry James.

54. For discussion of this style of sentimental writing, see Douglas, *Feminization of American Culture*, 234–40; William Hedges, *Washington Irving: An American Study, 1802–1832* (Baltimore: Johns Hopkins Univ. Press, 1965), 145–62. For Howells's early reading of male sentimentalists, see W. D. Howells, "George William Curtis," *North American Review*, 107 (1868): 104–17; WDH, *My Literary Passions*, 23–27, 64–66.

55. Quoted in Douglas, *Feminization of American Culture*, 376 n. 29.

56. [WDH], "A Summer Sunday in a Country Village: As Experienced by an Ennuyé," *Odd Fellows' Casket and Review*, 1 (1859): 354–57. Other Howells sketches reflecting the idler's manner include [WDH], "In the Country," *OSJ*, 9, 10, 11 June 1859; [WDH], "Hot," *OSJ*, 29 June 1859; [WDH], "A Day at White Sulphur," *OSJ*, 6 July 1859; [WDH], "I Visit Camp Harrison," *OSJ*, 31 Aug. 1859.

57. WDH, "In the Country," 9 and 10 June 1859.

58. Howells to Victoria M. Howells, 18 Sept. 1859, MS at Harvard.

59. Heine, *Travel-Pictures*, 327; Sammons, *Heinrich Heine: The Elusive Poet*, 26–87.

7. The Laying On of Hands

Epigraph: WDH, *Literary Friends and Acquaintance*, 101.

1. William T. Coggeshall, *The Protective Policy in Literature: A Discourse on the Social and Moral Advantages of the Cultivation of Local Literature* (Columbus: Follett, Foster, 1859); William D. Andrews, "William T. Coggeshall: 'Booster' of Western Literature," *Ohio History*, 18 (1972): 210–20.

2. The idealization of locality is variously treated in Thomas Bender, *Toward an Urban Vision: Ideas and Institutions in Nineteenth-Century America* (Lexington: Univ. Press of Kentucky, 1975); Robert A. Gross, "Transcendentalism and Urbanism: Concord, Boston, and the Wider World," *Journal of American Studies*, 18 (1984): 361–81; David Schuyler, *The New Urban Landscape: The Redefinition of City Form in Nineteenth-Century America* (Baltimore: Johns Hopkins Univ. Press, 1986); Raymond Williams, *The Country and the City* (New York: Oxford Univ. Press, 1973). Joshua R. Giddings to Laura W. Giddings, 22 and 23 Apr. 1837, Joshua R. Giddings Papers, MIC 7, MS at OHS.

3. Howells to John J. Piatt, 19 Sept. 1859, *Selected Letters*, 1: 43.

4. WDH, *Years of My Youth*, 139; Howells to Victoria M. Howells, 16–22 May 1859, *Selected Letters*, 1: 36; "Have We Household Poetry in the West?" *OSJ*, 20 Nov. 1858; [WDH], "News and Humors of the Mail," *OSJ*, 22 Dec. 1858.

5. WDH, *Literary Friends and Acquaintance*, 62f, italics added to quotation on 64. For the *Atlantic Monthly* during the 1850s, see Mott, *A History of American Magazines, 1850–1865*, 2: 493–502. David D. Hall, "The Victorian Connection," *American Quarterly*, 27 (1975): 561–74, treats the *Atlantic*'s secularism and its connection to the English reviews. On Holmes, see Peter Dobkin Hall, *The Organization of American Culture, 1700–1900: Private Institutions, Elites, and the Origins of American Nationality* (New York: New York Univ. Press, 1982), 198–206. For the *Saturday Press*, see Mott, *A History of American Magazines, 1850–1865*, 2: 38–40; Albert Parry, *Garrets and Pretenders: A History of Bohemianism in America*, rev. ed. (New York: Dover, 1960), 14–61; [WDH], "Editor's Easy Chair," *Harper's Monthly*, 112 (1906): 633–36. Howells to William H. Smith, 31 Jan. 1860, *Selected Letters*, 1: 51; Howells to William Cooper Howells Family, 21 Apr. 1860, *Selected Letters*, 1: 54.

6. Parry, *Garrets and Pretenders*, 14–61; WDH, *Literary Friends and Acquaintance*, 62f; [WDH], "News and Humor of the Mail," *OSJ*, 28 Oct. 1859; [WDH], "A Book Read Yesterday," review of *Ballad of Babie Bell and Other Poems* by Thomas B. Aldrich, *Saturday Press*, 30 July 1859, reprinted in Ferris Greenslet, *The Life of Thomas Bailey Aldrich* (Boston: Houghton Mifflin, 1908), 47–48.

7. Parry, *Garrets and Pretenders*, 14–61, quotation by Clare on 26. On Bohemian continuity with middle-class values, see Jerrold Seigel, *Bohemian Paris: Culture, Politics, and the Boundaries of Bourgeois Life, 1830–1930* (New York: Elisabeth Sifton Books, 1985).

8. Mott, *A History of American Magazines, 1850–1865*, 2: 39; [WDH], "News and Humor of the Mail," *OSJ*, 3 Sept. 1859; [WDH], "New York Journalism," *OSJ*, 29 Dec. 1858.

9. David B. Tyack, *George Ticknor and the Boston Brahmins* (Cambridge: Har-

vard Univ. Press, 1968), 173–87; Martin Duberman, *James Russell Lowell* (Boston: Beacon Press, 1966), 183–97; Ronald Story, *Harvard and the Boston Upper Class: The Forging of an Aristocracy* (Middletown, Conn.: Wesleyan Univ. Press, 1980); Hall, *Organization of American Culture;* Bender, "The Cultures of Intellectual Life: The City and the Professions," 181–95.

10. [WDH], "Andenken," *Atlantic Monthly*, 5 (1860): 100–102. On *Stimmungsbrechung*, see Sammons, *Heinrich Heine: The Elusive Poet*, 49.

11. Howells's first poem published in the *Press* was "Under the Locust," *Saturday Press*, 18 June 1859, reprinted in Howells and Piatt, *Poems of Two Friends*, 124. WDH, *Years of My Youth*, 155; WDH, *My Literary Passions*, 129–30; WDH, *Literary Friends and Acquaintance*, 27; Annie Howells Fréchette, "William Dean Howells," *Canadian Bookman*, n.s., 2 (1920): 10–11.

12. WDH, *Years of My Youth*, 144, 198; Howells to Victoria M. Howells, 23 Jan. 1859, *Selected Letters*, 1: 23; Howells to Victoria M. Howells, 18–24 Apr. 1859, *Selected Letters*, 1: 31; Howells to Victoria M. Howells, 3 July 1859, TS copy at Harvard; Howells to Joseph A. Howells, 14 Aug. 1859, *Selected Letters*, 1: 40; Howells to John J. Piatt, 19 Sept. 1859, *Selected Letters*, 1: 43; [WDH], "Drifting Away," *Saturday Press*, 10 Sept. 1859, reprinted in Howells and Piatt, *Poems of Two Friends*, 114–15.

13. Howells to Joseph A. Howells, 14 Aug. 1859, *Selected Letters*, 1: 40; Howells to James M. Comly, 8 July 1866, *Selected Letters*, 1: 263; WDH, *Years of My Youth*, 144, 198.

14. Howells to William C. Howells, 7 Aug. 1859, MS at Harvard.

15. Howells to Mary D. Howells, 24 Aug. 1859, MS at Harvard; Howells to James M. Comly, 5 Dec. 1874, *Selected Letters of W. D. Howells*, ed. George Arms, Christoph K. Lohmann, and Jerry Herron (Boston: Twayne, 1979), 2: 79.

16. Howells to John J. Piatt, 10 Sept. 1859, *Selected Letters*, 1: 41.

17. [WDH], "News and Humor of the Mails," *OSJ*, 16 Sept. 1859; [WDH], "News and Humor of the Mails," *OSJ*, 19 Sept. 1859; [WDH], "News and Humor of the Mails," *OSJ*, 28 Sept. 1859; [WDH], "News and Humor of the Mail," *OSJ*, 7 Oct. 1859; Howells to John J. Piatt, 19 Sept. 1859, *Selected Letters*, 1: 42–43; Howells to John J. Piatt, 22 Sept. 1859, *Selected Letters*, 1: 43–44; Howells to John J. Piatt, 5 Oct. 1859, *Selected Letters*, 1: 46; Howells to Victoria M. Howells, 5 Oct. 1859, MS at Harvard; Howells to Victoria M. Howells, 11 Oct. 1859, MS at Harvard.

18. [WDH], "News and Humor of the Mail," *OSJ*, 10 Oct. 1859; Howells to Victoria M. Howells, 11 Oct. 1859, MS at Harvard.

19. [WDH], "News and Humor of the Mail," *OSJ*, 17 Oct. 1859; [WDH], "News and Humor of the Mails," *OSJ*, 21 Oct. 1859; [WDH], "News and Humor of the Mails," *OSJ*, 25 Oct. 1859; [WDH], "News and Humor of the Mails," *OSJ*, 28 Oct. 1859; [WDH], "News and Humor of the Mails," *OSJ*, 1 Nov. 1859; Howells to William C. Howells, 26 Oct. 1859, *Selected Letters*, 1: 47.

20. Howells to Victoria M. Howells, 11 Oct. 1859, MS at Harvard; Howells to William C. Howells, 20 Oct. 1859, MS at Harvard; [WDH], "News and Humor of the Mails," *OSJ*, 21 Oct. 1859; [Samuel R. Reed], "Some ungenerous person . . . ," *OSJ*, 1 Nov. 1859.

21. Howells to William C. Howells, 6 Nov. 1869, *Selected Letters*, 1: 48; [WDH], "News and Humor of the Mails," *OSJ*, 2 Nov. 1859; Gilman M. Ostrander, "Emerson, Thoreau, and John Brown," *Mississippi Valley Historical Review*, 39 (1953): 713–26; Frederickson, *Inner Civil War*, 39–40.

22. Howells to William C. Howells, 6 Nov. 1859, *Selected Letters*, 1: 48; Louis Filler, ed., *Wendell Phillips on Civil Rights and Freedom* (New York: Hill and Wang, 1965), 96–113.

23. Howells to William C. Howells, 6 Nov. 1859, *Selected Letters*, 1: 48–49.

24. Roseboom, *Civil War Era*, 357–58; [Samuel R. Reed], "The Statesman Editor's Brownchetis," *OSJ*, 20 Oct. 1859; [Samuel R. Reed], "The Harper's Ferry War," *OSJ*, 21 Oct. 1859; [Samuel R. Reed], "Was John Brown Insane?" *OSJ*, 18 Nov. 1859; [Samuel R. Reed], "We presume that it is hardly necessary . . . ," *OSJ*, 7 Dec. 1859; [WCH], "Chivalric Cowardice," *AS*, 27 Oct. 1859; [WCH], "The Harper's Ferry Affair," *AS*, 27 Oct. 1859; [WCH], "John Brown," *AS*, 10 Nov. 1859; Howells to William C. Howells, 6 Nov. 1859, *Selected Letters*, 1: 48; [WDH], "News and Humor of the Mails," *OSJ*, 14 Nov. 1859. In *Young Howells and John Brown: Episodes in a Radical Education* (Columbus: Ohio State Univ. Press, 1985), Edwin H. Cady speculates that the Howells family was "complicit" in the Brown conspiracy. But the family's longstanding and steadfast commitment was not to abolitionism of the Brown variety or any variety but to radical Republicanism with its adherence to constitutional means to end slavery.

25. Wm. D. Howells, "Old Brown," *Echoes of Harper's Ferry*, ed. James Redpath (Boston: Thayer and Eldridge, 1860), 316; [WDH], "The Genii of the Woodpile," *OSJ*, 17 Nov. 1859.

26. [WDH], "Robert Blum," *OSJ*, 10 Nov. 1859; [WDH], "Foxes and Firebrands Going to Be Let Loose in Virginia," *OSJ*, 11 Nov. 1859; [WDH], "Abolition Lectures," *OSJ*, 15 Nov. 1859; [WDH], "News and Humor of the Mail," *OSJ*, 16 Nov. 1859; [WDH], "Bitters," *OSJ*, 18 Nov. 1859; [WDH], "News and Humor of the Mail," *OSJ*, 9 Dec. 1859; Howells to William C. Howells, 6 Nov. 1859, *Selected Letters*, 1: 48–49; Howells to Anne T. and Aurelia H. Howells, 13 Nov. 1859, *Selected Letters*, 1: 50.

27. [WDH], "News and Humor of the Mails," *OSJ*, 23 Nov. 1859; Advertisement in *AS* for *Poems of Two Friends*, 23 Dec. 1859; Advertisement in *AS* for Jan. 1860 *Atlantic Monthly*, 26 Dec. 1859.

28. Howells and Piatt, *Poems of Two Friends*, iv; WDH, *Years of My Youth*, 139–40; WDH, *My Literary Passions*, 45, 143; Howells to William H. Smith, 31 Jan. 1860, *Selected Letters*, 1: 51; [Harris], "Local Affairs: Poets and Parnassus—A Local Luminous by Lunar Reflection," *OSJ*, 26 Dec. 1859; [WDH], "New Publications," review of *Poems of Two Friends*, by J. J. Piatt and W. D. Howells, *OSJ*, 26 Dec. 1859.

29. *Saturday Press* review quoted in William T. Coggeshall, ed., *The Poets and Poetry of the West* (Columbus: Follett, Foster, 1860), 678.

30. Gail Hamilton [Mary Abigail Dodge], "The Review," review of *Poems of Two Friends*, by J. J. Piatt and W. D. Howells, *National Era*, 16 Feb. 1860; Howells to Gail Hamilton, 27 Feb. 1860, *Selected Letters*, 1: 52–53.

31. Lowell's comment on "genius" is quoted in Duberman, *James Russell Lowell*, 147; [James Russell Lowell], review of *Poems of Two Friends*, by J. J. Piatt and W. D. Howells, *Atlantic Monthly*, 5 (1860): 185. Howells's three new *Atlantic* poems were "The Poet's Friends," *Atlantic Monthly*, 5 (1860): 185; "Pleasure-Pain," *Atlantic Monthly*, 5 (1860): 468–70; and "Lost Beliefs," *Atlantic Monthly*, 5 (1860): 486.

32. [WDH], "Hawthorne's 'Marble Faun,' " *OSJ*, 24 Mar. 1860.

33. WDH, *Years of My Youth*, 188; Howells to William C. Howells Family, 21 Apr. 1860, *Selected Letters*, 1: 54.

34. Howells to William C. Howells Family, 21 Apr. 1860, *Selected Letters*, 1: 55.

35. Howells to Joseph A. Howells, 29 Apr. 1860, *Selected Letters*, 1: 56.

36. WDH, *Years of My Youth*, 170–71, 173; Howells to William C. Howells Family, 21 Apr. 1860, *Selected Letters*, 1: 55.

37. WDH, *Years of My Youth*, 173–74, 178; Howells to Anne T. Howells, 25 May 1860, MS at Harvard; Howells to Mary D. Howells, 19 June 1860, MS at Harvard; Robert Price, "Young Howells Drafts a 'Life' for Lincoln," *Ohio History*, 76 (1967): 232–46, 275–77.

38. W. D. Howells, *Life of Abraham Lincoln* (1860; reprint, Bloomington: Indiana Univ. Press, 1960), 21, 23–24, 30, 49, 50–51.

39. [WDH], "Letters from the Country," *OSJ*, 10 July 1860, reprinted in Robert Price, ed., "The Road to Boston: 1860 Travel Correspondence of William Dean Howells," *Ohio History*, 80 (1971): 95–98.

40. William D. Howells, "Niagara, First and Last," in *The Niagara Book*, by W. D. Howells, Mark Twain, Nathaniel S. Shaler, et al. (New York: Doubleday, Page, 1901), 240. On the romantic picturesque, see David Levin, *History as Romantic Art: Bancroft, Prescott, Motley, and Parkman* (New York: Harcourt, Brace and World, 1963), 7–9.

41. [WDH], "Glimpses of Summer Travel," *CG*, 21 July 1860, reprinted in Price, "Travel Correspondence," 103–4.

42. Ibid., 104; Howells, "Niagara, First and Last," 240, 251–52; [WDH], "En Passant," *OSJ*, 24 July 1860, reprinted in Price, "Travel Correspondence," 111–12.

43. [WDH], "Glimpses of Summer Travel," *CG*, 24 July 1860, reprinted in Price, "Travel Correspondence," 105–8; Howells, "Niagara, First and Last," 243.

44. [WDH], "Glimpses of Summer Travel," *CG*, 24 July 1860, reprinted in Price, "Travel Correspondence," 106; [WDH], "En Passant," *OSJ*, 24 July 1860, reprinted in Price, "Travel Correspondence," 113.

45. [WDH], "Glimpses of Summer Travel," *CG*, 9 Aug. 1860, reprinted in Price, "Travel Correspondence," 152.

46. Henry Wadsworth Longfellow, "German Writers: Heinrich Heine," *Graham's Lady's and Gentleman's Magazine*, 20 (1842): 134.

47. For this allusion, see WDH, *Literary Friends and Acquaintance*, 16, 36. Howells's later ambivalence toward the literary ideals represented by Boston is explored by Lewis P. Simpson, "The Treason of William Dean Howells," *The*

Man of Letters in New England and the South: Essays on the History of the Literary Vocation in America (Baton Rouge: Louisiana Univ. Press, 1973), 85–128.

48. WDH, *Literary Friends and Acquaintance*, 15, 23–25, 26.

49. Ibid., 26–28.

50. Ibid., 51–52.

51. Ibid., 35–38; Howells to 'William C. Howells Family, 3 Aug. 1860, *Selected Letters*, 1: 57.

52. WDH, *Literary Frie ds and Acquaintance*, 41–44; Howells to Oliver W. Holmes, Jr., 14 Nov. 186', *Selected Letters*, 1: 64.

53. WDH, *Literary Friends and Acquaintance*, 44–59; James R. Lowell to Nathaniel Hawthorne, 5 Aug. 1860, *Letters of James Russell Lowell*, ed. Charles Eliot Norton (New York: Harper, 1894), 1: 305–6. Emerson sharply delineated Thoreau's scornful treatment of young men: "His own dealing with [young men of sensibility] was never affectionate, but superior, didactic, scorning their petty ways,—very slowly conceding, or not conceding at all the promise of his society at their houses, or even at his own. 'Would he not walk with them?' 'He did not know. There was nothing so important to him as his walk; he had no walks to throw away on company.' . . . what accusing silences, and what searching and irresistible speeches, battering down all defenses, his companions can remember!" Whicher, ed., *Selections from Ralph Waldo Emerson*, 385–86.

54. WDH, *Literary Friends and Acquaintance*, 59–60. Fields's caricature of Emerson is quoted in W. S. Tryon, *Parnassus Corner: A Life of James T. Fields, Publisher to the Victorians* (Boston: Houghton Mifflin, 1963), 185. For Emerson's status as most-favored author, see Tryon, *Parnassus Corner*, 170, 402n. On Lowell's opposition to Transcendental Concord, see Austin Warren, "Lowell on Thoreau," *Studies in Philology*, 27 (1930): 442–61; Duberman, *James Russell Lowell*, 171–72. Brahmin antipathy toward Emerson's "unintelligible nonsense" is pointed out in Tyack, *George Ticknor*, 151–52.

55. WDH, *Literary Friends and Acquaintance*, 61–68; [WDH], "A Hoosier's Opinion of Walt Whitman," *Saturday Press*, 11 Aug. 1860, reprinted in Edwin H. Cady, ed., *W. D. Howells as Critic* (London: Routledge and Kegan Paul, 1973), 15; William Winter to Howells, 3 Mar. 1861, *Selected Letters*, 1: 55 n. 1; Howells to James T. Fields, 22 Aug. 1860, *Selected Letters*, 1: 58–59; Howells to James R. Lowell, 31 Aug. 1860, *Selected Letters*, 1: 60–61.

56. WDH, *Literary Friends and Acquaintance*, 29, 195; Duberman, *James Russell Lowell*, 166–67, 188–92.

57. [James Russell Lowell], review of *Venetian Life*, by W. D. Howells, *North American Review*, 103 (1866): 610–13.

58. Ibid., 611; James Russell Lowell, "Cambridge Thirty Years Ago," *Literary Essays 1*, vol. 1 of *The Writings of James Russell Lowell in Prose and Poetry* (Boston: Houghton Mifflin, 1890), 65–66; Duberman, *James Russell Lowell*, 158, passim; Barbara Miller Solomon, *Ancestors and Immigrants: A Changing New England Tradition* (Cambridge: Harvard Univ. Press, 1956), 1–22; R. W. B. Lewis, *The American Adam: Innocence, Tragedy and Tradition in the Nineteenth Century* (Chicago: Univ. of Chicago Press, 1955), 189–91; WDH, *Literary Friends and Acquaintance*, 184; Oliver

Wendell Holmes, *Elsie Venner*, vol. 5 of *The Works of Oliver Wendell Holmes* (Boston: Houghton Mifflin, 1892), [1]–6.

59. [WDH], "The Pilot's Story," *Atlantic Monthly*, 6 (1860): 323–25; Holmes, *Elsie Venner*, 5–6. For Lowell's concern for "character," see Duberman, *James Russell Lowell*, 66, 252–54.

60. James R. Lowell to Howells, 28 July 1864, *Letters of Lowell*, 1: 338. After his return to Columbus, Howells had written Lowell, "I remember every word that you said to me, and particularly all that touching my Heine-leeshore, and I try to write always outside of my affection for that poet." Howells to James R. Lowell, 17 Jan. 1861, *Selected Letters*, 1: 71.

61. Lowell's position was clearly stated in his 1855 Lowell Institute lectures and elaborated in essays he wrote following the Civil War. For statements in his Lowell Institute lectures, see the full version of "The Imagination," reprinted in James Russell Lowell, *The Function of the Poet and Other Essays*, ed. Albert Mordell (Port Washington, N.Y.: Kennikat, 1967), 68–88; Lowell, *Lectures on English Poets*, esp. 209–10. Lowell's later statements are discussed by Harry Hayden Clark, "Lowell's Criticism of Romantic Literature," *Publications of the Modern Language Association*, 41 (1926): 209–28. James Russell Lowell, "The Life and Letters of James Gates Percival," *Literary Essays 2*, vol. 2 of *Writings of Lowell*, 156–59; James Russell Lowell, "Rousseau and the Sentimentalists," *Literary Essays 2*, 253–66.

62. Lowell, "The Imagination," 69, 71, 72, 73–74; Lowell, "Percival," 144, 157–58, 159; Lowell, "Rousseau," 234, 250, 257–58; Lowell, *Lectures on English Poets*, 209–10.

63. Lowell, "Percival," 158.

64. James Russell Lowell, "Lessing," *Literary Essays 2*, 229; James Russell Lowell, "E Pluribus Unum," *Political Essays*, vol. 5 of *Writings of Lowell*, 71, 74.

65. Duberman, *James Russell Lowell*, 134–39, 158, passim; Leon Howard, *Victorian Knight-Errant: A Study of the Early Career of James Russell Lowell* (Berkeley: Univ. of California Press, 1952), chaps. 9–10.

8. The Province of Reason

Epigraph: WDH, *My Literary Passions*, 151.

1. James R. Lowell to Howells, 5 Aug. 1860, *Letters of Lowell*, 1: 305; Howells to James R. Lowell, 31 Aug. 1860, *Selected Letters*, 1: 60; Howells to Victoria M. Howells, 18 Sept. 1860, MS at Harvard; WDH, *Years of My Youth*, 181–82.

2. WDH, *Years of My Youth*, 178–79; [WDH], "Local Affairs: Changes in the State Journal," *OSJ*, 20 July 1861; James R. Lowell to Howells, 5 Aug. 1860, *Letters of Lowell*, 1: 305.

3. James R. Lowell to Howells, 5 Aug. 1860, *Letters of Lowell*, 1: 305; James R. Lowell to Howells, 1 Dec. 1860, *Letters of Lowell*, 1: 307; Howells to James R. Lowell, 14 Dec. 1860, *Selected Letters*, 1: 67–68; Howells to Oliver W. Holmes,

Jr., 6 Jan. 1861, *Selected Letters*, 1: 70; Howells to James R. Lowell, 17 Jan. 1861, *Selected Letters*, 1: 71.

4. These themes are variously treated in Haskell, *Emergence of Social Science;* Bender, *Community and Social Change in America;* Halttunen, *Confidence Men and Painted Women;* Neil Harris, *Humbug: The Art of P. T. Barnum* (Chicago: Univ. of Chicago Press, 1973); Gross, "Lonesome in Eden"; Carlo Ginzburg, "Clues: Morelli, Freud, and Sherlock Holmes," in *The Sign of the Three: Dupin, Holmes, Peirce,* ed. Umberto Eco and Thomas A. Sebeok (Bloomington: Indiana Univ. Press, 1983), 81–118. See esp. Jackson Lears, "The Stabilization of Sorcery: Antebellum Origins of Consumer Culture," Paper presented to the Organization of American Historians Annual Meeting, Philadelphia, 3 Apr. 1987.

5. See Lears's discussion of spiritual "weightlessness" and the urge to intense experience. *No Place of Grace,* 41–47f.

6. Lowell, "Percival," 144; Duberman, *James Russell Lowell,* 233; [WDH], "A Book Read Yesterday," review of *Ballad of Babie Bell and Other Poems,* by Thomas B. Aldrich, 47; [WDH], "Some Western Poets of To-day: Wm. Wallace Harney," *OSJ,* 25 Sept. 1860; [WDH], "Literary," *OSJ,* 6 Mar. 1861.

7. Howells to Oliver W. Holmes, Jr., 1 Sept. 1860, *Selected Letters,* 1: 61; Howells to Oliver W. Holmes, Jr., 14 Nov. 1860, *Selected Letters,* 1: 64; Howells to Oliver W. Holmes, Jr., 6 Jan. 1861, *Selected Letters,* 1: 70.

8. Howells to Oliver W. Holmes, Jr., 14 Nov. 1860, *Selected Letters,* 1: 64; Holmes, *Elsie Venner,* 5–6; [Oliver W. Holmes, Jr.], "Plato," *University Quarterly,* 2 (1860): 216.

9. Howells to Oliver W. Holmes, Jr., 14 Nov. 1860, *Selected Letters,* 1: 64; Howells to Oliver W. Holmes, Jr., 6 Jan. 1861, *Selected Letters,* 1: 70. Holmes's remark is quoted by Mark De Wolfe Howe, *Justice Oliver Wendell Holmes: The Shaping Years, 1841–1870* (Cambridge: Harvard Univ. Press, 1957), 44.

10. Howells to Oliver W. Holmes, Jr., 1 Sept. 1860, *Selected Letters,* 1: 62.

11. Holmes, Jr., "Plato," 217; [Oliver Wendell Holmes, Jr.], "Notes on Albert Durer," *Harvard Magazine,* 7 (1860): 41–47. On Holmes's break with the philosophical world of his father, see Mark De Wolfe Howe, ed., *Touched with Fire: Civil War Letters and Diary of Oliver Wendell Holmes, Jr., 1861–1864* (Cambridge: Harvard Univ. Press, 1946), 23–29, 79–80, 122, 135, 142–43; Howe, *Shaping Years,* passim; Frederickson, *Inner Civil War,* 85, 169, 174–75.

12. Holmes, Jr., "Plato," 216; Holmes, Jr., "Notes on Albert Durer," 45, 47.

13. Leland, *Works of Heinrich Heine,* 5: 145–46; Howells to Oliver W. Holmes, Jr., 25 Nov. 1860, *Selected Letters,* 1: 66.

14. Oliver W. Holmes, Jr., to Howells, 4 Feb. 1861, MS at Harvard.

15. All quotations in this and the following paragraphs are from Howells to Oliver W. Holmes, Jr., 24 Feb. 1861, *Selected Letters,* 1: 72–74.

16. The girl is mentioned neither in family letters nor in the *Sentinel.*

17. [WDH], "New Publications," review of *Westminster Review* (Oct. 1859), *OSJ,* 21 Nov. 1859.

18. Howells to Oliver W. Holmes, Jr., 25 Nov. 1860, *Selected Letters,* 1: 66–67; Howells to James Russell Lowell, 17 Jan. 1861, *Selected Letters,* 1: 71. On

Hamilton and his disciples, see S. A. Grave, *The Scottish Philosophy of Common Sense* (Westport, Conn.: Greenwood Press, 1973), 126–29; Kenneth D. Freeman, *The Role of Reason in Religion: A Study of Henry Mansel* (The Hague: Martinus Nijhoff, 1969). Howells passed over Asa Gray's elucidation of Darwin in the *Atlantic* with the terse reflection that it "will interest people concerned in the origin of their species." [WDH], "Atlantic for October," *OSJ*, 22 Sept. 1860.

19. [WDH], "Literary," *OSJ*, 28 Aug. 1860; [WDH], "New Publications," review of the *North American Review* (Jan. 1861), *OSJ*, 14 Jan. 1861; Howells to Oliver W. Holmes, Jr., 25 Nov. 1860, *Selected Letters*, 1: 66–67; Howells to Oliver W. Holmes, Jr., 6 Jan. 1861, *Selected Letters*, 1: 70; Heine, *Travel-Pictures*, 122. On Bowen and Holmes, see Meyer, *Instructed Conscience*, 17–29, 63, 95–97; Howe, *Shaping Years*, 35, 61–65.

20. Heine, *Religion and Philosophy*, 172–73; Howells to Oliver W. Holmes, Jr., 25 Nov. 1860, *Selected Letters*, 1: 66; [WDH], "Atlantic for October," *OSJ*, 22 Sept. 1860; [WDH], "Atlantic for November," *OSJ*, 23 Oct. 1860; [WDH], "Lamartine and American Literature," *OSJ*, 3 Nov. 1860; [WDH], "Literary Gossip," *OSJ*, 18 Jan. 1861; [WDH], "A Curiosity of Literature," *OSJ*, 5 Apr. 1861.

21. [WDH], "Literary Gossip," *OSJ*, 11 Dec. 1860.

22. [WDH], "Atlantic for October," *OSJ*, 22 Sept. 1860; [WDH], "Atlantic for November," *OSJ*, 23 Oct. 1860; [WDH], "Literary Gossip," *OSJ*, 18 Jan. 1861.

23. Holmes, *Elsie Venner*. Howells sided with the critic for the *North American Review*, who discounted "the stupid cry of infidelity" against Holmes and recognized his "larger and grander faith." In arguing for merciful treatment of exceptions, the reviewer noted, Holmes had never denied a moral universe. Review of *Elsie Venner: A Romance of Destiny*, by Oliver Wendell Holmes, *North American Review*, 92 (1861): 587–88; [WDH], review of *North American Review* (Apr. 1861), *OSJ*, 6 Apr. 1861.

24. Henry Maudsley, "Edgar Allan Poe," *Journal of Mental Science*, 6 (1859): 328–69; [WDH], "Diagnosis of a Poet," *OSJ*, 27 Nov. 1860. For discussion of Maudsley, see Elaine Showalter, *The Female Malady: Women, Madness, and English Culture, 1830–1980* (New York: Pantheon, 1985), 101–20.

25. WDH, "Diagnosis of a Poet."

26. Ibid.

27. For Howells's reading of Schlegel, see WDH, *My Literary Passions*, 111. Schlegel, *Lectures on Dramatic Art and Literature*, 113–14; see Schlegel's full discussion of Greek tragedy, lectures 5–10.

28. [WDH], "New Publications," review of *North British Review* (Aug. 1860), *OSJ*, 5 Sept. 1860.

29. [WDH], "New Publications," review of *Love and Penalty; or Eternal Punishment Consistent with the Fatherhood of God*, by Joseph P. Thompson, *OSJ*, 19 Dec. 1860.

30. [WDH], "New Publications," review of *Chapters on Wives*, by Mrs. Ellis, *OSJ*, 2 Mar. 1861.

31. [WDH], "Geoffrey Winter," Unpublished novel, MS at Harvard, 4. Citations of "Geoffrey Winter" in the following paragraphs refer only to quoted material.

32. Ibid., 10, 11, 26, 50; Howells to Victoria M. Howells, 18 Sept. 1859, MS at Harvard.

33. WDH, "Geoffrey Winter," 40, 41.

34. Ibid., 91, 93, 94, 100–101, 105. Howells canceled the word *objective* in the manuscript.

35. Ibid., 92, 94, 95–(a-96), 104.

36. Ibid., 1, 7, 16, 19, 36a, 107.

37. Ibid., 108, 128, 202; Howells to Oliver W. Holmes, Jr., 24 Feb. 1861, *Selected Letters*, 1: 73.

38. WDH, "Geoffrey Winter," 204, (222–223).

39. Ibid., 207–8.

40. Ibid., 72, (222–223).

41. Ibid., 59, 99–100, 165.

42. Ibid., 189; [WDH], "New Publications," review of *Nemesis*, by Marian Harland, *OSJ*, 5 Oct. 1860; [WDH], "Literary: New Publications," review of *Hopes and Fears; or Scenes from the Life of a Spinster*, by ?, *OSJ*, 7 Mar. 1861.

43. WDH, "Geoffrey Winter," 16, 213–14; Howells to Oliver W. Holmes, Jr., 25 Nov. 1860, *Selected Letters*, 1: 66; Howells to Victoria M. Howells, 24 Mar. 1861, *Selected Letters*, 1: 76.

44. [WDH], "Secession," *OSJ*, 25 Oct. 1860; [WDH], "Expulsion of South Carolina," *OSJ*, 17 Nov. 1860. I have distinguished Howells's editorials from Price's on the basis of Howells's position as "chief" editorial writer (see Howells to Victoria M. Howells, 18 Sept. 1860, MS at Harvard), his greater fluency of expression, and his more sophisticated reserve of literary expression. Some of Howells's editorials reveal consistencies with his literary columns and his political reporting for the New York *World*.

45. [WCH], "Republican Meeting," *AS*, 19 Dec. 1860; [WCH], "From the Editor," *AS*, 6 Feb. 1861; [WCH], "Compromise Canards—Compromise," *AS*, 13 Feb. 1861; Lowell, "E Pluribus Unum," 63, 70, 74.

46. WDH, *Years of My Youth*, 391; [WDH], "In Dickens' new story of 'Great Expectations' . . . ," *OSJ*, 31 Dec. 1860.

47. WDH, *Years of My Youth*, 181–82, 191; WDH, *Literary Friends and Acquaintance*, 70–71; Howells to Victoria M. Howells, 24 Mar. 1861, *Selected Letters*, 1: 76; William C. Howells to James M. Comly, 19 Dec. 1862, James M. Comly Papers, MSS 130, MS at OHS. On Howells and Elinor, see Ginette de B. Merrill, "The Meeting of Elinor Gertrude Mead and Will Howells and Their Courtship," *Old Northwest*, 8 (1982): 23–47.

48. WDH, *Literary Friends and Acquaintance*, 8; Howells to James R. Lowell, 17 Jan. 1861, *Selected Letters*, 1: 71, 72 n. 2; James T. Fields to Howells, 20 Sept. 1861, *Fields of the Atlantic Monthly: Letters to an Editor, 1861–1870*, by James C. Austin (San Marino, Calif.: Huntington Library, 1953), 140; [WDH], "New Publications," review of *New York Saturday Press*, *OSJ*, 7 Nov. 1860; William Winter to Howells, 3 Mar. 1861, MS at Harvard; Howells to Victoria M.

Howells, 18 Sept. 1860, MS at Harvard; Howells to John G. Nicolay, 13 Mar. 1861, *Selected Letters*, 1: 74–75, 75 n. 2; Howells to John Hay, 10 June 1861, *Life in Letters*, 1: 37; [WDH], "Summary of News by Last Night's Mail and Express," *OSJ*, 11 Jan. 1859; [WCH], "From the Editor," *AS*, 13 Feb. 1861; [WCH], "From the Editor," *AS*, 27 Mar. 1861.

49. Howells to Victoria M. Howells, 24 Mar. 1861, *Selected Letters*, 1: 75–77.

50. WDH, *Years of My Youth*, 200–201; [WCH], "From the Editor," *AS*, 17 Apr. 1861; [WCH], "From the Editor," *AS*, 29 Apr. 1861; [WCH], "From the Editor," *AS*, 2 May 1861.

51. [WDH], "The Significance of the Present War," *OSJ*, 15 Apr. 1861; [WCH], "From the Editor," *AS*, 24 Apr. 1861; [WCH], "From the Editor," *AS*, 29 Apr. 1861.

52. Howells to Victoria M. Howells, 21 Apr. 1861, *Selected Letters*, 1: 77.

53. WDH, *Years of My Youth*, 106, 117, 201–2, 382–83; "The 'Jefferson Guards,'" *AS*, 29 Apr. 1861; "The Giddings Zouaves," *AS*, 6 June 1861; "Ashtabula County in the Field," *AS*, 5 Sept. 1861; [WDH], "War Movements in Ohio," New York *World*, 15 May 1861.

54. Howells to Victoria M. Howells, 21 Apr. 1861, *Selected Letters*, 1: 77.

55. Howells to Oliver W. Holmes, Jr., 22 May 1861, *Selected Letters*, 1: 78–79.

56. [WDH], "Contributor's Club," *Atlantic Monthly*, 45 (1880): 859–60. John W. Crowley, "Howells's Obscure Hurt," *Journal of American Studies*, 9 (1975): 199–211, discusses reflections of Howells's guilt in his later fiction.

57. [WDH], "Decay of Southern Literature," *OSJ*, 30 May 1861; [WDH], "Periodicals," *OSJ*, 21 June 1861; Howells to John J. Piatt, 4 Aug. 1861, *Selected Letters*, 1: 81–82; [WDH], "The Fight at Bethel," *OSJ*, 12 June 1861; [WDH], "Name of Pierce," *OSJ*, 12 June 1861.

58. [WDH], "Our Defeat," *OSJ*, 23 July 1861. The actual Union loss in men killed at Manassas was 481. See Allan Nevins, *The War for the Union: The Improvised War, 1861–1862* (New York: Charles Scribner's Sons, 1959), 221.

59. WDH, *Years of My Youth*, 203–5; WDH, *My Literary Passions*, 148; WDH, *Literary Friends and Acquaintance*, 72–73, 78–79; Howells to John G. Nicolay, 24 June 1861, *Selected Letters*, 1: 80–81; Ticknor and Fields to Howells, 27 July 1861, MS at Harvard; Howells to William C. Howells, 7 Sept. 1861, *Selected Letters*, 1: 82–83; Howells to Mrs. Samuel M. Smith, 28 Sept. 1861, *Selected Letters*, 1: 84; [WDH], Daily Pocket Diary, 1860, entry for 22 Oct. 1861, MS at Harvard.

9. Desperate Leisure

Epigraph: WDH, *My Literary Passions*, 158.

1. W. D. Howells, *Venetian Life*, 3d ed. (New York: Hurd and Houghton, 1867), 32, 383; William Dean Howells, *Venetian Life* (Boston: Houghton Mifflin, 1907), 409; WDH, *Years of My Youth*, 189; WDH, *My Literary Passions*, 148. The phrase "friends with fortune" is quoted in Cady, *Road to Realism*, 143.

2. Howells, *Venetian Life*, 3d ed., 383.

3. William Dean Howells, "Young Contributors and Editors," *Youth's Companion*, 75 (1901): 267.

4. [WDH], Diary, Venice, 1861–62, entry for 15 Dec. 1861, MS at Harvard.

5. Ibid., entries for 3 Jan., 15 Apr. 1862; Howells to Victoria M. Howells, 18 and 21 Jan. 1862, *Selected Letters*, 1: 103.

6. WDH, *Venetian Life*, 3d ed., 38; Howells to John J. Piatt, 27 Jan. 1862, *Selected Letters*, 1: 108.

7. WDH, Diary, entries for 15 Dec. 1861, 9 Jan. 1862; WDH, *Venetian Life*, 3d ed., 58–59.

8. WDH, Diary, entries for 27 Jan., 24 Mar., 16 May 1862.

9. Ibid., entries for 25, 29 Dec. 1861, 24, 27 Jan., 24 Mar. 1862; James T. Fields to Howells, 20 Sept. 1861, Austin, *Fields of the Atlantic*, 141; [WDH], "Louis Lebeau's Conversion," *Atlantic Monthly*, 10 (1862): 534–38; Howells to William C. Howells, 12 Feb. 1862, MS at Harvard; Howells to James R. Lowell, 21 Aug. 1864, *Selected Letters*, 1: 194.

10. WDH, Diary, entries for 7, 30 Jan., 19 Feb., 12, 18, 24, 27 Mar., 1, 19, 26 Apr. 1862; Howells to Richard Hildreth, 22 Dec. 1861, MS at Harvard; Howells to John J. Piatt, 27 Jan. 1862, *Selected Letters*, 1: 106–7; Howells to Richard Hildreth, 1 Feb. 1862, MS at Harvard; Howells to Victoria M. Howells, 26 Apr. 1862, *Selected Letters*, 1: 114–15.

11. WDH, Diary, entry for 24 Jan. 1862.

12. Ibid., entry for 21 Feb. 1862; WDH, *Years of My Youth*, 230–31; Howells to Mary D. Howells, 4 Mar. 1862, MS at Harvard; Howells to William C. Howells, 7 Mar. 1862, *Selected Letters*, 1: 109–10.

13. Howells to William C. Howells, 13 June 1862, *Selected Letters*, 1: 116; Howells to William C. Howells, 11 July 1862, MS at Harvard; Howells to William C. Howells, 12 Sept. 1862, *Selected Letters*, 1: 125.

14. WDH, Diary, entry for 24 Jan. 1862; Howells to William C. Howells, 7 Mar. 1862, *Selected Letters*, 1: 111.

15. WDH, *Venetian Life*, 3d ed., 27–39.

16. Ibid., 50–51; WDH, Diary, entry for 4 Jan. 1862.

17. WDH, Diary, entry for 3 Jan. 1862.

18. Howells to Moncure D. Conway, 24 Mar. 1863, *Selected Letters*, 1: 145; WDH, Diary, entries for 7, 8 Jan. 1862; WDH, *My Literary Passions*, 150, 159, 162; WDH, *Venetian Life*, 3d ed., 158. On Protestant attraction to Catholic art, see Lears, *No Place of Grace*, 184–97, passim.

19. WDH, *Venetian Life*, 3d ed., passim; WDH, Diary, entry for 16 May 1862; WDH, *My Literary Passions*, 155, 158.

20. Howells to John Swinton, 22 Oct. 1863, quoted in James L. Woodress, Jr., *Howells and Italy* (Durham, N.C.: Duke Univ. Press, 1952), 52 n. 9; WDH, *Venetian Life*, 3d ed., 10, 15, passim.

21. Howells to Edmund C. Stedman, 1 Feb. 1864, *Selected Letters*, 1: 177.

22. WDH, "Young Contributors and Editors," 267; WDH, *Literary Friends and Acquaintance*, 85–86; WDH, Diary, entries for 1, 25 Apr. 1862; Howells to Victoria M. Howells, 26 Apr. 1862, *Selected Letters*, 1: 113; Howells to William C. Howells, 11 July 1862, MS at Harvard.

23. Howells to William C. Howells, 22 Mar. 1862, MS at Harvard; WDH, Diary, entry for 24 Mar. 1862; William C. Howells Family to Howells, 5 Nov. 1861, MS at MHS; Anne T. Howells to Howells, 16 Mar. 1862, MS at Alfred; Anne T. and Mary D. Howells to Howells, 21 May 1862, MS at MHS; Howells to Victoria M. Howells, 26 Apr. 1862, *Selected Letters*, 1: 113; Howells to Mary D. Howells, 3 Aug. 1862, TS copy at Harvard.

24. Howells to William C. Howells, 22 July 1862, *Selected Letters*, 1: 119–21.

25. Howells to ?, 6 May 1862, MS at Harvard; Howells to William C. Howells, 14 Aug. 1862, MS at Harvard; Howells to William C. Howells, 22 Aug. 1862, *Selected Letters*, 1: 122.

26. [WCH], "The Cincinnati War," *AS*, 17 Sept. 1862; Roseboom, *Civil War Era*, 397–99; Howells to William C. Howells, 28 Aug. 1862, *Selected Letters*, 1: 123–24; Howells to William C. Howells, 12 Sept. 1862, *Selected Letters*, 1: 124–26.

27. [WCH], "Towns to be Drafted," *AS*, 17 Sept. 1862; [WDH], "The Mulberries," *Atlantic Monthly*, 27 (1871): 377–79; Howells to Victoria M. Howells, 22 and 23 Oct. 1862, *Selected Letters*, 1: 130; WDH, *My Literary Passions*, 159.

28. Howells to Larkin G. Mead, Sr., 24 Dec. 1862, *Selected Letters*, 1: 132; Elinor M. Howells to William C. Howells, 4 Jan. 1863, MS at Harvard; Howells to James L. Graham, Jr., 22 Jan. 1863, *Selected Letters*, 1: 133; Howells to Charles Hale, 31 Jan. 1863, *Selected Letters*, 1: 134–35; Howells to William C. Howells, 12 and 20 Feb. 1863, *Selected Letters*, 1: 137–40; Howells to William C. Howells, 15 Mar. 1863, *Selected Letters*, 1: 140–43; Howells to Moncure D. Conway, 24 Mar. 1863, *Selected Letters*, 1: 145; Elinor M. Howells to Aurelia H. Howells, 15 May 1863, MS at Harvard; [Elinor M. Howells], Venetian Diary, 1863–65, MS at Harvard; Howells to Edmund C. Stedman, 1 Feb. 1864, *Selected Letters*, 1: 177.

29. Howells to William C. Howells, 15 Mar. 1863, *Selected Letters*, 1: 143; [WDH], "A Poet," *Dial*, 1 (1860): 371; Howells to Mary D. Howells, 18 Apr. 1863, *Selected Letters*, 1: 148.

30. Howells to William C. Howells, 22 Dec. 1863, *Selected Letters*, 1: 172.

31. Howells to Aurelia H. Howells, 18 May 1863, *Selected Letters*, 1: 150; WDH, *Years of My Youth*, 100, 273.

32. Charles Hale to Howells, 29 Apr. 1863, MS at Harvard; Charles Hale to Howells, 26 May 1863, MS at Harvard; Howells to Mary D. Howells, 18 June 1863, *Selected Letters*, 1: 154; Howells to Moncure D. Conway, 22 Aug. 1863, *Selected Letters*, 1: 155.

33. Frank E. Foster to Howells, 1 May 1862, MS at Harvard; Howells to Frank E. Foster, 11 Apr. 1863, MS at Univ. of Southern California Library, Morse Collection; Howells to Frank E. Foster, 13 May 1863, MS at Univ. of Southern California Library, Morse Collection.

34. Moncure D. Conway to Howells, 5 and 6 Aug. 1863, MS at Harvard; Frank E. Foster to Howells, 21 Aug. 1863, MS at Harvard; Howells to Moncure D. Conway, 22 Aug. 1863, *Selected Letters*, 1: 155; Moncure D. Conway to Howells, 13 Sept. 1863, MS at Harvard; Frank E. Foster to Howells, 20 Sept. 1863, MS at Harvard; Frank E. Foster to Howells, 3 Oct. 1863, MS at Harvard; H. M. Ticknor to Howells, 6 Oct. 1863, MS at Harvard; Howells to Charles

Hale, 25 Oct. 1863, *Selected Letters*, 1: 162–64; Frank E. Foster to Howells, 31 Oct. 1863, MS at Harvard; Howells to Charles Hale, 2 Nov. 1863, *Selected Letters*, 1: 164; Elinor M. Howells, Venetian Diary, entry for 6 Nov. 1863, entry by Howells for 11 Nov. 1863, MS at Harvard.

35. Howells to Solomon P. Chase, 3 Oct. 1863, *Selected Letters*, 1: 161; Howells to William C. Howells, 14 and 19 Nov. 1863, *Selected Letters*, 1: 166; Howells to Joseph A. Howells, 9 Dec. 1863, *Selected Letters*, 1: 167–68.

36. Howells to Joseph A. Howells, 9 Dec. 1863, *Selected Letters*, 1: 168–69; Howells to John G. and Laura P. Mitchell, 13 and 17 Dec. 1863, *Life in Letters*, 1: 79–80; Howells to William C. Howells, 22 Dec. 1863, *Selected Letters*, 1: 172; Howells to Moncure D. Conway, 16 and 22 May 1863, *Selected Letters*, 1: 187; Elinor M. Howells, Venetian Diary, entry by Howells for 9 Jan. 1864, MS at Harvard; [WDH], "Ordeals," Unpublished poem, MS at Harvard.

37. Howells to Joseph A. Howells, 9 Dec. 1863, *Selected Letters*, 1: 168–69; Howells to William C. Howells, 22 Dec. 1863, *Selected Letters*, 1: 172.

38. Howells to Moncure D. Conway, 26 Jan. 1864, *Selected Letters*, 1: 175; WDH, *My Literary Passions*, 162–64.

39. WDH, *My Literary Passions*, 162–64; Caroline Wigley Clive, *Paul Ferroll: A Tale*, 3d ed. (London: Saunders and Otley, 1856).

40. Charles Hale to Howells, 4 Dec. 1863, MS at Harvard; Howells to Edmund C. Stedman, 1 Feb. 1864, *Selected Letters*, 1: 177–78.

41. Howells to Edmund C. Stedman, 1 Feb. 1864, *Selected Letters*, 1: 177; Howells to Harper and Brothers, 20 Feb. 1864, *Selected Letters*, 1: 179–80.

42. Elinor M. Howells to Mary D. Howells, 27 Feb. 1864, MS at Harvard; [WDH], "Recent Italian Comedy," *North American Review*, 99 (1864): 364–401.

43. Elinor M. Howells and Howells to Anne T. Howells, 8 Mar. 1864, MS at Harvard; Howells to Aurelia H. Howells, [20 and ?] May 1864, *Life in Letters*, 1: 82–83; Elinor M. Howells, Venetian Diary, entry for 21 May 1864, MS at Harvard.

44. WDH, "Recent Italian Comedy."

45. James R. Lowell to Howells, 28 July 1864, *Letters of Lowell*, 1: 338; WDH, "The Turning Point of My Life," 165–66; WDH, *Literary Friends and Acquaintance*, 87; WDH, "Young Contributors and Editors," 267.

46. William C. Howells to Elinor M. Howells, 28 Apr. 1864, MS at MHS; Howells to William C. Howells, 4 May 1864, MS at Harvard; Howells to Samuel D. Howells, 19 May 1864, *Selected Letters*, 1: 189; Howells to Aurelia H. Howells, [20 and ?] May 1864, *Life in Letters*, 1: 82–83; Elinor M. Howells, Venetian Diary, entry for 21 May 1864, MS at Harvard.

47. Howells to John B. Howells, 2 Sept. 1863, *Selected Letters*, 1: 156–57 n. 1; Howells to William C. Howells, 25 May 1864, MS at Alfred; [WDH], "Elegy on John Butler Howells," *AS*, 29 June 1864; Howells to Anne T. Howells, 20 June 1864, *Selected Letters*, 1: 190.

48. Howells to James R. Lowell, 24 May 1864, MS at Harvard; Howells to Anne T. Howells, 20 June 1864, *Selected Letters*, 1: 191; Howells to Mary D. Howells and Girls, 12 and 13 July 1864, MS at Harvard; Howells to William C.

Howells, 22 July 1864, *Selected Letters*, 1: 192–93; Elinor M. Howells, Venetian Diary, entry for 21 Aug. 1864, MS at Harvard.

49. Howells to William C. Howells, 25 Aug. 1864, *Selected Letters*, 1: 196–99.

50. Ibid,

51. Ibid.

52. Ibid.

53. Ibid.

54. Howells to Joseph A. Howells, 13 Sept. 1864, MS at Harvard; Howells to Samuel D. Howells, 20 and 22 Sept. 1864, MS at Harvard; Howells to William C. Howells, 6 Oct. 1864, *Selected Letters*, 1: 199–200; [WCH], "Enlistments," *AS*, 3 Aug. 1864; [WCH], "Jefferson," *AS*, 31 Aug. 1864.

55. Howells to Anne T. Howells, 2 Dec. 1864, *Selected Letters*, 1: 204.

56. Howells to Anne T. Howells, 2 Dec. 1864, MS at Harvard. My reading of this passage differs from the editors' reading in *Selected Letters*, 1: 204. I read *endless* while the editors read *useless*.

10. Bound to the Highest and the Lowest

Epigraph: [WDH], "Editor's Study," *Harper's Monthly*, 80 (1890): 806.

1. WDH, *Literary Friends and Acquaintance*, 358; Howells to William C. Howells, 29 Nov. 1874, *Selected Letters*, 2: 77; Oliver W. Holmes to Howells, 14 Dec. 1879, John T. Morse, Jr., *Life and Letters of Oliver Wendell Holmes* (Boston: Houghton, Mifflin, 1896), 1: 44.

2. W. D. Howells, *Suburban Sketches*, 2d ed. (Boston: James R. Osgood, 1872), 165. For satirization of the aesthetic observer, see esp. Howells's sketch "A Romance of Real Life," 171–89, and for references to a sense of homelessness, see esp. his sketch "Flitting," 241–55.

3. WDH, "Recent Italian Comedy," 368.

4. Howells to William C. Howells, 11 Dec. 1870, *Selected Letters*, 1: 361.

5. Henry Ward Beecher, "The Advance of a Century," New York *Tribune*, 4 July 1876, reprinted in *Democratic Vistas: 1860–1880*, ed. Alan Trachtenberg (New York: George Braziller, 1970), 71.

6. Howells to Thomas W. Higginson, 17 Sept. 1879, *Selected Letters*, 2: 238.

7. W. D. Howells, *The Undiscovered Country* (Boston: Houghton, Mifflin, 1880), 106.

8. Howells to William C. Howells, 1 Feb. 1880, MS at Harvard.

9. WDH, *Undiscovered Country*, 53, 179.

10. Ibid., 235–36.

11. Ibid., 319.

12. Ibid., 419.

13. Howells to Henry O. Houghton, 14 Jan. 1881, *Selected Letters*, 2: 273; Howells to Horace E. Scudder, 8 Feb. 1881, *Selected Letters*, 2: 274.

14. Howells to William C. Howells, 29 Feb. 1880, *Selected Letters*, 2: 245; Howells to William C. Howells, 28 Nov. 1880, MS at Harvard; Howells to

Rutherford B. Hayes, 1 Dec. 1880, MS at Hayes; Howells to William C. Howells, 21 Aug. 1881, MS at Harvard; Elinor M. Howells to Olivia Clemens, 26 Aug. 1881, *Mark Twain—Howells Letters: The Correspondence of Samuel L. Clemens and William D. Howells, 1872–1910*, ed. Henry Nash Smith and William M. Gibson (Cambridge: Harvard Univ. Press, 1960), 1: 367–68; Howells to Samuel L. Clemens, 11 Sept. 1881, *Twain—Howells Letters*, 1: 373; Howells to William C. Howells, 17 July 1881, MS at Harvard.

15. Howells to James R. Osgood, 18 Feb. 1881, *Selected Letters*, 2: 277. On the middle-class ideal of marriage, see Mintz, *A Prison of Expectations*, 103–46.

16. Howells to James R. Osgood, 18 Feb. 1881, *Selected Letters*, 2: 277; W. D. Howells, "Alfieri," *Atlantic Monthly*, 35 (1875): 547.

17. W. D. Howells, *A Modern Instance*, ed. George N. Bennett, David J. Nordloh, and David Kleinman (Bloomington: Indiana Univ. Press, 1977), 89, 90. Citations of *A Modern Instance* in this and following paragraphs refer only to quoted material.

18. Ibid., 20–21, 23, 27, 29–30, 39.

19. Ibid., 13, 19.

20. Ibid., 96.

21. Ibid., 84, 101.

22. Ibid., 229, 304, 321, 322, 330, 343, 348.

23. For examples where Howells allowed his narrator's voice to intrude upon Bartley's reveries and assert his damnation, see Henry Nash Smith, *Democracy and the Novel: Popular Resistance to Classic American Writers* (New York: Oxford Univ. Press, 1978), esp. 86–88.

24. Cady, *Realist at War*, 210, has established the probable portion of the novel on which Howells was working when his illness occurred. Howells to William C. Howells, 15 Nov. 1881, *Life in Letters*, 1: 303–4; Elinor M. Howells to Annie A. Fields, 10 Dec. 1881, *Selected Letters*, 2: 340; Howells to John Hay, 18 Mar. 1882, *Selected Letters*, 3: 12; WDH, *My Literary Passions*, 178.

25. WDH, *A Modern Instance*, 417.

26. Ibid., 204, 351.

27. Ibid., 353, 416–17.

28. Ibid., 361, 453.

29. W. D. Howells, *The Minister's Charge or the Apprenticeship of Lemuel Barker*, ed. Howard M. Munford, David J. Nordloh, and David Kleinman (Bloomington: Indiana Univ. Press, 1978), 340; WDH, *A Modern Instance*, 418.

30. WDH, *The Minister's Charge*, 341.

31. Howells to George W. Curtis, 10 Aug. 1887, *Selected Letters*, 3: 194; Howells to George W. Curtis, 18 Aug. 1887, *Selected Letters*, 3: 193; Howells to Editor of New York *Tribune*, 4 Nov. 1887, *Selected Letters*, 3: 199; Howells to Editor of New York *Tribune*, 12 Nov. 1887, *Selected Letters*, 3: 201–4. A recent assessment of the Haymarket affair by Paul Avrich fully credits Howells's courage. See *The Haymarket Tragedy* (Princeton: Princeton Univ. Press, 1984), 301–4, 339–41.

32. Howells to Anne Howells Fréchette, 18 Nov. 1887, *Selected Letters*, 3: 208; [WDH], "Editor's Study," *Harper's Monthly*, 78 (1888): 159; [WDH],

"Editor's Study," *Harper's Monthly*, 79 (1889): 479–80; WDH, *The Minister's Charge*, 342.

33. Howells to Henry James, 25 Dec. 1886, *Selected Letters*, 3: 174; Howells to William C. Howells, 20 Feb. 1887, *Selected Letters*, 3: 182; Howells to George W. Curtis, 27 Feb. 1887, *Selected Letters*, 3: 183; [WDH], "Editor's Study," *Harper's Monthly*, 78 (1888): 159; Howells to Edward E. Hale, 28 Oct. 1888, *Selected Letters*, 3: 233. For general accounts of Howells's social concerns in this period, see the studies cited in Preface, n. 7.

34. W. D. Howells, "The Man of Letters as a Man of Business," *Scribner's*, 14 (1893): 429–45. For historical perspective on the business of literature during these years, see Nelson Lichtenstein, "Authorial Professionalism and the Literary Marketplace, 1885–1900," *American Studies*, 19 (1978): 35–53; Christopher P. Wilson, "The Rhetoric of Consumption: Mass-Market Magazines and the Demise of the Gentle Reader," in *The Culture of Consumption: Critical Essays in American History, 1880–1980*, ed. Richard Wightman Fox and T. J. Jackson Lears (New York: Pantheon, 1983), 39–64, 218–221; Christopher P. Wilson, *The Labor of Words: Literary Professionalism in the Progressive Era* (Athens: Univ. of Georgia Press, 1985).

35. Howells to Henry James, 10 Oct. 1888, *Selected Letters*, 3: 232; W. D. Howells, *A Hazard of New Fortunes*, ed. Everett Carter, David J. Nordloh, Don L. Cook, James P. Elliott, David Kleinman, and Robert D. Schildgen (Bloomington: Indiana Univ. Press, 1976), 25, 27, 28, 30, 101. Citations of *A Hazard of New Fortunes* in this and following paragraphs refer only to quoted material.

36. Ibid., 243.

37. Ibid., 55, 65, 69, 70.

38. Ibid., 18, 67–68, 180.

39. Ibid., 71, 147.

40. Ibid., 184.

41. Ibid., 306.

42. Howells to William C. Howells, 6 Apr. 1890, *Selected Letters*, 3: 278.

43. WDH, *A Hazard of New Fortunes*, 191–92, 194.

44. Ibid., 347.

45. Ibid., 379.

46. The theme of forgetting posed against complicity in *A Hazard of New Fortunes* is noted by Cady, *Realist at War*, 110–11.

47. WDH, *A Hazard of New Fortunes*, 145, 300, 324, 351, 363.

48. Ibid., 436–37.

49. Ibid., 437.

50. Ibid., 260, 430, 487.

51. WDH, "Bibliographical," *A Hazard of New Fortunes*, 5–6.

52. W. D. Howells, "Lyof N. Tolstoy," *North American Review*, 188 (1908): 851–52.

53. WDH, *The Minister's Charge*, 341.

54. WDH, *A Hazard of New Fortunes*, 436.

55. Howells to James Parton, 3 Jan. 1890, *Selected Letters*, 3: 269; Howells to Moncure D. Conway, 7 Apr. 1889, *Selected Letters*, 3: 250.

56. W. D. Howells, *"The Shadow of a Dream" and "An Imperative Duty,"* ed. Martha Banta, Ronald Gottesman, and David J. Nordloh (Bloomington: Indiana Univ. Press, 1970), 59.

57. See Lears, *No Place of Grace;* Lasch, *Culture of Narcissism;* Lears and Fox, eds., *Culture of Consumption.*

58. W. D. Howells, *The Altrurian Romances,* ed. Clara and Rudolf Kirk and Scott Bennett (Bloomington: Indiana Univ. Press, 1968), 246. Essays on the language of complicity include W. D. Howells, "Are We a Plutocracy?" *North American Review,* 158 (1894): 185–96; W. D. Howells, "Equality as the Basis of Good Society," *Century,* 51 (1895): 63–67; W. D. Howells, "The Nature of Liberty," *Forum,* 20 (1895): 401–9; W. D. Howells, "Who Are Our Brethren," *Century,* 51 (1896): 932–36.

59. See [WDH], "The Editor's Study," *Harper's Monthly,* 83 (1891): 639–40 (Garland); W. D. Howells, "Life and Letters," *Harper's Weekly,* 40 (1896): 630 (Dunbar); W. D. Howells, "An Appreciation," in Stephen Crane, *Maggie: A Child of the Streets* (London: William Heinemann, 1896), v–vii; W. D. Howells, "New York Low Life in Fiction," New York *World,* 26 July 1896 (Harrigan, Crane, Cahan); W. D. Howells, "A Case in Point," *Literature,* n.s., 1 (1899): 241–42 (Norris).

60. W. D. Howells, *The Son of Royal Langbrith,* ed. David Burrows, Ronald Gottesman, and David J. Nordloh (Bloomington: Indiana Univ. Press, 1969), 213.

61. Ibid., 228; Howells to William C. Howells, 14 June 1891, *Selected Letters,* 3: 314.

Epilogue

1. Unless otherwise noted, all quotations in the following paragraphs are from W. D. Howells, "The Pearl," *Harper's Monthly,* 133 (1916): 409–13; William Dean Howells, "A Tale Untold," *Atlantic Monthly,* 120 (1917): 236–42.

2. For discussions of "Old Times" in these terms, see Smith, *Mark Twain,* 77–81; Leo Marx, *The Machine and the Garden: Technology and the Pastoral Ideal in America* (New York: Oxford Univ. Press, 1964), 320–25.

3. On Twain's development between *Tom Sawyer* and *Adventures of Huckleberry Finn,* see Smith, *Mark Twain,* 113–37.

4. Howells had used this description to characterize Hamlin Garland's *Main-Travelled Roads.* [WDH], "The Editor's Study," *Harper's Monthly,* 83 (1891): 639.

5. W. D. Howells, "Lyof Tolstoï," *Harper's Weekly,* 31 (1887): 300.

Attributions, Permissions, and Notes for Illustrations

(Attributions and permissions are placed first followed by notes.)

1. W. D. Howells, *Years of My Youth*, illustrated ed. (New York: Harper and Brothers, 1917), facing 22; Clifton Johnson, Preface to *Years of My Youth*, illustrated ed., by WDH, [viii]; WDH, *A Boy's Town*, 37–38.

2. From William Dean Howells Collection, GA 20, by permission of the Rutherford B. Hayes Presidential Center; WDH, *Years of My Youth*, 25–26.

3. WDH, *Years of My Youth*, illustrated ed., facing 54; Johnson, Preface to *Years of My Youth*, illustrated ed., by WDH, [vi–vii]; WDH, *Years of My Youth*, 52.

4. From William Dean Howells Collection, GA 20, by permission of the Rutherford B. Hayes Presidential Center; WDH, *Years of My Youth*, 101.

5. By permission of the Houghton Library, Harvard University; WDH, *My Literary Passions*, 73. Howells's daughter Mildred noted Howells's age as eighteen and identified his companions as Goodrich and Miller on a copy of the photograph at Harvard. Mildred dated the photograph 1856 when she included it in *Life in Letters*, 1: facing 10. Howells signed and added the year 1856 on a cropped portrait of himself taken from this photograph, at Hayes.

6. Minot S. Giddings, *The Giddings Family: or, the Descendants of George Giddings, who came from St. Albans, England, to Ipswich, Mass., in 1636* (Hartford, Conn.: Case, Lockwood and Brainard, 1882), facing 150; [WCH], "Death of Mr. Giddings," *AS*, n.d. (ca. 26 May 1864), in Joshua R. Giddings Scrapbook, 1800–1864, Joshua R. Giddings Papers, MIC 7, at OHS.

7. Album for Mrs. P. H. Rickelson, 1864. Courtesy, The Winterthur Library, Joseph Downs Collection of Manuscripts and Printed Ephemera.

8. From Howells/Fréchette Collection, by permission of the Herrick Memo-

rial Library, Alfred University; WDH, Introduction to *Recollections of Life in Ohio*, by WCH, vii.

9. From Howells/Fréchette Collection, by permission of the Herrick Memorial Library, Alfred University; Mary D. Howells to Victoria M. Howells, 29 Oct. [1857], MS at Alfred.

10. From Howells/Fréchette Collection, by permission of the Herrick Memorial Library, Alfred University; Joseph A. Howells to Anne Howells Fréchette, 29 Mar. 1911, TS at Alfred; WDH, *Years of My Youth*, 98; Howells to Aurelia H. Howells, 21 July 1915, *Selected Letters*, 6: 82; Johnson, Preface to *Years of My Youth*, illustrated ed., by WDH, [ix].

11. From Howells/Fréchette Collection, by permission of the Herrick Memorial Library, Alfred University; Aurelia H. Howells, "Paper on William Dean Howells," n.d., TS at Harvard; [John Greenleaf Whittier], *The Poetical Works of Whittier* (1894; reprint, Boston: Houghton Mifflin, 1975), 403; WDH, *Years of My Youth*, 109; Howells to Aurelia H. Howells, 9 Jan. 1887, *Selected Letters*, 3: 178 n. 2; Clara and Rudolf Kirk, " 'The Howells Family,' by Richard J. Hinton," *Journal of the Rutgers University Library*, 14 (1950): 19.

12. From Howells/Fréchette Collection, by permission of the Herrick Memorial Library, Alfred University; Anne Howells Fréchette, 2d draft of an untitled speech concerning William Dean Howells, 3, MS at Alfred.

13. From Howells/Fréchette Collection, by permission of the Herrick Memorial Library, Alfred University; Anne T. Howells, Journal, 1863–67, entry for 10 July [1863], 4–5.

14. From Howells/Fréchette Collection, by permission of the Herrick Memorial Library, Alfred University; Anne Howells Fréchette, 2d draft, 6, MS at Alfred.

15. By permission of the Houghton Library, Harvard University; Howells to John B. Howells, 2 Sept. 1863, *Selected Letters*, 1: 157.

16. By permission of the Houghton Library, Harvard University; [WDH], "The Ghost-Maker," unpublished short story, 19–20, MS at Harvard. At least part of this story was written in Venice. A portion of it is in the hand of Elinor Howells.

17. W. D. Howells, *Literary Friends and Acquaintance: A Personal Retrospect of American Authorship*, illustrated ed. (New York: Harper and Brothers, 1901), facing 212; WDH, *Literary Friends and Acquaintance*, 29, 194.

18. By permission of the Houghton Library, Harvard University; Howells to John J. Piatt, 27 Jan. 1862, *Selected Letters*, 1: 108. Although Mildred Howells dated this photograph 1864–65 when she included it in *Life in Letters*, 1: [91], comparison with Howells's physical features in other Venice photographs suggests that it was taken earlier.

19. WDH, *Literary Friends and Acquaintance*, illustrated ed., facing 90; WDH, *Venetian Life*, 3d ed., 99–100.

20. By permission of the Houghton Library, Harvard University; Elinor M. Howells, Venetian Diary, entries for 1 July, 9, 18, 19 Aug. 1863, 3 Dec. 1864, passim, MS at Harvard. A copy of the photograph at Harvard is dated 1865 by Mildred Howells.

21. From Howells/Fréchette Collection, by permission of the Herrick Memorial Library, Alfred University; [WCH], "To the Voters of Ashtabula County," *AS*, 1 Sept. 1861; [WCH], "To the Voters of Ashtabula County," *AS*, 19 Sept. 1861; [WCH], "President's Proclamation," *AS*, 1 Oct. 1862; [WCH], "Union Ticket," *AS*, 7 Oct. 1863; [WCH], "From the Editor," *AS*, 22 Feb. 1864.

22. By permission of the Houghton Library, Harvard University; the photograph is dated in [Elinor M. Howells], Pocket Diary and Memorandum Book, 4 Feb. 1863 to 8 Aug. 1869, MS at Harvard.

23. Photogravure made by Elson Photogravure, Boston, in W. D. Howells, *The Coast of Bohemia* (1893; reprint, New York: Harper and Brothers, 1899), frontispiece.

Index